$12⁵⁰
CON HST

Ian Lovato
@ Canmore
241 3580
827 Tuscany Dr

D1015881

Tommy Douglas
The Road to Jerusalem

Tommy Douglas

The Road to Jerusalem

Thomas H. McLeod
and Ian McLeod

Hurtig Publishers

Edmonton

Hurtig Publishers Ltd.
10560 - 105 Street
Edmonton, Alberta
Canada T5H 2W7

Canadian Cataloguing in Publication Data

McLeod, Thomas, H., 1918—
   Tommy Douglas : the road to Jerusalem

Includes index.
ISBN 0-88830-316-5

1. Douglas, T. C. (Thomas Clement), 1904– 2. Politicians—Canada—
Biography. I. McLeod, Ian, 1953– II. Title. FC3525.1.D68M24 1987
971.064'092'4   F1034.3.D68M24 1987   C87-091317-4

All illustrations are from the Douglas family album, unless otherwise noted.

Edited by Rosemary Shipton
Designed by Jack Steiner
Index prepared by Molly Wolf
Typeset by Pièce de Résistance Ltée
Printed and bound in Canada

To the memory of Ruth McLeod,
who grew up at 86 Disraeli Street, Winnipeg,
and Thomas McLeod, printer,
host to Weyburn's Hot Stove League

CONTENTS

Illustrations
Photographs *following pages* 114 *and* 226

FOREWORD

At his memorial service, Tommy Douglas was given a standing ovation led by John Turner (the Liberal leader) and Brian Mulroney (the Conservative prime minister). This unusual tribute had been nobly won in years of disinterested and dedicated service to the people of Saskatchewan, the people of Canada, and the people of the world.

The two McLeods have told the story of that service in this welcome biography. They have had a long-standing and close personal relationship with the Douglas family and the older McLeod played an important part in shaping the work of the Saskatchewan Co-operative Commonwealth Federation government that Douglas headed. Their firsthand knowledge of Tommy Douglas's character and career is supplemented by numerous interviews and a wealth of documentary sources.

The McLeods analyse the part played in Douglas's ideas and attitudes by his Scottish, working-class inheritance, his North Winnipeg boyhood, and his years at Brandon College. They trace his transformation from preacher to politician, his transition from his pulpit at Calvary Baptist Church in Weyburn to the House of Commons in Ottawa, a pulpit with a much wider congregation. They assess his development and achievements while he was the premier of Saskatchewan.

As one of J. S. Woodsworth's small band of CCF MPs before the war, Douglas learnt his political trade. At the onset of war, he faced the agonizing decision between his leader's pacifism and his participation in resistance to fascism. As head of the first socialist government in North America from 1944 to 1961, he grappled with unprecedented problems in a province that had been almost destroyed in the "Dirty Thirties" by drought and depression. When, with great reluctance, he left Saskatchewan to assume the national leadership of the New Democratic Party, he had to struggle with still greater difficulties.

In coping with these problems, Douglas showed himself to be a man of extraordinary stamina and resilience. He had a great gift for working with other people; indeed, he encountered his worst troubles when at the federal level he was effectively without a close group of colleagues. Perhaps his greatest strength lay in his practical common sense. He was a magnificent idealist—a devout Christian, but a practical Christian and one more concerned for others than for his own personal salvation. He was a socialist, but a practical socialist, never doctrinaire nor dogmatic, always flexible and ready to try another expedient if the first one failed. He kept close to the grass-roots (or the mine face or the mill machinery). The needs of ordinary people, and especially the needs of the deprived, the sick, the oppressed, and the despairing, were his concern. He was determined to help every human being to attain an adequate supply of food, clothing, shelter, and health care. He never ceased to believe that solutions could be found to human problems, that some means could be worked out to improve the quality of life for suffering humanity everywhere. He was resolute in his belief that the test of policy should be the well-being of human beings, not the accumulation of wealth. To secure the basic material and medical necessities for everyone was only the beginning. That foundation would make it possible for his fellow citizens to share in building a New Jerusalem in which spiritual and intellectual values would have full play.

Douglas's transparent integrity, his utter lack of self-seeking and ego-tripping, made him a great political leader. Combined with his lively mind and creative imagination, these qualities made him an impressive speaker. His concern for others and his humanity meant that he could communicate equally effectively with dust-bowl farmers, coal miners, lumber jacks, and—as we learnt when my husband was agent-general for Saskatchewan in Britain—sophisticated City of London financial magnates. Though his speeches dealt with gloomy subjects, such as poverty, or technical problems involved in finding solutions, they were never dull. He clinched his points with a funny story, his sparkling wit and sense of humour captivated his audiences, yet no one could ever mistake his profound concern for a better life for all human beings.

The groundwork of social welfare structure that he and his colleagues in the cabinet and in the public service laid in Saskatchewan has played a vital part in the expansion of the welfare state in Canada as a whole. Douglas's legacy to all Canadians includes our national health service and the Canada (Quebec) Pension Plan.

Douglas's concern for others did not stop at provincial or even national boundaries. It reached out to developing countries and to the necessity of world peace. He always supported the work done by Saskatchewan House in London in attempting to help people from developing countries.

It was not only in the policies that he advocated and implemented that Tommy showed his essential kindness and humanity. He and his wife, Irma, were the most generous and kindest of friends. Typically, when a ten-year-old guest expressed a wish to see *The King and I*, Douglas at once discovered that he, too, longed to see the film and we all spent a splendid evening at the movies. It was a lot of fun to be with the Douglas family. There were always jokes and laughter. Tommy and Irma had a quality of direct friendliness and simplicity about them. The Right Honourable T. C. Douglas and his wife were as down-to-earth and unassuming as the student preacher at Carberry had been years before. There was never the slightest trace of pomposity in either Tommy or Irma, nor was there ever anything "holier than thou" about Tommy despite his roots in a strict Baptist congregation and in the social gospel. Though he had a unique political role and influence, he remained totally unpretentious. He was one of a group of illustrious colleagues, notably M. J. Coldwell, Stanley Knowles, David Lewis, and his successor in Saskatchewan, Woodrow Lloyd. As well, he worked happily with a host of supporters and friends at every level of society. He had his disagreements and his battles both within the party and with adversaries outside, but he never lost sight of his central aim—to improve the life of those in need.

To have had the friendship of Tommy and Irma has been deeply enriching. To have watched Saskatchewan in the Douglas era was to become hopeful for the future of the human race.

That a single province—in spite of seemingly overwhelming obstacles—could make such strides in setting higher standards of social welfare, and in creative social innovations that have changed the fabric of Canadian life, has been the result of extraordinary courage and creative ability on the part of Tommy Douglas, his colleagues, and his family. The story told in this book of those remarkable achievements is one of deep interest and significance.

Irene M. Spry
Ottawa

Acknowledgements

This book is the product of more than two years of interviewing and of digging in libraries, and we would like to thank the people who have helped us along the way. These include Ian Wilson, Lloyd Rodwell, and the staff at the Saskatchewan Archives; George Brandak at UBC Special Collections; Eileen McFadden at Brandon University; Colleen Dempsey (and many others) at the Public Archives of Canada; the Canadian Baptist Archives in Hamilton; and the staffs at the Glenbow Archives, the Manitoba Archives, the United Church Archives, the Shortt Library in Saskatoon, the Thomas Fisher Library in Toronto, the Queen's University Archives, and the Parliamentary Library.

We would also like to thank those who provided written documents or special help: Mark Talney, Shirley Douglas, Joan Tulchinsky, Eleanor McKinnon, Barney Arnason, Roy Borrowman, George Cadbury, and Cyril Symes.

Several people offered comments on various chapters: Beth Bilson, John Richards, Harley Dickinson, Ken Bryden, Ian Stewart, Elaine Husband, and Morna McLeod.

Carl and Mavis Goranson of the T. C. Douglas Calvary Centre in Weyburn helped to organize our work and extended warm hospitality. Dave Redel and Chuck Regehr, in Calgary, and Jim Weller, in Ottawa, kept us gainfully employed while we conducted our research. Many others have offered encouragement and put us up in their homes. Beryl McLeod in Ottawa and Susan Clancy in Calgary gave us constant support. They also helped to edit the manuscript.

The preparation of this book was assisted by a research grant and an expense grant from the Douglas-Coldwell Foundation.

1

Nothing of Everything

WEYBURN, SASKATCHEWAN, 1930: a prairie town, recorded population 5002, a place of constant hope and crushed dreams. Sometimes a bright sun stood high and proud in a vast blue expanse that reached beyond the horizons towards infinity; more often, in these days, the blue bled from the sky, and only the sun's ghost rolled through the grey murk.

Under Saskatchewan law, Weyburn was entitled to call itself a city, a description better suited to the early boom days when land companies and speculators had pushed the survey lines out beyond the requirements of any metropolis. It was a more tranquil place now, but it remained a centre where people came to buy food, machinery, and building materials, a divisional point for the Canadian Pacific Railway, and the home of one of two provincial mental hospitals. The sentinels of the prairies, the grain elevators, watched over the narrow, winding river and the commercial streets. When the dust haze permitted, the elevators announced to the traveller twenty miles away the presence of an urban centre, an important one to judge by their numbers.

North of the elevators, Weyburn's Main Street accommodated McKinnon's, "the largest department store in south-eastern Saskatchewan." Like so much else in the Weyburn of that time, the store is remembered (as MacTaggart's) in W. O. Mitchell's *Who Has Seen the Wind*. Nearby, two movie houses provided Saturday matinée fare for the young, including *Felix the Cat* and *The Werewolf* serials for a nickel. South of the river, on the crest of the town's only hill, the South Hill, sat the hospital and the watertower, and below them a few fine ostentatious houses. At the southern outskirts below the hill was the cemetery, unadorned by trees of any kind.

This was the town to which Tommy Douglas, a twenty-five-year-old minister, brought his bride Irma in August 1930. He had first come to live in the town the previous spring, just out of school, and the local weekly had heralded his coming: "he has conducted services at Austin, Carberry, and Strathclair, Man., where he is known as the boy preacher."[1] He had his own church, Calvary Baptist, a little white clapboard building on a corner near "down town"—although, of course, in Weyburn, most corners were near "down town." Calvary provided him with the only pulpit he was to occupy as a full-time minister.

Douglas and Irma arrived from Winnipeg, where they had spent their honeymoon. It had been a busman's holiday for Douglas, as he had filled in at a Winnipeg church to cover expenses. Now the young couple stepped off the train—the twenty-year-old bride making her first trip out of Manitoba, and the young minister with $5.39 in his pocket. The people of Calvary Baptist greeted them at the train station and a brass band serenaded them all the way to their first residence, an apartment above a downtown store.

On October 15, Douglas was ordained as a Baptist minister, or, in the words of the *Weyburn Review*, "received in to fellowship."[2] The moderator was the Rev. William Cameron Smalley, general secretary of the Baptist Union of Western Canada, later to be Douglas's defender within the Baptist communion. On the ordination council was Ted Stinson, destined to become his closest ally in the political battles of the next decade and a half. The young minister, it seemed, had everything he needed to make his way: a position in a progressive town and the respect of influential people.

But Weyburn's dreams of glory were to collapse over the next few years in a cloud of dust. The Weyburn Security Bank, one of the few chartered banks in the whole dominion, lost first its business and then its charter, and was rescued from disaster by the Canadian Imperial Bank. The manager of an allied mortgage and land company, the Weyburn Security Company, took his own life. The brewery dried up and vanished. The oil refinery, built during Alberta's first oil boom before the Great War, went bankrupt. A leading businessman, financially cornered, tried his hand at bank robbery—a career nipped in the bud by a three-year jail sentence.

Outside of Weyburn, the destruction was worse. In some areas of the West during the 1930s the farmer sold his crops and livestock for a pittance. In the dustbowl, where the rains failed year after year, the farmer had nothing to sell. The southern quarter of Saskatchewan was hit harder by the Great Depression than any other part of Canada.

Within a few years many of the towns and farms of the dustbowl fell to ruin. In 1937 D. B. MacRae of the Regina *Leader-Post* and R. M. Scott of the Winnipeg *Free Press* published their account of a trip through the country around Weyburn. It recorded an eight-year accumulation of woes:

In one municipality, 98 per cent of the farmers are getting public help; in another municipality, we were told that 95 per cent of the farming population is on public relief...taxes are in arrears for five years...It is pitiful to hear a man affirming that he had 125 acres of wheat acreage, and harvested 60 bushels of wheat...In one district, we found every farmer on relief except one...at (one community), potatoes will have to be brought in. At a hotel, one's nose came through a towel...the tea kettle is worn out and replaced by a lard pail...Information was given where one girl wore "the dress" to school while a sister stayed home...Broken panes of glass have been replaced with cardboard...Vacant farms stand out prominently about this part of the country, mute testimony to blasted hopes.

As for the small towns, the trading centres, a typical comment read: "Tribune was a 'good town'...the trading area was vast...a substantial community of the pioneer type was built up. Today, many of the stores and shops are vacant; windows are nailed up, people gone. There is scarcely a scrap of crop in the country." The reporters heard the best summary of the situation from the Chinese restaurant owner at Fillmore: "No crop, no garden, no oats, no potatoes, no feed. Nothing of everything."[3] The city of Weyburn escaped the worst of this suffering—the railways, hospitals, and schools survived, although in a crippled state. But as the farm economy rotted, businesses in the town caved in too, and the unemployed walked the streets.

Reminiscences of the Depression have found much virtue in it—in "the times that try men's souls." And indeed, the record is one of amazing resilience, of how the human animal makes the best of things, even finds a perverse pleasure in meeting adversity. But while for some the experiences of the times built character, for others they were soul-shrivelling. The true costs of economic depression were revealed not so much in statistical tables as in the eyes of the victims.

The new pastor plunged into his work with energy and compassion, determined to do something for the poor of the town. He was gifted with an evangelist's love of the language and a reformer's zeal, and he was bright, attractive, and persuasive. But the human suffering grew around him much faster than his confidence in himself. He made common cause with his fellow ministers, and then with a broad group of working people. They needed a leader. They chose Tommy Douglas. Before long he was part of a national reform movement with strong roots in the gospels of Jesus; its key principle was that the economic and social system must be reorganized to serve human need rather than human greed. In 1935 the people of Weyburn and the country around sent Douglas to Parliament bearing this message.

When the "boy preacher" settled in to this prairie community, neither he nor those around him could have guessed that it was the start of a relationship that would last for more than fifty years. For twenty-six of those years he would represent Weyburn as member of Parliament or as premier of Saskatchewan. He would remain, always, a member and supporter of Calvary Church. Near the end, in the 1980s, the people of the district banded together to save the little white church from demolition.

They towed it up to the crest of the South Hill and made it into a centre for the arts, dedicated to Tommy Douglas.

While the fortunes of politics took him to a succession of other cities during his career, Weyburn and Calvary Church remained at the centre of his affections to the end of his life. In a sense, though, his home lay beyond the line of sight, in a country that no one has yet visited. More than most politicians he reflected long and deeply on what the future might hold in store for humanity; on whether his grandchildren might see world tyranny, or doomsday, or what the prophets of his boyhood had called the Kingdom of God on Earth. "It's now possible to give everybody enough food, clothing and shelter to just get by," he said in one of his last radio interviews. "If we could do that tomorrow, it would be a great step forward, but it's not the end of the game. You're moving toward the horizon, and it's a retreating horizon. You never reach it."[4]

2

Socialist Beginnings

OM DOUGLAS, AN IRON MOULDER from the city of Falkirk, alighted from the westbound train at Winnipeg one afternoon in the fall of 1910. Along with his younger brother Willie, he had sailed from Glasgow two weeks before. The burly Scotsmen carried their suitcases through the crowds at the station, and walked north for a mile to Disraeli Street. They knocked at the door of Mariah Finn, a landlady who had welcomed many of their countrymen to Canada over the previous years.

Some of the sounds and smells around them might have been those of a Scottish steel town—the whistle at the Vulcan Iron Works, the hoot of lumber-company tugboats on the Red River, the reek of the gas works. But the brothers could see that this city of mud streets and frame buildings had sprung up only in their own lifetime. When Mrs. Finn had come to Winnipeg it had been a village on the edge of the wilderness; that wilderness now supplied the bread to feed an empire. The landlady bid them come in, and asked for her $4.55 weekly room rent in advance. They paid her with two golden sovereigns they had hidden away at the start of their trip.* With that, their foothold in the New World was secure. They would pay their second week's rent in Canadian money.[1]

Tom Douglas worked hard at the Vulcan Works through the winter. In the spring he brought his wife Anne and their two children to Canada.

---

* Mariah Finn was the great-grandmother of Tom McLeod (and the great-great-grandmother of Ian). She raised two motherless granddaughters, Ruth and Kate, and in time she presented each one with a gold coin, engraved with appropriate initials. Later, Ruth presented her coin to her new daughter-in-law Beryl, Tom's wife, who for years wore it attached to a bracelet. In 1986, in the course of a discussion with Aunt Kate (then in her mid-eighties) about early life in Winnipeg, she spoke of her grandmother's gift, regretting that her coin had been lost many years ago, and that she did not know where Ruth's was. Beryl held up the bracelet with the coin on it. Aunt Kate quickly indentified it and told us the above story of which until then we were ignorant. The coin was one of the two handed over to Mariah Finn three-quarters of a century earlier.

He had married Anne Clement of Glasgow in 1902, when he was twenty-two years old and she was twenty-three. Their son Tommy had been born in Falkirk on October 20, 1904, a daughter Nan in 1907; another daughter Isobel arrived soon after Anne reached Canada, in 1911. Whatever other dreams prompted them to migrate to Canada, their strongest motive was economic. The Scottish economy was beginning a long-term downward slide, and the shipyards, the locomotive plants, and the steel mills were the first to feel it. Scotland's peak was past, while a great era of Canadian railway building and farm settlement was now in full swing. Canada offered higher pay and better working conditions. It also promised more satisfaction, as Douglas recalled later:

> To be an iron moulder in Winnipeg, where there were probably only a couple of dozen, and he was one of the best, gave him a certain status. To be an iron moulder in Falkirk, where there were hundreds of them...
>
> Of course, my father had been a wanderer. He'd been in the South African War, he'd spent time with the British Army in India, got up to Afghanistan...He wasn't prepared to settle down in a small environment like Falkirk.[2]

Tom Douglas would return to Scotland in 1915, to serve in another war, and then migrate one last time back to Canada in 1919. His son, therefore, grew up knowing both worlds. Canada would provide the boy with all the opportunities he could hope for; but the Old Country's influence was also deep and lasting. He remained a Scottish nationalist all his life.

As a child, Tommy Douglas heard tales of Scotland's glory, and learned something at the same time of the power of the spoken word and the power of myth. As an adult, he wore his origins like a badge. He entertained crowds with droll tales: how the Scot wears the kilt to let him slide down hills more readily, since skin is cheaper than patches; how the Scottish minister, in explaining the line "the meek shall inherit the earth," suggested that "meek" is simply a plural of "Mac." In a more serious vein, he pondered out loud on the national virtues which the Scots boast about and which he cherished—a democratic respect for the individual, a faith in the benefits of public education.

Falkirk, his birthplace, lay fifty kilometres northeast of the "dubh glas" (dark water) that ran through his clan's oldest feudal estates, and an hour's trainride east of the furnaces and slums of Glasgow. Falkirk's economic heart was the Carron Iron Works, the oldest of the great industrial concerns in Scotland, whose founding in 1759 had marked the beginning of the Scottish Industrial Revolution. Tom Douglas worked at Carron, and so had his father.

Tom and Anne lived in one of a row of brick houses not far from the ancient narrow streets of the old town centre. Falkirk held on to something of its rural past. On market days Tommy heard the rumbling of the wagons as the country folk arrived from their dairy farms and their oat fields. Most Scots, though, had abandoned the fields and the villages by the time Tommy was born. While 12 per cent of them still farmed, fished, or worked in the mines, 60 per cent worked in the factories. Scotland produced almost half of Britain's steel and a quarter of its coal. As well, it manufactured steamships, locomotives, pottery, textiles, and furniture.

In a thousand ways, Scotland's industries, and her soldiers and scientists, had helped to build the British Empire, now the greatest power in the world. Scotland, like Canada, depended on and profited from a powerful southern neighbour's prosperity. But the future Canadian nationalist recognized as he grew up that too strong a dependence might destroy his homeland. Scotland must keep its neighbour at a distance, or risk oblivion.

The tales of Scotland's struggles with England filled Tommy's schoolbooks and provided the material for many evenings by the fireside. From the beginning, the leaders of clan Douglas had played a part in the country's endless political calculations, in the raids, treaties, and marriages. One of Tommy's greatest heroes, Robert Bruce, had warred on the English almost all his life. After losing an election, Douglas would remind his supporters that Bruce lost six times to the enemy and beat them decisively on the seventh try. "It was always part of your schooling that the English are really bastards, and if they'd had their way, you'd be under their thumb completely," said Douglas in 1985. "Any accommodation with the English was for purely selfish reasons, and not for any phoney patriotism...It's the same old question, how do you reconcile your differences, and work together on the things you agree with without being subjugated to the larger group?"[3]

Tommy's thinking and attitudes were shaped more by his family than by the formal educational system. His father exerted the greatest single influence, but his two grandfathers—old Tom Douglas and Andrew Clement—also pointed the way for him, giving him two models as Scotsmen, working men, and Christians.

Grandfather Tom Douglas, himself a master iron worker, was a self-taught intellectual, a radical Liberal in his politics. For him, the comforts of home consisted chiefly in a glass of whiskey and a raging argument—although he also passed many an hour sitting with his tiny grandson, reciting the poems of his favourite poet, Robert Burns. In family legend, old Tom could reel off the entire Burns canon, without a pause, in resonant bass tones. Here Tommy learned the lines he was to repeat so often in later years:

> Then let us pray that come it may
>   As come it will for a' that,
> That Sense and Worth o'er a' the earth
>   Shall bear the gree for a' that.
> For a' that, an a' that,
>   It's comin yet for a' that,
> That man to man the world o'er
>   Shall brothers be for a' that.[4]

Grandfather Tom attended the established Presbyterian church, and kept a strict sabbath: no labour, no frivolity.

Who shall ascend the hill of the Lord?
And who shall stand in his holy place?
He who has clean hands and a pure heart,
   who does not lift up his soul to what is false,
   and does not swear deceitfully.[5]

The litle boy might have heard his grandfather recite this psalm on a Sunday; and the next night, perhaps, the old man would regale him with Burns's mocking "Address to the Devil":

An' now, old Cloots, I ken ye're thinkin
A certain Bairdie's rantin, drinkin,
Some luckless hour will send him linkin
   To your black pit;
But faith! He'll turn a corner jinkin,
   An' cheat you yet.[6]

Grandfather Clement, Anne's father, was also a working man, and drove a delivery wagon in Glasgow. His outlook, though, differed substantially from the liberalism of Tom Douglas. In his younger days Andrew Clement had lived a drunkard's life, until the ultra-conservative fellowship of the Plymouth Brethren rescued him and brought him to Jesus. When he was older, he found more room to breathe among the Baptists, although his legal status as a religious nonconformist in Presbyterian Scotland remained unchanged. Grandfather Clement was a sober, quiet, generous man and a companion to his grandson. Together they would hitch up the workhorses and ride through the city streets.

Two strains of the Scottish character mingled in both men: one strain reflected in strong emotions, intellectual fervour, and independence of mind; the other in strict morality, regular Sunday observances, and rigid decorum. This did not eliminate some real differences between Douglas and Clement—for example, on the subject of the national poet. For Tom Douglas, Burns was the hero of the common man, while Andrew Clement dismissed him as irreverent, a womanizer, and a drunk.

Tommy Douglas—his full name was Thomas Clement Douglas—often praised the courage of Andrew Clement's nonconformism, and associated himself with those Covenanters of the seventeenth century who defied the established church and "held services in the caves and on the hillsides."[7] In keeping with his Covenanter background, Douglas later entered the Baptist ministry, but as a theological liberal and a sceptic rather than as a fundamentalist. In poetry and politics—in his love for Robert Burns and the cause of the working people—he inherited his tastes from his father's family.

Grace MacInnis likened Douglas to her own Scots husband, Angus, saying, "Tommy and Angus absorbed Burns with their mothers' milk."[8]

Both the writings and the life of Burns had a profound effect on Douglas, and evoked in him a feeling of kinship. He carried an antique volume of the poet's work in his luggage until it fell to fragments. He read and remembered much of the substance of many of the innumerable biographies of Burns. Over the years, Douglas built a reputation as a devotee of Burns—although a literary critic might complain that the cult he served was mired in "naive and sentimental moralizing" about the poet's work.[9] He was in constant demand as a speaker on Burns Night and at St. Andrew's Day banquets, and he crossed and re-crossed Canada toasting "the immortal memory."

Douglas was strongly attracted to the nationalist strain in Burns's writings. "I think Burns more than anybody else gave expression to the inner beliefs and the passion and longing of the Scottish people," he said. "Remember, they were a conquered people in a way. It's true they had fought back and gained a measure of political independence, but they were being absorbed, and they knew that they were being absorbed."[10] As well, Douglas found in Burns, in particular in "A Man's a Man for a' That," the essence of the Scottish ethic of democracy: "The rank is but the guinea's stamp, the man's the gold for a' that."

Douglas also saw in Burns's theology the reflection of his own thinking about the eternal truths. The irreverence which Grandfather Clement saw in Burns was, for the most part, an expression of contempt for the established church, its overweening officials, and all their works. In the matters of belief that Douglas (and his father) held to be important, Burns took a reverent attitude—even if it was the reverence of an eighteenth-century theological rebel. The poet of Scotland demonstrated a faith in a benevolent Creator with whom he preferred to deal directly, and a conviction that God's sacred nature pervaded the whole of his creation.

The land of Burns remained a place of grim social evils a hundred years after his death. Barons still collected steep "royalties" from the small farmers and independent miners who worked the feudal lands. The people still paid taxes to support the official Presbyterian church, and the law discriminated against religious nonconformists. The first Scottish Independent Labour Party manifesto, issued in 1888, described a state in which "every twentieth inhabitant is a pauper, a million men are out of work, one-fifth of the community is insufficiently clad, what are known as starvation diseases are rife among large classes, and in which one-third to one-half of the families of the country are huddled together six to a room."[11]

In the years before Douglas's father Tom entered the iron works at the age of twelve, Scotland's workers began to organize politically for reform. The Scottish Independent Labour Party was the first Labour Party in Britain; its leader, Keir Hardie, was a self-educated working man. He was also a devout Christian from a nonconforming sect. He was fired by the legend of the Covenanters, who preached against the godlessness of the rich at their seventeenth-century meetings on the moors. Independent

Labour won a measure of support from what Hardie called "the intelligent, well-off artisan," people such as Douglas's father. But many other workers, like Grandfather Tom, retained their traditional Liberal loyalties. The split between the two—before Tommy was born, they went for several months without speaking—typified a fracture that ran right across the Scots working class.

Tommy's father, a tall, reflective man, would sit by the stove and work at convincing his fellows: Liberal promises of radical change are fraudulent, an attempt to win votes. Behind the smokescreen the Liberals owe their political lives to the owners of capital. At his father's knee, Tommy learned that Liberals are conniving hypocrites—a point of view he never forsook. Over the course of his political career he remained on polite, even friendly terms with many Liberal opponents. On particular issues he might even support them. But at all times he spoke of the Liberal Party as a two-faced beast, a Jekyll and Hyde, and of its leaders as men of weak conviction who would sell out to the highest bidder.

Early in life, Douglas also learned of the joys and sorrows of watching the third party take a trouncing at the polls. Scottish Labour built a core of support in the shipyards, the coal mines, the foundries, and the radical clergy; but Keir Hardie lost every election he fought in Scotland and left the country. It was the dockworkers and the Christian reformers of London's East End who first sent him to the Commons. In Scotland the Liberals held most parliamentary seats until the 1920s.

Tom and Anne Douglas left Scotland's smokestacks and ancient towns behind when they brought their children to Canada in 1911. They carried their intellectual baggage with them, the idealism and scepticism of their people, ready to take a new form in the metropolis of the prairies. Winnipeg, with a population of 150,000 at the turn of the century, was workshop, warehouse, and counting-house for the prairies, the jumping-off spot for masses of immigrants. The red-brick mansions of the merchants rose to the south of the Assiniboine River, while north of its banks sprawled the community into which the Douglas family moved, a lusty community of small merchants and blue-collar workers.

Tom Douglas rented a house a few blocks west from Mrs. Finn's, and Anne, despite the family's limited means, soon made a comfortable home, adding to the family income by taking in a lodger or two. She was a whirlwind of a woman, full of jokes and arguments, forever advising and encouraging her only son. Little more than five feet in height, she dressed with great colour and dash, and she pushed herself to make her days as full as possible. She was to witness almost all of her son's career. She watched him ascend to the premier's chair in Saskatchewan, and then to the national leadership of the New Democratic Party. She died in the year the first astronaut set foot on the moon. In these early days she guided Tommy in public speaking and story-telling, teaching him to recite poems such as Kipling's "If" and Pauline Johnson's "Cry of an Indian Wife."

There were two other Scots families on the street, but there were also Germans, Ukrainians, and Poles. This gave Tom Douglas the opportunity to impart his "man's a man for a' that" ethic to his son: "He used to keep pounding it into me when I was a kid: 'You're playing with the Kravchenko kid. This is marvellous; this is what the world should be like. Sure, I can't understand the family next door, but you kids are growing up together, and you'll work for the same kinds of things, you'll build the same kind of world.' "[12]

In his new surroundings, Tom Douglas set up a small-time partnership with God in the back garden, and the two worked diligently to produce onions and cabbages. In later years, Douglas often extolled his father's abilities to make anything he touched grow, while at the same time lamenting his own lack of skill as a gardener. However, Tom's communion with God remained a private affair. He viewed organized religion with suspicion. He had attended Presbyterian services with Anne in Falkirk, but after a set-to with the minister he stopped going. The church, he decided, stood with the Liberals and the rich, and against the workers.

Anne Douglas, in contrast, was an active church-goer. She found her way to several North Winnipeg churches, including the chapel at the Methodist All People's Mission. The mission, scattered over several blocks, was part social centre and part school. It reached out to the poor and to Winnipeg's immigrants, people from a score of nations who were struggling to establish themselves in a new and sometimes unfriendly environment. Among its enterprises, the mission collected and distributed used clothing. It also offered immigrant mothers classes in nutrition, child care, and English. Soon, Anne was a volunteer worker in the mission's building on Sutherland Avenue.

Tommy sometimes went along to the mission after school, to swim, play in the gym, or read books in the library. It was an important turning point in his life—not because of the mission itself, but because of the presence of its superintendent, the Rev. James Shaver Woodsworth, one of Canada's great teachers and missionaries of the social gospel. "In the part of society that we moved in, he was a little god," said Douglas many years later. "Here was a fellow who could have been in a big church, had been in a big church, working among the poor people...My mother had a great regard for him."[13]

To the young boy playing ball or studying in the reading room, the gaunt, bearded Woodsworth seemed impossibly remote and austere. During those years, Tommy never spoke to him. Woodsworth's presence was remote, and yet he provided a model for Tommy—the man who battled selflessly to improve the human condition, who seemed to evoke the purest esteem, loyalty, and affection in those who worked with him, and who infuriated the complacent with his unshakeable conviction. The legend grew around this "saint of Canadian politics," and when the time came for Tommy to choose, he became a dedicated disciple.

At the time that Tommy first saw him, Woodsworth, already recognized as a leader within Canada's progressive Protestant movement, was still in his thirties. He was one of a host of preachers, social workers, and volunteer workers connected with a diffuse reform movement based in the Protestant churches in several countries. This movement had helped elect Keir Hardie to Parliament in Britain; in the United States, under leaders like John R. Mott (whose son would serve as Douglas's deputy minister of health in Saskatchewan), it built such institutions as the Young Men's Christian Association. The movement's pioneers had laid the groundwork a generation before. In the years after 1910 it was growing rapidly in popular appeal and political clout, and was winning its first major political victories in Canada. With the first workers' compensation bills and mothers' allowances came the dawn of the welfare state. Late in his career Douglas suggested that "Every major reform in the social order has drawn its impetus from the social gospel."[14]

The social gospel, "practical Christianity"—or, as Douglas later spoke of it, "the application of the gospel to social conditions"[15]—had evolved as a response to the stark miseries of the industrial age. Within its currents it counted conservatives, liberals, radicals, people who devised "a wide range of ideas and plans for social and moral improvement with which none of its advocates would be in total agreement."[16] One persistent strain yearned for a rustic past, and cursed the new cities as Babylon. However, the social gospel's main thrust was towards the future and the application of social engineering to the problems of society. It sought to use the emerging social sciences for Christian ends—adult education to raise up the worker; sociological surveys to point out the degrading effects of poverty on the family; urban planning to establish housing standards and parks.

The social gospel rallied to the idea of progress and the belief that social reform fit in with God's plan for the evolution of the human species. At its logical extreme, this gospel could be extended to include the "science" of eugenics — as a graduate student Douglas wrote his Master's thesis on the possibilities for developing a healthier human race by regulating marriage and sterilizing the unfit. More typically, the social gospel put forward a generalized optimism, teaching that God was leading an ever-improving mankind onward and upward to the New Day.

The movement did not seek to create a common dogma, nor to impose a particular theology on its constituents. Its watchword was tolerance. It was inevitable, though, that it would generate its own ad hoc theology, or, as its critics might say, anti-theology. If there is a place for each woman and man in the struggle to build the Kingdom of God on Earth, surely there must be room for all in the heavenly kingdom, too. "The Holy City," a theme song of the movement, expressed this view: "and all that could passed through that Gate, and no one was denied." At the core of fundamentalist Christianity there sat a stern God of wrath and vengeance, but the God of the social gospellers was benevolent, smiling down on all people of good will regardless of their conception of Him, Her, or It.

This view of a benevolent God, and a commitment to the brotherhood of God's people, was theology enough for many "practical Christians." With their burning concern for social improvement and their scepticism about certain biblical stories, religious radicals like Woodsworth gave scripture and doctrine a very distant second place behind the need for action. Woodsworth often used the phrase, "the secular is becoming more sacred every day." The whole world was God's church, the human race its congregation, social service a form of worship.

In a 1964 sermon entitled "The Social Gospel and Politics," Douglas affirmed his belief that the essence of the Christian ethic is the oneness of man: "God hath made of one blood all nations." God's judgement of us, he said, will depend less on our piety than on our commitment to the oppressed. The greatest sinners, whatever their religious pretensions, are those who deny the humanity of their brothers and sisters—in South Africa, in the ghetto, on the Indian reserves. "In Christ there is no East or West."[17] Douglas would become an evangelist for this idea of brotherhood. It drove him on throughout his public life.

In the years after the Douglas family arrived in Winnipeg, the Canadian movement's radicals gave an increasingly political slant to Christ's announcement of "good news to the poor." The Christian's aim, they concluded, must be to move councils and parliaments, to replace charity and welfare (and Liberal promises) with social and economic justice. Along with Walter Rauschenbusch, the voice of radical Baptists in the United States, they adopted the view that "Christianity is in its nature revolutionary."[18]

On the prairies, several social gospel radicals entered into direct political action. Dr. Salem Goldworth Bland of Wesley College, a leading writer and orator within the movement, was an especially effective critic of the ruling classes. As early as 1909 he urged the formation of a radical farmer-labour party to topple the established Grits and Tories. Woodsworth, Bland, and other activists found fertile ground for their agitation. In Winnipeg, workers like Tom Douglas had grown up with radical political movements, and by 1914 their Labour aldermen were a force on the Winnipeg City Council. In rural areas, the progressive traditions of the American Midwest and Ontario fused with a home-grown suspicion of the big "interests," and by 1916 Manitoba farmers were putting forward their own independent candidates for election.

The social gospel offered farmers and workers a vision of what Canada might become. Salem Bland, looking to the late 1980s, saw a nation "headed along the same road as the United States, ruled by millionaires." He continued, "We need an ideal, before our resources are seized, while the country is young and our new cities are growing up...Our ideal shall be: Canada for the people! We need a new party, a party that will have what no present party commands—moral enthusiasm!"[19] Woodsworth, too, had a dream as he stood on the mountain overlooking Montreal. He saw a vast city of the future where people flocked to their workplaces "not as slaves, not as jealous rivals, but as partners in a common enterprise." The churches in the new city were meeting places for all. "The earlier distinction between sacred and secular seemed to have no meaning."[20]

From his earliest years, Douglas lived in a household where these things were the meat and drink of table talk. The slogans of the radical social gospel made one essential point clear to him—that the Christian has a duty to engage in social service and social reform. Adopting even this simple idea put him into a minority camp among Christians. Many church-goers up to the present day continue to believe that the believer's only duty is to save his own soul. Douglas would grasp the underlying logic of the social gospel only slowly—first as a teenager trying to understand events like the great Winnipeg Strike, and later as a student of theology and social science at Brandon College. But all around him the movement's soaring oratory and its sense of limitless possibility was shaping the prairie society that would embrace him as an adult.

The onset of the Great War in 1914 posed an ideological problem for Tom Douglas. He had the radical Scot's suspicion of the British Empire, but he detested Prussia and its Kaiser. Radical leaders like Hardie and Woodsworth counselled pacifism, but most of the empire's socialists and progressives enlisted for battle. At the age of thirty-four he went to Europe to serve King George, although he decided "the only way he'd go was if he didn't carry a gun."[21] He joined a Scottish unit, the 12th Field Ambulance.

Anne and the children returned to Scotland and lived with the Clements in their Glasgow apartment. Grandmother Clement slept in the living room, Grandfather and Tommy in the only bedroom, Anne and the two girls in an alcove off the kitchen. They prayed together at the Baptist chapel near the River Clyde. The old men, women, and children in the pews sang "Nearer My God to Thee," and outside the horns on the steamships roared. The sun went down early on the cold Glasgow days, and gangs of boys gathered to rough and tumble in the half-light. Tommy fought his way in to one gang so he would have protection on the streets. He grew up quickly, caring for his two sisters and looking after his grandfather's rig. Just before his fourteenth birthday he withdrew from school to find work and help support the family. He got a job in a cork factory, where he acquired his lifelong habit of standing at his work table. He buried himself in the romances of Walter Scott and G. A. Henty. Douglas knew that his father might never come back. "I didn't rebel," he said, "because there was nobody to rebel against."[22]

In late 1918 the war ended, and with Tom still in uniform, mother and children returned to Winnipeg without him. Anne Douglas started work in the Singer factory, and rented a house on McPhail Street near the Elmwood Cemetery. Tommy found a job at the Winnipeg Grain Exchange, running messages for the traders and the grain company executives.

Around them in the factories of Winnipeg, and across Canada, workers and capitalists were on a collision course. Working people had found a new solidarity in the war effort, and many had risked their lives for the cause. Apologists for business warned that workers should be kept in their place, but liberals and radicals argued that working people had earned a voice in the management of industry. A prominent social scientist and Presbyterian layman, Mackenzie King, gained a national reputation with his book *Industry and Humanity*, in which he preached co-operation among the "four parties to industry"—owners, managers, workers, and consumers. The Methodist church, goaded on by Salem Bland and his allies, called for "A Complete Social Reconstruction." One report adopted at the 1918 Methodist conference stated, "We do not believe the separation of labour and capital can be permanent. Its transcendence, whether through co-operation or public ownership, seems to be the only constructive and radical reform."[23]

At this, the most revolutionary moment in Canadian history, the workers of North Winnipeg launched the country's greatest strike ever. On May 5, 1919, metal tradesmen in Winnipeg, including those at Vulcan, walked off the job. Within days, 35,000 workers in a city of 200,000 left their jobs in sympathy, and sporadic walkouts occurred in other cities across the West. Business leaders and newspaper editors charged that the sympathetic strike was led by Bolsheviks. In fact, the leaders were labour politicians who had worked democratically in the city for years. Woodsworth, who had left the church by this time, became editor of the strike newspaper after the arrest of the first editor, the Rev. William Ivens. He wrote to his friend William Irvine, "The workers were banded together to secure higher wages and the principle of collective bargaining—a principle that has been conceded in England for a great many years."[24]

Douglas was now old enough to recognize the significance of the strike and the sweep of events around him. On his way home from work he would weave through the immense crowds that filled the public parks at all hours of the day. There he heard speakers urge the strikers to stay calm and keep their spirits up. The climax came on Bloody Saturday, June 23, when mounted police attacked the crowds gathered in the Market Square in front of Winnipeg City Hall. Douglas and an older boy, his scoutmaster Mark Talnicoff, climbed to what they thought was a safe perch on a rooftop. The police fired first into the air, and the bullets whistled over the boys' heads. With another volley, a man fell dead below them on the sidewalk. That evening police arrested Woodsworth for his editorials. On June 29, with several of its leaders in jail, the strike collapsed.

The episode had important consequences for Canada. It played a part in the Liberal selection of a new leader the following month: the party chose Mackenzie King, the young labour relations expert, over a seasoned veteran. The strike also drew together the workers of North Winnipeg as never before. Their candidates won a string of victories in local and provincial elections, and in 1921 they sent J. S. Woodsworth to Parliament, an important step in the long road to organizing the Co-operative Commonwealth Federation (CCF).

Tommy Douglas never forgot Bloody Saturday and the show of strength by the corporate state. "Whenever the powers that be can't get what they want," he concluded, "they're always prepared to resort to violence or any kind of hooliganism to break the back of organized opposition."[25] He began to work in campaigns for Labour politicians at the school board and local council level, doing such jobs as dropping off leaflets at front doors.

A few weeks after the strike, Tom Douglas came home to Winnipeg. He was not yet forty years old, but the poison gas in the trenches had sickened him and the years of carnage had wounded his spirit. For the rest of his life he would suffer bouts of despair, walking alone at night for miles, trying to forget. His pension, after two tours of duty, amounted to something like $12 a month. Tom would spend his last remaining years labouring in the smoke and heat at the iron foundry, if there was work available. On Saturday nights he might play cards with Anne or go with her to see a movie. On most week nights he simply came home, ate, and slept.

At almost the same time as his father returned, Tommy Douglas got a job as an apprentice in a printer's shop. Soon, he too was a member of a union. His workmates were older than he was, and many were radicals, self-taught philosophers, men who wandered from town to town. He recalled little about the job itself in later years, but he remembered that he read everywhere he went, at home, on streetcars, in spare moments at work. Along with adventure novels, he came across several political pamphlets issued by such groups as the United Farmers and the Manitoba Independent Labour Party.

The city boy's real introduction to the politics of western Canada came with a book called *The Farmers in Politics* by William Irvine of Calgary. Irvine was a Scotsman, a former preacher who had studied under Salem Bland in Winnipeg. Elected as the Labour MP for Calgary East in 1921, he had strong links to the United Farmers of Alberta. Douglas took the book's message to heart: the farm movement, with its co-operative marketing enterprises, offered a radical alternative to capitalism. The farmer would show the way for other working people. "Co-operation is the gospel of the United Farmers," wrote Irvine, "and their leaders are the apostles of it. Natural law is on their side."[26] Irvine also wrote that social Christianity would help propel the growth of radical politics in the West. "The drunk traffic, graft, profiteering, greed and poverty are being arraigned from every quarter as incompatible with Christian principles. The protests may come from a Labour Hall, a church conference, a United Farmers' convention— but whatever the place of origin, the spirit is the same...The line between the sacred and the secular is being rubbed out."[27]

In the federal election of 1921 the United Farmers groups on the prairies, in Ontario and the Maritimes came together as the Progressive Party and elected sixty-five members of Parliament. The breakthrough marked a decisive setback for the two-party system in federal politics. The Progressive movement fell to pieces through the mid-1920s, but its spirit, captured in Irvine's writing, lingered on. It formed an important element in the rise of the CCF in Saskatchewan. Irvine became one of the young Rev. Douglas's favourite figures in the 1930s, and was one of those who encouraged him to enter politics.

For the most part, despite his reading, Douglas pursued interests outside politics. He joined the Order of DeMolay, the youth wing of the

Masonic Lodge, and became interested in amateur dramatics. "The experience gave me a feel for grease paint, but I never really liked the idea of being an echo of someone else's lines. I wanted to make up my own lines in life."[28] He remained a Mason for the rest of his life. Douglas also went to the One Big Union gym, where he parlayed his experience as a scrapper in the Glasgow streets into an amateur career in boxing. Later, leading his boys' groups, he would sometimes put the gloves on two fractious youngsters and tell them to go at it. "That doesn't mean I'd like any boy to get into professional boxing," he said. "But you don't avoid fights by never fighting. I think you avoid fights if somebody knows that you're willing to fight."[29]

The Douglas family, all but Tom, now belonged to the congregation of Beulah Baptist Church, a small grey wooden building on Kelvin Street. They became Baptists, said Douglas later, because Anne had been a Baptist in Glasgow, and Beulah was where the other neighbourhood teenagers went. The routine of the church came to govern their lives. Isobel, the younger daughter, recalled later that Tommy went on Tuesday for Scouts, on Wednesday for prayer meeting, on Friday for a young people's meeting. On Saturday, the Christian Endeavor youth group often organized an outing, and on Sunday the family attended church three times, for morning service, evening service, and Sunday school.

Douglas entered into the life of Beulah Baptist partly through Mark Talnicoff (later Talney), a Scout leader who subsequently married Douglas's sister Nan. The two young men organized a boys' cycle troop and on summer weekends would ride out to the country to camp under the stars. On Sunday morning they might attend a country church in their Scout uniforms, and after church play some baseball with the local boys. Talney and Douglas engaged in long, serious discussions about the relationship between the gospel of Jesus and the social changes they saw around them. They regarded themselves as young rebels, well to the left of the Beulah congregation. As Talney recalled:

> It was a very conservative church, and when you entered the worship service in the morning or in the evening, within the walls of that church you readily forgot that there was a world outside.
>
> I can never remember the pastor of the church in his sermons referring to any of the vicious problems and the evils which plagued the people of Canada. I can never remember him in any way supporting the workers as they struggled for a living wage...In other words, his total emphasis was on the after-life. And the hymns that were sung were quite indicative of that kind of egocentric religion which was fostered: for example, "When the Roll is Called Up Yonder, *I'll* Be There," and "Will There Be Stars in *My* Crown?"[30]

Talney and Douglas decided that they could best work for social improvement through the Christian ministry. They began to save their money, and in late 1922 Douglas preached his first service as a lay minister. In the spring of 1924, on their way home from church, they decided they would enrol at Brandon College, a Baptist school in western Manitoba with a reputation as a liberal outpost.

Tommy Douglas grew to manhood when the young West was in bloom and its settlers dreamed of building a rich and harmonious nation under the Union Jack. Almost every social and political change that Douglas witnessed bore a Christian stamp, influenced by the idealistic, though often self-righteous fervour of the social gospel. This movement expressed anger at existing conditions; but it also carried the hope, prevalent through the industrial nations, that people working in the service of God could shape a new world.

In the decades after 1920 the social gospel's combination of Christian reformism and tolerance for other religious views proved difficult to sustain. After all, if God can be anything you want Him to be, why have a church? For many people who came under the Christian reformers' influence, tolerance relaxed into apathy and they turned away from religion. Many more returned to the certainties of the God of Thunder and Vengeance, to the anti-social gospel: life as a scramble for personal salvation. In the secular world the lessons of the Great War, the Depression, and then another war deflated the belief that man was improving as a species.

Douglas would resist these pessimistic trends, and as late as 1943 he produced a summary of the classic social gospel hopes in a radio broadcast for the voters of Saskatchewan: "Improving our economic status is only the first step in man's upward climb towards a higher destiny...We maintain that we must have food, clothing and shelter, but in doing so, we are conscious of the fact that these are only prerequisites in the much greater task of building the Kingdom of God in the hearts and minds of men and women."[31]

In later years he reduced the specifically Christian content in his political speeches, but he always tried to play something of the visionary role of Woodsworth and Bland. He spoke of a society where the strong would bear the burdens of the weak, and the desire for social justice would overshadow the hunger for economic gain. In his keynote address to the New Democratic federal convention of 1967 he insisted that democratic socialism is "more than a halfway house" between communism and capitalism, "more than a sterile debate about whether Canada should have more public ownership or less...It is grounded in the belief that the economy should exist for the benefit of man, and not man for the benefit of the economy." This, he said, is a "revolutionary approach."[32]

Privately, he realized more and more how complex a task it would be to build a socialist world, but he still found the language of the social gospel useful. "The Kingdom of God is a society where moral values predominate," he said in 1985. "You're never going to step out of the front door into the Kingdom of God. What you're going to do is slowly and painfully change society until it has more of the values that emanate from the teachings of Jesus or from the other great religious leaders."[33]

3
College Years

I N 1924, committed to a life of Christian service, Tommy Douglas
returned to school to pick up the broken threads of his formal
education. He had taken his first job in Glasgow before he turned
fourteen; by the age of nineteen he had earned a union ticket, but he
lacked the qualifications required for university entrance. Douglas left
Winnipeg in the fall of 1924 and registered in the academy program at
Brandon College. Brandon was the chief market town in western
Manitoba, with a population of about 18,000. The little college sat on
a treeless plain at the city's western edge, near the Assiniboine River,
two limestone school buildings connected by a small chapel. Douglas
spent three years finishing the matriculation program, and in 1927 he
entered the Faculty of Arts, graduating three years later with a Bachelor's
degree.

The missionary Baptists of Ontario had begun to offer post-secondary
schooling in western Manitoba almost with the arrival of the first settlers.
Their model was the Canadian Literary Institute in Woodstock, the Baptist school which became McMaster University in 1890. By 1900 they had
founded Brandon College along with a new communion of Baptist
churches—the Baptist Union of Western Canada.

The college was set up to house liberal arts and theological departments side by side—to turn out young ministers with a capacity for
critical thinking, as well as educated Baptist lay people with some
knowledge of their religious roots. Whatever merit this prescription
held as a basis for developing a trained ministry, it contained the seeds
of tension and dissent. The Baptist Union of Western Canada—which
at its peak in 1914 took in fewer than 18,000 members—would have
found it hard to keep a full-scale college alive under any circumstances.
However, even this limited membership included liberal, conservative,

and fundamentalist factions, and they squabbled continually over the modernist nature of the college's program.*

Scholars in many countries, including some at Canadian Baptist colleges such as Brandon and McMaster, had worked for a generation to shed new light on the events recorded in the Bible. The sciences of geology and biology challenged the traditional understanding of the Creation; archeologists and linguists, and then theologians, wondered aloud about the origins of the tales of Methuselah or Jonah and the Whale. Some Christians grasped the new scholarship eagerly and some eyed it cautiously. The fundamentalists, who felt that the Bible stood above all forms of investigation and analysis, sought to avoid it completely.

This conflict would bedevil Brandon College until the church cut it adrift in 1938. Financial support for Brandon became, increasingly, a focus for argument and dissension within the Baptist Union. Some congregations refused to send their children to the college or to accept the products of its theological program. Support shifted, increasingly, to the more narrow-minded Bible colleges. "I am sure you appreciate the situation," wrote college president J. R. C. Evans to the chancellor of McMaster in the mid-1930s. "It is not always easy to bring the denominational point of view and the academic point of view together."[1]

The tensions between science and religion, between fundamentalism and modernism, came to a head at Brandon in 1922, two years before Douglas enrolled. A church commission acquitted Professor Harris Lachlan MacNeill and his colleagues in the "heresy trials" of that year; but some Baptists never accepted this verdict and returned to church congresses year after year to further undermine the ties between the college and its supporters. The episode is worth exploring, because it gives some insight into how the open-minded Tommy Douglas was able to live within the Baptist church—a body which in recent decades has become a preserve for conservative and fundamentalist Christians.

MacNeill, a member of the first graduating class of McMaster University in 1894, had come to Brandon in 1904 to teach Greek and Latin. In his philosophy he was a rationalist of Cartesian persuasion: a man with a deep religious faith, he believed at the same time that scientific method should be applied to the full range of human knowledge and experience. One of his former students has said, "[MacNeill] was very proud to be in the forefront of liberal thinking because he thought the whole church should move in that direction...he was the voice of Brandon, and led it out into these new fields."[2] For as long as MacNeill taught only Greek and Latin, he was, doctrinally, harmless. However, in response to the college's need for someone to teach New Testament history, he left Brandon to enrol in New Testament studies at the University of Chicago— a centre for liberal Baptist thought. He graduated in 1910 with a Doctor's degree and returned to Brandon and the Faculty of Divinity. The

---

* The Baptist Union suffered a steady exodus of congregations from before 1920 until the 1960s. Fundamentalist groups pulled out, small rural churches closed down, and German and Swedish Baptists formed their own federations.

rationalist philospher-theologian soon ran afoul of the fundamentalist jot-and-tittlers.

In 1922 a group of Baptist ministers in British Columbia levelled charges of heresy against several instructors at the college.* The charges, published in pamphlet form, included "perpetrating the reprehensible crime of sowing seeds of rank infidelity in the minds of the Young." MacNeill, the main target of the complaints, was named along with Principal H. P. Whidden as "men who love darkness rather than light." The crisis was brought into bold and almost comic relief with the charge that "the springs have been polluted with rationalism"—an odd complaint to make of an institution of higher learning.[3] However, the Executive Board of the Baptist Union of Western Canada took the complaints seriously and named a special commission to review the religious curriculum and teaching methods at Brandon.

Besides interviewing the college faculty, the commission asked Brandon graduates about the religious instruction they had received and whether their faith had been shaken by it. MacNeill also faced an inquisition by Vancouver's Baptist ministers, where he tried to explain his attitude to mysteries such as the Virgin Birth and the physical resurrection of Christ. He believed they had happened, he said, but he could not "get his mind around" how they had happened. The commission report of early 1923 exonerated Brandon College and its staff members. Of MacNeill, the commission satisfied itself with saying, "he believes in the fundamental place of the supernatural in the Christian revelation, but distinguishes between that fundamental faith and principle, and the liberty to investigate certain facts and events."

The report clearly added fuel to the fires within the Baptist Union. The fundamentalists remained wedded to a position which Douglas summed up as, "I want complete freedom of thought unless your point of view is different from mine, in which case you'll believe what I believe." Within a few months, sixteen congregations in British Columbia alone quit the union, and even then the controversy over Brandon continued. The pendulum had swung—for now—over to the modernist side; the commission, representing Western Baptist leadership, had delivered the back of its hand to those who brought the heresy charges. In doing so it set out a statement of faith—one which honoured the seventeenth-century individualist origins of the Baptist movement and also fitted the spirit of the college. The statement reflected the intellectual climate into which Douglas was moving:

---

* The year 1922 also saw the famous Scopes "Monkey Trial" in the United States which tested the right of schools to teach the theory of evolution and ignore fundamentalist protests. In the same year, American fundamentalists took on the popular liberal Baptist preacher and writer Harry Emerson Fosdick, who became one of Tommy Douglas's heroes. Fosdick questioned Christian belief in events such as the virgin birth of Christ and even expressed doubts about a literal Second Coming. However, in his 1956 autobiography Fosdick concluded that Protestant liberals of his generation went too far in pursuing intellectual fashion. "The centre of gravity was not in the gospel, but in the prevalent intellectual concepts of our time." H. E. Fosdick, *The Living of These Days* (New York, 1956), 245

We would reaffirm as a root principle of our denominational fellowship the competency of every soul in the sight of God and its direct responsibility to God; in the right of every man to hold the New Testament in his own hand, and to read it by the light of God shining in his own heart; the refusal to apply any doctrinal test by either political or ecclesiastical authority; a personal loyalty to Jesus Christ and his world programme as the acid test of all Christian discipleship; freedom in the interpretations of religious teachings so long as these are consistent with the pursuit of truth itself.[4]

This ringing manifesto, upholding the principle of freedom from dogmatic preconceptions in the search for truth, could not have found a more receptive mind than Douglas's. He was in no sense a fundamentalist. Influenced by his mother, he had led an active life within the church; but the influence of his iron-moulder, Labourite father also provided him with a lasting suspicion of anyone who would rule the lives and thoughts of others. This influence pushed him towards a questioning, rationalist approach to Christian belief. Douglas reflected late in his life that "my father was not well educated, but I have come more and more to think that he was a very wise man."[5]

When Douglas came to Brandon in 1924, the questions raised by the commission's work were still fresh. Would Brandon remain a place of open inquiry, part of an academic tradition reaching back 500 years? Or was it to become a training school devoted to hymn singing and Bible study? MacNeill became Douglas's favourite teacher, a man whom he regarded later as one of the great influences on the formation of his social philosophy. Near the end of his career, he said of his professor: "I would say that any intellectual curiosity I have came from [MacNeill]... He recognized that you have to have answers to the questions about what we are here for, what we are supposed to be doing...How do you work with your fellow man to build the Kingdom of God?" To Douglas, Professor MacNeill was "a giant among pygmies."[6] He spoke as the voice of rationalism.

If Harris MacNeill offered Douglas a grounding in rationalist philosphy and a questioning attitude to matters of religious belief, a second teacher exposed him to the rigours of scientific problem solving. John R. C. Evans had graduated from Brandon College in 1913, and, after teaching in the academy for several years, went on to earn a doctorate in geology at the University of Chicago. He returned to Brandon in 1923 and became president in 1928.

Evans inherited the aftermath of the "heresy trial," and the resulting decline in Brandon's fortunes. With the onset of the Depression, the financial problems became critical. When the Baptist Union finally cut its ties to the college in 1938, it was Evans who found Brandon a new life as a secular affiliate of the University of Manitoba. Evans's academic leadership at Brandon, and his heroic work in keeping it alive, are the subject matter for a book yet to be written.

Evans was a big man; standing well over six feet tall, with shoulders that seemed almost as wide, he loomed even larger when he donned his buffalo-skin overcoat to face the prairie winter. His academic stature was also impressive; from time to time he returned to the University of Chicago, where he served as head of the geology department during summer sessions. He influenced his students outside the classroom as well as inside, coaching basketball teams, supervising debating clubs, commanding the Officers' Training Corps. His students knew him as "the Doc," although only a select few ever addressed him directly in that manner. To generations of students, Evans was Brandon College, the embodiment of the educational philosophy that had originated with the Canadian Literary Institute—summed up in the homey motto carried on the college's insignia, "Education Crowned With Reverence." He was an ardent Baptist, a lay preacher, the confidant of the senior officers of his church. He took an active part in Baptist councils—he sometimes took students with him, and Douglas remembered watching the jousting among the various factions. But like MacNeill, Evans let his scientific scepticism flourish alongside his religious convictions, and he championed the cause of freedom of inquiry in all matters, including those of Christian dogma.

Evans provided Douglas with a sound training in scientific logic. The ability to identify and to ask the right questions, to grasp the essence of a matter rather than its superficial characteristics, remained a Douglas trademark throughout his career. Evans's class in geological history looked back on hundreds of millions of years of planetary evolution and posed as serious a challenge to the fundamentalists as any of MacNeill's seminars. For Douglas, it was an exercise in scientific reasoning. "MacNeill and Evans," Douglas said of his favourite teachers, "taught that the stories their students had absorbed over the years were in some cases just old wives' tales, fairy stories. At the same time, you had to recognize that to throw out the baby with the bathwater didn't solve your problems."[7]

Douglas's teachers inspired him and encouraged him to think for himself; his peers at Brandon accepted him as a natural leader. Brandon College was a tiny institution—until the end of the Second World War its student population seldom reached 200. In this atmosphere, students developed close and lasting friendships, and everyone had to take part in almost every field of activity if a real college life was to be maintained. No one plunged into college life with greater enthusiasm than Tommy Douglas.

From the beginning, he established himself as an able scholar. He won the general proficiency scholarships in each of his years in the academy and, despite the weight of non-academic activities, took his share of awards in his senior years too. Often, in later years, he would talk of his greatest coup—winning the senior prize in Hebrew in a class composed only of himself and two Jewish students preparing for the rabbinate. In speaking of the Tommy Douglas of these college years, one of his old associates said: "I would almost call [his] a charismatic gift. He had a smile and a way of dealing with people, a rare gift of language and an ability to relate himself to whatever was going on as if it was his particular contribution. He would get to the centre of a debate, of a musical program or a play or a lecture as if he had sort of brought it in to being himself."[8]

He quickly established a reputation as an orator and a debater, and even in his first year represented the college in intervarsity debating. In his first debate against a team from the University of Manitoba, he and his colleague successfully argued the negative of the topic, "Resolved: Western Civilization is Degenerating." Even before that, in his very first debate against another Brandon team, he showed that his expert foot-work was not confined to the boxing ring. The student newspaper, *The Quill*, observed, "We learned some rather startling facts, some of which seemed to be entirely original."[9] Douglas won. The young orator continued to lead winning debating teams; however, in his final year he suffered one notable loss by a unanimous decision. The opposing side included Irma Dempsey, the future Mrs Tommy Douglas. It is difficult to believe that even given the chance, he would have deliberately thrown the debate. It seems more likely that he had, in fact, at last met his match.

Douglas also pursued his interest in drama. He acted in several interyear drama competitions, or "Lit. Nights," and in the major productions staged for the public. The college offered elocution classes for the benefit of the theology students, the "theologs," where he developed his natural storytelling gift by working on the fine points of timing and voice projection. The immediate reward was financial—Douglas supplemented his slender income by giving readings and recitations at chicken suppers and church socials around the Brandon district. He often acted as the public spokesman for his student colleagues, voicing their farewells when MacNeill left the college in 1929 and enthusiastically greeting the appointment of Evans to the principalship.

Douglas played an active role in student government. He became a vice-president of the Student Representative Council while still an academy student, and in his graduating year he was elected "senior stick," the title given to the president of the student body. He was an active member of the Student Christian Movement, serving it both as an executive member and, later, as president. During his first university year he represented the college at the Tenth Quadrennial Convention of the Student Volunteer Movement, held in Detroit, Michigan, the theme of the convention being "Wanted—Builders for a Christian Internationalism." While such an experience might seem ordinary in an age of jet travel, in its time it was a major event in a young student's life.

The various claims on his time made it necessary for Douglas to neglect his athletic specialty, boxing. He had won the Manitoba flyweight title in 1922, and again in 1923, but dropped out of competition after entering the college. According to the college paper, there were occasional impromptu matches in the residence corridors after evening study hours, staged largely for in-house entertainment.

The theologs, being for the most part older and more mature than their fellows, played a leading role in student life. Some of them went on to distinguished careers in the ministry; and although the Baptist church was already turning to the right in the 1920s, several, like Douglas, would later join the socialist party and even stood for election. One of these was Stanley Knowles, a fellow member of the Typographical Union. The decorous behaviour of the Knowles of later years, the dean of the House of Commons, is difficult to reconcile with that of Knowles the college cheer-leader, leading his troops in a resounding rendition of the yell "Hippy Skippy."

Despite his active college life, Douglas devoted increasing time to working as a student supply minister. His first regular posting came not at a Baptist church but among the Presbyterians. In his last year in the academy, after a chance meeting with the field secretary of the Presbyterian church in Manitoba, Douglas agreed to take virtually full charge of Knox Church in Carberry.

Carberry, in February 1927—the month in which Douglas's mission began—was a town of a few hundred people. It was the trading centre for a prosperous agricultural community that had grown up in the last quarter of the nineteenth century, when westward migration, improvements in dry-land farming techniques, and the promise of the new transcontinental railway pushed settlement out of the Red River Valley and on to Manitoba's prairie uplands. Geographically, Carberry was fewer than 150 miles from Douglas's Canadian home in North Winnipeg. Socially, it occupied another planet. Carberry confronted the young preacher with the rural values and the rural issues that would preoccupy him for much of his adult life.

The community where Douglas had served his apprenticeship was one made up largely of blue-collar workers and small businesses. North Winnipeg was a unique microcosm, and a boisterous one, of the ethnic mix of Canada. It was a hot-bed of ideological debate, the core of the city's militant trade unionism. The presence of the other Winnipeg on the south banks of the Assiniboine, the stronghold of wealth and Protestant virtue, served only to spur on the workers' movements in the north end. Carberry, by contrast, was a stolid Anglo-Protestant village. The dominant strain of its public philosophy was the Toryism which the settlers had brought with them from Ontario. The hard core was, in a sense, a colourful lot—their politics were blue, their lodge Orange. As followers of Good King William they had trouble in accepting lesser mortals—that is, anyone from a different racial or religious background.

Douglas now entered a battle for minds and souls. *The Quill* commented: "It is alleged that Tommy Douglas's propensity for playing practical jokes has suffered under the weight of responsibility while managing a Carberry Church...It is hard to believe."[10] Whether or not his personal sacrifices extended so far is not clear. What is clear is that he added most of the burdens of a full-time ministry to his academic load, and he succeeded in both.

Douglas's performance in public life, as a parliamentary back-bencher, a provincial premier, and as a national leader, have tended to obscure his record as a minister of the gospel. This record is important not only because of his success as a minister, but because the notion of "ministry," as he developed it, underlay his later career. When the time came, Douglas accepted political life as a full-time calling, appearing only as a guest before various churches and synagogues. In a sense, though, he stayed in the ministry all his life. He exchanged pulpits, moving to a podium that gave him access to an immeasurably larger congregation, and one which promised greater opportunities to deal directly with those issues of human existence which were the source of his Christian concern. The foundations of his ministries, sacred and secular, were set: a firm belief in the Fatherhood of God; and total submission to the idea, in all of its shades and colours, of the Brotherhood of Man. To these beliefs all other concerns were secondary. According to these beliefs all human action was to be measured.

It was a simple faith, shorn of all dogma, easy to live with if monstrously difficult to apply in an increasingly complicated and secularized world. It was a faith that made Douglas unshakeably optimistic about God's purpose and about the goodness of human beings. He derived from it the operating principle of his existence—that people should be always aware of their responsibilities for one another.

The life of Knox Church under its young pastor is reflected, in some detail, in the columns of Carberry's weekly newspaper, *The News-Express*. Considering that he spent his week in classes at Brandon for most of the year, Douglas did a remarkable job of keeping his church active. He placed a strong emphasis on youth work, the activities of the Sunday school, the young people's organization, and the non-denominational Scouts and Cubs. He directed much of his preaching to the young people within and outside his congregation. He opened his Sunday evening services and after-service programs to the whole community, after the fashion of Woodsworth's "People's Sunday Evenings" in pre-war Winnipeg. Sunday morning services in Carberry, as elsewhere, were dedicated largely to the teachings of the individual churches, and there was little crossing of party lines. But as one who remembered those times recalled, on Sunday evenings "there was only one church in Carberry."[11]

From the beginning, Douglas placed the highest priority on his role as a preacher—on the effectiveness of the pulpit as a place from which to convey, by many devices, the messages of the gospel as they related to everyday life. His skills as an elocutionist and as an actor came into full play. Church notices carried such items as, "The Pastor will dramatize the Book of Esther," or, "Rev. T. C. Douglas gave a dramatization of 'The Fourth Wise Man' in place of the regular sermon." If a full house signalled a successful ministry, then Douglas succeeded, even at this early stage. He advertised his sermon topics in the local paper, and designed the ads to catch the reader's attention and interest. He preached his first sermon, ambitiously enough, on "Why We Fail as Christians," and disposed of the matter in one sitting. He followed this at a later date with "The Gospel in a Nutshell." Sometimes the title showed his wit: "God Provides Food for Every Bird, but He Doesn't Throw it in to the Nest"; sometimes it was downright intriguing—"The Woman who was a Hustler in the Church." He displayed the talents of the showman, with the result that he often had to set up extra seating for overflow congregations.[12]

Knox Church became a centre for cultural activities in Carberry. The young people's group mounted plays and variety nights under Douglas's direction, and musicians from Brandon often came at his invitation to put on recitals and musical evenings. It remained his view that an effective pastorate required more than preaching; it required a social outreach that made the church a focal point for the social, cultural, and intellectual life of the community.

One other element of this early ministry demands comment: the evidence of his growing sympathy with the Jewish community and its religion. He held this attachment throughout his life, and with the slightest encouragement he donned his yarmulke and entered the synagogue. His respect for the Jewish faith pre-dated his appearance in the Carberry pulpit. Brought up in a Scottish church tradition, he undoubtedly received a full exposure to the Old Testament, its prophets, and, especially, the Psalms which were so much a part of Scottish culture. In his days in North Winnipeg, his interest in social change brought him into constant contact with a sizable and vocal Jewish population. His career in Carberry tested his biases to the full, as the social gospeller from North Winnipeg was exposed to the voice of Manitoba upland Toryism.

The spokesman for the local moral gendarmerie, the guardian of the town's code of behaviour, was the editor of the *News-Express*. Mixed in with his columns of "boiler plate," the pre-printed copy that was the mainstay of the one-man paper, the editor offered an array of news-cum-editorial items like this one from the fall of 1927: "A member of the Carberry teaching staff took a couple of days off this week to celebrate the Jewish New Year with friends in Winnipeg. This is a precedent which will doubtless be followed by the Scotch to celebrate St. Andrew's Day, the Irish St. Patrick's Day and the English St. George's Day. What a howl would be raised in the district if a member of the staff, who happened to be a Roman Catholic took a day off to celebrate a church festival."[13] Quite apart from the implication that Christmas and Easter were strictly Protestant holidays, the column was in all respects waspish. In a town with only two Jewish families, it was not necessary to be overtly anti-Jewish—the tone of moral superiority was sufficient.

Whether in response to such overt comments, or impelled by his own convictions, Douglas took it upon himself to break down the barriers of misunderstanding. As one Carberry native who attended his services later recalled, he preached memorable sermons on the history of the Jews and their religious beliefs. On these Sunday evenings, and others, the two Jewish families of Carberry occupied two pews in Knox Presbyterian Church.

The student minister resigned from his charge at Carberry in April

1929. In preparation for his final academic year, he took charge of two small churches at Shoal Lake, Manitoba—his reasoning being that he could now deliver the same sermon morning and evening. Within a few months he was preaching alternate Sundays at Calvary Baptist Church in Weyburn. After graduating from Brandon College in 1930 he took a full-time position as pastor at Calvary.

There was more to the college years than study, preaching, and student affairs. There was also Irma, the bride who joined him when he moved to Weyburn and who would serve as companion and protector for fifty-six years. Irma was a teenage member of the Carberry congregation and was active in the musical life of the town. In the fall of 1928, accompanied by her mother, she moved to Brandon and registered as a piano student in the college's music faculty. Carberry was horse country, and Irma's father Hull Dempsey was a well-known horse dealer, noted among other things for his surrey and his exceptional team of "drivers." Dempsey had broken his limbs and back in a fall and moved about with great difficulty, but another horse fancier called him "the happiest man I ever met."[14]

In the course of a conversation which somehow wandered on to brewery wagons and draft horses, Douglas commented in 1985 on his own good fortune. He had sometimes looked after his Grandfather Clement's horses in Glasgow; and during that period when he was burning distillers' names on to corks for whiskey bottles, he met an older man who drove a team of Clydes. Douglas spent many of his days off in this man's company, cleaning harness and polishing the brass ornamentation, and their discussions were always about horses—as it turned out, a lucky circumstance. Douglas said later, "If I hadn't been able to talk to Irma's dad about horses, I doubt that he would have ever let me marry his daughter."[15]

Douglas's affair with Brandon College did not end with graduation in the spring of 1930. Soon after arriving in Weyburn he registered in a graduate program in sociology and returned to Brandon in 1933 to pick up his Master of Arts degree—granted by McMaster University. He stayed in touch with Brandon throughout his life, and among the active files in his desk drawer when he died was his copy of the college year book, *The Sickle*, for his graduating year, 1930.

Brandon, though, did not always return Douglas's love, especially after he entered socialist politics. Dr. Evans, a declared Liberal in politics, held to a tolerant position—he viewed Douglas as a Prodigal Son, beloved and destined in time to return to the fold, but in the meantime not a favourite topic of conversation. However, Evans's detached view was not held uniformly among his associates, or among those claiming to support the college.

In 1942, for example, a faculty member invited Douglas to the campus to give seminars and to join in a few "bull sessions" in the college smoking room. Within minutes of his appearance the official telephones of the college were ringing with complaints that "that man Douglas is on the campus spreading his Communist propaganda." Dr. Evans quickly traced the calls to members of the Brandon Liberal Association. Nonetheless, the dean of arts confronted the erring faculty member— Tom McLeod of Weyburn, an old friend of Douglas's—and a vigorous exchange of opinion took place. It would be many years before Douglas again visited Brandon as an official guest of the college; however, his informal visits continued, and the dean never pressed the issue again.

Rehabilitation came, in part with Brandon's transition from a Baptist school to a state-run college affiliated with the University of Manitoba, and in part with the political successes of Douglas and his CCF party. In 1961, during its last days as an affiliated college, Brandon awarded Douglas an honorary doctorate (Manitoba). Nine years later, the new Brandon University invited him back to award him its own LLD.

At the 1970 convocation, Douglas gave the address. It was a period of student unrest, and a faction of young radicals known as the Waffle was rocking the NDP, but he chose to remember his own youthful ideals and to make common cause with the young: "We must face the fact that the youth of today are in revolt against our way of life. Don't be misled by the beards, the long hair and the mini-skirts. These are merely the symbols of a generation which is disenchanted with the value systems of modern society. In this contest, I am on the side of youth. Their methods are often crude, and their aims are sometimes confused, but basically this is a protest against a society that has failed to meet man's deepest needs and impedes the realization of man's finest ambitions."[16]

Douglas treasured his honorary degrees as symbols of recognition from the governors of his Alma Mater, but he got greater satisfaction from a tribute paid by Brandon's students. In 1985 the student body dedicated its new student union building to Douglas and his old companion-in-arms and fellow Brandon alumnus, Stanley Knowles. Knowles, in the new era of socialist respectability, had even become the chancellor of Brandon University. The building is called the Knowles-Douglas Student Centre.

4
Dustbowl Preacher

TOMMY DOUGLAS FIRST TRAVELLED to Weyburn in the fall of 1929, just as the world was entering the Great Depression. The town was only a generation old, and its patchwork of streets, buildings, and vacant lots testified to the rawness of its frontier beginnings. Although the local Baptists had arrived in the earliest days, the trees around their little white church on Coteau Avenue were still young.

The congregation of Calvary Church had solidified over time into a body of steady, moderate folk. Its ministers had brought a zeal for practical Christianity to the new country, and some had taken leading positions in Saskatchewan's early social service movement. Calvary maintained its ties with the liberal academics at Brandon College during a time that more conservative Baptists were shying away. In 1929 the congregation's 140 members found themselves without a pastor, and they turned to the college and President Evans for help.[1] Evans sent two young men to try out for a permanent appointment. Over the winter, Douglas and his friend Stanley Knowles occupied the pulpit on alternate Sundays. On February 23, 1930, a special general meeting of the church membership issued the call to Tommy Douglas.

Douglas could now begin the settled life of a full-time minister. The church board set his starting salary at $1800 per year, at a time when school principals might earn $1200 and many farm families had almost no cash income. Had he wanted it, he might have followed his predecessors to bigger churches, bigger cities, and even more solid positions. This, however, was not to be his choice.

There is no doubt that Douglas did the things required of a new minister. He showed talent and energy as an evangelist, an important strength in a denomination anxious to spread the Good News. At his first meeting with his Board of Deacons, he announced that he would take Sunday afternoon services at churches and halls outside of Weyburn. He also conducted week-long revival programs in the city, and a report from the deacons rejoiced that "the Christian messages so ably interpreted and forcefully applied by Mr. Douglas...were practical and helpful far beyond human ability to measure...We are grateful to our Heavenly Father for the influence of these meetings upon our Church life, for the Decisions made and the additions to the membership of our Church through the Baptisms that followed."[2] Out in the community, Douglas associated at first with Weyburn's up-and-coming business people and professionals. As a member of the Young Fellows' Club, he met men like Junior Staveley, the son of a pioneer land speculator and later the most powerful Liberal in the district. Here Douglas helped raise money for a civic swimming pool, and earned the nickname "Slivers" after sitting down too abruptly on a wooden bench.[3]

It soon became clear that Douglas would not live a life of prayer meetings and service club luncheons. The spectre of poverty, in the city and in the countryside, challenged the young pastor to rededicate himself to the social gospel. Across Canada a revived Christian left was urging the country to action, and in many prairie towns the Protestant ministers stepped foward to speak for the poor before local councils and in the press. Douglas found himself working within a network of concerned people, with clergymen, teachers, labour activists, and co-op organizers. Similar networks were forming in towns across the province, and they would form the core of the CCF, the party that Douglas would lead into power in Saskatchewan in the next decade.

Late in his life Douglas told a story that illustrated his effort to bring over his neighbours to the cause of social action. One Sunday after church, the treasurer of the Young Fellows—a leading member of the Calvary congregation—took Douglas aside. The well-fed, well-dressed lawyer looked at the young preacher with concern.

"I just can't understand it," he said, "why do you get mixed up with this crowd?"

Douglas, in turn, asked, "What do you know about them?"

"Well, I see them when I go down the street..."

"Do you know anything about them, really?"

"I suppose not."

"Will you come with me for just a day?"

The next afternoon, when the two returned from a tour of the city, they sat down in the shade of the church. The lawyer was on the verge of tears and remained silent for several minutes. Finally he said, "I wouldn't have believed this. Kids without shoes who can't go to school...a woman going to have a baby with no place to put it when it arrives."[4] Even when suffering surrounds us, said Douglas, we close our eyes to it. Even in the pit of the Depression, many Canadians clung to their inherited belief that only the wicked and the shiftless are poor and that capitalism provides for everyone who is willing to work.

His years in the dustbowl convinced Douglas that he must, in the words of an earlier social gospel minister, "shine the light clear upon the evil"—and he saw evil in abundance in the growing poverty of his flock.[5] Before he thought of entering politics he learned to speak out and to organize, to persuade and persist. The wealthy lawyer in the story agreed at least on the need for charity. Douglas would convince others, over time, of the need for systematic change. He came to realize that social action is the art of the possible; but for him, the boundaries of the possible extended beyond the range of vision of most people.

His mission in Weyburn extended beyond his own congregation, to all of the community's dispossessed, churched and unchurched. In this he worked with several members of the local Ministerial Association, especially Dr. William Cameron, later to be elected moderator of the Presbyterian Church in Canada, and the Rev. Herb Cobb, minister at Grace United Church. Douglas, Cameron, and Cobb worked in concert to find support for desperate farm families and struggling mothers, and they joined with the unions in approaching City Hall to seek help for the unemployed. As Douglas remembered it, they were told, "It isn't any business of yours." To which Douglas replied, "Anything is my business that affects the people I come into contact with."[6]

Church congregations in other provinces, particularly Manitoba, Ontario, and British Columbia, joined in the effort, and food and used clothing came in to Weyburn by the carload. He recalled, "I became the repository for all the junk that nobody knew what to do with. The Baptist Church downstairs was just filled with clothing, perfectly good clothing people had outgrown...it became the distributing centre for the unemployed."[7]

Douglas was spurred on by what he had seen in Chicago, where he spent the summer of 1931. He went there to register in a PhD program in sociology at the university. He never finished the degree, but the impressions from that summer lasted a lifetime and pushed him towards a new political awareness. Chicago, the second largest city in the United States, showed evidence of economic rot to a degree that far surpassed his previous experience. His field work sent him into slums worse than Glasgow's, and to the hobo jungles where homeless young men of his own age frittered away their days. "I'd studied socialism and syndicalism and communism and capitalism...but I'd never sat down and honestly asked myself what was wrong with the economic system."[8]

In trying to answer the question of what ailed capitalism, Douglas introduced himself to some of the intellectuals of the American Socialist movement and found them scanning the heavens for pie in the sky. Sitting next to a crisis which appalled him, these thinkers passed their days discussing socialist ideology, and made no move to bring about change in the real world. "I went to their meetings. They spent most of their time debating whether or not, come the revolution, you would have communal feeding in the basements of schools, or whether we would have communal kitchens and people come and get their food and eat at their own place...The idea of cooking at home was a waste of time...The fact that people didn't have anything to eat didn't seem to bother them at all."[9]

Douglas was attracted by the word *socialist*, but the attitude of the American Marxists ran counter to the lessons he had learned in his young manhood. Practical Christianity taught that change flows from attacking the problems of the poor here and now, not from drawing up grand revolutionary plans. The Christian left in Canada had acted not through splinter groups, but through common fronts made up of anyone willing to lend a hand.

Saskatchewan had strong leftist traditions, based on the experience of the social gospel and on the success of the early farm organizers. However, it was not until after Douglas arrived in Saskatchewan that the province's radicals formed their own political party. In 1932, farm and labour groups forged an historic alliance, led by George Hara Williams, president of the United Farmers, and Major James Coldwell, the head of the scattered Independent Labour movement.

Saskatchewan had grown up in response to a buoyant world demand for wheat. Rapid expansion had made it the third most populous province in Canada; two-thirds of its million people lived on farms or in crossroads hamlets, and its towns and cities depended to a very large extent on the wheat economy. From territorial days, the farmers of Saskatchewan had organized to improve their position, placing great emphasis on adult education, discussion, and community work. Political debate ranked just behind food and shelter as a necesssity of life, and political action was a favourite avocation. In a real sense it was a rebel province, one which from the start had experimented with the use of government—provincial and local—as an appropriate device for meeting its needs.

The dominant farm organization, the Saskatchewan Grain Growers' Association, had always been divided on whether to assert the farmers' rights through political or economic action. The SGGA flirted with politics before 1920 in its endorsation of the Progressive Party, but its real energies went into the creation of a farmer-owned and -operated marketing system. With the formation of the Wheat Pool in 1923, an immediate success in a healthy world market, it appeared that the farmers had taken control of their destiny by using economic means. The collapse of world commodity markets wiped out the Wheat Pool's assets and put it deeply into debt. It was the most traumatic event in the history of organized agriculture in western Canada, and it prompted a reappraisal of the Saskatchewan farmers' strategy. At the time that the Douglases settled in Weyburn, the SGGA—now the United Farmers of Canada, Saskatchewan Section—was in a state of flux.

The fall of the Pool coincided fairly closely with the rise of George Williams, elected in 1929 as the president of the UFC. Williams was a forceful and sometimes brusque man, an informed student of history and politics, a seasoned organizer and a tireless worker. He was also a socialist who, unlike most of the farm leaders before him, refused to enlist with the old parties. He carried off his 1929 takeover of the farmers' organization like a military assault. He defeated five less radical candidates, and, in the aftermath of the election, half of the UFC's board of directors and most of its staff quit. Williams had read the mood of the rank and file correctly, though. His position was firm and the turn-around complete. The convention voted for "the abolition of capitalist robbery."[10]

In 1931, after consolidating their position, Williams and his allies set a new political tone for Saskatchewan as the UFC's February convention decided on direct political action. The farmers' movement would operate as a political party, supporting its own radical platform, nominating its own candidates, and running its own campaigns. The move profoundly affected both the political history of Saskatchewan and the career of Tommy Douglas. And because Saskatchewan later became the political and financial anchor of the national CCF, George Williams's generalship made a lasting mark on Canada.

The economic collapse also spurred Saskatchewan's urban left into organizing new workers' associations and Independent Labour parties. The leading figure in this movement, M. J. Coldwell of Regina, had travelled the rural areas for several years as a featured speaker. The programs of the Labour groups closely resembled Williams's UFC platform.

The Calvary congregation was an example of the kind of constituency that would respond to this growing political ferment. Many of its members were railway, retail, or hospital workers. Douglas estimated that two-thirds of them followed him into the CCF. Ethel Campbell, for example, ran the boarding house where he had lived in the months before he married Irma. Her husband Clayton headed the railway clerks' union at the Canadian Pacific yards. Later, as a school trustee, he would defend the right of teachers to work in political campaigns for the CCF. Ted Stinson and John Powers, members of the Board of Deacons and the organizers of a co-op store, acted with Douglas in his early political ventures as his official agent and campaign manager, respectively.

In the fall of 1931 a violent strike in the Estevan coal fields showed how vulnerable working people were to abuse during this economic slump. One of the most vicious chapters in Canadian labour history was written in that bleak corner of the province, less than two hours from Weyburn by train, in a strike that took a heavier toll in lives than had the Winnipeg General Strike. For Douglas, this strike must have appeared as a reprise of the conflict that he had watched with Mark Talney from their Winnipeg roof-top in 1919. Working conditions in the coal fields had always been far worse than those in the city. With the Depression providing an abundance of cheap labour, the Estevan coal operators were anxious to make conditions worse still. The fundamental issue was the same as in 1919: the rights of the workers to organize in a union of their own choice and to bargain collectively. The responses of the employers and the governments of the day followed the pattern set in Winnipeg, with even more tragic results.

Frustrated in their attempts to bring management to the bargaining table, the miners in the Souris coal fields struck on September 7, 1931. They had failed to secure the support of the established trade unions—

the Trades and Labour Congress and the All-Canadian Congress—and they had called in organizers from the Mine Workers' Union of Canada, a union affiliated with the Workers' Unity League of Canada and the Red International of Russia. There is no evidence that this affiliation had any effect on the union's choice of tactics; but the Communist link, together with the prevalence of foreign (i.e., non-British) names among the miners, was enough to provoke charges of a Red conspiracy. The essence of the affair, the deplorable working conditions at the mines and the right of the workers to seek improvement, was totally obscured.

The Estevan strike became, in fact, industrial warfare. It ended when the workers tried to stage a protest parade and the police attacked with bullets and clubs. Twenty-three people, some merely bystanders, were injured. Three men died; for years afterwards their comrades would keep their graves fresh with flowers.

Although the big labour organizations had defaulted, the strikers were not without friends. The United Farmers of Canada, Saskatchewan Section, took an immediate and sympathetic interest in their problems. The UFC's radical leadership called publicly for the right of workers to organize and to bargain collectively. They sponsored an independent investigation into the conditions at the mines and the results showed that a miner might dig thirty-six and a half tons of coal and receive $71.75, minus deductions for doctor, tools (which had to be purchased from the company store), rental, and lights. The report upheld the miners' claim that it was possible to "work month in and month out without receiving any cash at all."[11]

Of all the Saskatchewan cities, Weyburn was closest to the field of action; many of the casualties of the riot were treated in Weyburn by the city's doctors. The justice of the workers' cause and its dismal resolution weighed heavily on the mind of the Baptist preacher. His sermon topics in the fall of 1931 reflect the impact of the turbulent times on his thinking. In the midst of the strike he preached on the topic "Jesus the Revolutionist," and asked, "Would Jesus revolt against our present system of graft and exploitation?" How would Jesus view the coal miners' strike in Estevan? Were he to come to Earth again would we crown him, crucify him, or merely deport him? Douglas spearheaded a campaign to collect a truckload of food for the miners and their families. He visited the strikers in the field. His presence there caused the mine owners to complain to Douglas's church board, and he was to write years later that they "forbade the men to attend any meeting I might hold."[12]

That same autumn, Douglas helped to organize a workers' association called the Weyburn Independent Labour Association. The group did not, at first, pose as a political party. The local Conservative member of the provincial legislature addressed their first meeting. In the words of the *Weyburn Review*, "The WILA was organized as a protective association for the benefit of the working men of the City." Nonetheless, the association's objectives reflected the current of events that was moving Saskatchewan's left-wing forces towards a coalition and the formation of the

CCF. Their goals included a non-contributory scheme of unemployment insurance; public ownership of public utilities; and equal rights of citizenship irrespective of sex, class, origin, or religion. In summary, the WILA hoped "to influence public opinion by peaceful and legal methods in favour of organized labour and to secure legislation in the interests of the working class."[13]

Douglas went to work to create a positive understanding of the association's aims. He asked leading figures of the farmers' political movement to speak on behalf of the WILA—people such as Agnes MacPhail, a veteran United Farmers MP from Ontario; George Williams, the United Farmers' leader; and Louise Lucas, a respected farm-movement organizer. Of all those in the audience at these meetings, it seems that none was more affected than Douglas himself. The deepening depression, and the social havoc it was wreaking, had convinced him that volunteer effort and local lobbying could not address the problems of national economic disaster.

For example, Douglas was deeply disturbed about the weakness of the medical-care system. Some municipalities in Saskatchewan kept doctors on salary, but Canada and its provinces had never provided systematic hospital care for all, and the free-market approach excluded the poor. With the Depression, the ranks of the poor swelled to include farm families, unemployed workers, and old and disabled people whose relatives had lost their money. Unfortunately, the only way for Douglas and his fellow activists to address the problem was on a local, voluntary scale. "We had about eight doctors in town," he remembered later, "and a hospital: empty beds, but people stayed home sick. They couldn't pay. And you couldn't blame the hospital, the hospital couldn't take them in and take payment in soap coupons. [The hospitals] had to pay for groceries, they had to pay their staff."[14]

Douglas and his colleagues organized an appeal to raise donations from anyone who could spare them, and some doctors offered their services free of charge in emergencies. But it became increasingly clear that voluntary effort would never meet the problem. "When we would put out a call for help for a family, people would come, the banker's wife, the banker himself, people in responsible positions. But what could they do? There was no use just saying fork up another 20 or 30 bucks or 100 bucks and we'll send this person to the hospital. They can't do that every week."[15]

Douglas recognized that his forces in Weyburn had to become part of a larger body, dedicated to direct political action on at least the provincial front. Seeking guidance, he wrote in the spring of 1932 to J. S. Woodsworth. Douglas had followed the the career of the North Winnipeg MP since his election to Parliament in 1921, and had seen him in action at meetings in Brandon. At this very time, after years of preparing the ground, Woodsworth was starting to build the country's first national coalition on the political left, the Co-operative Commonwealth Federation.

In his response, Woodsworth suggested that the young preacher should get in touch with Coldwell, the man who was to become Douglas's political mentor and lifelong friend. M. J. (he rarely used his given names, Major James) was an English immigrant who worked in Regina as a school principal. He had earned his stripes in the Progressive movement, managing a campaign and, later, standing as a candidate. Both campaigns ended in losses, but by the late 1920s Coldwell was, simultaneously, a teacher, a Labour alderman in Regina, a leader in the Saskatchewan Teachers' Federation, and an officer of the Farmers' Political Asssociation. Not surprisingly, the old parties recognized Coldwell as a rising political power. Jimmy Gardiner, the provincial Liberal leader, offered him a cabinet seat in his vain attempt to build a Liberal government in 1929. In the 1940s, when Coldwell was in the House of Commons, Mackenzie King made a similar offer. Coldwell spurned them both. He was a liberal by temperament, with an overriding concern for social justice and civil liberties, but he abhorred the Liberal Party's opportunism, its broken promises, and its machine politics.

Coldwell might have remained a Progressive, except that the battered Saskatchewan Progressive Association fell to pieces in 1929. Almost at the same time Woodsworth appeared in Regina on one of his innumerable tours, and he urged Coldwell to bring together other Regina labour leaders in a new political grouping. The result was an Independent Labour Party, which attracted a few dozen railway workers, preachers, teachers, and professionals. Coldwell was elected president, and his assistant principal at Thomson School, young Clarence Fines, became treasurer. A few weeks later Woodsworth returned to Regina and they conducted a small conference of western Labour parties, with nineteen delegates present from four provinces. This was the network into which Woodsworth invited Douglas and his Weyburn associates in early 1932.

Almost as soon as Douglas wrote to Coldwell, the schoolmaster showed up on the preacher's front step in Weyburn. His manner of arrival delighted Irma and provided Douglas with a tale he often told through the years. Irma answered the door when Coldwell knocked, and he asked, "Is your father home?" The meeting initiated a bond between M. J. and Irma which lasted throughout Coldwell's life. In his final years, when M. J. was alone, Irma guided him on his weekly shopping expeditions.

Coldwell's visit to Weyburn was a fruitful one. He helped to organize a Weyburn Independent Labour Party, with Douglas as founding president. This group soon joined forces with Coldwell's Regina-based ILP, and the provincial leader began making periodic visits to Weyburn to speak at picnics and gatherings in country schoolhouses. Coldwell and Douglas became fast friends, addicted to endless political small-talk, and at the same time motivated by a broadly based social Christianity. Coldwell's stature in the farm movement also helped to establish Douglas's position in the eyes of the local farmers.

Saskatchewan's Independent Labour movement was never large in numbers. At its height in early 1932 it took in perhaps 500 members in half a dozen cities. Its greatest asset was Coldwell, who reached thousands of listeners with his weekly talks from Regina on CKRM radio. He was one of the first prairie politicians to grasp the potential of radio, and the beauty of his voice allowed him an admirable command of the new mass medium. Douglas, who first heard of Coldwell through his broadcasts, said later, "He was easily the best broadcaster we ever produced...he had a marvellous voice, that lovely English without being too English, a cultured voice. And he had a great capacity to state his case in relatively simple language which was a result of his being a teacher." The station charged six dollars for each fifteen-minute broadcast, and if the listeners did not send in enough nickels and dimes, Clarence Fines had to cover the deficit. Nature had endowed Fines with a water-dowser's talent for finding money, a talent that for the next thirty years would keep the Saskatchewan CCF alive. "Coldwell was the orator," said Douglas, "Coldwell was the gladhander, Coldwell was the idea man, but Clarence was the person who built the political structure."[16]

In the spring of 1932 the United Farmers and Independent Labour conducted their first joint exercise, confronting the provincial cabinet to demand an end to farm foreclosures. In July of that year they established a formal partnership, calling it the Farmer Labour Party. From the beginning the question of who should lead the party caused problems. George Williams insisted that Coldwell should be leader, because Coldwell had a less radical image. However, Williams became chairman of the new party's council, a position from which he could (and did) manoeuvre against Coldwell as the need arose.

Under Douglas's guidance, the Weyburn Independent Labour Party became increasingly active on the local front. Over the next two years it sponsored public meetings which featured such headliners as Coldwell, Woodsworth, William Irvine, Elmore Philpott, and Professor Joe Parkinson. The party also held its own monthly meetings and explored such topics as "Socialized Medicine" and "Scrip Money." The latter discussion led the party members to the City Hall, "to recommend the issuing of scrip in the near future to meet the needs of the times locally."[17] It was an early sign of the fervour for monetary reform which would lead Douglas, before long, into serious conflict with the provincial movement.

The speakers, the propaganda, his reading in economics, history, popular science—all of them pointed Douglas towards the conclusion that Canada's leaders were ignoring the potential solutions to the country's problems. He grew weary of the argument that his neighbours in Weyburn were suffering because of the "hidden hand" of the marketplace and that the capitalist system was the inevitable result of human nature. He had learned to subject problems to rational inquiry, and a condition of "poverty in the midst of plenty" was clearly irrational. He became more and more attracted, through the decade of the 1930s, to the idea of social engineering—to an optimistic (and sometimes misplaced) faith that government can solve all problems if it puts enough experts on the payroll.

At the same time, Douglas was inspired by the grass-roots traditions of prairie radicalism. The American-influenced Progressive tradition—strongest in Canada around 1920—held that local political associations, rather than cigar-smoking power brokers in the capitals, should control the legislatures. Local voters should have the right to write legislation and vote on it in referendums. As a result, politicians would be bound to act in the public interest. This line of thinking fit in well with Douglas's Baptist individualism, and it would figure prominently in his first nomination speech.

Much of this democratic idealism, though, was technically impractical, and it could not by itself generate any economic or social ideas. It blamed most problems on the immorality of politicians rather than on the structure of the economy. The Farmer Labour movement, borrowing from British Labour, took a more scientific line which emphasized the role of the state and the civil service. The state would provide medical and hospital care for everyone on an equal basis. It would supply credit for the farmer and protection against eviction; insurance for the worker against loss of income due to unemployment; and universal pensions for old people. "I became convinced," said Douglas, "that unless you put in a socialist society that will deal with every aspect of life, then there'll be all kinds of people falling between organizations."[18] But who would manage this society from day to day? The grass roots or the expert? As an opposition politician, and on the campaign trail, Douglas would emphasize the importance of popular control. As a government leader, he would become renowned for his use of planners and experts.

An early example of Douglas's faith in the expert was his Master's thesis, written in 1932. He had taken his courses from McMaster University in Hamilton by mail. His forty-three-page thesis, "The Problems of the Subnormal Family," earned him his degree in sociology. It proposed a devastating solution to what he saw as a key cause of poverty: the segregation of the "mentally and morally subnormal," and the sterilization of the mentally handicapped.

Douglas's decision to write on this topic reflected the state of North American sociology and psychology. Some of his teachers had gone to school in the days when psychology was known as "mental and moral science," and mental illness was often seen as the result of unsound ideas about God and society. The eugenics movement, which provided the basis for his thesis, had been growing as an influence on the social sciences for a generation. It aimed, simply, to breed a better human species. Eugenics sprang originally from the same nineteenth-century optimism that drove the social gospel crusade. If humanity could seize the levers of the divine evolutionary process, we could become more God-like. Strong human specimens must be encouraged to breed; the weak must be prevented from breeding. In the 1920s the movement gained momentum with the spread of a popular sociological notion that deviants and morons were reproducing fast enough to overrun civilization. Some eager theorists wanted to sterilize not only the mentally handicapped but also the "socially inadequate"—including, in a broad sweep, the "criminalistic," the disabled, the deformed, and the dependent.[19]

From this base Douglas began his argument, noting that the Weyburn district was home to a "growing group of indigents." For analytical purposes, he identified twelve "immoral or nonmoral women" who had produced, among them, ninety-five children, who in turn had brought forth 105 grandchildren. He observed that thirty-four of these were normal, judged by their progress in school, but another thirty-four were "moral delinquents," either because they had police records or had produced illegitimate children. In general, the same group suffered a high incidence of rickets and venereal disease. In setting out his conclusions, Douglas stated:

> The subnormal family presents the most appalling of all family problems...By subnormal we mean 1) a family whose mental rating is low, i.e. anywhere from high-grade moron to mentally defective; 2) a family whose moral standards are below normal, and who are delinquent; 3) as a usual, but not necessary corollary, a family subject to social disease; and, 4) so improvident as to be a public charge...
>
> Surely, the continued policy of allowing the subnormal family to bring into the world large numbers of individuals to fill our jails and our mental institutions, and to live upon charity, is one of consummate folly.

In response to these "appalling" problems, Douglas proposed that couples should be certified as to mental and physical fitness before marriage; that certified subnormals should be segregated in state farms or colonies; and that the mentally defective and the incurably diseased should be sterilized.[20]

Douglas's flirtation with eugenics was not simply an effort to please a professor. He returned to the same theme in 1934, in an article published in the Saskatchewan CCF *Research Review* under the heading "Youth and the New Age." He wrote: "The Kingdom of God is in our midst if we have the vision to build it. The rising generation will tend to build a heaven on earth rather than to live in misery in the hope of gaining some uncertain reward in the dim, distant future." The church, he said, must take an active part in social change if it is to uphold the law of God. As an example of social change, he praised the "science of eugenics" with its plan to control breeding among "subnormal" families. Future generations would cast superstition aside, he said, and prevent the mentally or physically unsound from rearing families.[21]

Douglas held two beliefs in remarkable contradiction at this time. He felt that the common citizen should have more control over his own life, but he also felt that a large group of citizens should be excluded from citizenship altogether. He was not alone. The United Farmers' government in Alberta, a Progressive regime with a mandate to improve the democratic system, had passed a "Sexual Sterilization Act" in 1928 and applied it frequently to inmates in provincial institutions. A "Human Betterment League" in California had increased the sterilization rate in that state. Sidney Webb and George Bernard Shaw, the leading British Fabians, were long-time supporters of the eugenics movement. They shared with Douglas a faith that agents of the state, working in the public service rather than for profit, would tend to work reasonably and humanely when putting any social reform into effect.

Douglas and the social scientists on whom he drew were guilty of overstating the extent of their knowledge. Their interpretation of such terms as "criminal" and "subnormal" showed a white, middle-class bias, and the programs that went into operation were highly arbitrary. A Calgary doctor, for example, recalled that an Alberta board of review ordered a twelve-year-old ward of the state sterilized in the 1950s because she had deformed feet. Tens of thousands of North Americans were sent under the knife by official order between the 1920s and the 1960s, and countless more were the object of private arrangements between parents and doctors.

Nonetheless, soon after Douglas wrote his thesis, the campaign to put new eugenics legislation into place ran out of steam. When the Nazis began, systematically, to sterilize their opponents, left-wing eugenicists like Julian Huxley and J. B. S. Haldane departed the movement. Neither science nor the state, they concluded, were mature enough to dictate human breeding patterns.

Douglas's enthusiasm for the idea also waned considerably. After the election of the CCF government in 1944, he received two official reviews of the Saskatchewan mental health-care system, one from a liberal expert and one from a radical left-wing scientist. Both recommended that the new government undertake a limited program of eugenical measures, including some sterilization of the mentally handicapped. Douglas, as minister of health, rejected these ideas and moved towards a system that emphasized therapy for the mentally ill and vocational training for the mentally handicapped.

Despite his increasing political activity, Douglas still found time for a wide range of pastoral and community duties. In the little study in his church on the corner, a couple of blocks from downtown, he wrote his sermons, his papers for McMaster, and his speeches on farmer-labour co-operation. The church itself was a distress centre and relief depot as well as a political headquarters. It was a place where ideas took root, and the results swept through the community. The study also became a counselling centre from which Douglas worked with the delinquent boys sent to him by a local judge, trying to find homes and work for them.

His job as a social worker caused him some headaches, but it did provide him with another story for future occasions. One day, in a fit of overzealousness, he agreed to take delivery of eleven delinquents who had appeared in court. In addition to scrubbing them clean in his own bathtub and re-clothing them from the church basement stocks, he undertook to develop an athletic program that would help fill their spare hours and teach them the virtues of fair play. He also hoped to keep them out of trouble with the law. Inevitably, in their boyish yearning for the good things of life, they slipped their leash and committed another break and enter. Once discovered, the plunder of cigarettes and chocolate bars that remained was handed over to the aggrieved shopkeeper, and the boys trooped back to the pastor's study. In Douglas's words, "I proceeded to give them my very best lecture...Pretty soon they began to cry and the tears flowed...It was a fine reconciliation." It was a time to apologize and repent—and the repentance included returning to the pastor his watch, his knife, his pen, and some other odds and ends they had lifted off of his desk while he delivered his sermon on the wages of sin.[22]

Along with the Revs. Cameron and Cobb, he also started a boys' group which met twice a week—once for recreation and athletic events and once for discussion. Many of the non-athletic sessions were held in the Douglas home, where the master orator gave the boys, some still in high school and some just out and unemployed, instruction in public speaking and debating. Knowing that most of the group could not afford to go away to university, Douglas produced, from his own university texts and lecture notes, a first-year course in economics. He hoped to expand this program to include other subjects, and, having profited from taking correspondence classes himself, he tried to have the courses recognized for credit by the University of Saskatchewan. The university turned down his request, but he continued to teach and planted the idea of university attendance in several young minds. Out of his small class would come three ministers of the United Church, two university professors, and one university official. Although one or two parents expressed some unease about the possible influence of the radical Douglas on their offspring, the program produced no CCF or NDP candidates.

A larger and more newsworthy venture was the formation of a local theatrical society. In the spring of 1932, the *Weyburn Review* announced a new day in the cultural history of southern Saskatchewan. In offering his preview of "Old Crusty Takes the Air," editor-reporter Walter Frederickson waxed lyrical: "With the presentation...of the play...by an entirely local cast, the development of dramatic art in Weyburn and district will undoubtedly receive a new impetus. In conversation with Rev. T. C. Douglas, who will direct and assume the leading role...the *Review* was informed that it is the purpose of those promoting the play to encourage the development of local talent in dramatic art, and to give the people really good plays within the reach of all. Arrangements are also being made to present this new comedy in a number of the leading centres in the southern part of the province." As testimony to the enthusiasm engendered by this effort, the paper went further to record: "the owners of Cleland's Hall [the only public hall of any size in the city] are going to considerable expense in rebuilding the stage and making new scenery for this and other performances to take place in the future."[23]

Many among the 500 who attended the presentation would long remember the preacher as "war hero," a role in which, the editor was satisfied, Douglas "demonstrated his ability as a clever actor." There were other plays, including a presentation of *Mr. Plimpton's Husband* ("the audience being kept in a continuous state of merriment''[24]), but the grander scheme for cultural revival never materialized as the career of Douglas the politician intruded increasingly on the time of Douglas the thespian. As late as 1942, however, he was directing some of the same actors in Christmas pageants at Calvary Baptist.

Douglas even managed a bit of time for his favourite sport, boxing, and appeared in some of the cards arranged by the local boxing club at the armouries. The weekly paper did not report on these local talent nights, so there is no won-lost record available. Soon other interests claimed his attention; his appearances in the ring became increasingly sporadic, and then stopped altogether.

When the Douglases bought a house near Calvary Church, they discovered in the garage a Model-A Ford, which remained unclaimed. The boys of the congregation rallied and painted it bright green. The Ford remained the family conveyance, taking them to Carlyle Lake in southeastern Saskatchewan for vacations. As Douglas grew busier over the next three decades, this resort gained increasing importance as a refuge where he could relax, read, play an occasional game of golf, and enjoy the company of his family.

In April 1934 his first daughter Shirley was born in Weyburn, and she quickly became a centre of attention for both her parents and the Calvary congregation. Shirley developed into a bright, pretty, and talented actress in her early childhood. Many years later the granddaughter of a family friend wrote to Douglas with a story about Shirley at Carlyle she had heard from her grandmother:

> [Shirley] was playing on the beach of Carlyle Lake when you called her. She blissfully ignored you, continuing to fill her bucket with sand. You called again, and again. Gram was nearby and said, "Isn't that your dad calling?"
> Shirley said, "Yes, but it isn't his mad voice."
> You called several more times before she turned to Grandma and said, "That's his mad voice," and slowly picked up her toys and ambled up the beach.[25]

Father's capacity for anger appears to have been limited. Daughter Joan, at a later time, recalled, "Daddy never yelled—his discipline, because it was so seldom, so quiet and so reasonable, was devastating. It left you feeling awful that you could disappoint this man so much. But mostly, he tended to spoil both Shirley and I—much to Mom's chagrin."[26]

In addition to the trips to the lake, the green Ford took Douglas to nearby rural points on Sunday afternoons, where he preached a third sermon, often to a non-Baptist congregation. On these excursions, he was usually chauffeured by his good friend Ted Stinson. The arrangement enhanced both Stinson's peace of mind and the public's safety—Douglas's driving was fast and erratic, though he continued to pass the required driver's tests when he was in his eighties. Fortunately, Irma, as a most proficient driver, usually provided the skill that Douglas lacked.

Through all his ups and downs, Irma was beside him. Physically, she was even smaller than her flyweight husband. Her keen sense of fun was complemented with an infectious giggle, characteristics which she carried into her later years. Modest to a fault, undemanding and uncomplaining, her daughter Shirley said of her that "she never made a fuss. She could have lived in a tent and made it comfortable." She sang in the church choir, worked in the church women's group, and avoided the spotlight. The official duties of a pastor's (and later, a politician's) wife she performed with grace and dignity, but she never revelled in them. Her chosen role, and one of growing importance in the life of her husband, was that of providing a shelter from the inevitable turmoil which surrounded her family. Shirley said, "Our house was run totally around my father by my mother. Our house was always my favourite house. There was something about the atmosphere—it was the coolest, quietest, calmest house I've ever been in."[27] As Douglas himself put it, Irma's presence made it possible for him to carry on. "The marvellous thing about Irma is that nothing seems to faze her, even when things are at their worst," he told interviewer Grant Maxwell. "You'd come home off the road, all hell would be breaking loose because of news reports that we were going to do this or that, and someone was threatening to sue for libel. But she'd never be perturbed. She may have worried a lot underneath, but you never saw it."[28]

From time to time, Douglas sought escape from his work, and found it, naturally enough, in a Weyburn printing shop. Printers used to say that "printer's ink gets in your blood," that a printer becomes addicted to the smell of paper, of ink and padding glue, together with the sound of voices raised over the busy clatter of the press. Douglas went in to breathe the air, and to listen to the debate and the retailing of wisdom that was offered almost every morning around the plant's huge pot-bellied stove. The crowd that gathered there took the name of the "Hot Stove League," although the owner of the plant, Thomas McLeod, was more inclined to refer to it as the "Hot Air League." Some were retired, some unemployed, some had businesses that, considering the city's economy, made no great demands on their time. In that winter season that sometimes seems forever in Saskatchewan, they came together for refuge from the cold, for a spirited discussion, and to wait for the morning train to bring in the mail and the Regina *Leader*. It was a place and a circle in which Douglas felt quite at home.

Douglas preached the social gospel of Bland and Woodsworth, directing his Christian family to look towards the real problems of real people. His long-time friend from Brandon days, the Rev. Edgar Bailey, commented: "I believe Tommy Douglas was issue oriented, that he became involved in things that related to people, and he put all of his abilities into that area when the issue came up. I don't believe that he was interested in politics from a political ambition point of view, I think he was interested in people."[29]

Certainly, he had no difficulty in filling the pews. An annual report of Calvary Baptist Church records "a splendid increase in attendance at all services."[30] He was more than a performer. In the words of one member of his congregation, "he provided a messsage of hope, and was a revered spiritual leader."[31]

In an interview in the last year of his life, Douglas set out the essence of his views of Christ and Christianity: "Jesus, more than anyone else who lived up to his time, and more than anyone since, epitomized the idea of the value of the individual...that the universe isn't made up of a great cruel God who tells everyone what to do, or of a great organization called the Church that steps with relentless heel on anyone who doesn't do what it tells them to do...Jesus was in his day, and he hasn't been surpassed since, a great moral teacher who recognized man's place in society, the kind of society that man could build...that the great motivating force in society is love for your fellow man...and that there is something that for want of a better term they call the Kingdom of God, which is simply an association of people who have certain ideas in common."[32]

If Douglas was, in the words of a church report, "winning his way into the hearts of many people," it was due not only to his pulpit performances or his social activism but also to his personal conduct. Grace MacInnis has noted in him an "ascetic strain," drawn both from his religious beliefs and his Scottish background.[33] This self-discipline did not lead to dourness. He neither smoked nor drank, but this was more a matter of taste and Scottish prudence than of ethics. The orthodox Christian's obsession with personal sin and purity distressed him; he waged his battles against what he saw as social sins, and spent little time proclaiming his personal morality. Later in life Douglas puffed on a pipe—most noticeably in cabinet meetings, where it was largely a matter of self-defence in an atmosphere clouded with cigarette and cigar smoke. On really festive occasions, he might even toy with a glass of sherry.

One personal characteristic which has made it difficult to record Douglas's life was his reluctance, even stubborn refusal, to criticize the conduct of others. He was generous towards his political opponents, and exceptionally loyal to any worker in the CCF cause. As a leader, he won loyalty in return. At the same time, he sometimes risked his political reputation and that of his party by protecting bumblers and by overlooking cases of bad judgement.

The combativeness for which Douglas became known was, except for the rarest of occasions, confined to the world of ideas. He readily lost himself in the excitement of debate but his interest lay in establishing a truth, not in crushing his opponent. Douglas almost never carried animosities away from the field of battle. Even when discussing the politicians who deserted the CCF, he could temper his criticisms with a compliment. As the old Scottish phrase put it, "He could find something good to say about the Devil."

5
The 1934 Election

I N THE SOFT EVENING LIGHT of early summer a crowd began to gather in front of the *Weyburn Review* offices on Souris Avenue. The centre of attention was a blackboard mounted across the building's second-story false front. Before the board, on an improvised trestle, one of the paper's staff walked back and forth, chalking up the voting tallies taken from the wires of the Canadian Pacific Telegraph. There were no quick computer projections available for the Saskatchewan election of June 19, 1934, and no television network decision desks. The results from across the province trickled in one by one. As the sky darkened, someone turned on the spot-lights set atop the Hi-Art Theatre across the street.

Slowly, a pattern emerged. The numbers told a tale of disaster for the old regime, the jerry-built "Co-operative Government." Every government candidate had lost his seat. The Saskatchewan Conservative Party was retreating into the electoral shadows, where it would remain for the next forty years. The Tories' coalition partners, the Progressives, were finished forever. Saskatchewan's political life was entering a new phase. The Liberals, under the leadership of Jimmy Gardiner—brilliant, calculating, ruthlessly partisan—had recaptured the legislative majority they had held from 1905 until 1929. But for the first time their only opposition in the legislature would come from a left-wing party, the Farmer Labour group, part of J. S. Woodsworth's national CCF. Liberals and Tories had reviled Farmer Labour as Communist during the campaign, and the election of even five radicals to the legislature was a victory.

There was disappointment, however, among the left-wingers of the Weyburn constituency. Their candidate, Tommy Douglas, placed third behind the winning Liberal and the incumbent Tory—a fate he shared with his colleague and leader, M. J. Coldwell of Regina. Darkness had settled over the scene before Douglas gave up hope. Then, in the floodlit night, the crowd of nearly 4000 watched the small, wiry figure climb to the trestle in front of the chalkboard. With the grace and dignity that would characterize his public appearances, he conceded defeat.

At this moment a politician was born. He called on his troops to keep up their courage and good cheer with a phrase he would often repeat in the course of ensuing battles: "As Jonah said when he was swallowed by the whale, you can't keep a good man down." Douglas reacted to his loss gracefully, but he could not accept it casually. The results challenged him to do better next time—and there had to be a next time.

J. S. Woodsworth had realized his long-time dream of a national left-wing political party in July 1932, in Calgary, when Labour Party delegates from the four western provinces, including Saskatchewan Farmer Labour, met with United Farmers representatives from Alberta and the national rail union leader, Aaron Mosher. This alliance agreed on a brief statement of principles and a new name—the Co-operative Commonwealth Federation.* "The name had coinage on the prairies," said Douglas later. "I think it was an awful mouthful."[1]

The new CCF resolved to spend a year on intense organization at the grass roots—an effort led in Saskatchewan by Coldwell, the Farmer Labour leader, and by Louise Lucas, a gifted orator from the United Farmers. In July 1933 the CCF held its first national convention at Regina. Here, it adopted a structure—one of federation among provincial sections, rather than unification—and ratified a detailed policy statement, which came to be known as the Regina Manifesto.

The manifesto was drawn up by a small group of intellectuals from Toronto and Montreal, members of the League for Social Reconstruction, which had been formed by Frank Scott and Frank Underhill to lay out a path to social and economic reform. Their proposals were realistic rather than utopian, and they anticipated many of the developments that would change Canadian life over the next few decades. The manifesto called for state health insurance, unemployment insurance, and public pension plans. It urged that governments greatly expand the network of crown corporations. It demanded the adoption of a Canadian constitution, with an entrenched charter of rights.

All of these proposals had become reality by the mid-1980s—partly, many would argue, because of the work of the CCF and then the NDP. However, the result fell short of forming a socialist whole. Many of the manifesto's ideas have been ignored by governments, and have been set aside even by democratic socialists. The prospects for a planned economy under public control seem as remote as ever half a century after the birth of the CCF. Workers still lack the right to participate in the management of industry, and Canadians generally await "a foreign policy...designed to promote disarmament and world peace."

To many outside the movement, the essence of the manifesto was

---

* The phrase "Co-operative Commonwealth" figured in American radical writings at least as far back as the 1880s. Walter Rauschenbusch, the American social gospel radical, used it in the early 1900s to describe the coming world of Christian social justice.

to be found in its famous peroration—a last-minute, almost accidental addition to the main document: "No C.C.F Government will rest content until it has eradicated capitalism and put into operation the full pro- gramme of socialized planning which will lead to the establishment in Canada of the Co-operative Commonwealth." This statement of wishful intention, beyond anything else in the manifesto, provided the ammuni- tion for those who wanted to describe the new movement as Communist—though the real Communists regarded the CCF as "social fascist." Certainly, at the bottom line, the CCF envisioned a socialist world—one which would organize its activities to satisfy public need, and not the private urge for profit. But it should have been clear that the new movement owed more to the Christian social gospel than to *Das Kapital*. While the manifesto spoke of "a planned economy...owned and controlled by the people," most party leaders rejected the Marxist termi- nology of "class consciousness."

The CCF differed most importantly from the Communists on the ques- tion of how to achieve socialism. In later years, the pioneers returned often to a sentence in the manifesto: "We do not believe in change by violence."[2] For the Christian left, the idea of civil war in Canada was absurd. "It is on the issue of violence that we part company with our Russian friends," said Salem Bland, the social gospel patriarch, at a party meeting in 1933.[3] Douglas echoed these thoughts in a 1985 interview:

> It was characteristic of the same division of thought that was taking place all over the Western world. That is, there were those who believed that our present economic system was unChristian, was anti-social, was harmful to all the traditions of humanitarian values. But there were also those who were equally convinced...that...there was no way by which peacefully you were going to bring about this social and economic change, and who had accepted the idea of the class war.
>
> Those of us who were social democrats weren't really saying that all of this can be settled without any trouble, that you're never going to have any bad feeling, you're never going to have any riots, you're never going to have any civil wars. But what we did believe was that these changes could be brought about if you got a measure of good will on both sides.[4]

Tommy Douglas did not register as a delegate at the Regina Conven- tion of 1933. His name is missing from the minutes and from a delegate list published in the Regina *Leader-Post*. The registrar, Clarence Fines, did not see Douglas there. It seems likely that the president of the Weyburn Independent Labour Party was tied down with local com- mitments and travelled to Regina City Hall only on Friday, the third day of the convention, where he observed the afternoon session. That even- ing Douglas drove two convention delegates to a public meeting in Weyburn, where he declared the convention to have been "the finest thing I have ever seen."[5]

The CCF convention provided the Saskatchewan Farmer Labour alliance with publicity, a sense of direction, and the knowledge that it belonged to a national movement. But the job of organizing the province remained formidable. With many people struggling to feed their families, there was little money left over for political causes. In some areas the socialists struggled against a current of popular resentment. Douglas remembered holding meetings in grain elevators in towns where the schools and church basements were closed to him. Snowdrifts blocked the road to the New Jerusalem in winter, and mud in spring. In summer the dust was so thick that, as a party worker put it, "You couldn't see the horses to throw on the harness."[6]

Coldwell travelled ceaselessly, despite his teaching job and the bad weather. His party was concerned about the leader's health, and he worried about his wife, now on a long slow decline due to multiple sclerosis. A former student offered to fly Coldwell to public meetings in a small plane, and crash-landed three times within a month. More often, Coldwell drove his own car. When some party members proposed the creation of a "Coldwell Fund" to help pay expenses, George Williams, the chairman of the party council, resisted. It was an early sign of the bitter rivalry that was to grow between the two men.[7]

Clarence Fines, Coldwell's Regina lieutenant, organized whist and dance nights at twenty-five cents a head, and paid the rent for the party's provincial office. The provincial secretary, Frank Eliason, wrote his letters on the backs of old UFC agendas. In one letter he wrote that the party's bank balance, which had been $16.27 at May 15, 1932, had grown to $17.49 one year later.[8]

The Farmer Labour organization, in short, depended on a few strong personalities for its survival when Douglas became its Weyburn candidate in November 1933. He would often say in later years that he stumbled into the job, that the local party simply could not find anyone else. Modesty aside, he was the obvious choice. He had been a guiding spirit in the formation of the Weyburn Independent Labour Party. He had carried labour's message to the farming community, and been active in the creation of the local Farmer Labour axis. At the nominating convention at Cleland's Hall in Weyburn on November 4, he won on the first ballot. According to a newspaper report, his supporters gave him "a tremendous ovation."

The Douglas nomination speech, reprinted in detail in the *Weyburn Review*, shows the young minister's radicalism to be, at this stage, some distance from his social democratic outlook of a decade later. True, he had identified the rich and "the interests" as the adversaries, and he held a vision of a co-operative society of the future. But his proposed methods for building the new world reflected the influence of William Irvine, now a leading force in the new CCF. Douglas's acceptance speech borrowed heavily from Irvine's radical progressivism, which emphasized monetary reform and decentralized democracy: "The economic system under which we have been living for over a hundred years is breaking down...the time has come for it to pass from the stage, and make room for a newer and more progressive system. The present system has failed to so distribute wealth that the people could buy back what they produced." We have a sacred obligation before God," Douglas concluded, to provide for children, the old, and the disabled. "Are not our obligations to them as sacred as to any group of coupon clippers? Must children starve while big interests take their pound of flesh?" Douglas also produced a signed recall paper, which gave his local supporters the right to force him to resign if he betrayed their trust.[9]

One special guest at the afternoon nominating convention was Clarence Fines, the Farmer Labour fundraiser from Regina. The twenty-eight-year-old schoolteacher had already shown a genius for organization. He had helped put together the momentous 1932 Calgary conference of the CCF, and had chaired that meeting. Fines would become an increasingly important ally in Douglas's political life, and eventually in his government. On this occasion, his first encounter with Douglas, his hosts insisted that Fines address the evening meeting—and he waited patiently as nine other speakers took their turns before him. (In those days, a political meeting was a failure if the lights were turned out before midnight.) Afterwards, he wrote an enthusiastic report for the provincial executive on the promising new candidate.

Douglas would have his work cut out for him. The incumbent Tory MLA in Weyburn was a respected pioneer, a former municipal secretary and lay preacher, and the Speaker in the Legislative Assembly. Robert Leslie's campaign slogan was, "A vote for Leslie is a vote for Progress." In setting out his platform in the *Review*, he extolled the virtues of his party in providing good, clean Conservative government.[10] The Liberal candidate, and the eventual winner, was Dr. Hugh Eaglesham, a leading citizen in the district. Eaglesham had arrived in Weyburn in 1902, when the settlement was only a few shacks around a grain elevator. As the prototype of the prairie family doctor he had covered the territory from the Souris River to the United States border, travelling by buggy in the summer and sleigh in the winter, and he had brought many of his constituents into the world. There were rumours that Eaglesham might be health minister in a new Liberal government. He warned that if Farmer Labour took power, "before you could cut the hay in the meadow, you'd have to call Regina."[11] The twenty-nine-year-old preacher, by contrast, had come to Weyburn only recently, and represented an untried party. He was, however, "a wonderful speaker," and he understood the issues.[12]

Understanding the issues was no easy matter in a world beset by the problems—international, national, and local—unleashed by the events of 1929. By 1934 there were scattered signs of industrial recovery, and commodity prices had strengthened somewhat. But in southern Saskatchewan improved commodity prices held little meaning for people who had nothing to sell. Alongside the claims of governments that the depression was over, the prairie newspapers still provided a daily diet of despair. The convoys of farm families and their possessions continued to head out of the dustbowl for the north country and a new start. Some farmers used oxen, even milk cows, to pull their ploughs.

Experts and non-experts scrambled to diagnose the social and economic ills that beset industrial society. Everyone from evangelists to economists offered prescriptions, ranging from prayer to monetary pump-priming. Most of the traditional remedies had little to offer those in government; the more elegant models of Keynes, and the war which was to provide their proving ground, were still some way off. One thing was becoming increasingly clear, though: whatever the appropriate policy, it was beyond the power of Canada's provincial governments to put it into effect.

Saskatchewan's "Co-operative Government" provided a case in point. In the election of June 6, 1929, the Conservatives under J. T. M. Anderson had taken fewer seats than the Liberals, but had succeeded in winning over the Progressives and Independents to their side by promising to run an honest administration. For the Tories, it was "a disastrous victory."[13] Within weeks of taking power, the new coalition was greeted by the Great Depression.

Anderson provided clean government, at least compared to the Liberals. He launched an inquiry into the sordid behaviour of the previous Liberal administration. He commissioned Coldwell, a defeated Progressive candidate, to design a merit system for hiring civil servants. However, the coalition found that trying to cope with a deepening depression was a lonely and almost futile job. It tried to prevent court action by creditors against citizens in debt, but its Debt Adjustment Act was struck down by the Supreme Court of Canada. The coalition saved the farmers' wheat-marketing agency, the Wheat Pool, from annihilation, and distributed emergency food, clothing, fuel, and seed grain to victims of the economic crisis on an impartial basis. But without any equalization system among the provinces, and without systematic federal support, Saskatchewan watched its debt double from $74 million to $140 million in five years. Torn between public demands for action and its reactionary roots, Anderson's Conservative organization came unglued. A former Conservative party president, D. S. Johnstone, repeatedly attacked the coalition as a free-spending rabble and denounced Anderson as another Coldwell. During the 1934 campaign many Tories threw their support to Jimmy Gardiner. When June 19 dawned rainy and cool, there were not even enough Conservative workers to drive supporters to the polls.

The other faction in the coalition, the Progressives, were enjoying their first taste of political power; they were also living out their last hurrah. The Progressive Party, born before 1920 out of the western farmers' disenchantment with the government of Canada, had enjoyed brief influence on the national scene during the twenties. But its radicalism had never matured into a full political program, and in Saskatchewan it had never developed a provincial presence. The fragmentary movement collapsed soon after the 1929 election, and its MLAs eked out their terms as bit players. The dissolution of the Progressives allowed the Farmer Labour alliance to move into a political vacuum on the left.

Besides its economic record, Anderson's government was also haunted by the circumstances of its birth. It had come to power in 1929 on a wave

of reaction—anti-Semitic, anti-immigrant, anti-French, and anti-Catholic—
and with the backing of the Ku Klux Klan, which had signed up thousands
of members in Saskatchewan. Although the Klan claimed to have no
political preferences, observers including Coldwell reported that Anderson
had close ties to the extremist group.[14] Gardiner, in contrast, had campaigned against the Klan. Many Catholics and immigrants remained
suspicious of the Tories, and regarded Gardiner and the Liberals as the
defenders of their rights.

The coalition chose in 1934 to run on its record and the promise of
greater things to come from R. B. Bennett and his Ottawa Tories. In truth,
though, Anderson's crowd was never in the race. The old pro, Jimmy
Gardiner, saw the contest as one between a rejuvenated Liberal Party and
the upstart CCF.

Gardiner, for his part, had a priceless talent for appealing to both left
and right, for promising change without upsetting the establishment. In
one 1934 press statement he undertook to extend social services, build
better highways, improve the relief system, create a public works program,
and reduce the provincial deficit, all at the same time. "Low tariffs and
free trade" were, as tradition demanded, the Liberal battle-cry. The Liberals
portrayed the Farmer Labour group as a Bolshevik menace, a threat to
private property, church, and charity. In this respect the new party's farm
policies, built around their use-lease concept, played right into the Liberals'
hands. Mackenzie King, the national Liberal leader, joined the chorus,
warning on a swing through the province that the CCF would confiscate
private property.

The use-lease proposal, first put forward by George Williams and his
United Farmers in 1931, was a defensible response to a crisis in which
foreclosures and evictions were becoming depressingly common. With
one stroke a banker could wipe out a lifelong investment of time and labour,
and send a proud farm family down the road with little more than the
clothes on their backs. Williams knew that the small-scale farmer would
always rely heavily on credit and would always have trouble making his
payments in years of drought and low prices. The Farmer Labour Party
proposed that a public agency should assume both the title to the farmer's
land and his credit obligations; the farmer and his family would retain the
permanent right to work the land and sell his crops.

In a farming province, built on the private ownership of land, the use-
lease proposition was easily interpreted to mean that the state would take
control of the farmers' property. To make things more awkward, Williams's
United Farmers had spoken, at the height of their fervour in 1931, of
nationalizing land. The Liberals, Tories, and the Catholic church lambasted
the idea and those who proposed it. The resulting "Red scare," in Weyburn
and elsewhere, crippled CCF candidates in 1934 and for the next decade. *

---

* The other parties also dwelt on the fact that George Williams had visited Soviet Russia in
1931, and had written a booklet assessing the strengths and weaknesses of the Soviet system.
Williams was aware of his notoriety after this trip, and when the Farmer Labour alliance was
formed in 1932 he deferred to Coldwell when the time came to select a leader. Nonetheless,
he remained a high-profile campaigner, and a target for red-baiters.

Douglas argued, in defending the proposal, that 35 per cent of the province's farmers were close to eviction. The lease would guarantee lifetime use of the land; it might be traded as any other property, and even become part of the family estate. The United Farmers had initially proposed that the system be compulsory; but now, said Douglas, every farmer would have the right to enter the scheme voluntarily, or to keep the title to his land if he wished.[15] But in explaining the details, there seems to have been some confusion and contradiction among Farmer Labour spokesmen, including Coldwell, Fines, and Douglas. Would the farmer be able to sell his land if he gave up title? The CCF failed to provide the public with any clear and convincing response.

Douglas had already, in the previous year or two, joined the growing ranks of the monetary reformers. Like many westerners, he traced the debt squeeze to private control of the financial system. Private companies controlled every kind of farm, business, and consumer lending. The banks even controlled the money supply, one of the major levers in the national economy, and they did so in a way that seemed both capricious and heartless.

One of the most eloquent voices in the monetary reform camp belonged to William Irvine, the Alberta MP. In a 1934 pamphlet he wrote that the issue of credit should be the CCF's top priority. In planning Canada's future, he said, "it is necessary to grasp only a few essential general principles...1) abundance can be produced for all; 2) abundance is not being distributed; 3) abundance can be distributed." He summed up this viewpoint with the slogan, "Poverty in the Midst of Plenty."[16]

Since the early 1920s Irvine had been a partisan of the social credit theory of Major C. H. Douglas, which proposed that the state should establish the value of the nation's capital and resource assets, and pay out a "social dividend" based on its calculations. Over the years Irvine convinced many fellow radicals, including several United Farmers MPs from Alberta, of the soundness of social credit economics. Douglas was among those swayed, a fact that would contribute to his embarrassment, and that of his party, in the federal election of 1935.

Irvine deeply impressed Douglas when he visited Weyburn early in 1933. Douglas admired the older man's powers of oratory and his talent for making complex issues understandable to the ordinary listener. In his later years, Douglas spoke of Irvine as "one of the people that was instrumental in making me a socialist, both through the things he wrote, and my conversations with him."[17] The immediate effect was reflected in a meeting of the WILP, chaired by Douglas, at which it was resolved that Weyburn's city council should issue scrip, or local currency.

Douglas continued to develop the social credit theme in a series of lectures entitled "Modern Economic Trends," and played on it often in the 1934 election. In a newspaper article he attacked the Anderson government's "suicidal" borrowing at rates of up to 8 per cent. He proposed the creation of a provincial bank, with or without a federal charter, which would lend money at much less than the prevailing rates. A Farmer

Labour government, he wrote, would also issue provincial tokens which would serve as money within the province to facilitate the exchange of goods and services: "There is an abundant supply of all the commodities that we require for a high standard of living...A vote for the Farmer Labour party is a vote for purchasing power."[18]

While the economic propositions of Major Douglas's Social Credit gained some favour in the Farmer Labour camp, the other Saskatchewan parties mocked and rejected them. Robert Leslie called them the work of quacks and charlatans. W. F. Kerr, a prominent Liberal, warned that a Farmer Labour government might try to pay its teachers and civil servants with tokens.[19]

On another front, Farmer Labour ran into resistance from the province's Roman Catholic leaders. Catholic opposition was presented most clearly in the columns of *The Prairie Messenger*, a Benedictine newspaper which was the voice of the English-speaking Catholics of the province. The Canadian Catholic bishops had ruled that socialism must lead to class war, communism, and the abolition of the sacred right of private property, in direct violation of papal teachings. The pastoral letter from the archbishop of Montreal, issued in 1934 on behalf of his fellow bishops, took direct aim at the CCF. "It can be said at once that socialization on such a large scale proposed by the CCF leaves no freedom to private enterprise or to the possibility of competition...The right of ownership has its foundation in the will of the Creator and the nature of man."[20] George Williams proposed that Farmer Labour respond with an anti-Catholic campaign, but Coldwell imposed a general silence on the issue. Only a few tough-minded Catholics chose to act against the apparent wishes of their church and support the socialist cause.

The tribulations of the Farmer Labour Party in entering its first campaign did not arise only from external sources. The letters of Frank Eliason, the party secretary, complain of a continuing lack of money and organizing talent. A scant three weeks before the election he wrote to Fines that the telephone might be cut off by June 10. Eliason also complained to Williams that while party members happily immersed themselves in discussion, reason, and education, they avoided house-to-house canvassing. The local representatives, he said, "seem to feel that it is a lot easier to stay at home and read about the establishment of the Co-operative Commonwealth than go out and take off their coats and fight for it."[21] Somehow, however, Fines managed to keep the leaky ship afloat. He put the discreet touch on sympathetic professionals — accountants, lawyers, and doctors — and paid the phone bills. Meanwhile, the party complained, fat-cat money poured in to Liberal coffers: $25,000 from Imperial Oil, an alleged $50,000 from the Bronfmans.

Despite its handicaps, the new party appeared to be making substantial gains during the campaign, drawing large crowds to its public meetings. Two thousand people heard Woodsworth and Douglas in Weyburn, and six thousand turned out for a meeting in Regina. Douglas concluded later, though, that the same Farmer Labour partisans were turning up for every meeting. A group of them would charter a bus, or pile into a car, and travel half way across the province to hear the same message they had heard the night before.[22]

Douglas's schedule in 1934 was a hectic one — a fit preparation for his life as one of the great political campaigners of his time. He addressed 120 meetings in villages like Minton, Lake Alma, Ratcliffe, and Ceylon, emphasizing the need for farm security and the failure of "the system" to distribute purchasing power. He spoke in favour of a crop-insurance scheme and supported the use-lease proposal (as he understood it). In discussing the provincial debt he argued for a cut in interest payments and the issuing of interest-free bonds. It has been noted, critically by some, that he said little about social ownership. Generally, his position at the end of the campaign was a moderate one, reflecting some of the ambiguities of his nomination speech: "No social institution will be discarded which continues to serve society in the best interest of all. The demand for change comes when we find our institutions are based on wrong principles, and are not serving the needs of humanity...the profit system has defiled whatever it has touched. And the profit system has touched everything. It has corrupted governments, debauched politicians, degraded morals, devitalized religion and demoralized human nature."[23]

On election day the Liberals took nearly half of the provincial vote. Although the Tories ranked second in the popular vote, they were wiped out. The Farmer Labour Party—or CCF, as it now officially became—was the new force in Saskatchewan politics. It became the official opposition.

In Weyburn, as Douglas conceded defeat, the crowd hoisted Dr. Eaglesham on its shoulders. (Eaglesham would serve one term in the legislature, as a backbencher.) Douglas had won in only eight of the constituency's forty-three polls. In the rural stations, he had won 32 per cent of the vote, but he took only 16 per cent in the city. He accepted his defeat calmly, and resumed his work at Calvary Baptist Church. He had never expected to win, he said later. "It was purely an educational campaign to put the story of this movement before the people."[24]

The 1934 election left the Saskatchewan Farmer Labour Party divided at its highest level. Coldwell, Douglas's patron and party leader, lost badly in his Regina constituency. George Williams, now emerging as Coldwell's rival, won his Wadena seat. In a chance meeting a day or two after the election, Coldwell suggested that one of the successful Farmer Labour candidates should resign his seat and allow him, as party leader, to contest a by-election. Williams was expecting to become the new CCF house leader in the legislature, and he laughed at Coldwell's idea, calling it "ridiculous."[25] From this point on, the two men barely spoke to each other. Until Coldwell's election to Parliament a year and a half later, they struggled for position within the Saskatchewan CCF. The animosity between them carried through to the end of the decade, and beyond, and helped to set off the bitter controversy that clouded the selection of Williams's successor, Tommy Douglas.

6

The 1935 Election

ON OCTOBER 9, 1935, amid the dusty elegance of a rented board-room in the Hotel Saskatchewan, members of the CCF executive prepared to eject Tommy Douglas from the party. The young minister, now the federal candidate for Weyburn, sat with his campaign manager Ted Stinson. Confronting them were five senior party officials. The group had clear evidence that Douglas had consorted with the enemy, and all but one of them wanted to withdraw CCF support for the Douglas campaign.

The poster before them bore the words, "VOTE DOUGLAS! Weyburn CCF-Social Credit Association." Andy Macauley, an old farm radical, growled, "That thing will be held in front of us in the Legislature next year." George Williams, the legislative house leader, said to Douglas and Stinson, "You have very successfully crucified the provincial organization." "You're wrong if you think I'm supporting a capitalist movement," said Douglas. "I merely promised to give Social Credit a free hand and support legislation to do so. That's exactly what George and M. J. said we should do."[1]

Five days later, with his status within the CCF still cloudy, Douglas won election to Parliament. The campaign had shown him to be a bold strategist, but his boldness had nearly done him in. Over time, the story of this election would fade into obscurity; but a few critics like Williams would never forget Douglas's brush with Social Credit.

By the time he ran for Parliament, Douglas was already a national figure within the Co-operative Commonwealth Federation. At the party's second national convention, in Winnipeg in the summer of 1934, Woodsworth had asked Douglas to accept the presidency of the CCF Youth Movement, or CCYM. Over the winter of 1934-35 the job put him in touch with youth clubs and CCF sections across the country. Together with his frequent speaking tours in his home district, the national post made him the most prominent CCFer around Weyburn and a natural choice to run in the federal election.

The convention at Winnipeg had been a disorganized affair; a keen observer, Frank Underhill of Toronto, wrote that this "collection of individual missionaries" was deeply divided over its short-term goals.[2] To add to the leader's troubles, some extreme left-wingers in the party's youth group were pushing the CCYM towards secession from the parent body. Woodsworth, Coldwell, and Fines decided to head off this threat by sending the minister from Weyburn into the youth convention to contest the presidency. Douglas had already dropped in on a few of the youth sessions, keeping to the back of the hall. On the third and final day of the convention, he stepped forward, and the hundred or so youth delegates elected him president by a two-to-one margin.[3]

Afterwards, he remained convinced that the incipient youth revolt had been the work of the Soviet-controlled Communist Party of Canada. "You're talking about boys right off the farm," he said in 1985, "to whom running for reeve was a moving experience. Suddenly, there are people who have been to these Communist schools...week-end seminars, week-long seminars...where they're really drilled in what I would call sabotaging social democratic movements, and moving them to the left or breaking them up."[4] Within months of the meeting, several of the most vocal CCYM delegates openly joined the Communists; one later became Saskatchewan leader of the Communist Party.

Douglas was sent into action, then, as an anti-Communist lieutenant, and his experience at the convention made him wary of Communists. However, for the next few years he remained open to links with the Communists in the so-called "daily struggle" outside electoral politics. His high profile as a young MP in the League Against War and Fascism, a common-front organization of Communists and socialists, would create some tension with the leaders who sponsored his rise.

Douglas won his first election at a time of turmoil in Canadian politics. Between 1933 and mid-1935 half a dozen political protest movements sprang up across the country, and Canadians took almost every opportunity to toss provincial governments out of office. Quebec dumped the Liberals in favour of the Union Nationale and Maurice Duplessis, Ontario rejected the Tories for the maverick Liberalism of Mitch Hepburn. The people of Alberta transferred their allegiance from the United Farmers to "Bible Bill" Aberhart and his Social Credit movement.

At the federal level, the weight of the voters' wrath fell in 1935 on the luckless Conservative government of Richard Bedford Bennett. The Calgary lawyer has emerged in Canadian myth as a figure of fun, as a man who raged against the Depression but whose actions only made it worse. Given the worldwide confusion about how to cope with the collapse, it is unlikely that Bennett's chief rival, Mackenzie King, would have done any better. Bennett's style, perhaps, was more abrasive: Douglas sometimes said that if Bennett saw a demonstration outside his windows, he would order that the crowd be dispersed, while King, in the same circumstances, would pull down the blind.

The Bennett government enjoyed a few successes—for example, it laid the foundations for the Bank of Canada and for public broadcasting. However, the prime minister's effort to revive Canada's economy through increased trade, to "blast his way into the markets of the world,"[5] failed badly—partly because of the protectionist feelings within his own cabinet.

In 1934 Bennett's trade and commerce minister, Harry Stevens, conducted a highly publicized inquiry into the behaviour of Canadian corporations. The Commission on Price Spreads and Mass Buying probed the very entrails of Canada's big business structure and its practices. Its findings split the Conservative Party, and strengthened public demand for more vigorous government intervention in the economy. The Stevens report revealed in detail the abuses of power, position, and privilege among Canada's major corporations. It told of price-fixing, of profiteering, and of terrible conditions among industrial workers. Among the parliamentarians on the investigating committee the lone dissenting voice was that of Edward Young, the Liberal member for Weyburn. Young's minority report, said to be the product of a corporate research team, defended the record of the packing houses and retail chains named by the majority. In the eyes of many westerners, Young had sold out to the hated eastern "interests."

The prime minister responded to the Stevens report, and to the climate of concern it created, with a battery of new legislation. His government passed bills intended to regulate wages and hours, ease farm debt and market farm products, and increase federal intervention in the economy. But when Ottawa tested the ill-fated reforms in the Supreme Court, the court ruled that Bennett was meddling with provincial powers. It was now clear that under the constitution, many of Canada's most pressing problems lay in the domain of the provinces, most of whom were too poor to take action.

By the summer of 1935 Bennett's government was falling to pieces, and the Liberals were ready to re-take power. The popular Harry Stevens left the Tories and set up a new Reconstruction Party to noisy fanfare. CCF leaders were attracting large crowds to their meetings, and a new party with some curious similarities to the CCF—the Social Credit party—was rising quickly in Alberta and showing signs of moving into Saskatchewan. Public feeling was running high against the government, and when the inmates of the western relief camps launched an On-to-Ottawa Trek, they won widespread sympathy. Police in Regina broke up the march, attacking a trekkers' rally with clubs and guns, and many people laid the blame for the violence at Bennett's doorstep.

CCF folklore has depicted Social Credit and the CCF as diametric opposites, but in the mid-1930s many voters perceived striking similarities. After all, the United Farmers—the Alberta organization which helped to found the CCF—had introduced social credit ideas into Canada from Britain in the 1920s. Well into 1935, even as it became clear that William Aberhart's Social Credit movement would mow them down, veteran UFA-CCF members of Parliament still insisted that Ottawa should reform both the economy and the welfare system by "drawing on the national or social credit of Canada."[6]

Alberta Social Credit, thrown together less than a year before the provincial election of August 1935, made many of the same promises as the CCF. It offered a guaranteed income, fair prices for both the farmer and the consumer, and debt forgiveness. More important, Aberhart stridently denounced the farmer's traditional enemy, the banker. Douglas had called for a provincial bank in Saskatchewan and the issuance of provincial tokens; Aberhart now promised a program of monetary reform for Alberta. Since Ottawa had sole responsibility for banking and currency, such proposals were constitutional absurdities, but many voters seeking radical reform overlooked this fact.

It would be wrong to overstate the similarities between Douglas and Aberhart. Both of these preacher-politicians put a Christian appeal at the heart of their political message; but Douglas came from one of the most tolerant and socially oriented traditions in Protestantism, while Aberhart had spent his adult life denouncing personal sin and speculating on the imminent second coming of Jesus. Where Douglas envisioned Canada moving outward into a family of socialist nations, Aberhart counselled his fellow Albertans to draw together and prepare for persecution from the money-changers and their hirelings. Douglas summed up his political aims in 1935 in the slogan, "The CCF Aims to Replace the Present Capitalist System." In the new era, private industrialists and financiers would lose their power to a network of public institutions. Elected officials and their advisers would reach a consensus with co-operatives, labour, and farmers' groups on how to produce and distribute abundance for all. Aberhart's long-term goals, despite his fiery rhetoric, were much more limited. Social Credit sought to liberalize the capitalist system, to make it more responsive and locally based. The CCF under Douglas would bring forth the Saskatchewan Power Corporation, a unionized, state-owned enterprise; Social Credit set up Alberta Gas Trunk, a government-regulated firm in the private sector, owned by thousands of small Alberta shareholders and closed to unions.

On the afternoon of Saturday, June 15, 1935, Tommy Douglas won the CCF nomination for the Weyburn federal riding at a meeting attended by 400 people. The announcement of the lopsided vote total, reported the *Review*, "brought forth wild acclaim from the assemblage."[7] At a public meeting that night, which "packed the Cleland Hall to suffocation,"[8] Douglas declared that "the pulpit was his first love, but that he would devote all of his spare time to the campaign ahead."[9] Like the candidates of the old Progressive Party, he also presented the chairman of the meeting with signed recall papers. These stated that the local CCF could force his resignation from Parliament if he ignored their wishes.

On that very first day the CCF agreed on a key point in its attack. Clarence Fines, in a meeting with the Douglas campaign team, produced a parliamentary quote from E. J. Young, Weyburn's Liberal MP, stating that "Canadians must learn to accept a lower standard of living." This quote became a mocking anti-Liberal slogan; it surfaced even on the Weyburn CCF blotting paper, above a drawing of a boy and a girl, and the legend "C(hildren) C(ome) F(irst)."[10]

In mid-August the Liberals re-nominated Young as their standard bearer. The Douglas forces were primed for the occasion. At a public meeting a week before the Liberal nomination, Douglas had challenged the Liberal candidate—and he expected it would be Young—to a joint debate anywhere within the Weyburn constituency. Ted Stinson, Douglas's campaign manager, repeated the challenge at the Liberal nominating meeting. Young—foolishly, as it turned out—accepted. The date for the debate was eventually set for September 25.

Ed Young, a farmer from a village west of Weyburn, had sat in the House of Commons for a decade. He had made his name locally as a supporter of low tariffs and free trade—always a vote-getter among prairie farmers. Somewhere during the Bennett years, though, Young had signed on as a messenger boy for central Canadian big business. His lonely pro-monopoly stand at the end of the Stevens inquiry earned him the friendship of C. L. Burton, the president of Simpson's department stores. The Ontario millionaire even parked his private railway car at the Weyburn station for part of the campaign, the better to coach Young on his strategy. It sat there in the shadow of the grain elevators, a symbol of Young's divided loyalties. The prospects for a CCF upset in the flatland country appeared excellent.

On August 23, 1935, the people of Alberta voted Social Credit into office with fifty-six of the sixty-three seats in the provincial legislature. The tired and scandal-ridden United Farmers of Alberta, like Anderson's Tories in Saskatchewan the year before, lost every one of their seats. The UFA government, under pressure from its members of Parliament in Ottawa, had half-heartedly allied itself with the CCF, but its policies had been rigidly conservative. On September 4 the new government was sworn in, and the next day the *Leader-Post* trumpeted the news that Aberhart planned to march on Saskatchewan and nominate a candidate in every federal seat. The federal election had taken a new turn. For the CCF in Weyburn, Edward Young no longer posed the only threat.

The Saskatchewan CCF leadership decided on a diplomatic response to the new challenge. Coldwell, the Saskatchewan CCF leader, and George Williams issued a joint statement. On the one hand, they tried to reassure those sympathetic to Social Credit in Alberta that no CCF member of Parliament would support the use of federal power to stifle Aberhart. On the other hand, they pointed out the differences between CCF and Social Credit aims. They emphasized that Aberhart's was still a capitalist party. "The attitude of CCF federal members," they concluded, "should therefore be stated as viewing with interest the experiment, and opposing interference with the expressed wishes of the Alberta people."[11]

In Weyburn, Douglas saw the danger that Social Credit might establish a beach-head in his riding and lure away voters who wanted reform but were still uncommitted. He also knew that if no genuine Social Credit candidate appeared, the Liberals might put up a dummy Social Credit nominee to split the radical vote. His response, rightly or wrongly, was to strike first.

Stinson, the local CCF president and Douglas's official agent and confidant, travelled to Moose Jaw in the first week of September to meet Aberhart's Saskatchewan organizer, Colonel H. W. Arnold. Whatever Stinson's arguments may have been, Arnold agreed to back Douglas if the preacher could win the support of Social Credit in Weyburn. When Stinson returned home, his executive committee approved a statement from the candidate which echoed Coldwell and Williams. Douglas was "prepared to initiate and support legislation in the House of Commons which would make possible the Social Credit system being operated in any province caring to do so."

This statement can be interpreted to mean everything or nothing, depending on your point of view. It should be noted that it was the only formal commitment Douglas made in seeking Social Credit support. He did not, as at least one other CCF candidate did, commit himself to supporting the Social Credit Party program. However, he sought, and received, official Social Credit support, and he spoke frequently of his sympathy with Social Credit aims. "I endorse the principle of socializing the credit of the nation," his statement said, "and issuing currency against the resources of our country, with a view to creating sufficient purchasing power to enable the people to purchase the goods which we have created in such abundance."[12]

While the CCF wooed the Social Credit vote, Aberhart's party made various offers to snare CCF candidates. In Rosetown the Social Credit group asked Coldwell to run for both parties at the same time, but Coldwell refused. Social Credit had more success in Yorkton. At their nominating meeting in that riding they asked CCF candidate Jacob Benson, "Will you agree to support Social Credit members in the House of Commons?" Benson answered yes; he also presented signed recall papers to the Social Credit executive.[13] His actions won the applause of his local CCF executive. Nonetheless, the provincial leadership called him onto the carpet, and at the end of September the party stripped Benson of his status as an official candidate, on the grounds that "the policies of the CCF are clearly defined...and do not permit of collaboration on the part of any candidates with any other political party."[14] Douglas took much the same road as Benson; certainly he collaborated with Colonel Arnold. However, thanks to luck and his friendship with Coldwell, he avoided expulsion.

Arnold had promised Douglas that he would get Aberhart's blessing if he could persuade local Social Crediters to support him. As it happened, though, there was no effective Social Credit machine in place in the

Weyburn area. Stinson and his confederates, acting with Douglas's knowledge, set out to create a Weyburn Social Credit Association where none had previously existed, one which would throw its weight behind the CCF candidate. Charter members of the Social Credit group included wives of CCF executive members. "We knew we had enough people to support us if we could keep it together," said Douglas later, "and so did the Liberals."[15]

The Liberals, meanwhile, organized a dummy Social Credit group of their own. They performed this service wherever Aberhart's party was weak in Saskatchewan, on the theory that a strong Social Credit turnout could only hurt the CCF. In Melville, for example, the Social Credit candidate was Thomas McCaffery, a senior Liberal Party official from Calgary. In Weyburn a prominent CCF supporter, Eric Mackay, told Douglas that the Liberals had offered him $2000—at that time a small fortune—to run under the Social Credit label. When Mackay turned them down the Liberals found another aspiring politician, Morton Fletcher, to pose as a "100% Social Credit" candidate.

In the midst of this turmoil, George Williams wrote to Douglas that "candidates would probably be much better off to frankly oppose the fallacies of Social Credit than to try to compromise."[16] But the CCF-inspired Social Credit rump in Weyburn had already called a convention. On Saturday, September 28, Douglas told this meeting—attended, at least in part, by his own supporters—that while he could not stand as a Social Credit candidate, he welcomed the local group's "whole hearted support."[17] The chairman of the meeting then read a telegram from Colonel Arnold, confirming that Tommy Douglas had the official support of Premier Aberhart and the Social Credit movement. The telegram left the Liberals' dummy candidate, Morton Fletcher, out in the cold.

One of Douglas's advisers who worked especially hard to set up the Social Credit ruse was a political nomad by the name of Daniel Carlyle Grant. Grant was a spiritualist and a tea-leaf reader who had worked in the Ku Klux Klan's campaign against brothels and gambling dens in the late 1920s. The Conservative government rewarded him with a provincial government job in Weyburn, but the Liberals had fired him on their return to power in 1934. Grant vowed revenge, and joined the Douglas campaign.

It was Grant who insisted on making Young's "lower standard of living" gaff a recurring slogan. He also concocted the scheme for providing Douglas with transportation: at Grant's urging, the Montgomery Brothers garage agreed to provide a new car, a silver Hudson Terraplane, in return for a promise of payment at some future date. The CCF then put the "Silver Bullet" up for a raffle, to take place at the end of the campaign. In the meantime, it served as the campaign car. At each stop—Douglas averaged three meetings a day—he mesmerized the crowd, and Dan Grant flogged raffle tickets. In this manner, they paid for both the car and most of their travel expenses.

From mid-August until October, the *Weyburn Review* granted both

Douglas and Young a chance to state their opinions in a series of weekly columns. Young stayed pretty much to discussions of free trade and the lunacy of the CCF program. Douglas covered a much wider range of issues; and although a couple of the columns were tinged with social credit theory, most kept to the political line laid out in the Regina Manifesto of 1933. The first priority, he wrote in his initial newspaper piece, must be economic planning. A national committee of experts should lay out plans for "the production, distribution and exchange of all goods and services." In the second column, he called for the socialization of all credit, banking, and insurance. A national investment board, he said, should redirect investment towards "socially desirable purposes as determined by the planning commission." These "purposes" might include utilities, or the development of mining, forest, coal, and petroleum, all to be controlled by the state. He made no mention of the role of private business.

For the next five weeks, Douglas established many of the themes he would pursue in Parliament, and later in the government of Saskatchewan. Government, he said, should offer both credit and freedom from foreclosure to farmers, and credit to co-operatives. Farmers should also get higher prices for their goods, although he did not explain how. On health care, he insisted that "Health services should be made at least as freely available as are educational services today." Workers should have unemployment and disability insurance, and better health and safety protection; he also proposed "state regulation of all wages," an idea that soon after disappeared from his repertoire. He demanded the abolition of Section 98, the anti-dissident law from 1919 which Bennett had used to round up the national Communist leadership. And, naively, he tried to predict the benefits that would flow from CCF government: "In the type of economy that we envisage, the need for taxation, as we understand it, will have largely disappeared." Like other CCFers—and like the British socialists of fifty years earlier—Douglas believed that once the profit system faded away the bottlenecks in the economy would disappear too, and all classes would share in an outpouring of abundance.[18]

The highlight of the campaign came on September 25, when Douglas and Edward Young staged their debate before 5000 people at the Arena Rink. As Douglas walked to the meeting from his home, he watched a steady stream of old trucks trundle past, their boxes packed with farmers in heavy coats. Inside, the big unheated barn was dark, and jammed with people standing on the dirt floor or perched in the bleachers that ran alongside.

Young had a reedy, indistinct speaking voice, but he refused to agree to the use of a loudspeaker. The young preacher had already learned the tricks of speaking to a large hall: he lengthened his vowels, almost as if he was shouting down a canyon, and his voice soared over the crowd. He opened with a pitch for both CCF and Social Credit votes: the first priority of a new government, he said, should be to restore purchasing power to the people. "Right here in Weyburn constituency, the purchasing power of the people is so low that people are, in some instances, forced to wear gunny sacks for clothing and go about in worn out shoes." In Sweden, he said, the central bank put money into circulation through social allowances, or as he translated it into social credit jargon, a "national dividend." Through the rest of his speech, Douglas called in various ways for economic stimulation through government spending. Government could ease unemployment, he said, with a program of public works; it could restore the farm economy by raising farm prices and holding down the profits to middlemen. He called for public pensions at sixty, and a national health plan; and he finished with a shot at Young, whose political views boiled down to support for "survival of the slickest."

The Liberal candidate spent his allotted time abusing the CCF. The cost of unemployment relief and health insurance alone, Young said, would amount to more than a billion dollars a year, and the country simply could not afford it. Waving a CCF pamphlet, he warned that the proposed national planning commission "would tell the farmers what to do on their own farms."[19] The pamphlet Young was holding had not been released to the public. Douglas knew, in fact, that the Liberals had stolen it from a local print shop. The day before, he had gone with an RCMP constable to the McTaggart village school and called the principal, J. J. McCruden, who was also Young's campaign manager, out into the playground. With the children watching from inside, McCruden had admitted to the theft.

And here was Young using the stolen document on stage! At the end of his rebuttal, Douglas told the crowd in the arena, "Any man who would stoop to such methods is unfit to be a teacher of the youth of this country! And any man who would make use of stolen property on a political platform is unfit to represent the people of this constituency in Parliament!"

"Well, the whole thing just broke up at that point," Douglas recalled later, "with Young shaking his fist and McCruden racing down the platform. He stood about six feet two, and he was threatening to knock my head off, and a whole bunch of farmers jumped over the railing and gathered around the platform saying, 'Don't you dare touch him!'...It was a great wind-up."[20]

It should have been a great wind-up, too, but the black chickens of the Social Credit dodge came home to roost. Relations between Douglas and the provincial party were strained to the breaking point. It appears Coldwell and Fines knew of the Douglas strategy and did not disapprove of it—Douglas said later that he went over the details with Coldwell at his Weyburn dinner table. Other CCF leaders from Woodsworth on down, however, had spoken out against any political fusion at election time. What did Aberhart want in return for endorsing Douglas? Or, more important, what had Douglas given away? Andy Macauley, a CCF MLA, charged that Douglas was "destroying the organization."[21]

Pro-Douglas posters appeared from a group calling itself the "Weyburn CCF-Social Credit Committee." A Social Credit official from

Alberta, Adam Zeigler, appeared on a platform with Douglas to show that he, not Fletcher, had Aberhart's stamp of approval. The *Leader-Post* helped out with a report that Douglas had "officially declared his willingness to support the Social Credit platform 100 per cent."[22] Douglas had not made any such pledge, but it still seemed to many in the party that he was guilty of collaboration. Senior CCFers like Tom Johnston, a member of the party executive, and Sandy Nicholson, an organizer in the northeast, demanded in letters to the CCF central office that Douglas be repudiated as a candidate. Stinson organized a support rally for Douglas in Weyburn and told reporters that "the Weyburn executive is independent of the central executive when dealing with matters in the riding."[23]

Douglas and Stinson faced a hostile reception when they met with five members of the provincial executive in Regina on October 9. A transcript shows that Williams, Macauley, Mrs. Fisher from the United Farmers, and Jack King of the CCF research office all hotly criticized the Weyburn manoeuvre.* Only Dr. Hugh MacLean, an old ally of Coldwell's, spoke up in defence of Douglas. The majority were prepared to convict him on the basis of Colonel Arnold's telegram: "This will confirm endorsation of convention held Weyburn [September] twenty-eight of you as Social Credit candidate."

"The idea of Social Credit is feasible in a planned social economy," insisted Douglas.

"That doesn't mean anything," said George Williams, and he held up the poster from the Weyburn CCF-Social Credit Committee. "Who issued this?"

"Our joint committee."

"How did you arrange for the speaker? Through Arnold?"

"We wrote and asked for a man to repudiate this man Fletcher."

"And you had this man sent from Alberta?"

"Yes."

"Communists have endorsed me," Dr. MacLean interrupted. "I am not a Communist."

"Did you do this because you felt you couldn't win without Social Credit?" asked Mrs. Fisher.

"Social Credit doesn't amount to a row of pins," Douglas retorted.

"Then why not go on a straight CCF program?"

"We are," said Douglas. "I am the CCF candidate for the Weyburn federal constituency, and the Social Credit forces have the right to endorse me and a joint committee has the right to issue literature to repudiate this man Fletcher. I refused 100 per cent acceptance of Arnold's program. I refused to sign the Social Credit recall. All I did was promise to give Aberhart a hand. Whatever action the executive takes does not affect me."[24]

The cocky young candidate would likely have been thrown out the

---

* This transcript is the only one of its kind in the Saskatchewan CCF files. Whether it was made up for the benefit of Douglas or his prosecutors is not clear.

door but for the presence of Dr. MacLean, who was one of the elder statesmen of the movement. The transcript of the meeting peters out, but it is clear that MacLean blocked a vote on whether to discipline Douglas. He warned that Coldwell, who was absent, had threatened to resign if the executive moved against his young friend from Weyburn.

The provincial leader confirmed this threat in a telegram to Williams the next day. Jake Benson, he wrote in a follow-up letter, had accepted a Social Credit nomination and offered to support the Social Credit caucus in Ottawa. Douglas had accepted only Social Credit support, with no strings attached. In future, he said, no candidate would accept the endorsement of any other party without clearance from the CCF executive. To eject Douglas now, though, would have "regrettable repercussions for the whole movement."[25] At the same time, Coldwell ordered Douglas to make his position plain with a public statement, and Douglas complied. He told the *Leader-Post* that he had not signed any agreement with Social Credit, and went on: "I am the CCF candidate for this constituency who has been endorsed by the Social Credit forces, who have pledged me their support. The fact that the Social Credit forces have undertaken to endorse me does not make me a Social Crediter."[26]

On election night, October 14, the early returns from Weyburn city polls gave Young the lead, and the Liberals staged a victory parade led by the McKinnon family of Calvary Church. Then the tide turned, and "Mr. Douglas's supporters 'chaired' him and carried him through the city amidst tumultuous enthusiasm."[27] He took 44 per cent of the ballots cast, although his share in the city was only 31 per cent. The final count gave him 7280 votes, compared with 6979 for Young. George Beischel, an invalid Conservative who had campaigned from his bed, got 1557 votes, and Morton Fletcher, the Liberal-sponsored "Social Credit" candidate, picked up only 362.

Elsewhere in Saskatchewan, the picture for the CCF looked bleak. Despite a vigorous CCF campaign, the party took only one other riding in the province, Coldwell's Rosetown-Biggar constituency. Social Credit also elected two Saskatchewan members, and split the protest vote in several constituencies. In Alberta, Social Credit wiped out half a dozen veteran CCF MPs. East of Winnipeg, Woodsworth's party failed to gain a toehold. Douglas and Coldwell would join two members from Winnipeg and three from British Columbia in the new federal caucus.

The federal Conservatives—fractured, demoralized, damned from every side—collected only forty federal seats. Harry Stevens's Reconstruction Party, although it cut heavily into the Tory vote, elected only Stevens to the Commons. The big winners were Mackenzie King and his Liberals, who had campaigned under the slogan "King or Chaos." The Liberals, facing a fragmented opposition, took 173 seats with only a small increase in their vote from 1930. It was the start of more than two decades of uninterrupted Liberal rule.

Despite the success of the Weyburn campaign, several members of the Saskatchewan CCF executive still wanted Douglas out of the party. On October 21 an executive meeting heard a letter of grave disapproval from Woodsworth, who had written before the election, "this kind of action on the part of individual candidates ought not to be permitted." The vote that had been delayed on the 9th was now taken, and Douglas was cast from the party. But Coldwell was present and forced a reversal: the matter would be taken to provincial council in December.[28]

The Social Credit Party also showed some confusion over the Weyburn results. The party's official newspaper, published in Edmonton, reported that Douglas "is understood here to have pledged his support to social credit. Local Social Crediters Tuesday evening claimed Mr. Douglas' election as an additional win for Social Credit, and that he should not have been referred to as CCF."[29]

By December, feelings within the CCF had cooled. The provincial council limited itself to a motion of censure against Douglas, and labelled the Weyburn campaign "embarrassing." The same meeting invited Jacob Benson of Yorkton back into the fold.[30] George Williams and his cronies were disgusted. Williams, chosen by council as the provincial leader because of Coldwell's impending departure for Ottawa, wrote, "If Douglas says that he was just double-crossing Social Credit, it is just possible that we would be on the receiving end of the cross next time."[31] Williams learned to work with Douglas over the next few years, but he never forgave Coldwell for his handling of the controversy. He bitterly denounced both men when he left the leadership in 1941.

Douglas, much later, offered a brief comment on his strategy in the 1935 election. Essentially, he and his supporters had rigged up a mock political party, which had successfully persuaded most Social Credit supporters to vote CCF. His motive, he said, was to unite all those who wanted genuine reform rather than let some stray into Fletcher's dead end. As for the differences between Social Credit and the CCF, he said, "here was a mob of people, farmers, small businessmen, railway workers, who knew that something was wrong...and wanted to support something. And they didn't give a tinker's damn about all of the fine points."[32]

Besides the attempt to throw him out of the CCF, there was also a move in 1935 to eject Douglas from the Baptist ministry. Early in the year a Baptist Union official urged Douglas to disengage himself from politics and offered him a post at the Strathcona Church in Edmonton. As Douglas often recalled in later years, this only strengthened his determination to run for the CCF.

In late fall, at a Baptist convention in Calgary, a few zealots called for the removal of his name from the ministerial rolls. A Douglas sympathizer who attended the meeting wrote that many Baptists preferred the model clergyman to be "a kind of religious eunuch, a token abstainer from booze, tobacco and politics."[33] However, the church patriarch, General Secretary William Smalley, squelched the motion.

Calvary Church made its last regular payment to Tommy Douglas on

December 30, 1935, after offering speeches and gifts at a farewell ceremony. However, the family kept their home in Weyburn until 1944 and their membership at the church. In fact, Douglas was a member until the end of his life. He preached at the Mortgage Burning Service in 1943, the fiftieth anniversary service in 1956, and the seventieth anniversary service in 1976. He also kept his place on the reserve list of ministers at the Calgary headquarters of the Western Baptist Union, but he never again held down a job as a preacher. The Douglas campaign put away its campaign materials, and Ted Stinson went back to work at his store. The campaign committee drew a lucky ticket on the "Silver Bullet." Dan Grant joined the Saskatchewan Social Credit Party. In early January, Douglas learned that his father had died suddenly of a burst appendix. He travelled to Winnipeg for the funeral and a sad reunion with his mother and sisters. A few days later, still in mourning, he set out for Ottawa and the start of a forty-four-year career as a professional politician.

7

A Western MP

TOMMY DOUGLAS FOUND Ottawa in the mid-1930s to be a drowsy, self-satisfied little city, largely untouched by the crop failures and factory shutdowns in the outside world. It combined, he said later, "Anglo-Saxon charm and Gallic efficiency," red tape and social snobbery.[1] The round of parties and receptions on Parliament Hill and at Rideau Hall churned along, seducing young and idealistic politicians with their "flattery, soft couches, and good food."[2] Douglas resisted these temptations and lived the life of an outsider, working late in his office under the eaves of Parliament's Centre Block.

J. S. Woodsworth's little band of radicals faced laughable odds. Rank on rank of Liberals perched on the government side of the Commons. They commanded the support of most of Canadian business, the media, the professions, the middle classes. They introduced enough reforms to avert social unrest, but not so many as to frighten the stock exchanges. To the CCF, it seemed the government always acted reluctantly and without any plan. For the rest of his life, Douglas would regard the 1930s as a decade of lost opportunity for Canada's young people, many of whom were either unemployed or scratching away at menial jobs. Only with the war, and the chance to die in uniform, would their country offer them a place in society.

Douglas entered immediately into the life of the Commons chamber. The reports that he intervened sixty times in debate during his first year in Parliament exaggerate his prowess—Hansard's indexes list most questions and comments as well as speeches. However, he delivered his maiden address within days of the opening of the House on February 6, 1936, and he spoke half a dozen times on agriculture and foreign policy in the unusually long five-month session that followed.

The family maintained the home in Weyburn, but Irma and Shirley came to Ottawa for the parliamentary sessions. Douglas now earned $4000 a year, a good salary at the time. For $40 a month Irma could rent an apartment in one of Ottawa's big brick houses in Centretown. All the same, Douglas was expected to give much of his money to the party and to other worthy causes. He worked long hours, but he also spent time with his wife and daughter. Shirley recalled taking a streetcar with her father to see a Shirley Temple movie; when the young heroine on the screen lost her way, the Canadian Shirley broke down in grief-stricken sobbing and had to leave the theatre.

The CCF caucus in Ottawa had only five core members, and if the party was to be effective in its opposition, each one would have to bear a heavy load. Besides Woodsworth, Coldwell, and Douglas, Angus MacInnis and Grant MacNeil from Vancouver were the only MPs who stood by the party until the 1940 election. Alf Heaps from North Winnipeg worked with the caucus, but he called himself a Labour MP for the *Parliamentary Guide*. Agnes MacPhail usually voted with the group, but her conservative United Farmers of Ontario backers opposed any formal tie with the socialists. J. S. Taylor of Nanaimo, elected for the CCF, jumped to the Liberals.

Douglas and Coldwell shared an office on the sixth floor of the Centre Block, next to Woodsworth's. Committee meetings began at 11 A.M.— Douglas sat on the Agriculture and Public Accounts committees—and the Commons sat from 3 P.M. until late at night, with a two-hour supper break. They had almost no time for research or correspondence. In a report to the Saskatchewan CCF, Douglas and Coldwell wrote that "Our present arrangement is a makeshift and painfully inadequately supplied with funds. Members here have been for years sending out literature, addressing meetings and doing propaganda work at their own expense. Small wonder that several of our former Members of Parliament are in straitened financial circumstances."[3]

One unexpected bonus was the arrival in Ottawa of a young lawyer, just returned from Oxford, who offered to take over Coldwell's job as national secretary for the CCF. David Lewis had come to Canada from Poland with his family when he was a boy and had made meteoric progress through the Montreal school system and McGill University. As a Rhodes scholar, he had been the first Canadian to be elected president of the Oxford Union. He had also immersed himself in the politics of the British Labour Party. Now twenty-six, Lewis soon emerged as both a shrewd adviser and a master of organization within the CCF.

Grace MacInnis, Woodsworth's daughter, worked as secretary to the caucus, and observed Douglas's performance during his early years. "He was at home right away in the House," she said later, "and yet he didn't have to do silly things to show off, to be aggressive like you are when you aren't sure of yourself. Tommy was always solid. He never jumped onto a spot unless he thought it was a solid spot. He was very cautious and canny."[4] Some of his opponents saw Douglas in another light, as a glib upstart, and they heckled him with phrases like "More from the gramophone!" and "Lecture number two." He obviously enjoyed needling the Liberal backbenchers in return and watching the effects. "There is an old saying," he once ventured, "that when you throw a stone into a pack of dogs and one yelps, he has been hit." Under pressure from the House, he withdrew the remark.[5]

Douglas also wrote biting anti-government newspaper columns for any editor who asked. In one piece for *The Advocate* he observed that Liberal members from Saskatchewan were keeping silent on the government's wheat policies, although they jumped eagerly into a debate on riding boundaries: "Feeding, clothing and caring for our people is of relatively little importance. Saving one's seat is of paramount importance. So this is parliament? Pardon me, I thought it was a kindergarten." A Liberal MP from Swift Current, C. E. Bothwell, denounced this article as unfair. Only two Saskatchewan Liberals had debated the boundary changes, he said, not the whole bunch. Given such cheap attacks, Bothwell said, he was not surprised that "when the honorable member for Weyburn starts to talk there seems to be a sudden exodus in the direction of the corridors."[6]

Douglas mellowed with age, and by the early 1940s he had the ear of the prime minister and other leaders in the House. After his departure in 1944, Bruce Hutchison summed up Douglas's record for *Maclean's* magazine: "He did not make himself popular in Parliament, but he made himself heard, and, at times, he could penetrate even the rhinoceros skin of the Government."[7] In the process, the preacher developed a tough hide himself; by the time he became premier of Saskatchewan in 1944 he was almost invulnerable to taunts and cheap shots.

Perhaps he was lucky to get off as lightly as he did, considering that he came into Parliament as a leading member of a suspected Communist front. Douglas became vice-chairman of the League Against War and Fascism in late 1935, a move which caused some friction between him and his CCF colleagues. The Liberals, and especially the Tories, had pestered Woodsworth and his followers about their "communistic" views for years. In a 1936 Commons debate on the Co-operative Commonwealth, a Tory MP named the League Against War and Fascism as a "communist organization," but the old parties never used this to launch any sustained attack on the young minister.[8]

The public had good reason to be confused about the relationship between the CCF and the Communists. The Communists sometimes dismissed the CCF as closet fascists, and sometimes proposed a union of the two sides; arguments for both views jostled for space in party leaflets. On the CCF side, Woodsworth and most of the older leaders were grimly anti-Communist, but some CCF radicals favoured the Marxist rhetoric of class struggle and the "liquidation" of capitalism.[9] "Some of our people were pretty close to the Communists," Douglas said in 1984. "They didn't want to go all the way out to taking orders from the Soviet Union, but they were pretty far left, and were prepared to almost accept, temporarily, a police state, although what they meant by temporarily God only knows. Police states have a way of staying."[10]

For his part, Douglas followed the lead of George Williams. The

Communists were winning converts through "the daily struggle"—a term that referred mostly to the organization of workers and the unemployed. CCFers like Williams felt that their party should show equal concern for the downtrodden. The Saskatchewan leader shared the platform with Saskatchewan Communist leaders at several meetings for farmers and for the unemployed in 1935. Douglas joined the League Against War and Fascism, a lobby group made up of Communist and socialist notables which set out to publicize both fascist aggression abroad and what it saw as the growth of far-right influence at home. The league urged the Canadian government to take a stronger stand against Hitler, Mussolini, and Japan. At the same time, it warned that fascism was already at work in Canada, as shown by police attacks on strikers and demonstrators, and by right-wing fringe groups.

At the league's second annual congress in Toronto in early December 1935, Douglas accepted the post of vice-chairman. The chairman was A. A. MacLeod, a leading Toronto Communist. The board of directors included a clutch of social gospel veterans such as Dr. Salem Bland, as well as A. E. Smith, a Communist organizer who had once been a senior officer in the Methodist church in Manitoba. Douglas spoke at the congress in favour of imposing sanctions against Italy, which had invaded Ethiopia the previous summer. Douglas's name remained on the league stationery through 1936. However, the Communist Party's files on the league do not mention his work, nor do the files of a league member in Calgary. (Unfortunately, Douglas's office records from 1935 to 1944 have disappeared.) It appears likely, in fact, that Woodsworth and Coldwell ordered him to drop his ties with the league early in 1936.

At a meeting of the CCF caucus and party thinkers in March 1936 the current ran strong against any further collaboration with the Communists or their front groups. Most of those present argued that the Communists had no real interest in reforming Canadian society. They wanted to sabotage the CCF and win members and prestige for themselves. Douglas later remembered quarreling with his older colleagues on the issue. Hitler and Mussolini, he said, were the main enemy. The CCF's integrity was at stake if the party deserted the anti-fascist movement merely to appease the red-baiters. "I was too idealistic," he said in 1985, "and so Coldwell and I differed quite seriously, and with Woodsworth even more. Both of them had had a lot more experience than I had and been around longer. I had the great advantage of youth in which you know everything and nobody can tell you anything."[11]

In addition to the league, Douglas belonged to a second group that right-wing critics labelled a Communist front, the Canadian Youth Congress. In the summer of 1936 he went as a CYC delegate to an international youth meeting in Geneva. His fellow travellers included Paul Martin, a young Liberal MP, and Denton Massey of the Conservatives. His trip convinced him that his fears about fascism were fully justified. He watched the Brown Shirts march in the streets of Germany, and met with labour leaders whose comrades had disappeared into prison camps. "I recognized then," he said, "that if you came to a choice between losing freedom of speech, religion, association, thought...and resorting to force, you'd use force."[12]

In August 1939 the Soviet Union signed a non-aggression treaty with Germany. Within days, Canadian Communists switched from condemning Hitler to opposing any Canadian war against Hitler. Douglas wrote of the affair in a *Commonwealth* article headed "I Am Disgusted," saying he had expected a "higher standard of international morality" from the Soviets. He recalled his dealings with the Communists in the League Against War and Fascism: "I felt that they were sincere in their opposition to fascism and that their desire to preserve democracy was genuine. Subsequent events have shattered my somewhat naive faith."[13]

The CCF's declared long-range goal was to build a co-operative commonwealth. In this respect the party differed radically from the other parties in the Commons. While the others believed that the people should control Parliament, the CCF hoped that someday the people would also wrest control of the economy away from the "monopolies and financial barons." In Douglas's words, any large private firm that failed to operate in the public interest should be taken over by "the appropriate public authorities" and run as a co-operative or a public service.[14]

With only a handful of members in the Commons, the best the CCF could do in the short term was to push the government to go a little further in helping Canadians through the Depression. The caucus agitated endlessly in Parliament for better relief programs and for federal job-creation schemes. Douglas, along with Coldwell, spoke for the party on agricultural questions. He called on the government to raise prices for farm products and infuse some capital into the bankrupt western economy. For lack of support staff or political contacts in other regions, he was forced to focus almost entirely on what he knew at first hand— the problems of prairie farmers.

In the running debate on agriculture, Douglas and Coldwell worked closely with the western Tories, especially Ernie Perley of Qu'Appelle, Saskatchewan, and R. B. Bennett of Calgary. Douglas later described the former prime minister as a reactionary in many ways, a man who really believed that the rich should dominate the poor. At the same time, he defended Bennett against his many detractors as a great parliamentarian and an honest broker. "He had been almost ruthless in his condemnation of anything he didn't agree with," said Douglas. "He was ruthless in dealing with people who differed with him. But he was never malicious about it. He always treated me as an erring preacher who had just got the wrong theology." Above all else, he insisted, Bennett was the sponsor of the modern Canadian Wheat Board, which formed part of the abortive New Deal of 1935. King's Liberals suspended the Wheat Board's operations in 1937, but they never quite killed it, and it went back into business in 1939.

Bennett retired from the Conservative leadership and from Parliament in the spring of 1938 and left for England, never to return. Douglas went down to the Ottawa train station on Sussex Drive on the morning of Bennett's departure and found that only two Tory MPs, neither of them Bennett supporters, had come to see the old politician off. "I was never so embarrassed in my life as I thought of the Tory party, of all the people he'd appointed to key jobs, the people he'd put in the Senate, the people he'd made cabinet ministers who wouldn't have made good messenger boys...But underneath they hated and despised him. And not one of them turned up."[15]

Douglas could afford to sympathize with Bennett, powerless and friendless as he was after his government's defeat in 1935. He held a different view of Mackenzie King. Douglas saw King as a self-styled humanitarian who lacked the courage to act on his convictions, the Dr. Jekyll whose rhetoric masked the cruelty of his government's policies.[16] "I was not a great admirer of King's, although nobody was kinder to me," he recalled. "He took a fancy to me for some reason. I think he saw in me what he had been like as a young man...He would follow what I was saying and what line I was advocating. And later when I became Premier, and I had conferences with him on various problems, he was helpful and courteous, and shilly-shallied on every question."[17]

Shilly-shally, said nothing, no action: these were the phrases Douglas used endlessly in his attacks on the King government as the hard times in the West continued year after year. In a triangular area marked by Brandon, Lloydminster, and Calgary, 300 municipalities suffered drought for most of the years between 1930 and 1937. For every $1000 the western farmer had borrowed before 1930, he owed $1700 by 1937; Saskatchewan farmers as a whole owed $120 million dollars on land with an estimated value of $100 million. Despite prices for Saskatchewan farm products rising in the late 1930s, they only reached 50 per cent of pre-Depression levels by 1940. Douglas found that King avoided any forthright response to these problems. In 1935 King had promised to liberalize federal policies on credit and currency. Instead, Douglas told radio listeners, even pro-Liberal newspapers complained about "the victory of orthodox high finance," as the King government held the money supply and public spending to a minimum.[18]

The CCF proposed that Ottawa undertake job creation through public works, and that the government subsidize farm labour to help hard-pressed farmers survive. King set up a National Employment Commission to study the labour force, and then disbanded it. The words "No Action," said Douglas, should be written on the commission's tombstone. Ottawa agreed to give some young people temporary jobs as farm labourers and tree planters, but shied away from either a public-works program or unemployment insurance. Douglas charged that King had abandoned youth, and was playing with fire: "There will arise in Canada," he said, "groups and parties advocating a much less desirable form of government."[19] When the Liberals amended the Prairie Farm Rehabilitation Act to provide support for the building of small dams and dugouts and the assembling of land for community pastures, Douglas estimated that Canada should spend $5 million a year to match similar American programs. It took the Liberals three years to spend $2 million.

In 1937 Saskatchewan experienced another crop failure, and many farmers applied for relief. Local welfare officers told the farmers they would not qualify if they owned cattle. But crop failure meant there was no feed available for the cattle, and nobody wanted to buy livestock. Many farmers had to sell off their herds at prices that did not cover the costs of their delivery to the slaughterhouse. Douglas told the Commons, "Thousands of farmers were faced with either liquidating their herds or seeing their children starve."[20]

The Liberals would demonstrate, after 1939, that they could find the billions of dollars needed to fight a war. They acted more cautiously in meeting the crisis on the prairies. Perhaps they feared that any massive redevelopment program in the West would cost them support in central Canada. Chronically depressed rural Quebec, for example, reacted sceptically to the sudden cries for help from the "gentleman farmers" of the prairies.[21]

The government enlisted western Liberals to argue that the CCF demands were unrealistic. If the dominion wanted to spend $100 million on raising farm prices by 10 per cent, said Alison Glen of Manitoba, it would have almost to double income taxes. "Unless the honorable member for Weyburn obtains the fountain pen of Mr. Aberhart in order to create the money," he said, "I do not know where it is going to come from."[22] Douglas sometimes argued, in return, that the East had taken far more out of the West over time than it had put in. He used a figure calculated by Professor Norman Rogers from the days before Rogers joined the federal cabinet. This estimate showed that the four western provinces had lost $54 million through high import tariffs in 1934 alone—far more than they received in federal emergency aid.[23]

Douglas indicated from the first that he would act as a regional MP, as well as a CCF MP. In 1936 he voted against a government plan to issue bilingual banknotes. The days of the Klan and its anti-French, anti-Catholic message of hate were still fresh in his mind. If the government issued dollar bills displaying both French and English script, he said, there might be another outbreak of bigotry in the West. The Liberals would best serve the country by "leaving well enough alone, by letting sleeping dogs lie."[24] He seconded a motion from Grant MacNeil that the banknotes should simply show the word "Canada," with appropriate numerals. When the House rejected this idea, Douglas and Coldwell voted with the Tories against the bilingual notes.

Usually, though, Douglas restricted his pro-western stand to farm issues. This pitted him against former Saskatchewan premier Jimmy Gardiner, now federal minister of agriculture. Both were skilled debaters, and legend has the pint-sized antagonists blazing away at each other day after day. But while Douglas made a couple of sallies at Gardiner's expense, for the most part they discussed the government's farm bills in a dignified fashion. When Gardiner delivered a moving speech on drought conditions, Douglas praised him in a newspaper column. When Gardiner spoke sharply against high farm machinery prices, Douglas cheered. When Gardiner had to defend policies that were unpopular on the prairies, Douglas replied with scathing criticism. A prime example was a speech on the Wheat Board that the CCF soon reprinted as a pamphlet called "The Betrayal of the West." The Liberals had agreed, after a great outcry, to subsidize the prairie farmer through payments from the Wheat Board. Douglas insisted, though, that the proposed payments were still far too small, and that Gardiner had betrayed the farmers of western Canada. "If the Liberals are going to desert the farmers of Western Canada in order to save a few million dollars, by virtue of which they hope to gain support in Eastern Canada, they are betraying the people who have long and patiently borne a burden under the present tariff system which is out of all proportion to any small return they may have received."[25]

During these years in Parliament, Douglas argued that Ottawa had no effective western farm policy. He said that the Liberals were stingy, that they kow-towed to central Canadian interests, and only set up their farm programs as political pressure forced their hand. Even granting his arguments, it seems unlikely that any government, Liberal or CCF, could have met Douglas's bottom line. To some extent, governments have responded over time to demands for orderly marketing of farm products, production subsidies, and cheaper credit. Nonetheless, Canada is still searching for the formula that will guarantee the survival of the family farm—and, by extension, the survival of rural culture.

Douglas and the CCF demanded as a first step that the federal government should reduce farmers' debt loads. Bennett, and then Gardiner, had tried to work in this direction, but the decisions of the debt review boards were often rejected by the banks and mortgage companies. Some private lenders adjusted their loans, but Douglas did not believe that they absorbed any real share of the Depression's costs. "Where there was nothing," he told the Commons, "they agreed to take nothing."[26] Douglas and the CCF scored heavily in Saskatchewan with their verbal attacks against the banks. When Douglas became premier, one of his first actions was to make it harder for lenders to foreclose on farmers.

But even where the banks were lenient, Douglas realized that the farmer's debts would only mount up again unless he could make a profit on his operation. Ottawa had started to subsidize farm operations with the Wheat Board, and in 1939 Douglas suggested that the federal government guarantee the farmer a fair rate of return by setting "parity prices" for all farm products. Under a parity pricing scheme, the selling prices for farm products would be established (and recalculated regularly) on the basis of their relationship to the farmers' costs for such items as fuel, seed, labour, and credit. But while the principle of parity pricing is easy to lay down, applying the idea is another story. Every farm operation faces different challenges—in distance to market, soil types and average rainfall, weeds and pests, availability of labour. The CCF, and later the NDP, continued to cling to the principle of parity prices, but they could never reduce it to specifics. As Douglas admitted to the Commons in 1941, the idea "can start so much argument that there is not much use talking about it."[27]

Douglas readily conceded that some farmers could make a profit even when prices were low. In 1940, when he was calling for a guaranteed payment of ninety cents a bushel for wheat, he admitted that larger farmers could make a living at the forty-nine cents market price.

He even defended the interests of the large-scale farmer on occasion, such as when he spoke against a government plan to limit the amount of grain an individual farmer might deliver to the Wheat Board. Many farms in Saskatchewan, including some in his Weyburn riding, took in two sections of land or more, and he did not want to see their owners penalized for their efficiency or their hard work.[28] Douglas tried to argue at the same time for the maintenance of the family that operated "not a wheat factory but a smaller farm of a quarter or a half section."[29] The dilemma—one that the CCF never resolved—was that the interests of the large farmer and the small farmer are opposed. Historically, the larger farmer has used his savings to buy out his neighbours and move them off the land.

The riddle of how best to protect the prairie farm was something that Douglas carried back to Saskatchewan when he re-entered provincial politics. The CCF's policies continued to resound with such phrases as "farming as a way of life, and not merely a way of making a living." However, while the Douglas government intervened vigorously to restrict the banks and mortgage companies, it could not answer the problem of how to protect farmers from each other.

8

Not Peace...But a Sword

THE DECADE OF THE 1930s was one of turmoil, opening with Japanese incursion into China, and moving inexorably towards the day when almost every industrial nation would march into the general combat. The peace that had been bought with the blood of a generation was an illusion. The war to end wars had spawned a chain of vicious, rapacious dictatorships. It was a time of disappointment, even cynicism, but many people chose not to look into the future. Those who predicted the outbreak of another great war went mostly unheeded, marked as doomsayers or jingoists.

There was no field in which the infant CCF looked more innocent, more utopian, than in its foreign policy declarations. In a world of state thuggery and diplomatic doublecross the Canadian socialists looked earnestly for the dawn of a new age of international harmony. In an echo of the decade's undergraduates and youthful idealists, the CCF resolved that Canada should never take up arms in any war. Its leader in Parliament, J. S. Woodsworth, had left the Methodist church in 1917 as a pacifist renegade. His parliamentary lieutenant on foreign policy issues after 1935 was the young member from Weyburn, Tommy Douglas.

Douglas's concern with foreign affairs took him far away from the down-home issues of farm debt and relief handouts. In the major foreign policy debates from 1936 onward, he demonstrated his remarkable skills for absorbing and analysing data, and for presenting his case with the assurance of a hardened courtroom lawyer. The challenge was enormous, for the party's position came very close to contradicting itself. On the one hand, the CCF hoped for a new system of international order to guarantee the peace. On the other, the party insisted that Canadians must never, under foreseeable circumstances, bear arms in a foreign land.

The CCF had agreed on the outlines of a foreign policy in the Regina Manifesto: "to obtain international economic co-operation and to promote disarmament and world peace." The manifesto set out three main principles: an insistence that Canada maintain complete autonomy from Britain and the empire; promotion of international co-operation (which was held to be incompatible with capitalism); and refusal to participate in "capitalist" or "imperialist" wars. Since war was, in the party's view, the product of capitalism, this could be taken to mean abstention from all wars. The election platform prepared by the National Council of the party in 1934 added, if such an addition was necessary, "The CCF is unalterably opposed to war. Not a Canadian shall leave the shores of Canada to fight on foreign soil."[1]

Douglas set out some of his own early views in an article he wrote for the Saskatchewan *CCF Research Review* in June 1934:

> Few generations have been so disillusioned about war as the present. It looks back upon a hundred years of wars fought to gain markets, not one of which was worth destroying a single human life...
>
> To youth it is becoming apparent that nothing is ever settled by war, and the only people who profit are the munitions manufacturers...at last youth is learning that international financiers and munitions makers have no patriotism but greed, no ideal but money, no god but Mammon; and for this is increasingly refusing to be butchered, mutilated and disembowelled...
>
> Modern youth will be as willing to die for what is noble as any generation that has preceded it, but will refuse to be cannon fodder in order to enrich capitalists and cover statesmen's blunders.[2]

Douglas got an early opportunity to test these convictions against the reality of war—not a classic war among capitalist, imperialist powers, but an act of aggression against a defenceless and economically backward nation. In October 1935 Italy invaded Ethiopia from its bases in Eritrea, in a move to expand its African empire and gain access to the East African coast. In Geneva, the League of Nations saw the Italian action as a test of its strength and prepared a program of limited economic sanctions against the Mussolini regime. Prime Minister Bennett signalled his approval, against the advice of his officials. The list of items under sanction excluded iron and petroleum, two key strategic materials. Canada's representative to the League, Dr. W. A. Riddell, initiated a move to cut off shipments of both commodities to Italy. However, at this time Canadians voted Bennett out of office and restored Mackenzie King and the Liberals. King, fearing that Canada might lose control over its own affairs by committing itself to some other country and that this commitment might lead the country into war, disavowed his representative's "pretentious gesture" and called Riddell home.[3]

The national CCF took a position which, in effect, supported King's actions. The party viewed the League of Nations as a club run by the major capitalist powers to serve capitalist interests, and as unworthy of support until it truly represented the community of nations. At its 1934 convention the party had agreed that "Canada must refuse to assist in applying the sanctions of the League of Nations in its present condition."[4] When Woodsworth spoke on Ethiopia, he declared that Canada should respond vigorously and be willing to sacrifice some of its sovereignty if it helped to bring about joint action. He did not specify what form this joint action might take, but he was unconditionally opposed to military intervention: "I believe the primary considerations which should determine Canada's foreign policy are the promotion of the safety and the welfare of the Canadian people and the maintenance of the unity of Canada as a nation...anything like a war would split this nation from stem to stern. We ought to be on our guard against any such disaster. Personally, I think Canada should declare her firm intention not to participate actively in any overseas conflict whatever."[5]

By his own account, Douglas differed increasingly with Woodsworth as the months went by. He came to believe that the evils of allowing fascist aggression to go unchecked would be greater than those of going to war. In the summer of 1936 he passed through a series of life-changing experiences during a visit to Europe. At the World Youth Congress meeting in Geneva he discussed war and disarmament with other young people. While in Germany he encountered the ideology of the master race and its plans to rule the world. A conflict with the Nazis, he realized, would not fit the definition of "capitalist war" that the CCF had laid out in 1933. This journey convinced him, Douglas told countless interviewers in later years, that Canada must do whatever it could to stop Hitler. "One cannot talk about conciliation with a mad dog. One cannot talk about mediation with a megalomaniac who says that the idea of peace is abhorrent to him...to take the teeth out of the League, to take from the League all capacity to enforce its decisions, is to make the League null and void."

Douglas berated the government for "moving steadily and relentlessly towards a policy of isolation." This could only lead, he said, to a state of international anarchy. Canada should work to strengthen the League of Nations. Along with other countries, Canada should surrender some of its national sovereignty, including the right to wage war, and should channel all disputes and disagreements among countries to a system of international courts.[6]

However, despite Douglas's criticisms of the King government, the CCF's approach to specific foreign policy issues remained very close to that of the Liberals. When civil war broke out in Spain in July 1936, the CCF held to its official position that foreign wars were not the party's business—even when, in this case, a democratically elected left-wing government was being throttled. At its convention that year the CCF passed a motion expressing sympathy with the people of Spain in their struggle against fascism, but agreed that "Canada should remain strictly neutral in case of war, regardless of who the belligerents might be."[7] Only a few CCFers, such as the Toronto group led by Graham Spry, waged an organized effort in an area the Communists had claimed as their turf. In a reversal of the normal roles, Spry engineered a social democratic takeover of the Committee to Aid Spanish Democracy and installed a long-time prohibitionist minister at its head. The committee, in turn, helped to fund the world's first mobile blood transfusion service, Dr. Norman Bethune's Madrid-based Canadian Medical Unit. Other CCF leaders, including the parliamentary caucus and Tommy Douglas, avoided taking any active role in the relief of Spain.

The CCF, with its pacifist leadership, was truly an anti-war party. In February 1937 Grant MacNeil and M. J. Coldwell introduced a motion in the Commons expressing "grave concern" at the "startling increases" in Canadian military spending. Douglas, in his part of the debate, emphasized the CCF's belief that Canadians wanted economic security rather than military might. The government, he charged, was readying the country for war, and using so-called defence needs as an excuse: "We are saying that we believe bread is more important than bullets, that homes are more important than aeroplanes, that giving people the means to attain physical well-being is more important than building up a military clique within the Dominion."[8]

In the latter years of the 1930s the world's march into the abyss of war accelerated, interrupted only temporarily by the illusions of Munich. Within the CCF, tensions increased as party members began to question the party's commitment to military neutrality. It seemed to some that the CCF had gone beyond idealism to the point of foolishness. Coldwell later wrote that when the moment of truth came, when Germany invaded Poland, and he had to announce the CCF's sudden turnabout in support of the war effort, he passed through the most difficult moment of his life. He spoke, no doubt, for many others.

Through 1938 and early 1939, some CCF members, especially Tommy Douglas, showed increasing concern for the "mad dogs" who ruled Germany, Italy, and Japan. Canadian nickel was an essential component in the fascist war machines, and Douglas tried without success to persuade the Liberals to halt shipments of nickel, scrap metal, and other strategic goods. At the same time, CCF MPs also continued to fight against any military buildup in Canada. They complained that by hiring soldiers, training cadets, and buying more guns, Ottawa would encourage a war-like attitude in Canadians. The CCF National Council agreed in early 1938 that the party should support some military spending, but only if it was "confined solely to home defence."[9]

On September 29, 1938, Chamberlain and Hitler signed the infamous Munich agreement which auctioned off Czechoslovakia to buy "peace in our time." Prime Minister King cabled Chamberlain, expressing his "unbounded admiration...the voice of Reason has found a way out of the conflict which no people in their heart wanted, but none seemed able to avert."[10] Tommy Douglas did not share in the Liberals' enthusiasm. Still among the youngest members in the House, he challenged the mood of optimism in the government benches as he replied to the Throne Speech. His words were grim and prophetic: "I am sorry that I cannot concur with hon. members opposite in lauding the pact of Munich as a milestone on the road to world peace. In my mind, the pact of Munich did not avert a war, it only postponed a war to that time when, collective action having become impossible, and our allies having fled, the

English speaking nations of the world, isolated and discredited, will face the fascist aggresssors alone. The pact of Munich was the final culmination of a long series of concessions, each concession leading to a situation that demanded still further surrender. Yielding to dictators does not buy peace; it merely brings about demands for further concessions."[11]

By late March 1939 the division of opinion within the caucus was becoming sharper. Woodsworth clung to the view that rather than confront the dictators, the nations should work for a reorganized League and address the problems which created dictatorships. Douglas, Coldwell, and Grant MacNeil argued that the time was past when that course of action (or inaction) was possible. Germany's opponents, they said, would soon have to stand up to Hitler and risk war. Canada must decide where it would stand at the moment of truth. In early April, Douglas made his last foreign policy speech to the House before the outbreak of war. He hinted that the CCF, or at least the member for Weyburn, might be ready to depart from their neutralist position. He repeated the well-known view that Canada must always determine its own course of action; but then he struck a new note on the question of whether Canada should or should not go to war. "It seems to be the consensus [in the House] that Canada's main contribution in the event of war will be economic and that *her military contribution will at best be relatively small.*"[12]

When the Wehrmacht swept into Poland on September 1, Canada could no longer treat its response to the threat of war as a hypothetical issue. The prime minister announced that he would summon MPs to Ottawa if the crisis led to war. When Britain declared war on the Axis, King called for the House to assemble on September 7. Canada would make its own decisions, he insisted; but it was already clear that Canada would follow Britain.

The day before Parliament was to open, leading members of the CCF met in special session in a Commons committee room. The National Council, provincial leaders, and distinguished advisers all turned out to help the parliamentary group work out a response to what they knew the government would propose. The meeting lasted for a day and a half, right up to the moment when Douglas and his colleagues had to enter the House. Of all the fundamental issues that could face Canadian socialists, this was the most critical, and the one with the greatest potential for tearing the movement apart. The delegates proceeded with a great sensitivity to party unity, even though they argued from a wide range of individual opinions.

The opinions expressed fell into four distinct categories. Woodsworth, supported by Stanley Knowles, took an unequivocal pacifist position. "I am opposed to all war, this war as the last war," said the CCF leader. "First, because I am a socialist and have taught that war is the inevitable outcome of the present economic system. Secondly, I oppose it from the standpoint of Christianity. It is against my ideals." Allied with Woodsworth were the anti-war socialists who held to the old dogma that "all wars are capitalist imperialist wars." One delegate stated

All illustrations are from the Douglas family album, unless otherwise noted.

E. T. Stinson

Boy preacher

Calvary Baptist Church, Weyburn

Tommy and Irma on their wedding day

Irma in 1967 JON JOOSTEN PHOTO

Handout, 1935 election

Relaxing on Carlyle Lake
SASKATCHEWAN ARCHIVES, R-B2907,
TORONTO STAR PHOTO

Following the swearing-in, 1944:
Dr. Hugh MacLean (left), Tommy,
Frank Scott, Clarence Fines,
John W. Corman, John Sturdy,
Shirley, and Irma SASKATCHEWAN
ARCHIVES, MACLEAN ALBUM, 38-4

At the rural telephone, 1940s
SASKATCHEWAN ARCHIVES

Tommy and cabinet colleagues
Clarence Fines and Woodrow Lloyd
SASKATCHEWAN GOVERNMENT
PHOTO, DON WEBB

Fireside chats PUBLIC ARCHIVES OF
CANADA, C 126128

Tommy Douglas jokes with
members of the 1st Canadian
Division, Barneveld, Netherlands,
29 April 1945 PUBLIC ARCHIVES OF
CANADA, PA-138035,
G. BARRY GILROY PHOTO

The new leader, 1961: Claude
Jodoin, Tommy, David Lewis

NDP leadership campaign, 1961:
Tommy, Hazen Argue,
M. J. Coldwell

The 1962 campaign in Saskatoon
SASKATCHEWAN ARCHIVES,
S-SP-B5228-4, *STAR-PHOENIX*
COLLECTION

this case in its most extreme form: "The ultimate victor is fascism, whether British or German fascism. There is not much choice between the two." Frank Scott of McGill University put the position more elegantly: "If we support a capitalist war, it will mean the end of democracy. The war springs out of Europe's conflicts...I am not interested in a victory as between two sets of gangsters." After making his argument, Scott then moved grudgingly towards what became the official CCF position.

George Williams sat at the other limit of the spectrum from the anti-war group. Although some party members back home had trouble distinguishing the Saskatchewan leader's position from that of Douglas, Williams was the only person to argue at this meeting for full military participation in the war. "Would the failure of the Allies and the victory of Germany destroy democracy?" he asked. "I think it would...We recognize that war is the outcome of capitalism, but what we are fighting to support is the right to change the economic system." The official position, predictably, settled between the extremes. Canada, the party decided, should offer whole-hearted economic aid to the Allies, but should stop short of providing troops. This compromise attracted the majority for many reasons: it set out a constructive formula for resisting fascism, it could be defended as patriotic in a country at war, and above all it promised to salvage party unity. Douglas, Coldwell, and MacInnis, who would become the party's most important spokesmen on war issues, all stood behind it.

The compromise proposals came first from Angus MacInnis on behalf of the B.C. executive. MacInnis was noted for his common sense as well as his eloquence, and his talk included a short rebuff to the anti-war socialists. "If a bandit enters a building with a shot-gun we send the police to get him," he said. "We do not leave him alone because he is a product of Canadian capitalism. Hitler may be a product of European capitalism but that does not mean that you should let him dictate to the whole world." The B.C. recommendations rejected the idea of any coalition with King. They opposed conscription or the sending abroad of any expeditionary force, and opposed any restriction on civil liberties in the name of wartime necessity. Canada should send supplies to Britain and her allies, including military supplies, but the Canadian government should control the arms industry. These suggestions provided the basis of the party statement, drafted largely by MacInnis, that was eventually adopted by the meeting in a 15 to 7 vote.

Douglas told the group that he supported Great Britain and France in their struggle. He urged his colleagues to adopt the B.C. proposals, and along with MacInnis and David Lewis he helped to carry the compromise proposal. The leader of Saskatchewan's pacifist caucus, Carlyle King, would complain to a friend that Douglas was an imperialist and a war-monger, but Douglas's words at the special session show that he kept to the moderate party line.

Within the committee room, Woodsworth had lost a struggle of wills.

No one would deny that he was a profound thinker on social and moral issues, and some revered him as a saint in Canadian politics. But on this occasion, when he tried to use his position to override the consensus of the group, he was left behind. He opened the meeting by stating that he would resign as leader if the CCF chose to support the war, a comment which apparently drew no response. Later the same day he tried again to divert the meeting to his point of view, by pressing a motion "that this Council refuses to endorse any measure that will put Canada into the war." It was an open attempt to test the personal loyalty of his colleagues, but the motion died when no one would second it. Even Woodsworth's oldest allies, including his son-in-law Angus, served notice that they would go on without him. The old leader had been defeated on the most important of his principles.[13]

On September 8, 1939, the drama shifted from the committee room to the floor of the House of Commons where the CCF acted out the finale of its play within a play. The caucus granted Woodsworth the leader's customary right to follow the prime minister in the order of speaking, but he spoke only for himself. From this point on, M. J. Coldwell would speak for the party in the Commons.

Woodsworth's address, and the hushed response it received, has always been regarded as one of Parliament's great moments. The small, stooped man who had fought so many battles, now stood alone in an assembly that was obviously intent on going to war. And even now there was a greater drama, hidden from the eyes of most of those present. In speaking to Ralph Allen twenty-two years later, Douglas drew back the curtain, revealing further the courage of his falling leader. A few days before these events, Woodsworth had suffered a severe stroke. "When he rose to speak he could scarcely see and one side was partly paralyzed. The night before Mrs. Woodsworth had made a few notes at his dictation—a cue word here and there—and put them on cards in thick crayon letters at least an inch high. I slipped into the seat beside him and handed the cards up to him one by one while he made his moving but hopeless plea for peace. I knew that in a few minutes I would be voting against him, but I never admired him more than I did that day."[14]

A perceptive member of the Press Gallery called this speech Woodsworth's valedictory, and time proved him right. Woodsworth spoke only once more in the House where he had sat for eighteen years. Slightly more than a year later, worn down by the intense life he had led, distracted by the horrors of a war that he detested, and wearied by the demands of yet another election campaign (which he had won by an even larger majority than before), his physical stamina drained and his health gone, he tendered his resignation from the party leadership. Six months later he died. One of the great chapters in Canadian political history was closed. In the by-election that followed, Douglas's college chum Stanley Knowles won a decided victory for the CCF.

Almost half a century after Woodsworth's death, Douglas shared some thoughts on the importance of his old leader to the party. While he leaned towards the view that mass movements are created at the grass roots and produce their own leaders, he recognized that in the early 1930s Woodsworth was the only leader acceptable to the farmers, to labour, and to thinkers on the left, and the only radical who was known to the Canadian public. "With Woodsworth," he said, "you put political principle first and political consequences second...and I think the CCF survived only because of Woodsworth's unyielding attitude. Compromise wasn't part of his makeup."[15] Douglas denied, though, that he based his style of leadership or speaking on Woodsworth's. If anyone influenced him in these areas, it was Coldwell.

In Saskatchewan, where Woodsworth had a large personal following, the news of the split in the caucus caused shock and grief in the CCF. Douglas tried to explain his own position in two articles he wrote for the Saskatchewan *Commonwealth*.[16] In the first, he recalled his visit to Hitler's Germany, a nation where colleges had become propaganda factories, the streets crawled with secret police, and labour leaders went before firing squads. In the second article, he set out a theological justification for Canada's entry into the war, beginning with a biblical quotation: "I am come not to bring peace on earth, but a sword. I am come to set a man at variance against his father—and a man's foes shall be they of his own household." His argument followed:

> We sometimes make the mistake of assuming that conflict is always a sign of human depravity and social retrogression. There have been times when social conflict has been indicative of positive good at war with the established evils of the day...The forces of justice will always come into conflict with those of oppression.
>
> There is a distinction in Jesus' teachings between individual ethics: turning one's cheek, giving one's coat, going the extra mile—and social ethics...When someone attacks a small child whom I have pledged to defend with my life, then the lion becomes me best. I can give my coat, but I have no power to give away an old man's coat at the command of a well-clad bully. I can give up some of my rights, but when a group of lawless men endeavour to destroy the fabric of law and order by which alone human society is possible, then I have a responsibility to discharge.

9

"The Canadian People Are Prepared to Fight"

BY THE SPRING OF 1940 the position of the national CCF had swung to one of virtually unqualified support for the war effort. The previous winter the government had sent a first detachment of troops to Europe without consulting Parliament, but the CCF had issued no public statement of protest. The emergency session which brought Canada into the war had lasted only a week, providing little opportunity for debate. Parliament went into recess until January 15, 1940, and was dissolved the same day, as the prime minister called a general election for March 25. Once more, debate was effectively postponed. The opposition parties were caught completely off guard. In their view, King had tricked them. The CCF denounced the government for trampling on the rights of elected representatives, and complained that issues such as unemployment, farm prices, and war-time profiteering demanded attention.

From the start of the election campaign, the advantage rested with the Liberals. They had met the challenge of mobilizing for the defence of Canada, but they had not gone so far as to offend anyone. The Conservatives, as often happened, were quarrelling among themselves, and had little to propose other than the idea of "union government"—an idea that even some Tories disliked.[1] The CCF faced grave problems in the campaign. Though it had declared itself in favour of a policy of support for Britain and France, the memory of the party's earlier calls for neutrality lingered on in the public mind. The old parties labelled the CCF unpatriotic, un-Canadian, even seditious. Inside the party, many faithful workers and supporters still sided with the anti-war position of Woodsworth, and regretted the CCF's departure from its long-time pacifist stand. Their lack of enthusiasm hurt the party badly in the months before the election.

After a hell-for-leather contest in his home riding, Douglas increased his winning margin from 300 in 1935 to a more comfortable 950. Once again he lost to his Liberal opponent from the city of Weyburn, but the votes from the farms and villages tipped the balance in his favour. Across Saskatchewan, the CCF vote rose by 50 per cent from the previous federal election, and three new CCF MPs joined Douglas and Coldwell in the winner's circle. However, it seems likely that the Saskatchewan results had more to do with the wheat glut, farm debt, and Liberal farm policies than with the war issue. Douglas later told the Commons, for example, that the Liberal "inspectors" hired to run a farm subsidy program spent early 1940 working in the election. Many prairie farmers, meanwhile, waited months for their promised payments from Ottawa.

In most of Canada the CCF campaign—based on the defence of civil liberties in wartime, the need for national control of war industries, and opposition to conscription—failed to catch fire. Only the ailing Woodsworth, Angus MacInnis from Vancouver, and the Cape Breton labour leader Clarie Gillis would join the five MPs from Saskatchewan in the new CCF caucus. King's forces captured 181 of the 245 seats in the House, giving him the greatest majority enjoyed by any prime minister to that time.

The CCF entered the new Parliament with an approach to the war that differed profoundly from its position of one year earlier. The party had not openly opposed the dispatch of the 1st Canadian Division to Britain in late 1939, and the National Council agreed to support the expeditionary force at its meeting in May 1940. The council resolved to resist any talk of conscription of troops for overseas service; but this showed concern for feelings in French Canada as much as any lingering anti-militarism. Woodsworth had faded as the dominating force in the party. At this council meeting he suffered a major stroke, one which effectively ended his career. The pacifist strain that had coloured party policy now disappeared almost entirely.

On May 30, in a debate on the War Appropriations Bill, Douglas made his first major speech on Canada at war. He clearly set out the CCF's new position: "I believe that apart from the conscription of men for overseas service, the country should bend every effort towards the successful prosecution of the war...only the British commonwealth and her allies stand againt barbarism and the extermination of everything that makes life worth living to a civilized human being...I believe the Canadian people in the main are prepared to fight."[2]

Douglas had already shown his personal commitment to the cause by joining the 2nd Battalion of the South Saskatchewan Regiment. He was rejected for active service because of his medical history. But for that rejection he might have joined fellow officers who were seconded to other regiments and trapped in the disastrous surrender at Hong Kong. As consolation for being rejected, he was offered a post as a padre but declined it. For the remainder of the war, as a reserve officer, he did summer tours of duty at Dundurn, south of Saskatoon. He made a conscientious second lieutenant, although he was probably a shade too flippant for some tastes. When a sergeant-major from the permanent force announced that he was moving his classes from one hut to another for the second time in a day "to confuse the enemy," Douglas asked, "Why don't you just invite them to some of our lectures?"[3]

For the most part, though, Douglas fought his war in the House of Commons, and much of that fighting was on behalf of the House itself. Like Woodsworth and Coldwell, he chafed at the government's secretive habits. In his first speech in 1940, he declared that "the right to criticize the government and to subject the government's conduct of the war to the most rigid scrutiny" was fundamental to the democracy that Canada was fighting for.[4]

In 1942 he urged that MPs should have "some particular task to do" to help with the cause. The whole administrative machine for the war, he complained, had been set up "outside of parliament altogether...members on both sides of the house have expressed the opinion again and again that they feel frustrated, and in some instances, almost useless."[5] If there was a real problem of disclosure, Douglas felt that Parliament could easily respond to it. He pressed for *in camera* sessions where the government could brief the House of Commons on sensitive military matters without broadcasting privileged information. Failing such sessions of the full House, he suggested that the government name an all-party committee that could act on behalf of the House to receive confidential information. Douglas and his colleagues repeated these pleas unsuccessfully throughout the wartime period. Where the government moved at all to open its books, it was in a limited way, in the area of military supply contracts.

From the mid-1930s the CCF had spoken out against the private munitions industry and the idea that business could profit from the shedding of human blood. This appeal struck a chord with Canadian voters, who often suspected that the big mining and manufacturing companies had been the only clear winners in the First World War. Now, Douglas said, Parliament must ensure that "while the Canadian people are sending men out to risk their lives, and the common people are assuming an ever increasing burden of taxes, there are no profiteers in Canada fattening themselves upon the tears and misery of the nation."

The Canadian government was spending billions on arms and military supplies, but it was almost impossible for the House to find out where the money was going, and who among the government's friends were getting fat off wartime contracts. Douglas felt that the Canadian people had the right to demand an efficient war effort, so that neither taxpayers' money or soldiers' lives would be squandered. He made two proposals: the first, that the government set up a special committee to monitor the efficiency of war production; second, that either the Public Accounts committee or a new special committee examine all major war-related contracts.

The government had dragged its feet on these issues. A parliamentary War Expenditures Committee had accomplished little during a few meetings in 1941. By April 1942, a second committee was going to work. Already, though, Ottawa had signed nearly half a million wartime contracts. "If the committee sat twelve hours a day," he said, "it could not make even a respectable dent in this great mountain of contracts."[6]

At the start of the war Mackenzie King avoided making any commitments on whether his government would conscript young Canadians into military service. Nine months later, in a sudden show of haste, he pushed the National Resources Mobilization Act through Parliament. This measure was designed to give the government the power to introduce a military draft, as well as to commandeer factories and materials. Although most observers believed that King was still pledged not to send draftees into battle, the bill posed a potential challenge to the CCF's anti-conscription policy. The prime minister did not fear the CCF but he desperately wanted to avoid stirring up the anti-conscription movement in the Quebec wing of his own party. To minimize divisive debate, he decided to ram the Mobilization Act through both the Commons and the Senate in one day.

Douglas was among those who challenged the bill. Having stated a month earlier that Canada should "bend every effort" to resist the enemy, he could not find much in the Mobilization Act to oppose in principle. He could only restate his party's opposition to sending conscripts overseas: "We are prepared to support what the bill purports to stand for, namely the conscription of the human and natural resources of Canada *for the defence of Canada.*" He did protest vigorously, though, against what he saw as the government's butchery of the rights of the Commons. The people's representatives, he said, could not possibly give the bill proper consideration in the course of one day. How did the government plan to use its new powers? What kinds of resources did it intend to mobilize? It was clear that the government would mobilize manpower as required—limited only by King's promises not to draft young Canadians for overseas duty. But would the Liberals act as resolutely to bring the mines, mills, and factories under control, and would they make use of the wealth being accumulated by private business? The Liberal steam roller was in high gear, however, and while King did not get the bill passed that evening, he did get it the next morning.[7]

As the war went on, the pressure mounted on the Canadian government for all-out mobilization and conscription for overseas service. King held firmly to the opinion that most Canadians opposed conscription, but many in his cabinet and party disagreed. In the Speech from the Throne of January 1942 the government promised a national referendum on the following question: "Are you in favour of releasing the government from any obligations arising out of any past commitments restricting the methods of raising men for military service?"[8]

The CCF, like King, was being rushed towards changing its views on conscription. The party was signing up thousands of new members, especially in Saskatchewan and Ontario, diluting the old pacifist idealism more and more. Even long-time members were caught up in the urgency of the battle against the Axis. In his reply to the 1942 Throne Speech Douglas declared that the CCF could not oppose a democratic referendum on this issue. However, he said, the proposed wording of the question was far too vague. If the Liberals wanted the voters to know what they were voting on, they should change the wording of the proposition to read, simply: "Are you in favour of conscription for overseas service: yes or no?"[9] His advice was ignored. King, mindful of Canada's past history, feared that a vote on such a straightforward question would only polarize and divide the country. He chose to put off any decision, and positioned himself to take a "conscription if necessary, but not necessarily conscription" approach, devoutly wishing the necessity for making the choice would never arise.

The CCF caucus was leaning towards support for conscription of manpower. But again, what of conscription of wealth? As in 1940, the CCF had to ask, was Canadian business going to avoid making sacrifices when farmers and workers were expected to give up their sons to the war? Douglas seconded an amendment moved by Coldwell that "the plebiscite should seek the support of the people of Canada for the effective conscription of war industries, accumulated wealth and financial institutions at the same time and on the same basis as the suggested extension of the conscription of manpower."[10] The House voted down the amendment by a lopsided margin.

The Liberals, with the support of the CCF parliamentary group, set the vote on the conscription resolution for April 27, 1942. In supporting the government, the caucus violated a National Council decision. The council had declared there should be no plebiscite unless it encompassed both the conscription of men and of wealth. The campaign leading to the plebiscite split the CCF, as well as the country at large. Some within the party opposed conscription unconditionally, because they feared that it might permanently damage Confederation. Frank Scott of Montreal, for example, understood the depth of anti-conscription feeling in his home province and saw King's ballot as a recipe for domestic disaster in Canada. Following Woodsworth's earlier lead, he offered his resignation as national chairman of the party. Fortunately, the crisis passed, and Scott's disciplined brilliance continued to adorn the party's internal debates.

Douglas understood the need to play down the party's problems in public. For example, he declined to appear on a panel with Scott for fear of getting into an open confrontation. He appears to have vacillated himself on whether to support King's plebiscite. He wanted the CCF to apply as much pressure as possible for conscription of wealth, but he also saw that pushing too hard for this CCF demand might hinder the war effort. He wrote to Clarence Fines in Regina:

> I believe the public should be told the facts frankly and bluntly, and King should be released from any commitments, real or fancied, which he thinks restrict the scope of our participation in the war.
>   As a matter of fact, we are so close to losing the war right now that it makes me shudder every time I look at a map.[11]

Some members of the Saskatchewan CCF executive opposed the referendum on pacifist grounds. While they failed to secure a party statement in support of their views, they successfully launched what may have been a related attack on Douglas's leadership hopes. He had taken the provincial presidency in 1941; but Oakland Valleau and Carlyle King, prominent pacifists in the Saskatchewan party, now convinced the executive that he had not been officially elected leader. The executive, with a suicidal flourish, declared the party leaderless. So it remained in disarray for several months, until a summer convention voted Douglas into the leadership.

The results of the national plebiscite confirmed Mackenzie King's worst fears. The English-speaking provinces, led by Ontario, voted overwhelmingly in favour of releasing King from any previous undertakings. The voters of Quebec were as solidly opposed. The country was deadlocked; King knew that he now faced the real threat of national disunity. He chose to delay any action on conscription, and by playing off members of his cabinet against each other he hung on until the end of the war without having to challenge public opinion in Quebec.

Douglas's career took a strange turn during the controversy over the wartime draft, as Prime Minister King began to invite him over to Laurier House for private discussions. Douglas had never been kind to the Liberals or to King in his speeches in the Commons. However, as he told Ralph Allen, the editor of *Maclean's*, "He did a number of things he didn't dare tell his friends about, so occasionally he selected me, a theoretical enemy, as his confidant. At the height of the conscription crisis in 1944, he kept me up half one night to tell me the whole incredible and devious story of his manipulations in and out of his cabinet and frequently behind cabinet's back. I suppose I could have destroyed him if I'd felt free to use it. But it didn't seem to occur to him to think of the risk he was taking."[12]

King appears to have trusted Douglas for sentimental reasons. The old bachelor, as Douglas often recalled, said that the young MP reminded him of his brother Max, to whom he had been greatly devoted and whose death had grieved him deeply. Douglas was touched, although he believed that his only resemblance to Max was in his receding hairline. Perhaps King was only exercising his wiles, as part of his undying crusade to absorb the CCF into the Liberal Party. Douglas always insisted, though, that Mackenzie King never tried to entice him into crossing the floor.

Throughout the war, the CCF made it a matter of high priority to speak out in defence of civil liberties. At its special council meeting in September 1939 some delegates expressed concern that the party itself, with its large anti-war contingent, might become the target of a crackdown in a repressive climate. When Parliament finally reconvened in 1940 after its long recess, Coldwell demanded that the government safeguard "the fundamental rights of British citizenship," regardless of any special powers granted by the War Measures Act.[13]

Through much of the episode that marked the worst wartime violation of civil rights, however, the CCF and Tommy Douglas sat silently by.
During 1942 the federal government transported thousands of Japanese,
a majority of whom were Canadian citizens, away from the west coast
and seized their property. Ivan Avakumovic, in his history of *Socialism
in Canada*, has written that the CCF "did not mince their words" in
opposing these evacuations.[14] In fact, the CCF's official policy was one
of support for the government's action as being a matter of wartime
necessity.

There is no doubt that the CCF reacted vigorously through 1940
against certain actions taken under the War Measures Act, a law which
gave the federal government sweeping powers and suspended virtually
all civil guarantees for Canadians. Prime Minister King invoked the act
and its attendant regulations in August 1939, without reference to Parliament. The CCF immediately attacked the law's provisions for press and
radio censorship, and called on all "friends of democracy, to start defending now their liberties and civil rights." The party's national convention
the next year stood firm for the right of fair trial, freedom of speech,
and freedom of assembly.

Douglas spoke in Parliament in June 1940 on the War Measures Act
and the Defence of Canada regulations. The government, he agreed,
needed special powers in wartime to deal with spies and saboteurs. At
the same time, this need did not stand above all other considerations.
Douglas insisted that the people of Canada, through Parliament, should
approve any special powers granted the government before they became
effective. The nature and extent of these powers should be made
specific—"so specific that they cannot lend themselves to the persecution of any individuals or group of individuals in Canada."[15]

In that same 1940 session, Ernest Lapointe, the minister of justice,
published a list of organizations now declared to be illegal. The list
included Communist and Communist front groups, as well as some ethnic
organizations with German, Italian, or Communist ties. The minister also
served notice that the government would keep watch on others who
might subvert the war effort, including Quakers and other conscientious
objectors, Jehovah's Witnesses, and even some unnamed labour leaders.
Douglas spoke eloquently in defence of the conscientious objectors. No
doubt he remembered the ostracism Woodsworth had suffered as a pacifist
in the First World War, as well as his own father's decision not to carry
a gun. He pleaded in the House for the right of conscience, saying, "the
reason we are opposing Hitler today is that he has denied that right of
conscience...you cannot defeat Hitler by emulating Hitler."

Douglas asked the government to amend the War Services Act so that
no citizen would be forced to bear arms, regardless of whether or not
his stand was based on the teachings of a particular church or religion.
At the same time, he held that this exemption should apply only to military
service. Conscientious objectors, he said, should be expected to volunteer
for non-military service. "I do not believe in this hour of crisis any man

has a right to exemption from service," he said, "but I do believe he has a right to determine what service he can conscientiously perform."[16]

In a similar vein, Douglas came to the defence of the Jehovah's Witnesses when the government banned their publication, *Consolation, a Journal of Faith, Hope, and Courage.* He would get no political mileage from siding with this unpopular sect, but Douglas did it as a matter of principle. He suspected that the official attack on the Witnesses had more to do with their evangelizing work in Catholic Quebec than it did with the war effort. The government had no evidence, he told the Commons, that the Witnesses' practices or beliefs threatened the nation. "We keep on telling people in the democratic countries that we are fighting for the four freedoms, one of which is to worship God in the manner in which we choose. It seems to me that it is going to be increasingly difficult to convince the world that we are seeking to get religious freedom for the people of Europe when we deny it to the people of Canada."[17]

If the story had ended there, with the work of Douglas and his colleagues in protecting religious and political freedoms, the CCF would have won great credit. Sad to say, though, the party gets little credit for its part in the destruction of the Japanese community in British Columbia.

Early in the war, the Liberal government gave explicit promises that no group would suffer for the war, regardless of national origin. In September 1939 Japan joined with Germany and Italy in the Triple Axis. In June 1940 Lapointe told Parliament that no Canadian resident would be arrested without reasonable grounds, or detained without trial, even if he was a citizen of an enemy nation. The RCMP, he said, had all potential subversion under control. Canada's military bases and other potential targets for sabotage were well protected. He added that "Any persecution of racial minorities in this country is unworthy of our people and foreign to our traditions and our national spirit."[18]

A year and a half later the Japanese air force bombed Pearl Harbor, and a wave of pent-up racial hatred poured across the continent. The Canadian government declared all of British Columbia west of the Cascades a "protected area." The Japanese-Canadian community on the Pacific coast was ripped apart. Government clerks separated husbands from wives and children. While the victims waited to be shipped off to work gangs or to camps in the interior, the authorities penned them up in livestock pavilions at the Vancouver exhibition grounds. The government seized the land and boats of the Japanese, and put them up for auction. The fact that more than half the 22,000 people affected were either Canadian-born or naturalized Canadian citizens mattered not at all. As Ken Adachi has written, "Not one effective voice of protest had been raised by white Canadians; even the CCF Party, for some years an uncompromising champion of citizenship rights for the Japanese, expressed itself in favor of the evacuation 'for reasons of defence.'"[19]

Even granting that the Japanese government might have had some sympathizers, and perhaps even a few active agents on the west coast, the government had no excuse for its actions. The RCMP had advised the government that it had identified all such agents, that they were few in number, and that they presented no grave threat. The prime minister himself had quoted approvingly in Parliament in 1941 from a committee report that labelled the Japanese Canadians "good citizens and desirable settlers" from every point of view but race.[20] The chief of the General Staff had told his colleagues, even after Pearl Harbor, that the Japanese Canadians did not pose the slightest menace to national security.[21]

Nonetheless, the entire country gave way to panic over rumours of Japanese sabotage. Behind it all lay generations of racial tension on Canada's west coast. The Japanese had done well as farmers, fishermen, and merchants, while at the same time maintaining their traditions and customs. The Anglo majority on the coast feared the Japanese and, even more, resented their success. A. W. Neil, a Tory MP, summed up this shabby sentiment in 1942: "In the words of Kipling, 'you cannot breed a white man in a brown or yellow hide.' And you cannot let the brown man boss you. The white man must be dominant, his word must go."[22]

When the issue got its only real airing in the House, on July 29, 1942, the CCF felt it best not to intervene. Like the other parties, Coldwell's group succumbed to the political pressures of the moment. The party was gaining in the public opinion polls, and trying to play in the big leagues.

Looking back, it seems strange that a party so committed to the cause of civil liberty could accept, without expressions of the gravest concern, the policies adopted by the King government. It is hard to believe that once the round-up of the Japanese began, the CCF did not pursue in detail every action which appeared contrary to the party's ideals. It is clear that the national CCF took its lead from the British Columbia wing of the party and its spokesman, Harold Winch. Winch not only surrendered to the panic of early 1942, he fanned the flames: Vancouver was soon to become the second Pearl Harbor, he said, and the federal government was guilty of "criminal negligence" for not having moved against the Japanese sooner. The B.C. party newspaper echoed his words, and called on Ottawa to get the Japanese away from the coast immediately.[23]

After the evacuation, Canadians began to debate what would happen to the Japanese community when the war ended. The prospects were for mass deportation, described more genteelly as "patriation." Within the CCF, Grace and Angus MacInnis now sprang to the defence of the Japanese, though the rest of the B.C. party members kept to their aggressive stand. They demanded in early 1943 that the Japanese be relocated across the dominion. This proposal was upheld at the CCF national convention of 1944. A sudden return of poor and homeless people to the west coast, the party agreed, would simply provoke disturbances. The delegates did not discuss the question of how the Japanese had fallen into their impoverished state.

Douglas remained uncharacteristically silent throughout this debate. He was increasingly busy, in 1943 and 1944, working for victory in Saskatchewan. He decided, perhaps, that to step forward as Canada's only pro-Japanese politician would not win votes. Like other CCF leaders, he set the issue aside as "a British Columbia issue" and, as such, one to be left to the B.C. membership; they were closest to the scene, and felt more passionately than party members in other parts of Canada.

Soon after the war, Douglas was able to use his new powers as premier of Saskatchewan to make some small restitution for Canada's crimes against its Japanese community. Saskatchewan was among the first, and perhaps the very first province to offer a safe haven to its share of refugees under the federal resettlement program. In a letter to a friend and Brandon classmate, the Rev. Scott Leith, the premier wrote, "I am hoping that other provinces will do likewise, so that these people will not be persecuted and hounded from place to place."[24] Douglas received some hate mail after he took this decision, but the reaction in the province appears to have been favourable on balance.

Douglas also hired a Canadian lawyer of Japanese descent as a senior legal adviser in March 1946. George Tamaki, a British Columbia-born graduate from Dalhousie, was recommended for the job by George Cadbury, the CCF government's chief industrial executive. The Liberal Winnipeg *Free Press* praised the well-publicized hiring as "eminently democratic and liberal,"[25] and Japanese Canadians across the country took new hope.

The prejudices of the Winch faction in British Columbia died hard. After the Tamaki appointment, a B.C. party official phoned Douglas and pleaded with him to change his mind. Douglas wrote to Angus MacInnis that "the entire CCF caucus in British Columbia were convinced that they might as well shut up shop." MacInnis advised Douglas to stick to his guns. Sandy Nicholson, the Saskatchewan MP, reported to Douglas that Winch was "depressed about what he felt was the almost certain demise which the CCF would suffer in B.C." Douglas replied briskly to the lobbying from the coast: "If the existence of the CCF in B.C. depends on bowing to racial intolerance, the sooner it folds up the better."[26]

10

Return to the Prairies

THE SASKATCHEWAN CCF confirmed Tommy Douglas as its leader in the summer of 1942, slightly less than seven years after his first election to Parliament. Those years had seen turmoil in the provincial opposition; the governing Liberal Party, lacking effective leadership, had settled into a process of slow decay.

After M. J. Coldwell went to Parliament in the election of 1935, George Williams replaced him as the provincial leader of the CCF. Besides acting as political leader and house leader in the legislature, Williams was party president, chairman of the CCF Council, and, effectively, provincial secretary. Until 1940 he wielded enormous power in the party without facing any organized challenge. Underneath the facade of unity, however, the CCF was increasingly a party of discordant factions. Perhaps the greatest political accomplishment of Douglas's career would be his success in rebuilding this troubled organization.

On the government side, the Saskatchewan Liberals lost Premier Jimmy Gardiner, who departed for Ottawa in early 1936 for a job as federal minister of agriculture. The Liberals had always found strong and talented men to lead them: Scott, Martin, Dunning, Gardiner. With the naming of Gardiner's successor, William J. Patterson, the chain was broken.

Patterson was an insurance agent from Saskatchewan's conservative southeast, and he was a Gardiner man. First elected to the legislature in 1921, he joined Gardiner's first cabinet. His selection as premier in 1936 may have surprised some observers. He lacked both the platform presence and political flair of earlier leaders, and the *Leader-Post* named him last in a list of six candidates for the job. But Gardiner, although he had been called to glory in the House of Commons, unwisely chose to retain his dominance over Liberal Party affairs in Saskatchewan. He looked to the loyal and humourless Patterson to be his proxy.

The Gardiner machine, undamaged at first by Gardiner's nominal departure, rolled on. Its intrusion into almost every corner of Saskatchewan life made it a central consideration in CCF strategy. Preoccupied with ridding the province of Liberal corruption, the provincial CCF returned to paths which it had renounced following the dealings with Social Credit in 1935. Tommy Douglas, like Jimmy Gardiner, kept up an active presence in provincial affairs, and he worked with George Williams to put together an anti-Liberal common front of political parties

In the 1930s, parliamentary sessions lasted for only three or four months at the start of the year, leaving MPs with the rest of the year to devote to party work or private business. The new member for Weyburn put his time to good use. He loved the campaign trail, and pursued it in his home province and several others besides. He took as many meetings as he could, pleasing both the crowds and local organizers. He also extended his network of political contacts as an intermittent member of the Saskatchewan CCF Provincial Council.*

Douglas had an important supporter in Fred Williams, the editor of the CCF newspaper, who often published his speeches and columns. He had met Williams during his preaching days, when the editor was producing a journal called *The Commonweal* from an office in Creelman, just east of Weyburn. Together with a printer named Frank Wood, Douglas and Williams met at the Calvary Church office to plan the *New Era*, a paper which they hoped would become the voice of socialism in the Weyburn district—and someday, perhaps, the whole province. They rented the premises and equipment of a defunct Weyburn weekly, and went into production in time for the election campaign of 1935. Douglas remained on the board of the *New Era* during his first years in Parliament, and it provided detailed coverage of his activities. The paper moved to Regina in 1938 and became *The Commonwealth*; although Fred Williams could not publicly take sides in the developing party leadership dispute, he continued to give space to Douglas's writings.

George Williams, the provincial leader, turned out to be a cordial ally after the Social Credit episode of 1935. He put aside his differences with Douglas, and soon they were on "Dear George" and "Dear Tommy" terms. They disagreed in 1936 on how to link federal and provincial riding associations, but Williams wrote to Douglas at the same time, "I do not think there is any misunderstanding between you and me. I feel perfectly sure that every one of your actions...is absolutely sincere and not engineered by any personal desire for advancement."[1]

---

* The record of T. C. Douglas on the Saskatchewan CCF Council and Executive:

	Council	Executive
	Council	*Executive*
1936	Defeated	—
1937	Elected	Elected
1938	Elected	Defeated
1939	Withdrew from nomination	—
1940	Did not stand	—
1941	Named to council and executive to represent federal CCF caucus, Feb. 1941; elected party president, July 1941	

Williams and other members of the CCF executive had brought Douglas to trial in 1935 for consorting with the enemy, and very nearly cashiered him. It turned out, however, that Douglas had been just slightly ahead of his time. This was the era of the common front; in Europe especially, socialists and Communists united to fight the fascist threat. There were no declared fascists in Saskatchewan politics, and few Communists, but CCF supporters set out to find allies to overthrow the Liberals, whom they regarded as the worst of all possible ruling parties. At their summer 1936 convention, CCF delegates voted overwhelmingly to invite all "progressive groups...to discover common ground on which we may unite." They reaffirmed this stand in 1937, although the definitions of the words "progressive" and "unite" remained unclear.[2]

The result over the next two years was the near self-destruction of the CCF in some constituencies, which may partly explain George Williams's autocratic leadership style after 1938. CCF members got tangled up with "Unity" and "Independent" groupings that took in Tories, Social Crediters, Communists, and old-time Progressives; in Regina the CCF split between two sets of rival "Labour" candidates. Douglas warned Williams in early 1938, "If we just elect about a dozen such members you may very well see our organization being blocked by the very people we have helped to elect."[3]

Williams veered in 1936 towards courting Social Crediters and Communists by pointing out the similarities between their views and the CCF's; a year later he was trying, ineffectually, to squelch the trend to political fusions. He had never wanted fusion, he insisted; co-operation with other parties should take a different form. In his eagerness to wipe out the Gardiner Liberals, Williams preferred the "saw-off" tactic. Under this system, opposition party leaders would agree among themselves where each would run candidates, depending on which local organizations had the best chance of defeating the Liberals. Ideally, the Liberals would face only one strong opponent in each riding. What was supposed to happen after an election, in a legislature fractured among four or five parties, remained a mystery.

Douglas was a strong supporter of the saw-off idea, and helped to arrange a deal with Social Credit that was intended to benefit the CCF in the long run. In June 1937 Williams travelled to Edmonton to meet Aberhart and to propose an agreement to carve up Saskatchewan. The meeting was inconclusive. As a token of CCF goodwill, Douglas, apparently with the help of Alberta CCF leader William Irvine, arranged in early 1938 to keep the CCF out of an Edmonton East federal by-election. "We incurred some criticism from our own people," Douglas reported to Williams. "But it has changed the entire attitude of the Social Credit forces here in Ottawa, and we are told it has inclined Aberhart very favorably toward giving us almost a free hand in Saskatchewan." Coldwell's role is obscure; he said in his memoirs that he always stood above such horse-trading, but Douglas told Williams, "M.J. and I feel that we made a good strategic move by preventing the CCF from nominating in East Edmonton."[4] As it turned out, though, Aberhart and Douglas were not reading from the same bible. The Alberta premier threw his full weight into the 1938 Saskatchewan election, appearing at forty meetings in the province and drawing good crowds.

Douglas also tried to arrange some saw-offs with the Saskatchewan Conservatives, working with Ernie Perley, the Tory MP for Qu'Appelle. Douglas felt that if the CCF stayed out of the way of a few prominent Tories, such as party leader John Diefenbaker, then the Tories would agree to support some CCF candidates.

A month before the election, Douglas urged Williams to make a comprehensive deal with Diefenbaker's people. "I still see nothing to prevent pulling our candidates out of such places as Turtleford, Watrous, Melfort, and Torch River, in return for a free field in Last Mountain, Elrose, Rosetown and Weyburn...Unless some satisfactory basis of co-operation can be worked out between now and nomination day, we are going to lose everything except 8 or 10 well-organized seats."[5] Douglas was wasting his time. The CCF, for its part, gave the Conservatives a clear field in several ridings. The Tories, unfortunately, failed miserably at the polls.[6]

Some CCF supporters complained that the Tories did not fit the party's definition of "progressive" and should not be part of any CCF strategy. Douglas had not yet met the new provincial Conservative leader, John Diefenbaker, but he liked the young Baptist lawyer's platform on such issues as farm debt, social services, and public works. Later, he concluded that Diefenbaker's forward-looking stand in 1938 was simply opportunistic: "He fastened on to anything that seemed to appeal to the public mood. If somebody had found out during the campaign that people were in favour of abolishing individual ownership of the home, he would have looked at it very carefully."[7]

The political muddle that accompanied these fusions and saw-offs is illustrated by events in Douglas's home town. Two of the MP's key organizers, Charlie Broughton and Bob Harris, went to the Weyburn Tories to propose a deal. They acted, most likely, on their own initiative. The deal would see the Tories nominate John Burnside, a rural reeve and a member of the Weyburn CCF executive, as the Conservative candidate. In return, the CCF would not nominate anyone. Tories and CCFers could vote for the same man, and the anti-Liberal cause would emerge triumphant. In February 1938 the Conservatives nominated Burnside. When he found out about this deal, Douglas decided to keep his nose out. He was "concerned," he told Williams, that Weyburn voters would be asked to vote Tory; however, he thought there was a good chance the Tories might be persuaded, in return, to stay out of the neighbouring Milestone riding.[8] But some Weyburn CCFers, ignorant of or unhappy with the plan to dress up Burnside as a Conservative, forced a CCF nominating meeting at the Weyburn IOOF Hall in April.

The day of the meeting came and the platform was loaded with dignitaries—George Williams, Douglas, Clarence Fines. At the start of the meeting, Burnside stood up to plead for CCF support in the provincial election. Broughton admitted that he had promised Burnside the support he was asking for. As Fines remembered it, "this was a very embarrassing moment for everybody." The membership asked the provincial leader for his advice on whether the CCF should name a candidate to oppose Burnside, but George Williams remained silent. Douglas also declined to give advice. He did, however, take the opportunity to kill one inaccurate rumour, that he had promised the Tories support in return for help they had given in 1935. He called this "a contemptible lie...If it's proved I'm prepared to resign."[9] The meeting nominated Fred Williams, the editor of *The Commonwealth*, and Burnside left, humiliated.

Douglas stood behind Fred Williams throughout the provincial campaign, and on June 7, the night before the election, marched with him at the head of a parade to the Weyburn fairgrounds. But the efforts of the popular MP went for naught; Williams finished second to the Liberal candidate, with Burnside trailing badly in third. In fact, the CCF did not take a single seat in southern Saskatchewan, and did not even run candidates in the four major cities. The election gave the party precisely the "10 well-organized seats" which Douglas had seen as the worst prospect, and even this was an electoral fluke. Social Credit, with 16 per cent of the vote compared with the CCF's 19 per cent, took only two seats.

At its summer 1938 convention the Saskatchewan CCF agreed there would be no more deals with other parties, but the practice died hard. CCF supporters backed two successful "Unity" candidates in the 1940 federal election, and in the same campaign Tommy Douglas and Ernie Perley agreed to a saw-off. The CCF stayed out of Qu'Appelle, and the Conservatives stayed out of Weyburn. Both incumbents won.[10]

In 1938 the party rank and file acclaimed George Williams as leader for the third straight year. Coldwell remained aloof and the two men bickered at party meetings, but Woodsworth assured Williams that the national organization was "delighted" with the election results.[11] Douglas and Williams had worked together during the campaign, and now respected each other's political strengths. Douglas invited the provincial leader to Weyburn to lecture his troops. "You could do me a lot of good," said Douglas, "as well as giving some of my committees a fatherly talk about getting to work."[12]

Williams's strength of character could not, however, conceal the Saskatchewan CCF's weaknesses. The party's share of the popular vote in 1938 had actually declined from the level of 1934. All of the party's MLAS came from rural ridings in central or northeastern Saskatchewan. More than six years after the party's founding, several regions of the province remained poorly organized or untouched. CCF members in Saskatoon, the west, and the northwest flirted with Communist- or Social Credit-led Unity groups. Coldwell and Douglas counselled diplomacy in approaching these coalitions; Williams told Douglas to "leave this business of co-operation and unity entirely alone,"[13] and began to denounce the Unity groups in radio broadcasts.

This may have been the point at which the struggles within the CCF began. The party convention again acclaimed Williams leader in 1939, but he felt compelled this time to respond to charges of "dictatorship." "I quote President Roosevelt," he said. "Be loyal to the organization or withdraw."[14]

Douglas and Williams had agreed before 1939 that Canada would sooner or later be forced to go to war against fascism in Europe. When world war came, however, Douglas supported the national party's compromise position. Williams insisted on the right to speak his conscience as a provincial leader. He went so far as to suppress opinions that differed from his own. He had already acted as a censor at least once, preventing a Douglas article on the munitions industry from appearing in the *Commonwealth*. Douglas was explaining the party policy of "national control"; Williams wanted nationalization. In September 1939 Williams refused to distribute copies of J. S. Woodsworth's parliamentary speech opposing Canada's entry into the war. He also refused to circulate the pamphlet setting out the national party's official position—Coldwell's position—which supported the provision of economic but not military aid to Britain. He explained to reporters that "undoubtedly the policy of the CCF will change," and soon after demanded the creation of a Canadian expeditionary force.[15] When Dr. Carlyle King, a member of the provincial executive, asked for a party membership list so that he could mail out Woodsworth's speech, Williams withheld it. From now on, he announced, all interriding correspondence must go through his hands.

From September to January, Williams dodged any discussion of his actions by neglecting to call meetings of the provincial council or its executive committee. He met only with a "Board of Strategy"—himself, his United Farmers crony and fellow MLA Tom Johnston, and Clarence Fines. Carlyle King wrote, "Fines has usually been consulted after a committee of the Board—guess who!—has given the decision...Williams regards the CCF as his own machine for gaining political power in Saskatchewan."[16] Coldwell, who had moved into the national leadership after Woodsworth's resignation, began to consider at this point how to unseat Williams from his throne. If every provincial section went its own way on the war issue, he warned from Ottawa, the CCF would collapse. He wrote of Williams, "He is without doubt the most cunning individual with whom it has ever been my misfortune to be associated...I have made up my mind that I will be no party to placing George H. Williams in the Premier's chair."[17]

The federal election of February 1940 strengthened Coldwell's hand. In the national vote the CCF did even worse than in 1935 and elected only eight candidates. In Saskatchewan, however, the CCF added three new seats to those held by Coldwell and Douglas. Williams claimed that this result vindicated his leadership; in fact, it gave Coldwell three parliamentary allies to counterbalance the Williams loyalists in the provincial House. Sometime during 1940 Coldwell began to push Tommy Douglas towards the Saskatchewan leadership. Sandy Nicholson recalled many years later in a conversation with Douglas, "It wasn't you that fanned this but your colleagues [the federal members] felt this was the thing to do at that time."[18]

Williams was overworked, and the CCF's membership was shrinking. The party lacked a full-time organizer, and its lines of communication were being strangled by the lack of executive and council meetings. Coldwell, Douglas, and the three new Saskatchewan MPs agreed that, at the very least, the CCF must separate the political leadership from the party presidency. The leader should speak out on public issues and the party program; the president should give his time to organizing the party. "It was apparent something had to be done," said Douglas later, "and there was a growing feeling that we were doomed...There was no ideological split. There was a tendency to get into cliques, which is almost inevitable in human organizations."[19]

Two months after the 1940 federal vote the parliamentary and legislative caucuses met in the oppositon lobby of the Saskatchewan Legislative Building. Williams came equipped for any challenge to his power. As chairman of the meeting he presented a neat package of resolutions already passed by his caucus; the most important declared that Williams should stay on as party president at least until after a provincial election victory. In other words, one man should control party documents, membership lists, and finances, as well as make all strategic decisions and policy statements.

The MPs promised to study Williams's resolutions, but soon after they drafted a brief to the Provincial Council which explicitly rejected the MLAS' position. They presented it to council one day before the summer convention. The brief bore no signatures, but Williams later called it "the work of T. C. Douglas and an attack on my leadership."[20] The brief explained that during the 1930s, when the party had almost no money, "it has been a very excellent thing to have the Leader of the Opposition also as the Provincial President." However, there should now be a separate president to build a strong party which could prepare ideas for a CCF government.[21] The council, dominated by Williams's followers, would have none of it, and shelved the document rather than present it to the July 1940 convention. So ended the period of cordial relations between Douglas and George Williams.*

Despite the council's move to protect him, though, Williams's leadership came under attack. A Saskatoon-based pacifist wing put an unsuccessful motion before the convention that the leader's powers should be reduced. The same group nominated Carlyle King for the party presidency, so as to relieve the leader of "tiresome duties."[22] King, a thirty-three-year-old English professor and a principled opponent of the war

---

* The MPs' brief also said that once the CCF formed a government, the party council should have some control over cabinet selection and should advise on legislation. After the victory of 1944, the council rubber-stamped Douglas's cabinet selections, and a party advisory committee looked over the first batch of legislation. However, this "direct democracy" feature of the CCF faded rapidly in importance.

effort, had taken considerable heat at the University of Saskatchewan for his views. Williams, building his case against the first internal challenge he had ever faced, argued that the president's job and the leader's job were indivisible. Whatever the merits of this argument, Williams won the day.

Williams suspected Dr. King of fronting for a Coldwell-Douglas conspiracy against him. In fact King, although he later worked closely with Douglas for fifteen years, had no use at this stage for the Weyburn MP or his views on the war. In one letter to a friend he had compared the Williams-Douglas rapport on the war issue to the pact between Hitler and Stalin; he dismissed the preacher as "practically an imperialist...My guess is that Douglas will not be with us long, for which we can be truly thankful."[23] It seems impossible, from these words, that the strong-willed King would have worked to put Douglas in the leadership.*

After the 1940 convention, Williams again suspended executive and council meetings. He joined a reserve military unit, the Canadian Light Horse, to show his commitment to the war effort. In January 1941, after months of delay, the Provincial Council finally met. It agreed to consider splitting the highest party offices and discussed forging closer ties to Coldwell's group in Ottawa and hiring a paid, full-time provincial organizer. The prime candidate for the job was John T. Douglas, Coldwell's campaign manager in Rosetown-Biggar and a man Williams despised. A month later, Williams announced that he was leaving for Europe as a quartermaster with the 11th Hussars. His biographer says he went because "his position was untenable" in Saskatchewan.[24] In fact, he appears to have been in the grip of a mounting paranoia, obsessed with the idea that the forces of evil were conspiring to destroy the party that he had built. Almost his last act before leaving Canada was to write a long and rambling letter to the CCF executive, charging that Coldwell had always coveted his job and that T. C. Douglas had worked to undermine his leadership. Although Williams had not faced any critical test of his strength, he could see that his days as supreme leader were numbered. Even his supporters had grown tired of being ignored and bypassed.

Tommy Douglas contested the Saskatchewan CCF presidency for the first time at the provincial convention in Regina in July 1941. CCF house leader John Brockelbank nominated the absent George Williams, who took more than a quarter of the ballots, but Douglas took the remainder. Williams had charged that Douglas was manoeuvring against him unfairly and secretly, but the delegates clearly rejected his claim. They chose the candidate who sat in the hall over a candidate who was stationed somewhere in England.

---

* Douglas was, in a sense, an imperialist. In a 1937 speech he expressed his hope that the British Empire might lead the way in establishing an international democracy. "The throne is the symbol and embodiment of liberty, right and justice, upon which British rule is founded...the King the expression of the will of the great masses." *Weyburn Review*, May 20, 1937

A new team was forming. Douglas was president; Clarence Fines, Regina alderman and fundraiser extraordinaire, became vice-president. The troublesome issue of the party leadership, however, was still not resolved. Since Williams had always held the presidency and the leadership to be indivisible, Douglas assumed he was now the leader. Fines and the party paper, the *Commonwealth*, saw it the same way. Unfortunately for Douglas, some in the party awaited the return of the old leader and others harboured their own ambitions. When Fines introduced Douglas at a Regina meeting in late 1941 as "our next Premier" it caused an outcry. The CCF MLAS wanted Provincial Council to "rectify Fines's mistake, and to ensure that no similar blunder is committed in the future."[25]

The council agreed that the party was leaderless and would remain so until the 1942 convention, six months away. If there was an election call in the meantime, the CCF would organize a special convention. Douglas remained calm and waited out his time until July. If the Liberals had been alert, they would have pounced on this opportunity for an election call.

Douglas's position at the head of the party, then, was uncertain for the first year. Nevertheless, he and Fines set out a plan for reviving the party: double the party membership, increase the circulation of the *Commonwealth*, and create committees on party finances, radio broadcasting, and literature. In a special executive meeting in August 1941 the two men set out to put these plans into effect. Douglas made MLAS, MPS, and party veterans responsible for organizing sixteen zones under the co-ordination of J. T. Douglas and Clarence Fines. A mild-mannered but persistent United Church minister, Sandy Nicholson, MP, would head a fund-raising drive, and Carlye King would direct publicity. "A productive, forward looking, harmonious meeting," said King forty years later.[26] A job was set out for every important figure in the party. Here Douglas showed, for the first time, one of his great strengths. He matched people to tasks without regard for previous conflicts or personal differences. He sometimes rewarded flattery and friendship, but he almost never punished those who had opposed or vilified him.

Douglas continued his organizing drive in the fall of 1941, when he set up a network of committees to prepare the CCF for power. The first was a labour committee with seventeen members, fourteen of them from the trade unions. MLA Joe Phelps, later natural resources minister, headed a Natural Resources committee; Teachers' Federation leader Woodrow Lloyd, later education minister, joined the Education Committee. The retail merchants' panel included Ted Stinson of Weyburn as well as a young Moose Jaw alderman, Ross Thatcher. In time, Douglas and Fines set up a six-member Planning Committee to run the growing network, with themselves at the head. Douglas took care that two seats on this committee went to Williams loyalists, Brockelbank and Phelps, and two to the pacifists, Valleau and King. He also split the seats evenly among non-MLAS and MLAS.

In circulars to local CCF associations, Douglas called for more members and more funds; in some ridings the number of paid-up members had fallen to a handful. At organizing meetings, he wrote, a few chosen friends of the party should flash their money around before dropping it into the basket; this would stimulate contributions. Often, after a first organizing meeting, the riding executive would call a public meeting and invite Douglas as the drawing card. It was his job to buoy up the workers, to inspire the multitudes. At each moment he had to preserve the conviction that nothing could stop the party now. At Fir Mountain when his chair collapsed under him on the stage, he picked himself up with dignity, rubbed his posterior, and declared in his best orator's tone: "Mr. Chairman, that is just where Mr. Gardiner's Liberals give me a pain."[27]

Douglas hoped that the 1942 convention at the Bessborough Hotel in Saskatoon would establish him unambiguously as the party's political leader. This time, he came before the convention with a name and reputation established across the province. The meeting first defined the leader's responsibilities: to "have supervision of all political and legislative matters ...lead the CCF group in the Saskatchewan legislature...lead a Government in the event of the CCF Group forming the Government in the Province."[28]

Then came the more serious business. Once again the absent George Williams was nominated, not by house leader John Brockelbank but by an obscure sympathizer. Brockelbank himself was a candidate, as was the pacifist MLA Oakland Valleau. The delegates cast their first ballot, then milled about the hotel ballroom waiting for the result. The buzz of anticipation mounted as Louise Lucas approached the centre of the platform. Silence descended. "The scrutineers beg to report that Mr. T. C. Douglas, MP, was elected as Political Leader on the first count."[29] A wave of measured applause rolled across the hotel ballroom, a sound of relief, maybe, rather than jubilation. The divisive struggle was over. Valleau came forward to pledge the loyalty of the CCF members of the legislature. Finally, after two years of talk, the delegates split the presidency from the leadership, voting Clarence Fines into the job.

The next year, in 1943, George Williams again offered his services as party leader. He wrote from England to both Brockelbank and Fines, asking them to make it clear to the annual convention that he was available if nominated from the floor. Fines stalked the convention with Williams's letter in his pocket, but there it remained. John Brockelbank stood as the only challenger to Douglas, and Douglas won by a large majority.

Douglas then moved to heal old wounds. He praised the MLAs for their "loyal and unswerving support," and nominated Brockelbank for the vice-presidency. The trio that he established, Douglas, Fines, and Brockelbank, would lead the CCF into government within a year. After this meeting, he was never again challenged for the provincial leadership.

While George Williams continued to serve in Europe, he ran as an absentee candidate in Wadena in 1944. He returned just in time to win the seat, and agreed to serve as minister of agriculture in the new Douglas government. At a banquet soon after the election, Williams collapsed from a stroke. He went to British Columbia to recover, but in early 1945 he wrote his letter of resignation. He thanked Douglas for giving him the chance to serve in the cabinet. A few months later, Williams died.

11
Victory

This is the greatest political battle you and I have ever witnessed because the outcome may decide our way of life for the next quarter of a century. This is no time for the timid and the weaklings who are willing to sell themselves and become the apologists for Big Business. These are times that call for men of courage and women of vision to strike a blow for our economic emancipation. Every vote for the CCF is another link broken in the chains of our economic servitude. The time has come for each of you to take sides.[1]

LESS THAN A WEEK before the election of 1944 the radio stations of Saskatchewan carried this strident call from Tommy Douglas to the people of the province. The people responded with a massive show of support. They gave his party 53 per cent of the vote, compared with 19 per cent six years earlier. They gave him forty-seven of the fifty-three seats in the provincial legislature. They drove the Liberals into opposition, where that party languished for the next twenty years.*

The election took place at a time in Canadian history that might be called the Days of Great Expectations. The wartime economy was humming. There were jobs and incomes for all. The spectre of a fascist world-state had dissipated, and Allied troops in Europe pushed on towards victory. The nation bathed in a euphoria of togetherness, of the shared joys and sorrows that make up wartime experience. Canadians were resolved that the postwar world should be a better place, that the social disorder of the past should give way to social communion. Governments had moved boldly to prosecute the war; voters reasoned that governments could also manage economic and social affairs to produce a better and more secure life for all. In short, Canada's political thinking had taken a sharp turn to the left.

---

* Many CCFers believed that their party should have taken forty-eight rather than forty-seven seats. Clarence Fines said in 1986 that the CCF campaign manager in Premier Patterson's riding could have won on a recount, but failed to apply in time.

No one was better at reading the signs than Canada's prime minister, Mackenzie King. The events of 1943 provided all the persuasion that King needed: in that year the CCF came perilously close to snatching power in Ontario, and briefly moved ahead of both the old parties in the national Gallup Poll. Along with his cabinet and a battery of economists armed with the latest theories of Lord Keynes, King set out to forestall a socialist takeover. He determined to make a new Canada, but one that Liberals could safely inhabit.

If Ottawa showed concern at the CCF surge, Bay Street reacted in terror. The country's leading capitalists, including the heads of Imperial Oil, Noranda Mines, International Nickel, and Massey Harris—all of them happy to accept government handouts in later years—formed a committee of twenty-one to battle the socialist hordes. Robert Simpson Ltd. offered its catalogue mailing system for the distribution of propaganda. Canada's most frustrated politician, Arthur Meighen, recently whipped by the CCF in a York South by-election, fronted for the operation, along with Charles Dunning, a former Saskatchewan premier. They rang all the bells the reactionaries had sounded in 1919, but they rang them louder. Socialism equalled Communism. The CCF would confiscate property, bank accounts, and life insurance. The left would impose a government of, by, and for the shiftless and the incompetent, and "advocates of free enterprise [would] be regarded as guilty of treason."[2] This business crusade hit its stride across Canada in early 1944. Along with Mackenzie King's promises of reform, it helped to burst the national CCF bubble.

In Saskatchewan, however, the scare campaign went nowhere. Perhaps the farmers of the province had grown so hardened to confiscation by the banks and mortgage companies that the big business call to arms raised little interest. Certainly the CCF had established itself as part of the community; local co-ops, women's groups, and rural councils were among its strongest supporters. Douglas's forces continued their march in Saskatchewan, even as his party elsewhere in the country faltered.

The Saskatchewan Liberals, for their part, ignored the popular will for change and declined to follow Prime Minister King's reformist lead. When they jumped on the red-scare bandwagon, it only served to highlight their ideological bankruptcy. They were a sad, tired, and discredited party, with a meagre list of accomplishments. They had introduced Canada's first retail sales tax; they tried to soften the blow by calling it an education tax, but the money went in general revenues and not directly into education. Indeed, many local boards could not pay the $700 a year to their teachers that the government suggested as a minimum. Next to "farmer," "schoolteacher" was the most common occupation given by CCF candidates in 1944.

Premier William Patterson provided the Liberals with uninspired leadership. He had, after all, been chosen to hold the fort for Jimmy Gardiner and not to offer ideas of his own. When prairie farmers began to protest against wartime price controls on their products, Patterson stood on the sidelines. Canada's largest producer co-operative, the traditionally neutral Saskatchewan Wheat Pool, held a series of joint meetings with the CCF and marched on Ottawa in early 1942. The most influential voting bloc in Saskatchewan had swung against the Liberals. The Gardiner patronage machine, at the same time, was losing its punch. Jimmy Gardiner remained active behind the scenes—a 1942 article in *Canadian Business* called him "Premier of Saskatchewan in absentia"[3]—but the end of the Depression had also sharply reduced his power over the people of Saskatchewan.

Douglas believed that the Liberals had maintained themselves in power through intimidation. The CCF had made progress during the 1930s in areas where the farmers harvested a crop; where there was no crop, the Liberal machine controlled the relief system. An army of "inspectors" had threatened to cut off even the bread of life from those who caused trouble for the ruling party and had rewarded the compliant with petty jobs and contracts. "It was a terrible thing to watch," Douglas said later. "It was a complete negation of democracy."[4] But things were different by the early 1940s. With people moving off relief in the cities and towns, public appointments and the public purse worked less well as instruments of persuasion. The citizens who had suffered threats and blacklisting vowed revenge. What had been grease for the wheels of political conquest turned to sand.

By tradition, Patterson's term should have ended with an election in June 1943 at the latest, but the Liberals chose to postpone the day of judgement. In April of that year they commissioned an Independent MLA to introduce Bill 13, a bill to prolong the life of the government for one year. The supporters of the bill argued that elections are expensive and that the legislature had no important business before it. An election campaign, they said, would distract Saskatchewan from the war effort. The Liberal majority in the House agreed to the extension. Douglas had seen this manoeuvre coming, but Frank Scott, the national party's constitutional law expert, advised him from Montreal that the Liberals were acting within their powers. "Your legislature can prolong its life indefinitely," he said. "The remedy is political (if that exists) and not legal."[5]

Douglas was still sitting in the Commons, and he pressed Prime Minister King to disallow the provincial bill. "Democracy has been defined by Thomas Jefferson as 'government by consent of the governed,'" he said. "The moment that a people are governed without their consent, we have moved from Democracy into Fascism." King responded with unusual clarity, stating that he was opposed to parliaments extending their own terms of office. However, he failed to act, despite Douglas's continued hounding.[6] Strangely, the bill met with public apathy, even though it implied that a Canadian legislature could avoid elections indefinitely. The CCF provincial caucus received only one letter of complaint, and the party backed away from trying to stage any mass protest.

Douglas would revive the issue of the government's delaying tactic during the 1944 campaign—less as a question of constitutional law than as a comment on the senility of the Liberal party. The government had abused teachers, farmers, and people on relief, and had then decided to insult the whole province by staying on for an extra year. As its life ebbed away, Patterson's party would issue a final appeal on posters and in newspaper advertisements: "PLEASE GIVE US ANOTHER CHANCE." It was perhaps the most pathetic slogan ever coined for a Canadian election, a plea for clemency for a government which had convicted itself.

From the day he assumed office as provincial CCF president, Tommy Douglas prepared his troops for the coming election. As late as 1943, however, he still faced a troublesome factionalism within the party. In Saskatoon, for example, the head of the CCF old guard complained persistently that Douglas was plotting against him. This disturbance is worth mentioning because the man in question would later advise Douglas on party affairs for a decade and a half.

Carlyle King was a member of the provincial executive and president of the Saskatoon CCF group. Douglas had also invited him onto the powerful six-member Planning Committee, the body charged with co-ordinating the work of all the other CCF advisory committees. King's strength lay in the areas of publicity and education. He had little talent or taste for grass-roots organizing; his big-city chapter of the party was one of the smallest in the province, with only fifty members. He later wrote that "the main business of socialist parties is not to form governments, but to change minds."[7]

The Saskatoon CCF spent its evenings debating socialist theory and world affairs. It did not run candidates in federal or provincial elections. Out in the real world, CCF sympathizers joined in a motley Unity effort along with some Communists, Tories, and Social Crediters. Their candidate, the Rev. Walter Brown, won in a federal by-election in 1939 and again in the 1940 federal general election, but he died soon after his second victory. His successor was the Rev. C. P. Bradley, who had met Douglas at military camp. Some in the party distrusted Bradley as a political butterfly, but Douglas encouraged him to join the CCF, along with those of his supporters who wanted to come along.

At the Saskatoon CCF general meeting of 1943, fifty of Bradley's followers overwhelmed twenty-five of King's friends and elected a majority to the executive. Carlyle King was bumped down to vice-president. King complained to the provincial executive, demanding that the old order be restored. On Fines's suggestion, the executive named a temporary Saskatoon committee combining old guard and new guard, and called a second general meeting in the riding. Fines advised King to sign up some supporters, instead of spending his time writing letters; but King lost the second presidential contest, and again cried foul. He blamed Douglas and Fines for his loss. Uncharacteristically, Coldwell sided against Douglas. He wrote to King, criticizing Douglas's support for Bradley as "dangerous," and offering King a job with the federal party.[8] But Douglas made no apologies, nor should he have. He understood King's strengths, and had given him a senior post in the provincial CCF; but he also felt that King had made a poor local president. He felt strongly that the CCF must open its doors to people with political skills and energy.

Although Carlyle King stayed away from the 1944 provincial convention, delegates elected him party vice-president and the next year he accepted the party presidency. After this, he seems never again to have attacked Douglas in his letters or public statements. Until 1960 he and Douglas met on regular Sunday afternoons in the premier's office. "We smoked our pipes at each other," King would write, "and plotted how to do good for the people of Saskatchewan."[9]

At the same time as he worked to douse the remaining brush fires in the party, Douglas prepared for the 1944 campaign. With Clarence Fines in the central office and Jack Douglas in the field, the state of party organization improved rapidly. The party lacked the big-business funding available to the Liberals, but this was offset by the steady rise in the number of dues-paying CCF members. When Douglas took over the party presidency in 1941, it had fewer than 5000 members; by April 1944 that figure had risen past 26,000. The CCF also passed the hat at its public meetings and gathered donations from individuals and small businesses. Most important, it could call on the volunteer efforts of thousands of dedicated people, organized from the poll level up. The policy committees, set up in the fall of 1941, continued their work. By the end of 1943 the CCF's Saskatchewan leaders knew in some detail what measures they would put before the legislature if they formed a government, and they were ready to submit their ideas to outside review.

Over the New Year's holiday of 1943-44, seventy-two leading members of the national and provincial sections of the CCF met in Regina for an exchange of ideas. They knew that a Saskatchewan election was imminent and that the party stood an excellent chance of winning. Such a victory would be a socialist first for Canada, and a CCF government in Saskatchewan would bear a great responsibility; it must light the way for future victories in other provinces. Everyone at the conference felt a sense of urgency, as well as a proprietary interest in what was going on in the provincial party.

The meeting subjected the policy papers from the Saskatchewan committees, as well as some entries from other CCF sections, to a searching examination. Conference panels studied ideas for labour legislation, health care, provincial budgeting, natural resources, and public ownership. The weekend helped to clarify some of the ideas held by the Saskatchewan group and to reinforce others. When the party entered the 1944 election, its program had already undergone a baptism of fire.

Unavoidably, the conference had to leave some of the most important questions about the future unanswered. For example, if the CCF came to power in Saskatchewan, how far could it go without running afoul of the federal government? Less than a decade earlier, Ottawa had used its power of disallowance against Alberta, when the Social Credit government there had tried to regulate the banks and the newspapers. Many of the activists at the Regina meeting believed that King's Liberals would use the same power to frustrate CCF provincial governments. The B.C.

group under Harold Winch even muttered that the CCF should be ready, if they met capitalist-inspired obstructions, to resort to "extra-parliamentary measures." They did not make clear what such measures might amount to, and the suggestion got no further attention.

The debate served to flag a potential problem, one which became a reality a year later when it seemed that the Government of Canada might use its power to disallow certain CCF legislation. The debate also pointed up a potential split within the party. While Frank Scott from McGill insisted that the power of disallowance was a necessary weapon for strong central government in Canada, Douglas and the Saskatchewan camp became convinced that it had no place in a healthy confederation.

Immediately following the Regina conference, the Saskatchewan party's "winter schools" went into session. They were held in Regina and in Saskatoon, and each lasted five days. The schools were not new in 1944, but this year they took on a special importance. Two hundred and thirty people attended, including candidates and campaign managers from the various constituencies. David Lewis, Wiiliam Irvine, and Colin Cameron, all remarkable for their platform presence, stayed over from the leaders' conference to stimulate and inspire the discussions.

Throughout the days of the school, Douglas met with the candidates and their managers to thresh out the campaign strategies that would lead to victory. Out of these talks emerged the card outlining the CCF's "nine-point program." In the coming campaign all the party's canvassers would carry this card, which set out the specific actions a CCF government would take on assuming office. The program promised farm security legislation, a new deal for labour, and the creation of a government department to support the development of the co-operative movement. It pledged to restructure the public school system, develop industry through publicly owned business, and work towards a system of socialized health care. Throughout his career as provincial leader, Douglas held to a simple theory of campaigning. He would agree with his advisers on a limited number of things they knew they could do in government; set them out in plain language that every voter could understand; concentrate their campaign on those issues; and try to insure that all the party's candidates and speakers told the same story.

When Premier Patterson called the long-delayed election in the spring of 1944, the CCF was ready for the fray. The rumblings which had distracted the party in the early forties were under control. The committee work, the strategy sessions, and the building of a strong provincial network had all put the CCF in a position to win a landslide victory. But on top of all these strengths the biggest single asset the party had, now and for the next two decades, was its leader, Tommy Douglas.

Douglas was among the greatest political campaigners Canada has known. He showed great ability as an MP and premier, but the election campaign stimulated him beyond anything else. Though he might be worn and weary from the day-to-day demands of his office, the calling of an election worked an amazing transformation. As the fire-horse of the earlier days responded to the station bell, Douglas would burst from the stall, eyes glistening with anticipation, eager to race the distance and join in the excitement. The only real contender for his title as number one campaigner was Agnes MacPhail of Ontario, who had served the Progressive cause and then the CCF since Douglas's boyhood; and the toughest assignment in the movement was to shepherd the two of them together through a day on the stump.

The 1944 election was one of the last of its kind. Within a decade, television, the new electronic monster, would change the basis of political campaigning. During this campaign, the pamphlet and the daily and weekly press remained essential tools in the work of campaigning. The public meeting and the Sunday picnic were also important in the political process, and helped to make the campaign into a personal encounter for the voter. Radio could be used to supplement and support such public meetings. As the most advanced electronic medium in 1944, radio offered a large audience to any group that could pay for time, and in this election the CCF could afford to present its message on most local stations. It also ended the near-monopoly that the daily and weekly newspapers, most of them dedicated to the Liberal cause, exercised over the flow of information. For those who understood how to use it, radio offered a new kind of access to the emotions of thousands of voters at a time. And Douglas, along with Coldwell, became one of the CCF's finest broadcasters.

Douglas put forward a different personality on radio from the one he exuded on the platform. At public meetings his first thought was to warm up the audience, to establish a rapport. He did this with light comment and good humour, designed to put everyone at ease and to make his audience more attentive. On radio, he avoided playing the joker. If he had a role model it was probably Franklin D. Roosevelt and his "Fireside Chats." Douglas sought to develop an intimacy between himself and the individual listener. He came across as a kindly, sympathetic fellow. He felt comfortable with radio, and it was here that he most systematically set out his ideas on the future of Saskatchewan. Over the winter of 1943-44 he presented fifteen-minute talks on provincial radio at least twice a month, and he kept to this routine right up to election day in June. He also took on an increasingly heavy load of public meetings as winter melted into spring.

The standard schedule from mid-April until June 15 took Douglas to three public meetings a day. In between, he presided at strategy sessions with candidates and local organizers, often in an automobile on his way to the next engagement. He spoke in country schoolhouses, church halls, community halls—any space with enough room for an audience, seated, standing, or listening through the doors and windows.

The telephones in rural Saskatchewan were still hooked up to party lines, and the CCF called its public meetings in the country with a "general ring." The operator announced, with a special long-short ring, that a call of interest to all subscribers was coming through; after the receivers had been lifted in subscribing farmhouses, a CCF spokesman would announce the time and place of the meeting, hang up, and repeat the performance on another line. In the towns, posters or newspapers provided the advertising.

The meetings often tested the dedication of the faithful to the cause. They began on time, and ended when they were finished. No matter what the status of the headline speaker, he or she was preceded by a long list of others, each with a message for the voters: local party officials, lesser provincial luminaries, guests, all had their turn. When the audience had reached an appropriately comatose state, the organizers of the meeting would pass the hat. The crowd's devotion to the main speaker could be measured by the number of seats still occupied when he or she was introduced, and few ever walked out before Douglas took the platform.

Sundays and holidays for the CCF were picnic days, when families would take their sandwiches and lemonade to a local park or a farm and hear speeches from candidates and party leaders. These were popular social events, but their true purpose was not lost from sight; parents expected even their children to be fully attentive. To enable the speaker to stand above the crowd, the organizers would scrounge up some form of podium—perhaps even that source of many jokes, the farmer's manure spreader.

Douglas's platform performances highlighted the 1944 campaign across the province: the lively, boyish appearance; the captivating cadence of the rhetoric; the head thrown back; the light glinting off the rimless spectacles; one hand on the hip while the other cut the air with a measured stroke; the almost cough-like laugh that signalled an impending rapier thrust; above all, the integrity of the man.

Important as the speech might be in winning a following, however, the meeting really began when the speeches were over. For as long as time would allow, Douglas would remain near the stage, surrounded by people anxious to shake his hand and give their advice or tell him their troubles. It was now that he established the bond between himself and his followers. He had a remarkable ability to concentrate his attention on whoever stood before him. As long as the conversation lasted, that person was the only person in his world. He had a great memory for names and for family ties and family affairs, and this knowledge came readily into play on a second meeting. Anyone meeting Douglas for the first time thought they had made a friend; on meeting him for the second time they were sure of it. As an opposition politician commented, "Douglas doesn't need to kiss babies, babies kiss him."

In the 1944 campaign both Douglas's radio and platform personalities came fully into play. There was something youthful and forward-looking about Douglas that supported his promise that the CCF, together with the people of Saskatchewan, could develop the province's resources and rebuild the run-down towns and cities. At the same time, many of his proposals had a reassuringly familiar ring. The "nationalization of resources" and "social reconstruction" were phrases that went back a generation to the period of Christian reform and Progressivism.

In setting its course, Douglas promised, the CCF would operate according to the wishes of the common people. His was a people's party, financed by the people, and it would never dance to the tune of the big "interests." The party organization was open to anyone who wished to join, and the membership would decide what direction the party should take and what programs its government should implement. The CCF's representatives in the legislature would be bound by the party's wishes: "Those of us who occupy positions in the CCF have no power to add or subtract one sentence from the programme laid down by the people themselves...We are merely their servants appointed to carry out their wishes as expressed from time to time in convention assembled."[10]

In the course of the campaign, Douglas kept most often to the themes which had dominated recent Saskatchewan CCF conventions: patriotism, the economic lot of the farmer, and health care. In at least one broadcast he managed to combine all three: 65 per cent of Canadians must go into debt to pay for surgery or prolonged illness, while another 25 per cent must rely on charity. Saskatchewan farm income from the 1937-40 period averaged $291 per family—what kind of care could farm families expect? "From 1914 to 1918 we lost some 60,000 of our finest young men in Flanders Fields. That was a tragedy and we all recognized it. We have raised thousands of cenotaphs to remind us of that loss. But from 1935 to 1938 we lost 61,514 babies under one year of age in Canada. That is a tragedy too, and one which might have been prevented had more adequate health services been available. It is estimated that in Canada we lost one mother every eight hours."[11]

He returned frequently to the problems of rural people and their one-crop economy. Saskatchewan was still a community of farm families living on individual holdings, and no one questioned the primacy of the farming interest. The dream of the prairie socialist was inseparably tied up with a belief in the special wholesomeness of rural life and the family farm. The effort to build a healthy rural society from the ashes of the Depression was a top priority for Douglas and the CCF, but it would also pose enormous challenges. The prairie and parkland where most of Saskatchewan's 900,000 people lived took up less than half the province, but it covered more territory than the United Kingdom. A new government would have to build new networks of highways, hospitals, telephone and power lines—to raise the quality of life for country folk.

The most critical issue of the moment was security of tenure for the farmer. Douglas pledged to face down the eastern creditors who beset Saskatchewan farmers and forced them from their land. Beyond wanting to head off immediate foreclosures, he knew that governments must make farming more economically attractive in the long term. He continued to make the plea he had made in the Commons—that the federal government work towards establishing parity pricing for agricultural products. The provincial government could improve the farm economy by helping to make it more diverse.

At its simplest, diversification meant the production of commodities other than wheat. The government would have to design programs for water conservation and livestock feed banks, and, to ensure orderly marketing for products such as honey, wool, and leather, it would have to encourage marketing co-operatives or set up marketing boards. Some of the proposals for diversification looked forward to a radical change in the Saskatchewan farm economy—widespread irrigation and vegetable canning, for example. At the forefront, Douglas himself prepared to lead the way into the new world of "chemurgy," where farm products would be put to industrial use, especially in plastics and fuels. Saskatchewan farmers would find vast new markets, and Saskatchewan cities would boom. For many, the memory of the 1944 campaign became bound up with the stage props Douglas carried from meeting to meeting in his dilapidated brown brief-case. In the manner of the temperance lecturer of bygone days holding up a jar of pickled livers for inspection, he drew forth little jars of alcohol and syrup, strips of plastic, and sheets of leather and insulating batting—all made from the products of the Saskatchewan farm. It was a mesmerizing performance, but while research in the next few years confirmed that grain and hides could be transformed into sophisticated products, it also concluded that there was no economic reason to do so, in Saskatchewan or anywhere else.

The well-springs of energy on which Douglas drew during this campaign seemed bottomless, but he could not be everywhere at once. Every candidate in the province needed the leader at his side, to fan the flames and insure victory. This raised a problem that would figure in Douglas's career until the late 1960s: what about the leader's own riding? Douglas had never run in the Weyburn provincial constituency; much of it lay within the city of Weyburn, always a weak spot in his federal campaigns. In this campaign, he relied on some seasoned veterans. The campaign manager was Ted Stinson, his close adviser since 1934. One of his two chief organizers was Charlie Broughton, a cowboy-booted Englishman who had worked the area for the CCF since the mid-1930s. Broughton's wife supported them both by teaching school, and he had vast resources of time for leaning on fenceposts, talking politics with farmers, and angling for donations. The second organizer had less experience: Tom McLeod had helped out as a teenager during Douglas's early campaigns, but had then left for college in Brandon and the United States.

Of course, the Liberals campaigned too. For the most part they used a negative strategy, denouncing the CCF as Nazis one day, Bolsheviks the next. The self-styled "independent dailies" in Saskatoon and Regina, both owned by the Liberal Sifton family, also trumpeted the alarm. On the day the Allied armies landed in Normandy, June 6, the *Leader-Post* carried one editorial on the great invasion and two lambasting the CCF. Three days later, the Regina paper featured four unsigned anti-CCF editorials, one pro-Liberal editorial, an anti-CCF cartoon, and two anti-CCF opinion pieces. Two days before the vote, an editorial cartoon portrayed Douglas in a surgeon's smock, preparing to wield an axe against a strapped-down guinea pig labelled "Saskatchewan."

To the Liberal charges that the CCF would confiscate farms, Douglas had only to point to the nearly 6000 foreclosures and mortgage defaults in Saskatchewan from 1935 to 1941. When his opponents claimed that the CCF would confiscate insurance policies, he replied that Canadian companies had cancelled $700 million in life insurance policies during the Depression. At the same time, Douglas played down warnings that he would lead a government of rampant nationalization. "The CCF does not want to own everything. In fact, we recognize that even if it were desirable...[it] would break down under the weight of bureaucracy and red tape...This leaves a wide field for private ownership."[12]

Douglas now stood on the brink of power. He was torn in those last days between his habit of indulging his high hopes for the future, and the realization that provincial governments face severe limits: "Don't think we can give you an entire new society," he told an audience a few days before the vote. "Nobody can do that in one province...Only the federal government can take over the banks and issue currency, give you parity prices, and control the tariff and the freight rates. I don't want the CCF party to get one vote in this election by saying they are going to do things they cannot constitutionally do."[13]

On election night, Douglas's constituency office became a provincial headquarters, as party workers from across Saskatchewan phoned in their local results. Minutes after the polls closed a pig-tailed Shirley Douglas began bouncing in and out of the office with agonizing regularity, asking, "Is my father the premier yet?" By nine o'clock it was clear that Douglas had carried more than 60 per cent of the votes in the Weyburn constituency, including a majority in the city. By ten, the party workers in the office could report: Yes, Shirley, your father is the premier.

That night, Douglas rode the shoulders of his supporters down Weyburn's Main Street. Two days later he retreated to his cottage at Carlyle Lake. The people had spoken for change, and he must now decide how fast to proceed. The CCF could not, despite his campaign rhetoric, bring "economic emancipation" within a year or a generation; it could improve life for the old and the sick, for underpaid workers and for farm families. It would never bring in the Kingdom of God on Earth; it would lead a dusty, bankrupt province into the mainstream of Canadian life.

12

The First Cabinet

HE SASKATCHEWAN LEGISLATIVE BUILDING faces north, overlooking a formal garden and a narrow, artificial lake. In summer, sailboats and canoes dot the green surface of Wascana, except when the northwest wind churns up its shallow waters. In winter, the observer sees only a subarctic waste. Across the lake lies the heart of the city of Regina—a town of 60,000 in 1944, its streets laid out in a perfect grid on the flattest of prairie land.

Inside, the legislature is a place of marble floors and marble pillars, with a grand central staircase leading to the Legislative Chamber. Up that staircase, carpeted in red for the occasion, walked Lieutenant-Governor Archibald P. McNab on July 10, 1944, to swear in Canada's first socialist government. Eight hundred people crammed the galleries. The premier's mother Anne was seated in a chair on the floor of the chamber, resplendent in a formal gown and a big hat.

Douglas faced what appeared to be an impossible set of challenges: the highest per capita provincial debt in the country, hostile corporations, hostile media. He would respect the wishes of all the people, he promised during his first broadcast after the election, and his government would move cautiously: as the old Scotsman had admonished him, "If you canna see the bottom, dinna wade far oot." At the same time, the government would be firm in dealing with big business. The number one election issue had been farm security, and post-election events now made it even more critical. Douglas affirmed in his broadcast that the government would honour its pledges. "Even now, mortgage companies and lending institutions are exerting tremendous pressure upon the debt-ridden farmers of this province. During the election they eased up a little...Now they are becoming almost ruthless in an attempt to seize all they can before we are able to pass legislation for the protection of debtors. Let me warn the mortgage companies, here and now, that unless they stop their campaign we shall be forced to take steps to protect those whose farms they are trying to seize."[1]

Election promises were not his only problem. Friends and strangers pressed him for jobs, favours, and recognition. He led a forty-seven-member legislative caucus, many of whom felt they belonged in the cabinet, as did their friends and relations back home. Party members in Saskatchewan and across Canada expected quick action against the corrupt and the wicked, and an immediate start on the building of a co-operative commonwealth using their disparate blue-prints. Douglas led a mass movement, and the masses clamoured to gain the ear of the government. Letters of advice and entreaty poured in by the bagful. One citizen submitted a plan for poisoning Saskatchewan's rats with fish scraps, and another hoped to melt the polar ice caps to freshen the rivers. Someone sent in specifications for a device that would raise water by its own pressure. People pleaded with Douglas to spring them or their relatives from jail, or to get their songs on the radio. Students of the Book of Revelation warned that Armageddon was near. Others reported that the Russians had invaded the province, and were beaming their lethal rays at farms and hamlets.[2]

Within a week or two, Douglas had gathered a few key helpers into his office. The first to join him was Tommy McLeod. McLeod knew Douglas from his boys' group in Weyburn, and had followed his path to Brandon College. After finishing graduate school at Indiana University, McLeod had returned to Brandon to teach economics. During his summer vacation in 1944 he helped with the Weyburn CCF campaign. The morning after the election, when McLeod called on Douglas to offer his congratulations, the new premier offered him a job. After a moment of reflection, McLeod accepted. Douglas said, "That's fortunate, I've already wired your resignation to Dr. Evans [the president of Brandon College]." McLeod was officially appointed economic adviser to the Executive Council on July 12. The title covered a multitude of tasks, and he served as research officer, theoretician, personnel adviser, and special envoy.

Douglas's greatest appointment was that of his secretary. Eleanor McKinnon was a daughter of one of the elders at Calvary Baptist, Norman McKinnon, who was also a noted Weyburn Liberal. Eleanor, too, was a graduate of Brandon College, and worked before the election as the secretary to the superintendent of the Weyburn Mental Hospital. Douglas asked her to leave her job and come to Regina—but only after getting her mother's permission. The appointment ruffled a few feathers among CCF partisans who felt the secretary's job was too prestigious, and too sensitive, to go to someone from the enemy camp. The muttering died down as Eleanor established herself. With only one break in service, she remained Douglas's right hand for the next forty-two years.

Eleanor McKinnon became the centre of calm in the near-chaos of the understaffed premier's office. The CCF government, as a people's government, felt it had to watch every dollar, particularly in its early days. If an employee could establish that he or she was doing the work of three, a second person might be hired. Eleanor supervised clerical staff once there was a clerical staff to supervise; she managed the premier's timetable, and sometimes the premier along with it; she directed traffic in and out of the office. She devoted a great deal of personal energy to the causes of petitioners with genuine problems, and, at the same time, she deflected the cranks from inside and outside the government service who felt they had a claim on the harassed premier's time. She did it quietly and gently, but with incontestable firmness.

Later in 1944 the premier's staff expanded with the appointment of a young Calgarian, Dr. Morris Shumiatcher, as legal adviser to the Executive Council. "Shumy" had earned the first doctorate in jurisprudence ever granted by the University of Toronto. Officially, his job was to help the premier to organize cabinet procedures. In fact, he did whatever needed doing, whether that was acting as pro-tem chauffeur for the premier, cooling out an irate taxpayer, or preparing a brief for the government.

The records from these days show that it was a time of confusion, of loose and shifting roles, of jobs started and never finished. The sense of disorganization was heightened by the fact that the Liberals had emptied the files of almost every document that might help the CCF govern the province. When Mackenzie King asked Douglas to comment on the agenda for an upcoming dominion-provincial conference, Douglas had to reply that he did not know a conference was planned. He wrote to the ex-premier, William Patterson, complaining that this act of pillage was "most improper," to which Patterson responded with a vague denial, assuring Douglas that "we followed the rules and practices established by custom."[3]

Douglas's first task, following the election, was to put together a cabinet. Many of the MLAs thought they had a right to an appointment, and a legion of party followers felt they had a right to advise on the matter. He made no promises. He shut himself away at his Carlyle Lake cottage with Clarence Fines and drew up a list of cabinet prospects. He consulted, among others, the president of the provincial party and the provincial executive. He established his own criteria for selection, emphasizing ability, region, occupational group, and religion. He knew that most of the experienced caucus members had resisted his rise to the leadership, but they would have to have a place in the cabinet.

The CCF had promised to reform Saskatchewan and to create new government departments that would work in neglected areas: co-operation, labour, and social services. In addition, party leaders expected there would be special economic and social pressures at the end of the war, and agreed to set up a Department of Reconstruction and Rehabilitation. To cope with all this new activity, Douglas increased the number of cabinet appointments from nine to twelve. This opened the government up to charges of lavish spending, however, and Douglas and Fines decided to reduce cabinet ministers' annual salaries from $7000 to $5000. The premier, *primus inter pares*, would draw $6500. Ten years later this sum would be increased to a princely $8500, at a time when senior deputy ministers were making $18,000.

Where the CCF had been split by factional feuds in the past, there was now a spirit of harmony. The members of cabinet accepted their roles and pulled their weight, held together by a bond of mutual trust, an attitude fostered and strengthened by the premier's own example. Half of the new ministers came from the cities, half from the farms and villages. None had experience in provincial government. All of them, though, had served in some elected capacity—in the legislature, on municipal councils, or as officers of province-wide organizations such as the Wheat Pool or the Saskatchewan Teachers' Federation.

Douglas, the premier, would also hold the health portfolio: the reform of the medical-care system lay near the top of the CCF's list of concerns. Fines, the long-time Regina alderman and inveterate party fundraiser, would act as provincial treasurer; Douglas also made him responsible for the Civil Service Commission. Fines hated this second job, since it seemed to conflict with his role as MLA for the civil service city, Regina. In 1947, after he had piloted through a new Civil Service Act and supervised the reorganization of the government's personnel system, he sloughed off this responsibility onto the schoolteacher, Woodrow Lloyd.

Lloyd, the minister of education, was the youngest member of cabinet at thirty-one, and the only one born in Saskatchewan. In the sixteen years he spent in the job the face of Saskatchewan education changed completely: bigger schools and school districts, better-qualified and better-paid teachers. Over the years, Lloyd rose in stature. He joined the Treasury Board, the body which pounded the government's spending estimates into their final form and carried them through cabinet. Douglas brought him into the informal inner cabinet, a small group that provided the premier with advice and sometimes comfort. He emerged in time as the cabinet's philosopher, and, eventually, in 1961, as the CCF's second premier. Here he would live out his finest hour as the man who put Douglas's Medical Care Act into effect in the face of an hysterical protest campaign. When Lloyd retired, Douglas praised him as "the conscience of the government, and the conscience of the party."[4] Lloyd had his detractors, however. While he successfully fought the battle over larger country school units—a controversy that hurt the government in the 1948 election—some CCFers criticized him for not implementing the teaching methods or the curriculum content that they felt should prevail in a socialist state.

Douglas made the former CCF leader, George Williams, his agriculture minister, but for reasons of health he was forced to resign before he could serve. His successor, Isadore C. Nollet, was a snoose-chewing cattleman from the northwest (his wife made him give up the habit after he took his oath to the king). As a radical farmer, he had helped push for the formation of the Farmer Labour Party in 1932. He was also Catholic, and so helped the government broaden its appeal. A kind and thoughtful person, he was never a cabinet heavyweight but became popular among the farmers and the younger members of the party.

George Williams's lieutenant of earlier days, John Brockelbank, took the municipal affairs post. Here he could consult with the mayors, reeves, and councillors, one of the most important groups in the province. He was a farmer who had cleared his own plot of land in the northern bush, a largely self-educated man who would tackle some of the most complex questions in government when he moved to natural resources after 1948. Brockelbank entered cabinet as a George Williams die-hard and a former leadership candidate in his own right. Carlyle King, who looked on as party president, said that "Brock was an ideal second in command; he could never have made a good leader."[5] Above all, he was a generous and dedicated party worker, and within a couple of years he became one of Douglas's strongest supporters. Brockelbank worked closely with the premier for the next seventeen years, a member of the inner circle of cabinet, and maintained his connection after Douglas returned to Ottawa.

Another politically sensitive post, the highways portfolio, went to Jack Douglas, Coldwell's campaign manager from Rosetown and the CCF's provincial organizer since 1941. Jack Douglas was in his early fifties and had come to Saskatchewan from Ontario in his childhood. Like the premier, he displayed some of the traits of the old Scottish Covenanters: the austere self-control, the unyielding personal independence. "Saskatchewan had been notorious for 20 or 30 years," said Tommy Douglas many years later. "Highways was the patronage department, it was the graft department, the department where favours were handed out. Sometimes in the old days the government contract for a piece of road would be in the hands of a farmer—a big farmer—or a local reeve or municipal councillor. And these people wielded terrific power, they were handing out money all the time, gravelling in the summer, clearing snow in the winter, building new roads."[6] Jack Douglas had the job of cancelling these Liberal contracts and putting them out for tender to attract the lowest bidder. The money the government saved in scrapping the old sweetheart deals—on highways, printing, construction, supplies—went a good way towards paying for the CCF's new programs.

Over the years, Jack Douglas and the premier also met to discuss prospective candidates in the various ridings. As highways minister, Jack Douglas travelled the province, and he would take a hand if he thought the CCF was in danger of nominating a crank or a windbag in any area. He did not pick the candidates, but he put potential candidates together with potential supporters and would drop a favourable word here and there. Never, said Clarence Fines, did the party leaders go into a nominating convention and order up a result.

This hands-off approach to constituency affairs did not meet with universal approval. Some of the premier's advisers suggested from time to time that he should take a more direct role, in the fashion of Mackenzie King. He could shore up his cabinet, they said, by fixing nominations for prominent citizens or up-and-coming party activists. The idea was anathema to Douglas. He would encourage young hopefuls to run, if they asked him—as with Allan Blakeney in 1960—but he held firmly to the principle that the grass roots must make the final decision on the candidate.

For the most part, his faith in the good judgement of his supporters was vindicated by the quality of the members they sent to the legislature.

John Wesley Corman, the only lawyer in the caucus, became the attorney-general by default. The sixty-year-old Corman was also the former mayor of Moose Jaw, and possessed perhaps the finest pair of political antennae in an astute cabinet. Decked out with his straw boater and carrying his cane, he resembled a cartoon figure of earlier days, Foxy Grandpa, and he probably deserved the name himself. Born in Ontario, he had served as a lawyer, alderman, and mayor in Moose Jaw since 1915. Corman had grown up as a card-carrying Liberal, and had even named his son Wilfrid Laurier Corman. In the 1930s he had run as a Social Credit candidate, at a time when Social Credit was regarded as a progressive movement. This prompted him to use a standard punch line at the end of his radio broadcasts: "You are born into the old parties. You have to think your way into the CCF. Good night."

Corman also had a finely tuned legal mind. With his photographic memory, he could absorb a brief while others were getting settled in their chairs. His cabinet colleagues, and Douglas most of all, listened to the Corman judgements with respect, and more than one argument faltered on a mild intervention from the attorney-general. Corman developed a strong attachment to the young premier. Seven years after his retirement from office, as he approached eighty years of age, he wrote on his Christmas card to the leader of the NDP, "You are still my political idol."[7]

The other ministers had strong local support, but played less important roles in the cabinet: Charlie Williams from Regina, Lauchlan McIntosh from Prince Albert, Jack Sturdy from Saskatoon. Oak Valleau from Melfort, the bright and earnest minister of social services, represented the CCF's left-wing pacifists. He might have moved to the inner circle had he not lost his seat in 1948.

The cabinet's maverick was Joe Phelps from Saltcoats riding, who became the minister for natural resources. Phelps was another radical farmer and had stepped forward as one of the most vocal members of the CCF opposition in the legislature after 1938, focusing his fury on the Liberal minister of natural resources, W. F. Kerr. He had been a moving spirit behind the party subcommittee on resource policy that Douglas had established in 1942. Phelps was a dreamer, and generated great enthusiasm among those around him, but the roadside was strewn with the bodies of those who could not keep up. Above all, he loved the idea of public ownership of industry, and he paid no attention when others counselled caution.

In the name of resource development, Phelps plunged the CCF government head first into a series of industrial and commercial ventures—a woollen mill, a tannery, a shoe factory, a brick plant. He acted without trying to establish whether he could sell the products or even manage the operations. The resulting tangle posed a challenge to George Cadbury and the Government Finance Office when the time came to impose some order on the government's business sector. Phelps ordered the purchase of at least one plant without consulting the cabinet, and he resorted to tears when his colleagues threatened to reverse his decision. Douglas recalled, "You could always count on him being on your side if you were raising some question that was extremely controversial... Phelps really wasn't so radical, you know, he just jumped to the left side of any issue that came up. He liked to make a noise."[8] After his surprise defeat in 1948, Phelps returned to the farm movement. He emerged in 1949 as president of the newly formed Saskatchewan Farmers' Union, the successor to the old United Farmers. He also served on the CCF provincial executive and, from these strategic positions, continued to demand that the government move faster to create a socialist community.

The rest of the caucus, mostly farmers and railwaymen, were kept to the back benches, and this caused some hard feelings. Those with energy and talent worked on committees and local party affairs. A few sulked and left politics after one or two terms. Douglas and Fines took pains to brief the back-benchers on all of the government's strategies; the most serious revolt would come in 1946 and 1947, when three or four MLAs fought hard against the consolidation of the remaining small school districts into larger units.

There were no women cabinet ministers at any time during the Douglas period, although several women worked as key local organizers for the CCF. Before the 1944 election, in fact, Douglas had to fight off a move by the Maple Creek riding executive to dump Beatrice Trew, the party's only female candidate.

The Douglas cabinet meetings were a study in collegiality. As president of the Executive Council, Douglas ruled with a light hand. He expected all cabinet ministers who were in Regina, unless they were in the hospital or the morgue, to attend every meeting, to be prepared, and to participate. He sought consensus, and carefully solicited the views of all ministers without imposing his own. He tried to avoid votes and, rather, in Quaker style, sought "the sense of the meeting." His chosen role was to analyse proposals and ask questions. Cabinet ministers frequently left meetings wondering why they or their advisers had not anticipated the premier's train of thought. In canvassing his colleagues he usually reserved his own views to the last, and where there was division of opinion he sometimes sided deliberately with a loser. His summary was, customarily, "Well, I'm inclined to agree with X, but since the rest of you seem to be agreed on Y, I guess that's it." The aggrieved minister, having lost his case, would at least feel that the premier had been on his side.

The members of the Douglas cabinet were always aware of his presence. His authority, however, flowed less from the power of his office than from the fact that he symbolized their common goal. He had the gift of synthesis, as Stephen Lewis later observed; he had the gift of clarity. He could take complex issues and reduce them to vivid populist imagery. He encouraged the best of the people's representatives to speak up and to put their ideas to work.[9]

13
Who's in Charge?

FOR THOSE CLOSE TO DOUGLAS, 1944 was a year of achievement. The days were filled with personal sacrifice but also with satisfaction. The work of building a new government with limited resources brought ministers and staff together in the kind of fellowship usually associated with a theatre of war. The government had made an amazing start. By year-end, it had issued cards to 30,000 people, widows, single mothers, and old people, giving them access to free medical care. It had introduced free cancer and psychiatric treatment, and raised mothers' allowances by 20 per cent. It had stabilized the farm debt situation, launched an insurance corporation, proclaimed a new day for labour, and started a massive program of administrative reform.

Douglas was sustained by a manic energy and a diet of raisin pie and coffee. In time his stomach rebelled, and he had to switch to milk and poached eggs. The strain told on other ministers as well. On cabinet days, regardless of what was on the agenda, the door opened at 10:30 sharp and the angel of the outer office appeared with a tray holding three half-pints of milk. Discussion stopped until straws had been inserted and first sips taken. This ceremony soothed three ulcers, but it threatened to create others, particularly in those who were interrupted while making a presentation. An exasperated Woodrow Lloyd commented, "If one more of you fellows would develop an ulcer we could buy a cow, and each of you could have a tit."

There was no half speed with Douglas. Every moment counted. One day, when McLeod chauffeured him to an appointment outside Regina, they got stuck behind a slow-moving truck on a country road, and Douglas fumed. Etiquette called for the truck to pull off and let the car go past; finally, McLeod made a lunge for it and crowded past on the outside. He turned to see the premier of Saskatchewan hanging from the open door on the passenger side, his head clearing the gravel by eighteen inches, trying to read the licence number on the truck.

Wherever he travelled in Saskatchewan during 1944, Douglas's followers lionized him as the man who had brought the CCF into its own. The party and the government enjoyed a honeymoon that year, highlighted by the remarkable fall session of the legislature when the government wrote much of the CCF's historic program into law. These were the party's greatest days. After this, the government would build up its own staff of in-house advisers and form new links with the world outside the party, and the CCF organization would lose its status as the main centre of influence.

Its populist history suggested that the party organization should play a special role in the Douglas government. The CCF had strong roots in the Progressive movement, with its concern for democratic reforms; the old Progressives had believed that putting the politician under the direct control of the local committee would revolutionize the political system. The CCF provincial constitution in 1944 still gave local party groups the right to recall their MLAS and force their resignation, and it was understood that the annual party convention should set the agenda for the legislative caucus. But, as Al Johnson points out in a thesis on the CCF in power, Douglas was confronted by another, more strongly established model when he became premier. Under the British cabinet system the government is accountable to those outside the legislature only at elections. Parties have traditionally stayed dormant except when the time came to get their politicians into office.

Douglas had always shown respect for the Progressive tradition of direct democracy. In 1934 and 1935 he signed recall papers, offering his supporters the right to overrule his decisions as an elected member. In 1940 he co-wrote the MPs' brief on party structure which suggested that the provincial council should have a leading part in selecting the cabinet. In 1943 he told a radio audience that the CCF politician's job was to obey the party's wishes, "as expressed from time to time in convention assembled."[1]

Now facing the realities of office, the new premier found himself saying, in his first radio broadcast, that the CCF government had to serve all the people, not just members of the CCF. This marked the start of a discreet tug-of-war, with the party on one side and the cabinet and caucus on the other. The party's activists pushed for rapid and widespread reform. Over the years, however, Douglas and Fines would prove that they understood the limits to the public's appetite for change, and it would help them win five general elections in a row.

Douglas and Fines had to deal with a spectrum of pressure groups outside the party, including big business. Plans for a Farm Security Act and the new mineral taxes brought the government into sharp disagreement with several interests—mining, oil, mortgage, and insurance companies. Some major companies, such as Imperial Oil, would refuse to invest in the province for several years. The premier and the treasurer had to persuade those who would listen that the new government would act moderately and within the law.

Fines described Douglas in these meetings as "the smoothest customer I ever saw."[2] The premier would rush from his desk, usher in his visitor, and spend several minutes on the weather and family matters. When it got down to business, he had a photographic memory for speeches, letters, and contracts, and often spouted a visitor's own words at him verbatim. Fines had a similar gift for numbers. He could pick figures out of the air, add, multiply, and compound interest, all in his head. The two leaders decided to fly to New York, Toronto, and Montreal in late summer 1944 to offset the scare stories about the socialist takeover. They reassured the financial houses that the new government intended to keep paying its debts. Most of the investment brokers received them cordially, but at Prudential Insurance in New Jersey the investment manager informed the pair that he had dumped $3 million in Saskatchewan bonds. Fines, as a Prudential policy holder, dressed the man down for his recklessness.

One crack in the party-cabinet relationship appeared at the CCF's 1944 summer convention. On the policy side, everything appeared harmonious. A legislative advisory committee elected by the convention had little to say. After all, its members had until recently worked on the same policy committees as the men who were now cabinet ministers. Douglas met only briefly for a chat with this advisory group, made up of two backbench MLAs and three party members. Elsewhere, though, there was division on the issue of democratic procedure. Toby Nollet, soon to be in the cabinet, moved that the convention delete all reference to the recall process in the party constitution. Peter Makaroff, a leading party member outside the legislature, got the question referred to provincial council, where the recall idea died a lingering death.

Party-cabinet tensions would wax and wane over the next few years, although they never provoked any public split. The picture grew more complicated with the decision in 1945 to set up a think tank, the Economic Advisory and Planning Board. Inevitably, this body would compete with the party as a source of advice for the government. All sides understood that the board would play a central role in designing the socialist state: it would provide a fresh analysis of the Saskatchewan economy, examine new ideas for expanding industry and raising capital, and develop new government management methods. Judging from party literature, setting up the board might be the most important single step the Douglas government would take. The question arose: Would the public, and especially the committed members of the party, be given some control over the planners?

The nearest thing to a guidebook on CCF economic theory—*Social Planning in Canada*, from 1936—stated that more concentration of power in the cabinet and the bureaucracy was unavoidable in the socialist state. The eastern academics who wrote the book, including several of the authors of the Regina Manifesto, dismissed the idea that planning could be done by parties or people's committees. A more idealistic strain in the CCF, however, suggested that grocers, mechanics, and housewives would be invited to offer their wisdom at the economic planning table. As late as 1943 Douglas had written in support of such a do-it-yourself democracy in the CCF *Commonwealth*: "One of the problems of our generation is to exercise control under a planned economy without at the same time falling under the blight of regimentation. We believe that the solution lies in having the people themselves, through workers' and farmers' organizations, do the planning and exercise the controls which are essential if we are not to fall back into the economic chaos of the Hungry Thirties."[3]

When it came to the crunch, Douglas and his colleagues created the Economic Advisory and Planning Board as a panel of paid experts answerable only to cabinet. The cause can be summed up in the old phrase about too many cooks: Saskatchewan was already building the most complicated government structure in Canada, and had no need to multiply committees and centres of power. Douglas assured the provincial party council that he would consult it on all major issues. The council agreed, in turn, early in 1945, that it would offer "helpful criticism" rather than try to direct the cabinet. However, a year later, with the planning board in operation, the council made a losing bid to place some citizen representatives on the board. The summer convention of 1946 indicated some restlessness in party ranks. A key resolution urged the government to "proceed with the realization of our program of Socialism...with increased speed and renewed zeal."[4]

Over time, the party activists found more than enough constructive outlets for their political energies—for example, on the boards of the burgeoning power, telephone, and insurance companies—and they began to make their own kinds of compromises. The roles of cabinet and party became more clearly defined, and the premier's dealings with his party grew more tranquil, but there was a cost attached. By 1950 the loss of ferment had brought a loss of enthusiasm and, more troublesome, a drop in membership.

In building his new government, the premier set out to find the best available talent. The Liberals complained that he was turning Saskatchewan into a laboratory for socialism, and belaboured him for turning the government over to the "carpet-baggers" and the "back-room boys." Douglas believed that conventional Canadian governments had grown stale, to the point where they considered inward-looking thinking a virtue. He was determined to lead Saskatchewan into the big leagues of public administration.

He started quickly in his own Health Department. In the summer of 1944 he hired Henry Sigerist, a leading American authority on public health, to examine the Saskatchewan health-care system and propose reforms. On Sigerist's recommendation, Douglas set up a Health Services Planning Commission and brought in Drs. Mindel and Cecil Sheps from Winnipeg, and later Dr. Fred Mott, the deputy surgeon general of the United States, to head the commission. Within a short period, these outside experts and the staff they gathered around them had laid the groundwork for the sweeping reforms that culminated with medicare.

Although progress in the areas of social and economic planning came more slowly, Douglas eventually succeeded in attracting dozens of experts into the province. The Saskatchewan government, with its high calibre of professionalism, became a model for other Canadian jurisdictions to follow. However, Douglas's staffing policies probably caused more heartache among CCF party members than any other issue. His supporters could live with the experts from outside, but they grew increasingly frustrated that the government seemed to be protecting Liberal appointees from the old days while it created only a few patronage jobs of its own. Saskatchewan's disgust with a rotten Liberal machine had contributed greatly to the election of the CCF; the public service, in CCF eyes, overflowed with Liberal hacks and in-laws, many of them unqualified for their jobs. Coldwell, on the night of the 1944 election, predicted "a real housecleaning."[5] Tom McLeod, in a memo that went to cabinet even before it was sworn in, advised ministers to purge the "undesirable elements" from their departments before the government adopted new rules that would protect public servants.[6]

Douglas promised immediately to get rid of workers who were "either incompetent or merely political employees."[7] Some boards and commissions had become havens for Liberal appointees and, within weeks, the government either abolished them or brought their staffs into the mainstream public service. It abolished the Saskatchewan Tax Commission and the Farm Loan Board, and cancelled the contracts of several dozen "liquor inspectors" and "Northern Areas inspectors." In the departments, the government asked some unqualified workers, such as untrained social workers, to resign. But the firings stopped well short of a bloodbath. A memo from Douglas's desk comparing staff turnover during the Liberals' last year and the CCF's first year shows only a small-scale purge among salaried workers:[8]

Permanent Staff	Resigned	Retired	Dismissed
May 43-May 44	197	25	1
May 44-May 45	193	69	18

Only one minister, Joe Phelps of natural resources, really laid on the axe, firing fifteen people, many of them at senior levels. Most other ministers kept their staffs almost intact. The new government retained several deputy ministers whom the CCF had denounced in the days of the Liberal regime. In three of the four new departments, the new deputy ministers were simply promoted from their old branch head jobs.

CCF partisans expressed annoyance at what they regarded as the cabinet's pussy-footing. They became even hotter when the new Public Service Act made it clear that Douglas meant to hire on the basis of merit. If party members wanted jobs for their sons and daughters after this, he referred their letters to the Public Service Commission. As he wrote to one party member: "We are seeking to eliminate patronage and to have our elected members work as lawmakers and not as party bosses who hand out patronage to their friends and political supporters. I am sure, on reflection, you will agree that this will make a much better government."[9]

The premier did not ignore all his supporters. In his first round of appointments, in fact, he rewarded his oldest political ally. The Liberals had made the business of government purchasing into a racket, with party insiders providing a range of goods and services—food for the mental hospitals, vehicles, advertising, and so on. Douglas set up a Government Purchasing Agency to place orders and contracts on the basis of open bidding. He was determined that its operations should be above suspicion, and its manager must, therefore, be someone who could win the public's trust. He turned to his old friend, church deacon, and campaign manager, Ted Stinson. No one argued with the results. Stinson cleaned up the system, and he always returned gifts sent in by suppliers—with one exception. As a temperance man, he poured any gift of liquor down the sink.

In the fall of 1944 the CCF executive resolved that only "proven socialists" should become deputy ministers or commissioners, positions not governed by the merit principle imposed by the new Public Service Act. It may be more than coincidental that the mover and the seconder of the motion, Peter Makaroff and Carl Edy, soon got high-level appointments to government boards. The government also took a couple of former MLAS under its wing, as well as a few other long-time workers. In general, however, the CCF appointed people to boards and commissions because of their background with labour, farm, or business groups rather than their party colours. Much of the government's legal work went to a firm whose senior members were leading Tories.

Government hiring remained a sensitive issue right up until Douglas left the premier's job in 1961. The CCF executive asked again and again that senior positions (at least) should be reserved for party activists or known sympathizers. The cabinet obviously violated this principle many times, or the executive would have stopped passing such resolutions. At the same time, the occasional plum appointments bestowed on party veterans irked the opposition. By 1960, the list of CCF appointees had grown far enough into the dozens to give the revived Liberal Party a political issue. However, Douglas always resisted the idea that these appointments constituted real patronage. He said in 1985, "Patronage is where people are put into government employment primarily for the purpose of building a political machine—hire members of their own party who in turn will hire others. Consequently, the party in office becomes a giant employment agency, and the concept of merit goes out the window."[10] Certainly the CCF, from this perspective, did not depend on patronage for its survival as the Gardiner machine had done.

In their first months in office, Douglas and his colleagues succeeded in paying their financial commitments from a depleted treasury, firing some old workers and hiring others, and meeting with the hordes of well-wishers and lobbyists who wanted to make an impression on the new government. They also prepared a raft of legislation for a special fall session of the House. The ideas behind most of the new bills had been gestating within the CCF for years, but the work of drafting was still a strenuous task. Douglas and his ministers pushed hard from their end. The unsung heroes of the piece were the law clerks of the assembly's legal counsel, especially Jimmy Runciman, an elderly, tweedy little Scot. He was a master craftsman who took bills that had been put together by the amateurs and, clause by clause, word by word, produced works of superb legal draftsmanship.

The Throne Speech which launched this session on September 27, 1944, was in effect the new government's manifesto. It set out the priorities for rebuilding a rundown province. The CCF would "create a government organization sufficient in scope to meet the needs of postwar society." It would come to the aid of debt-ridden property owners, urban and rural; at the same time, it would offer more help to the disadvantaged. And where the private sector had hesitated to invest in Saskatchewan, this government would recognize "the increasing importance of social enterprise."[11]

Over the next two months, Douglas and his colleagues passed seventy-six pieces of legislation, touching almost every area in the life of the province. These reforms were largely the work of the grass roots. CCF party committees had fed their ideas to provincial council, and from there proposals went to caucus and to cabinet. In 1944 the party council also reviewed the legislation before it went to the House. This final step was dropped in later years, but in Douglas's view, party committees remained the source of new ideas. Very little the CCF government did, he said later, was a surprise to anyone. "By the time you got it to the legislature, there wasn't anything hidden in it. It had been beaten to death."[12]

While the party would always offer ideas, never again would the government adopt so many of them in one burst. Slowly, a mood of political caution would close in on the CCF; along with this, the paid advisers counselled increasingly specific limits on the government's activities. This led to some frustration in the party, much of it unspoken. Carlyle King, the CCF president, would testify to this mood in an article he wrote in 1952 when he said that socialist parties worldwide were crowding the political centre and had not had a new idea in ten years.[13] However, it is testimony to the leadership of Tommy Douglas, and to the spirit of 1944, that the CCF avoided open splits and public resignations during his career as premier.

14

The Politics of Federalism

TOMMY DOUGLAS AND CLARENCE FINES sometimes travelled together to federal-provincial conferences in Ottawa. During one visit in the mid-1950s they arranged to meet privately with Prime Minister Louis St. Laurent. On the Friday morning of their appointment the two Saskatchewan politicians made the short walk from the Château Laurier to Parliament Hill, and then down an elegant, gloomy East Block corridor to the prime minister's office. C. D. Howe, the minister of trade and commerce, was present along with St. Laurent, and a moment after the meeting began a short, stocky man scuttled through the door and took a seat by the wall. James Garfield Gardiner, the minister of agriculture, "sat in the corner like a little boy who had just sneaked in. Neither the prime minister nor Mr. Howe paid the slightest attention to him."

Douglas had come to inquire about federal plans for the South Saskatchewan River dam, a megaproject that Gardiner had been promising his province for ten years. The federal government had changed its tune so often that not even the premier knew where matters stood. He asked the prime minister what he thought would be a fair division of costs on the project.

St. Laurent answered calmly that he was not interested in making a proposal. The province could put up 90 per cent and Ottawa would not contribute a nickel. The only way he would change his mind would be if the prairies faced a crippling drought.

"What's the point in building a dam," said an exasperated Douglas, "if there's no water to put in it?"

St. Laurent agreed that the premier might put out a news release stating that the Liberals had no intention of building the dam, and with that the meeting ended.

"Fines and I were walking down the corridor," Douglas recalled, "and I heard footsteps behind me. I felt Gardiner tugging my arm, and he said, 'Now don't you pay any attention to that, he doesn't mean what he says...why don't we just go into my office and talk about it?' "

"I said, 'You go to hell. I don't want to discuss this with you at all.' "[1]

Saskatchewan and Ottawa—as the story illustrates—had their ups and downs during the Douglas period. The great national reforms that the CCF hoped for at the end of the war failed to materialize, and the federal government lost its enthusiasm for ideas like hospital insurance and medicare. Saskatchewan, a poor province in the hinterland, had little success in persuading Ottawa to finance its experimental programs.

All the same, the 1940s and 1950s witnessed important changes in the face of Canadian federalism. Canadians had learned something about the nation's economic fragility during the Depression, and the conscription plebiscite during the war had pointed up the persistent split between French and English. In the years after 1944 Canadian leaders worked out new systems of joint action, and gradually the flow of federal funds going to the poorer provinces increased. The arrangements between Ottawa and the provinces became more flexible, obscuring the neat definitions of jurisdiction set out in the British North America Act.

Within a generation, Canada was to accomplish through agreement what it had never been able to do by constitutional amendment. These agreements did not come easily; there was considerable tugging and hauling, and "centralist" became a pejorative term among those who wanted federal money without the federal presence. Tommy Douglas was often called a centralist by those who misunderstood the changes that were taking place, but this label oversimplifies his position.

At the beginning of his career, Douglas had sometimes viewed the federal power with suspicion. When he entered the Commons in 1935 many members of the CCF supported a major centralization of taxing powers, so that the federal government could redistribute income among the provinces. Douglas found himself arguing, along with Saskatchewan CCF leader George Williams, that the old parties would probably hold federal office for many years and that the provinces should hang on to their taxing powers. If the CCF took control of a provincial government, he told David Lewis, it should not have to answer to some federal redistribution commission run by Liberals or Tories.[2] Williams, characteristically, stated the position more bluntly: "I can well see the argument in favour of centralization of power under a socialist government, but centralization of power under the present set up may easily mean 'secession' later on, because I have absolutely no faith in a government controlled by Eastern financiers and industrialists."[3]

Douglas, as he matured politically, overcame some of his suspicion of centralized power. He dreamed that some day Canadians would design a planned national economy, an economy organized for people, not for profit. As he considered this prospect, he developed the belief that "Only the federal state...can give us a sense of identity as well as the constitutional power to map out long-term programs."[4] This did not mean that he was prepared to abandon the provinces. His early battles as premier of Saskatchewan taught him the value of protecting provincial jurisdiction and the rights of the regions.

Saskatchewan in 1944 remained a have-not province. Its run-down state testified to the futility of a constitutional arrangement that gave the provinces authority and responsibility, but not the power to raise taxes. Douglas believed, along with the national CCF, that the major defects in the economy—unemployment, poverty, industrial stagnation—could not be repaired by provinces acting individually, especially poor provinces like Saskatchewan. Every day he encountered the fact of regional disparity, that natural resources and business activity were spread unevenly across the country. Repeatedly, in his public speeches and radio addresses, he decried the fact that, every year, mortgage, loan, and farm-machinery companies took millions of dollars out of Saskatchewan without paying income or corporation taxes.[5]

The Rowell-Sirois Commission on Federal-Provincial Relations had declared in 1940 that every Canadian had a right to a fair standard of government services. Douglas agreed with the commission that the central government should affirm this right by using the tax system to redistribute income. He saw, too, that the national government alone had the muscle to maintain the health of the Canadian economy and insure workers against unemployment. Under the wartime tax agreements the provinces had surrendered some of their taxing powers to Ottawa. He now saw these agreements as potential long-term tools for sharing money among the provinces, and he no longer spoke of the possible abuses of centralized power.

Douglas's years in the House of Commons had dampened his parochial sentiments and strengthened his feeling for the nation. As premier, he remained aware of the tensions that are characteristic of the federal state. In a letter that he wrote in 1955 he stated:

> It seems to me that during the next few years, the battle in Canada is going to be between two opposing concepts—one which thinks of Canada as a nation in which the entire economy will be integrated so as to guarantee every citizen no matter where he lives, certain minimum standards of health, welfare and education, and on the other hand the concept that Canada is merely a loosely knit collection of provinces in which those provinces which have large corporations will be relatively fortunate, while those who lack this tax base will become depressed areas. This latter concept will certainly suit the big business interests of Canada since they know they can exert sufficient pressures on provincial governments which are friendly to them to see that they are not taxed too heavily for social services.[6]

The roots of Douglas's federalism went deeper than political theory or economic calculus, back to the social gospel of his youth. He believed that just as the strong should help the weak in the local community, the rich should bear the burdens of the poor within the nation. Soon after he became federal leader of the NDP in 1961, Saskatchewan edged past the national average and became one of the wealthier provinces. The federal government began to skim money off for redistribution elsewhere. Some of his former cabinet colleagues complained to him about this turn of events, but Douglas reminded them of the days when Saskatchewan had lived partly on the gifts of other Canadians. "If Saskatchewan has newfound riches it cannot share with the rest of Canada," he said, "then there is no longer room in the party for me."[7]

When Douglas moved into his office in 1944, his desk was not quite bare. On it was a letter from the federal minister of finance, James Ilsley of Nova Scotia, demanding payment from Saskatchewan of $16.5 million, about one-half the province's annual budget. This money would repay Ottawa for the federal loans advanced to Saskatchewan farmers to buy seed grain in 1938.

The farmers, in the spring of 1938, had just experienced the worst crop year in the history of the province. The land had yielded two-and-a-half bushels of grain to the acre, and farmers had sold it at distress prices. Douglas, as the MP for Weyburn, predicted in late 1937 that the whole region would be left without seed grain, and he urged the federal government to spend some money and put seed in storage. The government failed to act, and when spring came, seed was in short supply and the farmers had almost no cash with which to buy it. Eventually, the federal government organized a program that provided cash advances for farmers to buy seed, but the provincial government had to guarantee these loans. The farmers paid as much as $1.43 a bushel for seed, and in M. J. Coldwell's words, "They received the seed late, seed that was dirty, seed that was unsuitable; they received 40 cents a bushel that year [fall, 1938] for top grade wheat."[8] Many farmers could never repay their loans, and the province was left with an enormous debt to Ottawa.

During the election campaign of 1944, CCF leaders promised they would seek to have the federal government reduce its claim, on the grounds that Saskatchewan had incurred the seed-grain debt under duress and during a time of national emergency. However, almost as soon as the CCF took power, the King government demanded payment in full, at a rate of at least $2 million per year. In the minds of Douglas and his colleagues, this was a blatant case of discrimination. The King Liberals in Ottawa had never tried to force their lame-duck counterparts in Regina to settle. The notes given as security had simply been renewed from year to year, the latest renewal coming five days after the election of the CCF.

The new premier suspected that while the hand raised against Saskatchewan was that of Ilsley, the dagger belonged to Jimmy Gardiner. It caused Douglas, Fines, and the rest of the cabinet grave concern that the Government of Canada might be engaged in a partisan ploy to damage the province. They dug in and refused to comply with Ilsley's demand, choosing instead to rally the people of Saskatchewan. Douglas told a radio audience that his government did "not intend to pay one dollar" unless Ottawa agreed to cut the debt in half.[9] After further dispute, the federal government began to seize part of its statutory annual payments to

Saskatchewan. The CCF cabinet took the federal side to arbitration on the legality of the seizure, but a three-member panel ruled in Ottawa's favour. In Douglas's view, the suspension of federal grants that had been paid since the founding of Saskatchewan in 1905 could only poison relations between Ottawa and all the provinces. At the same time, he hoped the controversy might help the CCF in the upcoming federal election. As it turned out, his party took eighteen of the twenty-one federal seats in the province.

By September 1945 both sides had had enough. It seems likely that Ilsley, although he had a reputation for stubbornness, did not really have his heart in the struggle. He worked out a compromise settlement, giving Saskatchewan eleven years to pay off a $12 million debt, and whisked it through a special cabinet meeting that he called when Gardiner was away from Ottawa. Douglas and Fines determined that about three-quarters of the money would come from the provincial treasury, with the farmers paying the rest. They also decided to reimburse any farmer who had paid off more than half his seed-grain debt from 1938.[10]

The seed-grain dispute did no lasting damage to the relationship between Saskatchewan and Ottawa. Douglas refused to take the disagreement personally, and maintained a high respect for Ilsley and for Mackenzie King.

As the fighting in Europe and the Pacific drew to a close, the Government of Canada came forward with a blue-print for a new national postwar order. The 1940 Rowell-Sirois Report had been savaged by Ontario, Alberta, and British Columbia, but much of its spirit remained alive. If anything, the flame burned a bit brighter in a country committed to avoiding its past mistakes. The bright young officials in Ottawa, inspired by the economic doctrines of Maynard Keynes, accepted the idea that a minimal level of social and economic rights constituted the first claim of all Canadians. If Canada could make a smooth postwar readjustment and set out on a long-term program of reform, it would avoid the economic depression and social upheaval that had caused so much unrest in Canada in 1919.

King's government in Ottawa had a second reason for pushing forward in 1945: it feared the continued strong support for the CCF in Ontario and the West. The time had come for Mackenzie King to find anew that middle road he loved to occupy. Under King's guidance, economic logic and political necessity made common cause in the "Green Book," the documents which the federal government put before the provinces in preparation for the Dominion-Provincial Conference on Reconstruction in August 1945.

Douglas would attend many joint meetings of government leaders, but none would hold the promise of this one, his première appearance as a first minister. The Green Book ranged over such issues as employment, social security, resource development, and tax sharing. In each area the documents set out an analysis and a set of proposals. The Green Book suggested to Douglas that Canada might soon become the kind of political community he wanted. The Government of Canada would take responsibility for maintaining the general health of the economy, with the aim of keeping unemployment to a minimum. The provinces could move ahead with their own business, freed of the worst burdens of economic breakdown and supported from Ottawa in their social and economic policies.

The asking price for all of this was, essentially, a continuation of the wartime tax agreements, which had increased Ottawa's share of Canadian tax revenues. Douglas regarded the proposed shift as fair, considering the promised benefits.

Douglas went to Ottawa prepared to co-operate with the dominion government. However, he was virtually alone among the provincial premiers in endorsing Mackenzie King's grand design, and the first ministers' conference broke down on the first day. Most of his counterparts found the federal proposals too radical, or a threat to the immediate advantage of their own voters, and would yield nothing to any common agreement. There were four Liberal premiers present, but among them, only Stuart Garson of Manitoba appeared ready to follow Ottawa's lead. The rest seemed to be interested mostly in emerging on the winning side. Douglas twitted the prime minister during one of the conference breaks with the comment, "It looks like you and I are the only Liberals here." The federal government, he said in 1958, had put forward "one of the most comprehensive pieces of work that has ever been done in Canadian history, in laying out the blueprint for the establishment of a planned economy in Canada...It was a tragedy that it was all ditched."[11]

The 1945 conference was overshadowed by one of history's cataclysmic events. Towards the end of the morning session the prime minister arose from his place at the end of the conference table and said he was about to make one of the most important announcements of his career. A few around the table snickered, thinking that King might be jokingly preparing to pass on a trivial message, such as an invitation to a reception. This turned to stunned silence as King read a statement on the dropping of the first atomic bomb on Hiroshima. The meeting took a recess; in the washroom a dean of law stared at the white tile wall in front of him and whispered, "I guess this is the end of God." A new age had dawned, although it was not the one Douglas had hoped for when he set out for Ottawa.

Tucked away in the British North America Act of 1867 are provisions which give the Government of Canada the power to disallow any provincial act. Ottawa can take this step when it pleases, irrespective of whether the provincial legislation in question touches on federal concerns. This power was designed to guarantee the supremacy of the central government, but federal governments soon learned that the political costs attached to imposing disallowance could be very high. After 1900 the practice fell more and more into disuse, although Ottawa disallowed some of the Alberta Social Credit government's legislation in 1937, and helped to destroy the radical momentum of William Aberhart's movement. At the 1944 New Year's policy conference in Regina many CCF speakers predicted that the election of a socialist provincial government would trigger a capitalist counter-attack from all sides. Frank Scott, the national party's constitutional expert, suggested that the federal power of disallowance would be one of the establishment's most important weapons.

The CCF took office and passed a first round of legislation, and then a second, without any comment from Ottawa. Then, on September 17, 1945, Douglas got a letter from the federal Department of Justice, informing him that it had received two petitions for the disallowance of legislation. The Canadian Pacific Railway was unhappy with the Douglas government's Mineral Taxation Act, while the Dominion Loan and Mortgage Association wanted to see Saskatchewan's Farm Security Act struck down. In response to these petitions, the federal government had set up a committee of ministers to look at both issues. The letter notified Douglas that the committee would open hearings in three weeks.

The Mineral Taxation Act imposed a levy on hitherto tax-free mineral (subsurface) rights. The CCF government regarded it as a companion to the property tax which had always been assessed against surface rights. Canadian Pacific still held large tracts of land from the days of Sir John A. Macdonald and could expect to face a major tax expense under the act. The Farm Security Act was designed to protect the farmer against the financial burden of having to make mortgage payments in years of crop failure. The farmers' movement had long demanded that mortgage and loan companies should share in the losses, as well as the profits, of agriculture.

Douglas found the idea of disallowance to be insulting, and he was further upset by the federal government's method of proceeding. Once again, it appeared the CCF was being harassed by a consortium of eastern interests and federal Liberals. In a letter to M. J. Coldwell, the national CCF leader, Douglas wrote that although the petitions had been received in Ottawa in July, the Justice Department had not notified him until mid-September. The federal government was giving the province "literally three weeks to prepare arguments against briefs which appear to have taken six or eight weeks to prepare." St. Laurent, the minister of justice, had suggested that the provincial government might be restricted to one hour in its presentations. Attorney-General Corman, replying for an exasperated CCF cabinet, had told St. Laurent that neither the hearing dates nor the one-hour restriction were acceptable.

Douglas carried his case to the people on the radio, and the government distributed a pamphlet called "The Case Against Disallowance." The campaign focused on the importance of the Mineral Taxation and Farm Security acts rather than on the legal technicalities. Douglas called on the citizens of the province to organize and to fight the federal government on the issue, and organize they did: resolutions protesting against "this arbitrary action" arrived in Ottawa from the United Farmers, the Saskatchewan branch of the Canadian Congress of Labour, and many municipal councils.[12] The brief that Corman's staff prepared for the federal hearings took a different tack. It made no mention of the substance of the legislation. It stated, simply, that only the courts should have the power to strike down provincial laws, and then only on constitutional grounds. The Government of Canada, it said, had no part to play.

Perhaps King and St. Laurent had already reached the same conclusion, or perhaps they decided that they did not want to pay the political cost of taking on the people of Saskatchewan. Before the hearings opened, Coldwell wrote to Douglas that he had talked to St. Laurent, who said "that disallowance is conceivable only if provincial legislation interfered with the rights of the Dominion or placed the whole of Canada in a bad light before the world. It was no concern of his...to decide on the constitutionality of provincial legislation...He said that he could not do other than to grant the request (to hear the petitions) because, after all, individuals have the right to approach the crown if they feel themselves aggrieved."[13] In the event, the panel of ministers heard the pleas of the railway and the mortgage companies, and rejected them.

It is interesting to note that a difference of opinion persisted between Douglas and Frank Scott on the federal power of disallowance. After Douglas hired Scott to help prepare Saskatchewan's position for a 1950 constitutional conference, the premier's office and Scott exchanged some firmly worded notes on the issue. Douglas felt that all mention of disallowance should be deleted from a new constitution—a position that distinguished him from the strict centralists. Scott contended that the provinces should not be allowed to develop into "glorified little states," and he urged Douglas to support retention of the power.[14]

While Ottawa only threatened to meddle in Saskatchewan's affairs, the Douglas government definitely crossed into Ottawa's jurisdiction when it began to take action in the area of Indian affairs. Douglas, along with his legal adviser Morris Shumiatcher, helped Saskatchewan's status Indians to find a unified voice in 1946. Shumiatcher's ongoing work in this area appears to have irritated some on the federal side, at least among the bureaucrats.

Saskatchewan had about 14,000 status Indians in the mid-1940s, most of them living on the province's sixty-one reserves. Under the constitution, Ottawa took responsibility for their health care, income support, and education. The decision to bring Douglas into the picture appears to have come from the Indian side. An Assiniboine chief from southeast of Regina, Dan Kennedy, befriended the premier, and in 1945 the Assiniboine gave him the tribal name We-a-ga-sha, or Chief Red Eagle. The relationship might have stayed at the level of friendly correspondence, except for the keen interest that Shumiatcher took in the native cause. He visited several reserves and found that the Indians had a long list of complaints, telling of corruption among federal Indian Affairs officials, a low quality of education in the mission schools, low standards of health care, and discrimination by Ottawa against the hundreds of Indian war veterans.

The CCF government was not in a position to solve the Indians' problems. However, Douglas called the chiefs from southern Saskatchewan together for a meeting on January 4, 1946, in the cafeteria of the legislature. A week later, Shumiatcher met with the northern chiefs at Duck Lake. At a general assembly of chiefs in Saskatoon in February, Shumiatcher read a message from Douglas: "Nothing is asked of you, except that you meet in a friendly spirit with your fellows, and that you frankly discuss your problems."[15] The assembly agreed to the formation of the Union of Saskatchewan Indians, the first Indian organization in the province that could present a united front in approaching the federal authorities.

In a March article in the *Canadian Forum*, Shumiatcher wrote that Douglas was becoming "increasingly incensed" at federal indifference to conditions on the reserves. However, it was the premier's adviser who remained active, to the point where the Indians complained to Douglas. The young lawyer was setting the agenda, they said, and giving orders, and they reluctantly asked that the white men now withdraw from their meetings. Shumiatcher continued, nonetheless, as an ad hoc ombudsman for status Indians, forwarding their complaints to the RCMP and senior federal officials. When a new federal minister came on the scene in 1949 he reviewed his files and asked Douglas to respect the chain of command: "What disturbs me is the tendency on the part of certain Indians to ignore the Indian Superintendent and communicate with your office."[16] At about this time, Shumiatcher left the public service for greener pastures, and the CCF withdrew from the field of Indian affairs.

In 1956 Douglas appointed a committee under Jack Sturdy, an MLA and former cabinet minister, to study the question of whether the province should take responsibility for status Indians. Sturdy answered in the negative, but he proposed that the CCF government set up job-training centres to encourage Indians to leave the reserve and seek better opportunities. "I am sure the municipalities would welcome these people," Sturdy told the legislature. "Then think how rapidly integration would take place, for Indian children are just as attractive, just as lovable as white people."[17]

Over the next thirty years the Indians moved to Saskatchewan's cities in large numbers, along with their Métis cousins. Instead of a municipal welcome they met with racism, unemployment, and poverty. No government, federal or provincial, Liberal, NDP, or Tory, ever put together a political consensus among the white majority to address the problem.

Of all Douglas's negotiations with Ottawa, none lasted longer or took more twists and turns than those leading up to the construction of the South Saskatchewan River dam. On the federal side sat the eastern heavyweights in the federal cabinet—King, C. D. Howe, St. Laurent. On the other side were Saskatchewan politicians of all stripes, with their vivid memories of the dirty thirties. They knew that while only God can make rain, man can learn to conserve water supplies against future periods of drought. Without water, the crops shrivel, the livestock starves, and even the family garden falls into ruin.

The history of the dam is a classic tale of federal procrastination, of promises made and promises broken, relieved by a few moments of low comedy along the way. The cast included three prime ministers, two federal ministers of agriculture, and numerous underlings. Through much of the piece Douglas found himself locked in a strange embrace, half waltz and half wrestling match, with his old political opponent Jimmy Gardiner.

Engineers had speculated for many years on the possibility of damming the South Saskatchewan. Almost a century before construction went ahead, Henry Youle Hind had suggested that future governments might divert water from the Saskatchewan into the Qu'Appelle system and open up a water transportation route from Winnipeg to the western prairies. Douglas saw other uses for stored water: in irrigation, power generation, recreation, and in increasing security of supply for Saskatchewan's cities: "Water is a prerequisite to growth. Without an abundant supply our cities cannnot grow...and our farming and livestock economy is subject to instability and periodic drought."[18]

Douglas's interest in the question went back at least to 1938, when he seconded a motion in the Commons from Coldwell calling on the King government to study the potential for water conservation and irrigation projects on the prairies. In speaking to his motion, Coldwell asked specifically for the damming of the South Saskatchewan.[19] Gardiner, the minister of agriculture—after whom the present dam is named—took no part in the debate. Indeed, he appears to have maintained an official silence on the subject for the next six years.

Perhaps coincidentally, Gardiner went to work on the idea a few days after the Saskatchewan CCF government was sworn in in 1944. Federal engineers, he told the Commons, were surveying to determine the possibility of building a dam near Saskatchewan Landing. A year later, he announced that he would consult with the provinces affected (mostly Saskatchewan and Alberta) to find out whether they were prepared to make good use of new water that would be supplied. He indicated his eagerness: "All we want is to get along with it as quickly as possible."[20] In early 1947, Gardiner told reporters that a decision on where to locate the dam would come that summer, and work would then proceed. In June the cabinet approved an order-in-council declaring that once Ottawa had reached an agreement with Saskatchewan, construction should begin "at the earliest possible date."[21] However, an engineers' report put a $66 million price tag on the project, and after mulling over this for several months, Gardiner suggested there would be at least a two-year delay.

The Douglas cabinet could only look on while Gardiner promoted the project in Ottawa. The federal minister had spoken always of "we" and what "we" intended to do. The province might have been excused for thinking that the federal government planned to finance the scheme itself, as an irrigation project under the Prairie Farm Rehabilitation Act. In the spring of 1948, however, Gardiner revealed that the federal government would take responsibility only for creating the reservoir, and any money for irrigation or hydroelectric works would have to come from the province.

At this point Gardiner ran into the roadblock that would prevent him from making any further progress: the coming to power of a new prime minister. Mackenzie King seems to have kept his nose out and left his Saskatchewan lieutenant free to act as he pleased. Louis St. Laurent, unlike King, took an interest in the project, but only because he wanted to kill it. It seems unlikely that St. Laurent had any interest in water conservation or in the prairie West. But Paul Martin, who was health minister at this time, later wrote that St. Laurent had "his doubts" about Gardiner, and that this aversion extended to his pet scheme.[22]

Gardiner was caught in the middle. He wanted to build a dam, but he was also a loyal soldier in the Liberal cause. Where the federal government had offered promises, it now became evasive. Gardiner could only tell the House of Commons that once the government decided to proceed, it would proceed. John Diefenbaker complained that trying to get information out of Gardiner was like "trying to pick up mercury with a fork."[23]

In mid-1950, six years after his first proclamation, Gardiner announced that he was ready to discuss plans for the South Saskatchewan dam with the Douglas government. He met with Douglas and the CCF cabinet, there was a flurry of telegrams between the two governments concerning "possible financial arrangements," but little was accomplished.[24] In early 1951 they met again, and Gardiner asked for a firm commitment from the province. Saskatchewan, he said, should agree to build secondary storage reservoirs, irrigation canals, and all power installations. Although this went far beyond what the federal minister had suggested in 1944, and beyond what Alberta had had to finance in its schemes, Douglas agreed in a letter to meet these demands. He got no reply.

Instead, Douglas learned that summer that Ottawa intended to appoint a royal commission to investigate the project—even though a federal official had told him that "no irrigation project in Canada has ever been so thoroughly and carefully documented."[25] The announcement caused some resentment in the West, since the federal government had set out on much larger schemes, such as the St. Lawrence Seaway, without any commission inquiry. Douglas saw little point to the inquiry, but he promised his full co-operation. The federal commission's report, tabled in Parliament in January 1953, suggested that Ottawa should avoid funding the project. On the one hand, it would provide "social returns...of great value to the region in which it is situated." On the other hand, the cost of building the dam would exceed "the economic returns to the Canadian people."[26]

Douglas publicly attacked the report's findings. He said in a press statement that the commission had used a vastly inflated estimate of prospective costs, cost figures which the head of the Saskatchewan Power Corporation had described as "an insult to the intelligence of any engineer familiar with the project."[27] Privately, Douglas had serious reasons to suspect that the report had been tailored to suit St. Laurent's demands. One member of the commission had met with Coldwell in Ottawa and admitted that he saw no reason for the inquiry, since the government had all the information it needed.[28] It appeared that Ottawa was looking for a reason to back out, partly for financial reasons and at least partly to please Alberta. Ernest Manning and his Social Credit government had high hopes for the irrigation projects along their part of the South Saskatchewan, and for years had opposed any allocation of water for a dam outside their borders. Alberta had intervened before the royal commission to argue against the province of Saskatchewan's plans. After the commission had finished its hearings, its secretary had returned to Saskatchewan and had tried to persuade Toby Nollet, the minister of agriculture, to "sit down with Alberta to discuss alternative projects."[29]

All in all, it was a situation that could only stimulate the fighting spirit in Saskatchewan's premier. From this point on, the initiative in promoting the South Saskatchewan scheme passed into Douglas's hands.

Having set out the errors contained in the commission's report, Douglas wrote to St. Laurent on January 23, 1953, saying that his government wanted to go ahead on the basis of the cost-sharing agreement reached with Gardiner two years earlier. He said flatly that "nothing in the findings of the Royal Commission has altered our position in this regard."[30] Three months later Gardiner replied on behalf of the federal government, saying that Ottawa was "prepared to consider a definite proposal from the Provincial government." Douglas, amazed, made Gardiner's letter public, and branded it "a pathetic attempt to evade the consequences of his failure to proceed with the project."[31] However, when Gardiner asked Douglas to make further concessions on the dam, Douglas made them. He pointed out that the federal government was building the St. Lawrence Seaway—an $850 million dollar project—at no cost to Ontario or Quebec. Douglas agreed, nonetheless, to pay a quarter of the cost of the main reservoir, plus the total cost of the electric and irrigation works.

Douglas now felt that he had gone more than halfway and in the spring of 1954 he wrote a straightforward letter to Gardiner telling the federal government to make up its mind and get on with a final agreement. St. Laurent took offense at the tone of this letter, and forbade Gardiner to have any further contact with Douglas. A few weeks later Gardiner sent a hand-written note to the premier from his farm at Lemberg, Saskatchewan: "I think it would be well if you and I were to meet unofficially."[32] They met at Douglas's office in Regina and drafted an amended letter setting out Saskatchewan's position. This letter may have soothed the prime minister's feelings, but he still would not be convinced that the project was in the national interest. He could not see the reason for spending millions to put "a lake in a dry area."[33]

Douglas realized that he was beaten. In a 1955 news release he said that "there seems to be little value in continuing negotiations at the present time."[34] The two sides continued corresponding, but as Douglas had surmised, they accomplished nothing. And so matters stood when the people of Canada turned Louis St. Laurent and his Liberals out of office in 1957.

On June 10, 1957, John Diefenbaker and his Conservatives took the most seats in a federal election and a few days later Diefenbaker formed a minority government. In early August, Douglas wrote to the new prime minister listing the issues that he regarded as topics for early discussion, including plans for a South Saskatchewan River dam. The chief negotiators were now all westerners—Douglas, Diefenbaker, and Douglas Harkness of Calgary, the minister of agriculture. Diefenbaker had long been a supporter of the scheme, and the talks made rapid progress. Less than a year after Douglas wrote his letter to Diefenbaker, the two governments signed an agreement. In July 1967, twenty-three years after the first signs of life from the federal government, Prime Minister Lester Pearson officially opened the main works of the dam.

And how did the dam come to be named after Jimmy Gardiner, the federal minister who failed to sell the scheme to his colleagues? Perhaps Douglas had something to do with it. In July 1950 Alvin Hamilton, an organizer for the provincial Conservatives, wrote to Premier Douglas seeking support for his proposal to name the dam after an eastern Tory who had supported the project. The premier's answer tells us something of his sense of history:

> I know that what I am going to suggest will sound very strange, coming from me, but I have had in the back of my mind for some time the idea that this dam, if it is proceeded with, ought to be called the Gardiner Dam. Mr. Gardiner has represented Saskatchewan in the federal cabinet since 1935, and if the dam is completed, it will be in large part due to his efforts. I don't need to tell you that I have disagreed with Mr. Gardiner on almost every item in domestic politics over the past twenty years.
>
> I don't know how many of my colleagues or other persons in Saskatchewan would share my ideas in this matter, and I have never voiced them publicly, because I would like to see the dam started before we begin worrying about the name for it."[35]

However the names were chosen, the dam became the Gardiner Dam, the reservoir behind it is called Diefenbaker Lake, and the picnic areas and campgrounds that look out on the lake are part of Douglas Provincial Park. The whole complex, said Douglas in 1967, "should be a constant reminder of the co-operation and help we have received from our fellow Canadians. It should make us ready and willing to extend the same help to other parts of Canada when they require it."[36]

15

Minister of Public Health

T HE REGINA MANIFESTO of 1933 declared that "every civilized community" owed its citizens a properly organized public health-care system. When Tommy Douglas took office in 1944 he was determined to improve the standard of health care in Saskatchewan, and he assumed the portfolio of minister of public health along with the title of premier. The programs he introduced over the next five years set a standard for the rest of Canada. In 1983, in a speech on the fiftieth anniversary of the manifesto, Douglas named the maintenance of the health-care system as a top priority for New Democrats, along with the campaign for full employment and the quest for world peace.[1]

Douglas had arrived in Saskatchewan with vivid memories of a childhood bone disease and of how his leg had been saved by chance. For him, this story became a symbol of the unfairness of the health-care system, and he told it often over the years: "I lay in a children's hospital in Winnipeg on and off for three years. My parents couldn't afford the services of an outstanding surgeon. I had my leg hacked and cut again and again, without any success. The only reason I can walk today, Mr. Speaker, is because a doctor doing charity work, one of the great bone surgeons of Winnipeg, who was later killed in the First World War, came into that hospital one day with a group of students, took an interest in my case, and took it over."[2]

Within his flock in Weyburn, Douglas had again seen the unjust results of a system that rationed medical care on the basis of personal wealth. By the time he became premier, he was more committed than ever to the idea that health care should be available to all.

Douglas served as minister of public health from 1944 to 1949. Over that period of time he introduced many innovations, including at least one North American first, a program to guarantee free access to hospitals. When he stepped down as health minister, the final advance—the creation of a universal medicare system—still lay ahead. The CCF would wait until 1961 before it had the money available to go ahead with public health insurance.

Douglas came to power in a province that had wide experience in financing health services with public funds. Saskatchewan had been in the forefront in providing government-assisted care for the mentally ill, the mentally handicapped, and victims of tuberculosis. From the pioneer days, many of the cities and towns had owned and operated their own hospitals. Starting in about 1920, many municipalities retained the services of a salaried general practitioner, and at a later date entered into contracts with medical specialists. By 1944 almost one-quarter of Saskatchewan's population was covered by municipal doctor plans, and some also paid into local hospital insurance plans. Co-operative associations and the organized medical profession itself had inaugurated medical-care insurance schemes. The CCF proposed that medical insurance should be extended to everyone, and even the Patterson Liberals promised in the legislature that they would support medicare—if Ottawa paid for it.

The stage was set, then, for a period of rapid development in the health-care field. Some critics complained that the public health post should have gone to a medical doctor, but the CCF caucus had none to offer—the nearest facsimile would have been old Doc Houze, a country veterinarian from Gravelbourg. Douglas, fortunately, had the ideals and energies for the task, and the determination to carry his ideas through. He took the measure of what the public wanted, came up with a set of programs, and motivated the people around him to get on with the job.

His time as public health minister also provided him with one of his classic after-dinner stories. As he told it on countless occasions, he was visiting the mental hospital in Weyburn when he met a patient walking around the grounds. The patient asked him who he was, and Douglas replied, "I'm the premier of Saskatchewan." The patient responded, "That's all right, you'll get over it. I thought I was Napoleon when I came here."

Douglas turned first for advice to Dr. Hugh MacLean, a founding leader of the Saskatchewan CCF who had retired to California. MacLean had opened his medical practice southeast of Regina the year after the province was formed, and had also entered the farmers' movement in the early days. In 1921 he stood in Regina as the federal candidate for the Progressive Party, and along with his young organizer M. J. Coldwell he ran the Progressives' only losing campaign in Saskatchewan. As a member of the CCF provincial executive in 1935, MacLean had fought to keep Tommy Douglas in the party when others wanted to expel him over his dealings with Social Credit.

MacLean returned briefly to Saskatchewan after the victory of 1944 and addressed the jubilant CCF summer convention on the subject of socialized medicine. He also conferred with Douglas on how to tackle the public health portfolio. The premier decided as a first step to conduct a systematic study of Saskatchewan's health-care needs, and he determined that he would hire the best professional help he could find. By the end of his first month in office Douglas had secured an order-in-council providing for the creation of a Health Services Survey Commission and had appointed its secretary, Dr. Mindel Sheps of Winnipeg. Mindel and her husband Dr. Cecil Sheps, who came to the Saskatchewan scene in 1945, were experienced physicians, as well as socialists of outstanding ability and great energy, and played a key part in laying the foundations for a new health-care system.

From his home in California Hugh MacLean maintained a brisk correspondence with Premier Douglas. In one letter he identified the questions that the survey commission should ask: Where did the gaps in the health-care system lie? How much were the people prepared to pay for? How could the government find new revenues to pay for health services?[3] MacLean also suggested the names of several doctors from inside and outside Saskatchewan who might help with the commission. For chairman, he proposed Dr. Henry Sigerist, professor of medical history at Johns Hopkins University in Baltimore. Douglas already knew Sigerist's name; the Swiss public health specialist had appeared before a House of Commons committee the previous year and had made a good impression. He phoned Sigerist and, as he said later, "I think he was so astonished that anyone would have the gall to ask him, and then to tell him that we couldn't pay anything except his expenses, that he came."[4]

The commission also included representatives from the medical, nursing, and dental professions, and a hospital administrator. To Douglas's disappointment, MacLean declined to serve. He did, however, continue to offer useful advice until his death in the mid-1950s. When the University of Saskatchewan inaugurated its degree program in medicine in 1952 Douglas recognized MacLean's services to the province in a letter; he said, "In a sense you are the spiritual godfather of both the Medical School and the University Hospital, as well as of our general health program as completed."[5]

Sigerist arrived in Regina on September 6, 1944. He had just a month in Saskatchewan before moving on to a job in India. In that short time, his commission toured the province, received sixty-six submissions from various interests, and laid its report on the premier's desk. The Sigerist report, brief as it was, laid out the pattern that Douglas and the CCF were to follow in developing their health programs. At the centre of the report lay the principle that every citizen has the right to medical care: "The policy for the future must therefore be to finance an increasing number of medical services for an increasing number of people from public funds. This will be a gradual development, the pace of which will be determined by the personnel, equipment and financial resources that can be made available for the purpose. *The goal is clear, it must be to provide complete medical services to all the people of the Province, irrespective of their economic status, and irrespective of whether they live in town or country.*"[6]

The Sigerist commission's report recommended a decentralized system for planning and managing the provision of health services.

Saskatchewan's population was widely scattered, and most of its earlier health programs had grown up at the local level. The commission proposed that the province should be divided into health districts, each with a headquarters and staff. The report also proposed the creation of a special body, the Health Services Planning Commission, to carry out ongoing research and to monitor new programs. It called for the construction of training centres for the mentally handicapped, and for free medical services for pensioners, widows, and orphans. It also pointed out the need for better care for expectant and new mothers in hospitals, for more public health nurses, and for school dental clinics.

As Sigerist travelled the province, nothing caught his attention more than the lack of plumbing. He had made acquaintance with the prairie outhouse and had read about the prairie winter. At one meeting with Douglas, he expressed surprise that the people of Saskatchewan did not suffer from chronic constipation. This comment may have spurred the government to provide financial support for the gradual installation of running water in the villages and on the farms. Often, during Douglas's years as premier, the glow from the bonfires lit up the prairie sky as the country people ceremonially burned their privies.

Dr. Sigerist and Premier Douglas also discussed the need for universal health insurance. They agreed that any launching of a general insurance system probably lay far in the future. The problem was not one of finding public support, for it appears that most people in Saskatchewan were eager for medicare. The largest obstacle, simply, was lack of money.

Saskatchewan had a large and active pro-medicare lobby called the State Hospital and Medical League. This group had brought together churches, co-operative associations, local governments, and women's groups, and claimed to have a mailing list of 5000 people by 1942. The doctors had recognized the strength of public feeling, and the Saskatchewan College of Physicians and Surgeons came out in 1942 in favour of "state-aided Health Insurance" on a fee-for-service basis.[7] However, the doctors demanded a share in the control of any medicare scheme—a demand that would prove a sticking point when Douglas finally moved to set up a medicare plan twenty years later.

The Douglas-Fines CCF executive agreed in 1943 on the outlines for a medicare system, and Douglas made very few changes in his ideas on health insurance after this date. The group agreed that such a plan should cover every citizen; that it should be paid for from general government revenues; that there should be no deterrent fees or premiums. The question of whether doctors should work on salary or receive a fee for each service provided was left open. The final proviso—and a crucial one— was that Ottawa must give some financial support.[8]

The Mackenzie King Liberals were considering a major expansion of social programs at this time. As part of the grand scheme for postwar reconstruction, the Government of Canada proposed, at the Dominion-Provincial Conference of 1945, to fund a national medicare scheme. However, King would not move ahead without general agreement from the provinces, and several provincial leaders opposed the idea of public health insurance.

Throughout his career as premier, Douglas hounded federal leaders to help Saskatchewan with a medical insurance plan, but he had no success. And without federal help, the CCF could not finance medicare. The province was already stretching its health-care budget, building new hospitals in Redvers, Eastend, Wawota, and dozens of other towns. Douglas could tell the legislature by 1954 that his government had doubled hospital capacity in the province. Where Saskatchewan had had the lowest number of hospital beds per capita of any province in 1944, it had the highest in 1954. Moreover, the CCF paid the bills for a costly program to provide free hospitalization. In the late 1950s the federal government under Diefenbaker agreed to pay some hospitalization costs, leaving the CCF free to move ahead with medicare. But it was not until July 1, 1968—after the Saskatchewan scheme had proven its effectiveness—that Lester Pearson's Liberals began to provide federal support for a broader scheme of health insurance.

In the absence of federal support for universal medicare, the CCF government was obliged to move step by step to make health care as accessible as it could. From the beginning, it took over the full cost of treatment for tuberculosis and cancer patients and for the care and treatment of psychiatric patients. A recently mustered-out RCAF pilot suggested in a meeting with Douglas that the province should have an air ambulance service; he agreed, and put the former pilot in charge of the operation.

In keeping with Sigerist's recommendation, the government established a Health Services Planning Commission. Its early inspiration came from its secretary, Dr. Mindel Sheps. Later, when her husband Cecil was appointed chairman, the two provided direction and drive as the planners moved forward on several fronts. Among the first tasks facing the commission was that of supporting the minister of health in his negotiations with the medical profession. By the end of 1944 these talks had borne fruit and the doctors agreed to provide service to 25,000 old-age pensioners, blind people, and mothers on social assistance, all at public expense.

Douglas acceded in these negotiations to the doctors' demand that they be paid on a fee-for-service basis, even though some in the CCF felt that doctors working for the public should earn a flat salary. Before the 1944 campaign the College of Physicians had suggested that the CCF was "a dangerous element."[9] Douglas showed with this action that he could compromise, but many of the doctors remained suspicious, and vocally so, that the socialists wanted to make them slaves to state medicine.

These were the first, though certainly not the last, of Douglas's negotiations with the doctors' union. One physician later described him as intelligent and idealistic, and praised him as the most accessible of premiers. But although the relationship remained proper—Douglas ensured that the medical profession was represented when its interests were at stake—it was never a cordial one. In the background lay the influence of the well-heeled American Medical Association, which Lord Stephen Taylor later described as "hysterically opposed to medicare."[10] The Saskatchewan physicians believed—correctly—that the CCF was moving, step by step, towards a state-controlled medical insurance system.[11] Henry Sigerist had written that the municipal doctor plans, a form of local medicare, already formed "the backbone of all medical services in the province" in 1944, and he recommended that the plans be extended and developed.[12] The College of Physicians and Surgeons opposed the idea and, by putting pressure on its members, made it almost impossible for them to pursue careers as municipal doctors on salary.

The Health Services Act that Douglas brought before the legislature in the fall of 1944 set out the framework for a new, decentralized Saskatchewan health-care system. The responsibility for planning and building hospitals and clinics, and for setting up public health programs, would lie with the regional boards in each health region. The province would provide financial support. The Health Services Planning Commission, along with the Department of Public Health, would try to insure that the local projects met provincial standards and fit in with the overall plan.

The government put considerable effort into publicizing the creation of the fourteen health regions. From the summer of 1945 through the spring of 1946, officers of the Health Services Planning Commission— chiefly Mindel Sheps and Tom McLeod, joined later by Dr. Orville Hjertas—travelled the province. They met with interested community leaders—municipal councillors, co-op directors, weekly newspaper editors—to talk about setting out regional boundaries and electing regional boards.

In most of the new regions the citizen boards took public health programs well beyond the traditional limits. They continued to immunize children against disease and to inspect drinking water, but they also launched health education campaigns and opened clinics for mothers and babies and, in some cases, instituted school dental programs.

Health Region No. 1, based in Swift Current, went the whole way. In 1946 the regional board and local doctors set up a district-wide medical insurance program, Canada's first. The program, partly financed by a special tax collected across the region, served as an excellent demonstration project for the later provincial plan. However, the doctors' union opposed the creation of any more such regional plans, and the Swift Current health insurance scheme remained a one-of-a-kind experiment.

It should be noted that there was no great outcry over the next decade for regionally organized medicare. Two other health regions voted against paying special taxes for health insurance in a 1955 referendum. Douglas blamed this setback on the fact that the farmers were broke, but it probably had more to do with the effectiveness of the medical lobby and the cautious mood that had taken hold of Saskatchewan after the first flush of reform.

With the health regions swinging into operation in early 1946, Douglas turned his attention to the problem of making hospital care available to everyone. Sigerist had advised the CCF to introduce free hospitalization gradually, starting with maternity cases. Douglas, however, decided to set up a complete program in one jump. The dominion government had offered in 1945 to help pay the cost of hospitalization, as with medicare. However, King's Liberals scrapped this proposal too, because some provinces resisted it. Douglas remained hopeful that Ottawa might change its stance eventually. Until then, Saskatchewan was on its own.

In embarking on the hospital insurance gamble, Douglas overruled the advice of his own planning commission. The planners reported that the province faced a huge hospital construction bill over the next few years. In addition, they pointed out that Saskatchewan lacked the technical, professional, and administrative staff to put a hospital insurance program into effect. Douglas, as minister of health, took due note of this information, but he judged that the risks of not proceeding outweighed any obstacles. In the spring session of 1946 he introduced a Hospital Services Act, and promised the legislature that he would have a province-wide program in operation on January 1, 1947.

Once again Douglas decided to seek additional expert help to work with the Drs. Sheps in putting the program into effect. He approached Dr. Fred Mott, deputy surgeon-general of the United States, a name that he said later was put forward by Henry Sigerist. Douglas flew to Washington and put his charms to work on Mott. Among other things, he told the American doctor how much he had admired his father, Dr. John R. Mott, a missionary and a leading figure in the American social gospel movement. The younger Mott had lived in Montreal and was married to a Canadian. He not only agreed to come to Saskatchewan but he brought along an experienced colleague, Dr. Len Rosenfeld.

Even with this infusion of talent, the planning commission despaired of meeting its deadline. In the fall of 1946 a delegation of planners came to the premier's office to ask for a one-year extension to January 1, 1948. Douglas rejected this appeal on the spot. He knew that he would be calling an election for mid-1948, that any major new program must have a trial period before the voters accepted it, and six months would not be long enough. He told his advisers to give him a plan for putting the scheme into effect for the start of 1947—or he would find others who would.

Douglas, again, was taking a risk. If he announced the start of a program which then broke down, if the new insurance scheme could not pay its bills, then hospitals and patients might suffer. His staff stepped up the pace of their work. Malcolm Taylor, at the time the new secretary of the planning commission, later wrote, "It was a period of feverish activity, reminiscent of mobilization in 1939."[13]

Across the province, many hospital directors expressed grave concern about the hospital insurance plan. They worried that the CCF was working towards a government take-over of the hospitals. The hospitals had been built by municipal governments or charitable groups such as the Catholic nursing orders. All had strong ties with their local communities. The Catholics, in particular, had long been schooled in the belief that socialism and confiscation went hand in hand. When he met with leaders of the hospital association in his office, Douglas reassured them that what the government proposed was an insurance program, one designed to pay their bills and not to take over their property. The local citizens' boards would still manage their institutions. He did not have time, he said, "to keep track of every bed-pan in Melfort."[14] The hospitals would find, in fact, that one of their biggest headaches—collecting fees from their former patients—would become a thing of the past.

Despite the fretting of the hospitals and the fact that Fred Mott's people worked under battlefield conditions—their office was an old retail store, their desks were plywood panels on trestles, and their filing cabinets were cardboard boxes on the floor—the scheme was launched on schedule on January 1, 1947. At the end of that year Mott wrote in the *American Journal of Public Health* that 93 per cent of the population of Saskatchewan was covered by the new scheme, the only exceptions being some remote northern communities and some people who were covered by other programs.[15]

There was scattered resistance to the new hospitalization tax. Although Douglas in his later career would strongly oppose medicare premiums, his 1947 hospital plan depended on the collection of a special tax from every family. At least one dissident paid a $50 fine after convincing some of his fellow citizens in the hamlet of Arran to withhold their tax.[16] However, by the time of the 1948 election, the CCF would boast of the new insurance plan as one of its major achievements.

One project dear to Douglas's heart was the creation of a university medical centre. He overcame those in cabinet and among his advisers who said the province could not afford to build a medical school and teaching hospital, and work began in 1948. The first dean, Wendell Macleod, set out to teach a new generation of family doctors about the social aspects of medicine and the special needs of Saskatchewan. His work flourished until the medicare crisis of 1962. Macleod and some of his colleagues were blacklisted by the medical profession when they came out in support of medicare, and several of them left the province.

In late 1949 Douglas left the health portfolio and became the minister of co-operative development. His successor in the health portfolio was Tom Bentley from Swift Current, a long-time member of Saskatchewan farm movements and of the CCF. After serving a term in the House of Commons, Bentley was elected to the legislature in a 1949 by-election. He was a strong administrator and parliamentarian, and soon established a close rapport with his staff.

Saskatchewan's Public Health Department compiled an outstanding record of success under Tommy Douglas, and it continued to expand over the next decade. The regional boards, with provincial support, developed preventive programs in areas such as sanitation and immunization, and the department created new divisions of health education and nutrition.

Douglas and his government also introduced sweeping changes to the mental health-care system, but these reforms were not so widely acclaimed. The budget of the Public Health Department's Psychiatric Branch increased five-fold while Douglas was minister and doubled again before he left the province. During the 1940s and 1950s, Saskatchewan developed a reputation for thoughtful progress in its programs for the mentally ill. However, owing to circumstances that were largely beyond the government's control, it got little credit for its work either from mental health support groups or from the public at large.

Douglas had a special interest in mental health care, dating back at least to the early 1930s and his graduate thesis on the "mentally and morally subnormal." When he became health minister in 1944, he set out immediately to improve conditions at Saskatchewan's mental hospitals. More than 3000 patients were crammed into the human dumping grounds at Weyburn and North Battleford, some sleeping in porches or corridors, with no distinction made between the mentally ill and the retarded. A report from C. M. Hincks of the Canadian Mental Hygiene Association, who made his third tour of Weyburn and North Battleford in 1945, suggested that patient populations should be cut by almost half if the hospitals were to function properly.[17]

The major form of treatment for the patients was work therapy, and the hospitals contained upholstery and knitting workshops, bakeries, and large farms. The goods produced were sold to help with the hospital upkeep, so that the best workers, the sanest and steadiest patients, were those least likely to be discharged.

In early 1946, with a new administrator in place, six employees at the North Battleford hospital were convicted of theft. Douglas assigned his legal adviser, Morris Shumiatcher, to investigate, along with his friend Major Bill Bethel, the business manager of the Weyburn mental hospital. They reported that pilfering from the hospital—of linen, food and alcohol, building supplies, and more—was almost universal and had cost the taxpayer hundreds of thousands of dollars over time. The corruption had started at the top, they said, with a former director who regarded the hospital as "his own private estate."[18] They recommended the dismissal of thirteen workers. The savings that Douglas achieved at this hospital alone were enough to buy a second plane for the air ambulance service.

In trying to raise the standard of care in the mental hospitals, Douglas also took steps to improve working conditions for the nurses and orderlies. Before long, he found himself torn between his pro-union feelings and his desire to have the hospitals staffed by trained people. An early act of his government allowed the workers to unionize, and within a year they had won higher wages and shorter work weeks. Attendants who had earned as little as $70 a month while working a seventy-two-hour week watched their hourly rates triple. Douglas knew, though, that many hospital workers had been hired by the previous government on the basis of their Liberal affiliation, and not for their qualifications. In 1946 his office asked the Public Service Commission to "weed out" people with less than a grade 11 education; under pressure to hire war veterans, it also called for the dismissal of married women.[19] Not surprisingly, relations between the new hospital workers' union and the CCF cooled, and the CCF got no benefit at the polls from having raised wages and shortened hours.

The union eventually won the battle. In 1948, when the Psychiatric Nurses' Act prescribed qualifications for mental hospital nurses—the first law in Canada to do so—a "grandfather clause" went into effect. All of the attendants then on staff at Weyburn and North Battleford won automatic status as registered psychiatric nurses.

Douglas made a real effort to carry out enlightened policies. He made immediate physical improvements at Weyburn and North Battleford, and, after intensive special studies, he had separate centres for the mentally handicapped planned and constructed.* His government passed a law stating that only physicians—and not relatives, police, or judges—could commit people to mental hospitals. Unfortunately the hope expressed in the 1944 Sigerist report, that the mentally ill might be integrated into the community, remained wishful thinking. Sigerist had suggested that the mentally ill could be treated at regional clinics, with more serious cases residing at local hospitals. However, the family physicians were strongly opposed to the idea of having to deal with mental patients. Douglas ordered a publicity campaign in an effort to improve public attitudes towards the mentally ill and mental health care. But the campaign generated hostility and anxiety at the grass roots. Management and staff at the mental hospitals, for their part, still resisted the idea of discharging the more lucid patients—perhaps because they feared it might turn the hospitals into madhouses.

Throughout its time in government, the CCF found it difficult to attract top-calibre psychiatrists to Saskatchewan. A CCF MLA complained as late as 1960 that the treatment programs at the North Battleford hospital were still a mess, and he blamed a long history of "puling, indecisive, ineffective management."[20] Douglas agreed that he would like to see changes, but he said that no qualified doctors were available.

In the late 1940s Hincks's Mental Hygiene Association changed its name to the Canadian Mental Health Association, and began to broaden its base as a national support group for the mentally ill. Douglas, in an effort to promote the mental health issue, enlisted every member of his cabinet in the CMHA by 1951. However, the lobby group soon became a thorn in the government's side. Dr. Griff McKerracher, the head of the government's Psychiatric Branch, became a spokesman for the association and publicly chastized the CCF for the shortcomings of the programs that he was paid to carry out. His successor after 1955, Dr. F. S. Lawson,

---

* Sigerist and C. M. Hincks recommended that the CCF move towards a program of sterilizing the mentally ill and the mentally handicapped in order to stop them from propagating. However, despite his earlier enthusiasm for eugenics, Douglas never set up any sterilization program in Saskatchewan.

also carried on a public crusade, focusing mostly on his demand for the construction of regional mental hospitals.

The critics had some valid arguments. By the late 1950s the big mental institutions remained dismal and depressing, and many unqualified workers remained from the old regime. However, the fundamental problems—the lack of any cure for most mental illnesses and the stigma still attached to mental illness by the general public—lay beyond the government's control. Although the discovery of new drugs would allow the mental hospitals to start releasing their patients into the streets after 1960, the underlying problems would persist across Canada into the 1980s. The complaining by his own staff hurt Douglas, since he felt his government had done its best. "There is no government activity," he wrote in 1957, "which has had such a rapid increase in expenditures as the Psychiatric Branch. However, instead of telling the public how much has been done to improve conditions in mental institutions, and in the treatment and care of mental patients, the whole aim of the Psychiatric Branch seems to be to tell the public how little we have done in this regard."[21]

16

Labour Reform

TOMMY DOUGLAS was the son of a trade unionist and had earned his own union card in Winnipeg's printing trade. He believed that a socialist society would right the historic wrongs suffered by workers, and he saw organized labour as indispensable to the building of a socialist movement. The rich had gathered their wealth by taking control of industry and appropriating the proceeds; one aim of the CCF was to restore to working people the dignity and position that was rightfully theirs.[1] Once in power, however, Douglas learned that labour's claims often clash with, rather than complement, those of consumers, taxpayers, and the poor. Leadership placed him in the delicate position of having to defend working people while discouraging organized labour's tendencies to form a new elite.

By 1942, when he took the CCF leadership in Saskatchewan, the federal party had adopted a clear set of priorities for labour. In the postwar world, new CCF governments, federal and provincial, would recognize labour's long-deferred rights. The party promised "the enactment of legislation which will compel the recognition of bona fide trade unions, enforce collective bargaining, establish fair wage levels...protect the workers against victimization and discrimination, and generally establish organized labour as a partner in industry with a proper share in its control and management."[2] From the time Tommy Douglas took the premier's oath in Saskatchewan, he and his colleagues were under pressure to fulfil this CCF program.

Up until the Second World War, Saskatchewan was predominantly a rural community. The workers in the railway shops and yards across the province belonged to trade unions, as did some urban construction workers, but, on the whole, industrial workers had only a slight influence on the order of business. The first premier, Walter Scott, was a veteran of the International Typographers' Union; in the years before 1920 he introduced some moderate labour reforms, such as safety standards and a ban on child labour. However, Scott's successors, Liberal and Conservative, built little upon this foundation. In 1938 the Saskatchewan Liberals established the legal right of workers to organize, free from employer intimidation. But the law was toothless: there were no penalties for employers who refused to bargain with their workers. Even more than their counterparts in Ottawa, Premier Patterson and his colleagues were reluctant to mount an honest defence of the trade union movement. They felt it would be suicide for the government of a one-crop province, intent on spreading the economic risks by developing new industries, to scare off potential investors and employers.

For its part, organized labour before 1944 showed little interest in political action anywhere in Canada. Among the new industrial unions of the Canadian Congress of Labour (CCL), several prominent leaders in Ontario worked for the CCF. However, the movement as a whole was torn by internal squabbles, intercongress rivalries, and Communist infiltration. The oldest and largest body, the Trades and Labour Congress (TLC), maintained its traditional suspicion of direct political action and held back from endorsing any party. Saskatchewan industry expanded with the war, and the CCL established itself in the meat-packing plants and some big retail stores. But even when the CCL adopted the CCF nationally as "the political arm of labour," it caused no immediate swing to labour participation in Saskatchewan CCF activities. Individual unionists came forward, but only a handful of union locals voted to affiliate with the party.

On taking office, Douglas acted quickly on a new deal for labour. The blizzard of new legislation that hit the assembly in the fall of 1944 included the bills that created the present system of labour laws for Saskatchewan. The CCF created a Department of Labour, a ministry which would devote its full attention to worker-management relations. Amendments to the Public Service Act gave civil servants, for the first time in Canada, the right to join unions. Douglas also invited some of the national CCF's leading labour specialists to Saskatchewan to advise the government. Andrew Brewin, a Toronto labour lawyer, was largely responsible for drafting a new Trade Union Act. Working together with the premier's staff, the advisers from Ontario produced a Magna Carta for Saskatchewan labour, guaranteeing labour's right to organize and bargain collectively and creating a Labour Relations Board with worker representation.

By 1946 a Douglas aide could write that the CCF was certifying trade unions in cases where 50 per cent of the workers signed union cards, and protecting workers against being fired for union activity. The government had imposed strict penalties for unfair practices, increased workers' compensation levels, and guaranteed a minimum wage and two weeks' holiday.[3]

From the beginning, though, some prominent members of the national party expected more than Douglas could give. Saskatchewan signalled the breakthrough that would set the stage for further victories, provincial and national: Douglas and his colleagues were to set up a model of government that would meet the specifications of socialists across the country. This meant not only labour legislation, but an ongoing partnership with the Canadian Congress of Labour in industrial affairs. David Lewis, the national secretary and party theoretician, wrote to Douglas a month after the 1944 election, suggesting that the CCL should help draft the new legislation: "From the point of the view of the CCF in other provinces, the accomplishments of your government in the field of labour policy will be of absolutely decisive importance."[4]

The Congress was a new and untried body in Saskatchewan. The CCF's personal and political ties with local units of the rival Trades and Labour Congress were much stronger. Before long, the relationship between the government and the CCL solidified into one of continuing irritation. The province's TLC officials carried on their tradition of passivity from Liberal days, turning up once a year for a discussion with cabinet. The CCL's leaders nagged the government constantly, perceptibly chilling the legislature's attitudes towards organized labour and its demands.

One important source of friction throughout Douglas's seventeen years as premier was the performance of Charles Cromwell Williams as minister of labour. Williams was a railway telegrapher by trade, one of half a dozen railway workers elected as rookie MLAs in 1944, all of them from rail unions associated with the TLC. Unlike the others, Williams had a track record as a politician, as mayor of Regina, and had developed a gift for rolling up huge electoral margins. Charlie Williams had to be recognized as a political power and included in the Douglas cabinet. Unfortunately, he possessed only slender talents in other areas, such as running his department or advocating the cause of labour within cabinet.

Williams had run afoul of the CCL during his term as mayor over his perceived lack of support for a strike at a wartime assembly plant. When Douglas appointed him labour minister in 1944, the CCL accused the premier of selling out to the rival congress. The Regina Labour Council and the local CCL office called on Douglas to fire Williams immediately, but he refused, then and later. He could see no alternative to Williams, certainly not one who would carry the same popularity with the general public. Williams was a favourite in town and country; he drew support from the TLC's railwaymen and tradesmen, and from farmers and small business people too. "I have never met a man more willing, nicer, or more decent," David Lewis wrote to Douglas, but he added, "At the same time I have seldom met a man less adequately equipped for an important job such as he has."[5]

Douglas never liked firing ministers or anyone else. His resolve was stiffened in this case by the harsh demands of the local agents of the Canadian Congress of Labour. The statesmen of the congress—Fred Dowling, Charlie Millard, Pat Conroy, and especially Aaron Mosher—had done fair service for the CCF in Ontario, but they were also engaged in a power struggle among themselves. The CCL spokesmen in Regina, Alex McAuslane and Cy Palmer, were proteges of Pat Conroy, the general secretary of the congress, and had limited support from other national labour leaders. McAuslane, the first vice-president of the CLC, was a blustering character who liked to dismiss his adversaries as "labour rats" and "scabs."[6] Douglas considered some of the organizers that McAuslane hired to be Communists, and he wrote to Lewis, "With the communists running the show and McAuslane charging around like a bull in a china shop the CCL is well on its way to committing hari kari in Saskatchewan."[7]

Charlie Williams kept his job as minister until 1964, with Douglas compensating for his weaknesses along the way. The premier took some of the Labour workload onto himself; for example, he mediated in a 1948 coal strike in Estevan. He also named strong deputy ministers of labour, people with a sympathy for industrial unionism. Ken Bryden was referred to Douglas by David Lewis. Bryden's successor, Hub Elkin, came out of the Saskatchewan CCL, where he had once written stinging criticisms of C. C. Williams.

Another strain on the link between the government and the CCL was a noisy difference of opinion as to whether the congress should have a monopoly in organizing the civil service. In the name of the crown, civil servants in every province had always been denied the right to argue for a better deal. Douglas had promised during the 1944 campaign that government workers would get full rights to organize and bargain collectively. He knew of their plight from his own riding, where the Weyburn mental hospital staff made up an important part of the population. Saskatchewan's civil servants rewarded the CCF campaign in 1944 with substantial support, not only in Weyburn but throughout the province. Douglas and his colleagues took office confident that they had the good will of their troops.

With the election over, the CCL moved in. McAuslane and Palmer spearheaded the drive. Throughout the fall of 1944 these two officials did far more shouting than listening, and at a time when Douglas and the government were preoccupied with dozens of pressing matters. McAuslane announced from the start, against the advice of his local officers, that he wanted the entire civil service certified as a single bargaining unit. The CCL signed up the telephone workers, Saskatchewan Power workers, and the staff in the two mental hospitals. However, workers in the government departments chose to go with the TLC, and when the Labour Relations Board counted the union cards the TLC was the clear winner.

The workers in the departments made their decision for obvious reasons. The Civil Service Association, through no fault of its own, had always been denied the right to bargain like a regular trade union, but it had developed its own leadership, program, and esprit de corps. It welcomed Douglas's election promise to establish a government personnel system based on the merit principle. The civil servants understood, better than anyone else, that previous regimes had abused the service for political purposes. It did not help the CCL, in its attempt to take over, that its spokesmen made so much of their preferred relationship with the ruling party.

McAuslane made no attempt to work with the Civil Service Association, branding it a "company union" and a "scab" union. He bypassed the association's leadership and called a meeting where he directed rather than invited the audience to sign up with his organization. This meeting lost the civil service to the Congress of Labour. Both McAuslane and Pat Conroy, the CCL secretary-treasurer in Toronto, complained to Douglas that he had promised the congress the right to organize the Saskatchewan civil service. The civil servants' rejection of their efforts, they said, marked a failure on the part of Douglas and his cabinet to deliver on a promise. When McAuslane confronted Douglas in the premier's office, Douglas said that he had promised simply to welcome the CCL to Saskatchewan if the congress decided to organize the civil service. He did not regard this as a promise to deliver his workers, gift-wrapped, to the CCL. Indeed, he said, if he had made such a promise, it would have violated the terms of the Trade Union Act the unions were clamouring for—an act which gave all workers complete freedom of choice in deciding which, if any, union they would join.

Douglas offered, however, to get McAuslane out of the mess he had made for himself. He went to the Labour Relations Board and asked that the civil service be split into three bargaining units, "for ease of negotiations."[8] The board agreed. The mental hospital, power, and telephone workers went to the CCL, and the government departments stayed with the TLC. Down the road, this division would make the government's bargaining sessions with its workers harder, rather than easier, as the rival congresses competed to see who could win the fattest contracts.

Locals of the Canadian Congress of Labour became the agents for the power and telephone workers in 1944, and for workers in other crown industries as they opened up. It was the contract talks between the government and the CCL unions, representing crown corporation workers, that killed hopes for a new era of socialist labour relations. By their very nature, these talks were confrontational. At the national level, CCL leaders continued to claim a special relationship with the CCF, and Douglas met conscientiously with the Saskatchewan representatives of the congress. The premier took the role of labour's chief spokesman in cabinet, and he retained the confidence of the unions—so much so that he was labour's overwhelming choice to lead the new national NDP in 1961. Within the party, however, support for labour was waning. By 1948 even the radical Joe Phelps blamed concessions to labour for the party's election losses in that year.

The CCL unions expected from the beginning that the Saskatchewan government would be the pace setter for the country in offering wages and benefits to its workers. They saw this as the duty of a provincial socialist government to its national movement and to its labour arm. But Saskatchewan was only starting to recover from the Depression. It still carried a heavy debt load, along with the psychological scars left by drought and farm foreclosure. Saskatchewan's people had more recent experience with sharing poverty than with sharing the wealth, and while many people supported labour's right to organize (as the farmers had done two decades earlier), they were not prepared to give labour a preferred economic position—either at their own expense, or at the expense of the publicly owned corporations.

Whatever the prior expectations—that the government would be a model employer, that its unions would be co-operative—the two sides soon found themselves tangled in the old labour-management dance of confrontation and bluff. George Cadbury, the government's chief industrial officer, lamented that the traditional system "forced both parties to manoeuvre and adopt belligerent attitudes once a year." But Cadbury's proposed solution, to replace collective bargaining with a yearly fixing of contracts by an "independent" tribunal, would have amounted to a direct assault on the union position. Douglas declined the idea.[9]

In November 1948, workers at the Saskatchewan Government Insurance Office walked out on strike. The union had proposed a 49 per cent wage increase, at a time when inflation was running at under 3 per cent. When talks broke down, the labour side blamed Oak Valleau, the former cabinet minister who now chaired SGIO, saying that he did not understand the collective bargaining process. The government saw the walkout as simply an attempt to force a crisis. Douglas wrote, "The issue is whether the increase will be reasonable or unreasonable, and also whether the rather extreme tactics of the union are the way for the government and trade unions to work together."[10]

Following the settlement of this strike—thanks in large part to the intervention of Pat Conroy—Douglas wrote to Aaron Mosher, the CCL president, expressing his unease about the "fundamental lack of good-will and understanding of the kind that is necessary...to develop the good relations which are implied in the alliance between the CCF and the CCL." He continued: "There is no possibility of the Insurance workers, or any other government employees securing a level of wages substantially out of line with their contemporaries in this province...We shall not...be able even to discuss the kind of wages currently demanded by several unions...It would be tantamount to exacting a levy on the vast majority of our citizens for a mere handful of their fellows."[11] As it turned out, though, the government failed to hold the line. Five years after this strike, wages at SGIO were 25 per cent above those at Saskatchewan's private insurance companies, none of which the CCL ever organized.

Beyond the wage issue lay an even greater one, the question of whether Insurance Office employees or any other government workers had the right to shut down government services. Some ministers, including Fines, questioned this right. Their thinking seems to have influenced Douglas when he said, "There can be no opportunity for any group to use their economic or political power to establish a favoured position among their fellows except by consent of the community as a whole, expressed through their democratic franchise. That is what the CCF stands for."[12]

For the first time, the potential conflict between labour's rights and the government's responsibility to maintain services became a reality. As it turned out, though, the Douglas government would not feel itself obliged to ban civil service strikes. With the help of mediators who had some knowledge of both labour and politics, the CCF avoided any further major work stoppages.

In May 1950, workers at Saskatchewan Power threatened to go on strike and turn the lights out on the prairies. The newspapers reported that "informed union sources" were warning that the CCL would withdraw its support from the government unless contract talks resumed. John Brockelbank, the chairman of the Power Corporation, replied that the government had "no intention of granting special favours in return for support."[13] The strike was averted, with some help from national officers of the trade union movement and the party.

In 1954, after a crop failure, the government ordered the crown corporations to withhold any general wage increase. The Saskatchewan Federation of Labour (CCL) attacked the move as "anti-labour, reactionary, and completely dictatorial." Douglas replied in a public statement that "no group in the community is entitled to a larger share of a smaller cake."[14]

The next year, Saskatchewan Power and its workers got into another dispute, and again a strike was averted, but only after David Lewis had travelled west from Ontario to mediate. The government was maintaining labour peace, but some CCF supporters suspected that it was caving in to the unions for the sake of its political friends in other provinces. The people remained wary of the potential influence of organized labour on the government, a mood that carried over to the end of the decade when the CCF's alliance with labour in the New Party aroused widespread resistance in Saskatchewan.

The scuffling between the CCF and the CCL obscured the gains made by Saskatchewan labour inside and outside government. Union membership doubled during the Douglas period to almost 30,000 by 1961. The minimum wage law, and the forty-four-hour week improved the lives of many workers, along with the provisions for statutory holidays and annual vacations. The workers' compensation system greatly increased its benefits, allowing injured workers to support their families. The Douglas cabinet showed it was serious about protecting unions, taking over a privately owned box factory in 1945 when management refused to bargain with its workers.

Labour victories grew less frequent after the CCF's first term. The Federation of Labour was still pressing in 1960 for a forty-hour week. The minimum wage law left farm workers unprotected. The government, anxious to provide jobs for veterans, was reluctant to hire married women for several years after the war, and had support in this from many conservative labour leaders. Union militants found themselves consistently outvoted at CCF conventions. "We would leave the convention licking our wounds," said Walter Smishek, later an NDP cabinet minister, "saying, 'another convention, another beating.' "[15]

At the end of the Douglas years in Saskatchewan, the dream of "democracy in the workplace" was as distant as it had been in the strike year of 1919. The government made several attempts to start joint consultations within its own operations, but they appear to have arisen as a response to crisis, like the expropriation of the Prince Albert box factory. These efforts quickly petered out.

Few in the cabinet were keen on these experiments—Fines later called the abortive labour-management committees "fifth wheels"—but organized labour was even more reluctant.[16] Years after George Cadbury proposed to the CCL that it should name representatives to crown corporation boards, the unions were still looking at the idea. Cy Palmer, for one, argued that putting workers on boards would "soften up our people too much."[17]

Tommy Douglas, looking back, concluded that the new unions had trouble attracting interest among their members even for conventional purposes, let alone experiments in management. The Saskatchewan unions saw any offer of consultation, he said, as "a government plot to get the workers tied up." Corporation managers, meanwhile, were preoccupied with their own growing pains. "We were never strong enough in any industry or any factory to have the workers running anything," he said later. "We had the hope that as time went on, crown corporations would get strong enough that the trade union could have a part of the action, to put some money in, to get partial ownership. But that was viewed with great suspicion by even the most advanced agricultural organizations."[18]

The strains on the government-union relationship eased after 1955. The CCL developed a home-grown Saskatchewan leadership more attuned to the politics of a rural province. In 1956 the industrial unions elected their first MLA, William Davies. In the same year, the Canadian Congress of Labour and the Trades and Labour Congress merged, ending the years of conflict. The government's negotiators grew more skilled, and labour-management relations in the public sector stabilized, but the result was more in keeping with the traditions of private sector bargaining than with any socialist pattern.

Douglas succeeded over the years in avoiding an open split, as his five election victories show. There is reason to believe, however, that these tensions played a part in his first major political defeat in 1962, when Saskatchewan voters rejected him and his New Democratic Party. As premier, Douglas maintained the respect of both farmers and organized labour. However, some Saskatchewan voters regarded his departure as a sellout, a sign that labour now dominated a socialist movement that had been cradled and nurtured in the prairie soil.

17

Planning for Development

THE PROGRAM which brought the Douglas team to power might well have been called "Operation Bootstraps." The hazards of depending on a one-crop economy showed themselves everywhere in Saskatchewan, in the enormous provincial debt, public and private, in the neglected roads and the shabby homes and public buildings. The CCF and its supporters were determined to plan and build a new province, but it seemed they would have to go it alone.

If one word pointed the way, it was *diversification*—of agricultural production and of economic activity generally. The previous Liberal government had realized this too and had tried to attract investment, particularly in wartime industries. However, in the eyes of private investors, the national wheat bin was not an attractive prospect as a manufacturing centre, mostly because of its location. They chose to invest elsewhere, and the province was denied any important share of the wartime industrial boom. The people of Saskatchewan, unfortunately, had very little money to invest. Investment requires an accumulation of investible funds. Saskatchewan had only an accumulation of debt—the heaviest burden of debt in Canada. It may be just as well that Douglas and his CCF cabinet colleagues had not been schooled in the "laws" of traditional economics, or what happened in Saskatchewan might never have taken place.

From the early days, Saskatchewan governments had experimented with socialization of industry—although they would never have called it that. They set up hail-insurance schemes and operated creameries. They even considered establishing grain-handling systems and operating railway lines. The government had operated the telephone system since before 1910, and had made an end to Prohibition in the 1920s with the opening of the provincial liquor stores. Saskatchewan also had what was probably the most broadly based co-operative movement in the country. Its largest co-operative, the Wheat Pool, was also the largest business in the province.

As Douglas took office, the community was poised for a new round of industrial development. Saskatchewan had tired of waiting for someone from outside to get things rolling. Douglas had promised action, and he would deliver—probably more than he expected, considering the efforts of Joe Phelps, his minister of natural resources. The intention was to expand and diversify the province's economic base, to increase the provincial income, and to spend the resulting tax dollars on roads, schools, and social programs.

The CCF, in 1933, had agreed to work for "a planned, socialized economic order." If the government was to secure economic growth, it would have to own many of the key industries. The Regina Manifesto declared that the first step of a socialist government would be "the setting up of a National Planning Commission consisting of a small body of economists, engineers, and statisticians." Alongside this commission, citizen boards would operate the state-owned corporations "for the public, and not for the private profit of a small group of owners or financial administrators."[1] As declarations of intent, these words have a fine ring. As a guide to organization and management, they leave most questions unanswered. Somehow, Douglas and his colleagues would have to turn these prayerful incantations into workable plans for action. To the government's lasting credit, it succeeded, even if it made some mistakes in the process. Along the way, it set some new standards for the administration of government in Canada.

In reflecting on the CCF government's experience in Saskatchewan, Meyer Brownstone, one of its leading public servants, has identified two key elements. First, the government was committed to using socialist means and the power of the state to achieve its goals. Second, the CCF cabinet (and Douglas in particular) were committed to making the government machine a rational, planning institution "of the highest order possible," while at the same time keeping in touch with the voters and the people's organizations.[2] To this should be added a third element. The government was determined that the new boards and agencies it set up should not escape the traditional control of the cabinet and the legislature. If anything, these controls should be strengthened.

In devising means for maintaining control over the bureaucrats, and at the same time giving them the scope to exercise their professional skills and initiative, the Douglas government made a great contribution to the practice of public management. One senior civil servant later commented, "It was this sense of tremendous freedom that made the Saskatchewan public service so attractive to those of us that worked there."[3] This sense of freedom fostered a high degree of loyalty to the government, and especially to Tommy Douglas. Compared to more recent bureaucracies, the Douglas administration was small enough to encourage a high degree of informality. Most of the senior public servants knew Douglas personally, and had a chance to exchange opinions with him—in the cafeteria, if not in his office.

Douglas and his ministers appreciated professionalism, and sought out and encouraged advisers who worked in a professional manner. Many of the new recruits shared or sympathized with the CCF philosophy; but there were others, equally loyal to Douglas, who wanted simply to gain professional experience, and who would openly disavow any connection with the party. Douglas sometimes had to defend the presence of these political outsiders. One top adviser recalled watching the premier meet with some irate party members who were unhappy about the appointment of an expert who would have failed their blood test. Douglas cautioned them, "It's easier to make a socialist out of an engineer than it is to make an engineer out of a socialist."[4]

The road to political success can be a rough one, and during its first two years in power the Douglas government hit some jarring potholes. To get started on its economic program the government needed a plan, an organization, and money, and it lacked all three. Clarence Fines and Douglas were able to shore up Saskatchewan's credit rating in their talks with big lenders. Beyond this, they could only try to put some of their store of ideas into effect.

During the election campaign, Douglas had beaten the drum for "chemurgy," the process by which Saskatchewan grain would be converted into plastics, fabrics, and fuels. "Whether we know it or not," he enthused, "science has opened the door to a new world of infinite possibilities."[5] This crusade had caused some unfavourable comment from the experts—one Manitoba scientist labelled the CCF's hopes "chembicility"—but Douglas and Phelps maintained their enthusiasm.[6] In September 1944 the new premier announced that H. W. Monahan, one of the leading lights of the chemurgy movement, had taken a position in the Department of Natural Resources. Monahan was to begin at once to "map out plans for the development of Saskatchewan industries" based on the use of agricultural products.[7] After this, the chemurgy project fell into obscurity, although Monahan popped up again in 1945 as the expert who advised the government to make its ill-fated foray into the wool-products business.

In other areas, the CCF got better results. The government's Economic Advisory Committee studied the economics of automobile insurance and fire insurance. Reassured by their report, the cabinet agreed to a proposal from Fines and made insurance its first commercial venture. Early in 1945 the Saskatchewan Government Insurance Office came into being, and over the years proved to be a popular and profitable undertaking. The government made another prudent move when it directed the Saskatchewan Power Commission to start buying up the small local power companies around the province. Until 1944 the commission had acted mostly as a regulator of the numerous privately and municipally owned utilities. It now took the first steps towards creating a state-owned, province-wide electric power network.

These initiatives would have absorbed the full attention of most governments, but the Saskatchewan CCF had a long list of ideas for potential businesses. Before 1944, Phelps's party committee on natural resources had proposed "the eventual and complete socialization" of all natural resources under provincial control.[8] By election time, various party spokesmen were talking about running airlines, coal-processing plants, fish plants, and woollen mills. As minister of natural resources, Phelps found himself in the driver's seat, and he determined to follow the trail his committee had mapped out: to develop Saskatchewan's resources, using Saskatchewan labour, to meet Saskatchewan's needs and to generate the income necessary to finance the province's social development. This formula won favour with a segment of the public that went well beyond the membership of the CCF.

By the end of 1945 Douglas found his government in charge of several enterprises based on the processing of primary products—timber, fish, fur, wool, hides, and clay. Each enterprise stood alone as a separate entity, with a general manager responsible to Phelps. Within his department, Phelps also set up a northern air service and a radio-telephone network. His colleagues usually learned of developments only after they had taken place, but if they asked him to slow the pace, he would reply, "Never say whoa in the middle of a puddle!" The puddle proved to be deeper, and the prairie gumbo much stickier, than Phelps had anticipated. By the end of 1945 some of his new businesses were running up embarrassing financial losses.

The CCF's unsuccessful ventures—the "problem children," as the senior advisers dubbed them—never really threatened the financial health of the government, although they took up a disproportionate amount of its time and attention. These junior members in the family of Saskatchewan crown corporations accounted for only about 5 per cent of total government investment in industry. The power, telephone, and insurance companies would generate profits that far exceeded the losses sustained on the woollen mill, the brick plant, and the shoe factory. However, the problem children provided a prime target for opponents of the CCF, from the day Phelps tabled the first financial reports and for decades after. They proved, said the Liberals and the Tories, that the CCF was incompetent, and that government had no place in business. Douglas and his colleagues said too little about the fact that these corporations had a social purpose—especially in the north, where ventures like the fish marketing service created badly needed jobs.

After a year in office the premier could see the root causes of what were now obvious mistakes. All of them were related to poor planning, a shortage of trained managers, and an ignorance of management methods. Douglas had a philosophical commitment to planning, but until 1944 he had not been required to put it into operation. Now he was confronted with the need to put words into deeds. Phelps's problem children were running wild. In addition, all the cabinet ministers were coming forward with new programs and new ideas, and there was no mechanism for meshing them together.

From the fall of 1944 through most of 1945 the government relied for its economic advice on an Economic Advisory Committee, made up mostly of academics who had also served the Patterson government. Working under the direction of a distinguished economist, Dr. George Britnell, they had a wealth of knowledge about Saskatchewan's economy and a great deal of energy. However, they had made it clear to Douglas that they did not regard themselves as planners and would not act in that capacity. They worked mostly for Fines, reviewing the province's tax structure and preparing briefs for dominion-provincial conferences.

In mid-1945 Douglas found the planning expert he was looking for, and began negotiations to bring him to Saskatchewan. George Cadbury would play a leading role in sorting out the government's problems and in establishing the planning system that would let the CCF set long-term goals. Cadbury had been born into the world of business, and had worked for the family firm in England as well as for several other companies. He graduated in economics from Cambridge University at a time when giants such as Maynard Keynes and Joan and Austin Robinson were generating great intellectual excitement. Cadbury and his wife Barbara were committed socialists. Both were active in the Labour Party and in the co-operative movement, and were steeped in the ideas of international socialism. David Lewis had heard about Cadbury while he was at Oxford, and advised Douglas to invite him to Saskatchewan. Fortunately, Cadbury consented.

On January 1, 1946, Cadbury assumed a double-barrelled title, chairman of the Economic Advisory and Planning Board and chief industrial executive. One part of his persona would be dedicated to planning, the other to bringing order to the crown corporations. Here was a public servant who could help to make the government into a rational institution "of the highest possible order," one that was both efficient and politically responsible. Until he left Saskatchewan in late 1951, Cadbury occupied a position just a step below that of a cabinet minister. Indeed, some cabinet ministers felt that he enjoyed a higher status than they did. He met freely with any of the ministers, particularly those who headed the crown corporations. For the most part, though, he dealt with Douglas, whom he regarded as "his minister," and with Fines, who had general responsibility for economic matters. Cadbury's two agencies, the Planning Board and the Government Finance Office—responsible for organizing the management of the government businesses—answered directly to the cabinet. Their governing bodies were twin cabinet committees, one headed by the premier, the other by the treasurer.

As premier, Douglas was the unquestioned leader in cabinet, in caucus, and party on matters of policy. He was the government's practical dreamer. The essence of his leadership, the source of his power over others, was his ability to dream and to cast his dreams in practical forms, to reduce his ideas to precise language, and to articulate them in such a way as to inspire those around him. He also had the ability to explore the ideas of others with an open mind, to analyse and to learn—and, at times, to act as a prodigious critic. The planning function, embodied in the Economic Advisory and Planning Board—the government's think tank—was built around his office and answered to him.

Fines, as treasurer, was the practical man who had the administrative skills and the manager's toughness that Douglas lacked. Luckily for the CCF, he had no desire to dump Douglas from the premier's chair. He understood his role, and was satisfied to complement Douglas's strengths with his own. If Douglas was the designer, Fines was the mechanic. During the almost twenty years that they worked closely together, from the time Douglas took the CCF provincial presidency in 1941, they probably never had a serious discussion of their unwritten contract, but both men adhered to it faithfully.

From the time of its foundation in the territorial days in 1885, the government in Regina had grown steadily and had sprouted departments, boards, and agencies, all with no central support staff. The process of drawing up budgets was primitive. Fines recalled seeing a minister's secretary in the Liberal days simply re-typing the budget from the previous year. The government had no systematic way of gathering economic or population data, and would not have had much use for such data in any case. There were no regular lines of communication with other governments.

The challenge for Douglas and those around him, then, was to organize the government to meet new and positive challenges, and to instil a sense of purpose into its work. Douglas often spoke of planning as an essential feature of socialism in action. He wanted to make room in his government for a small group of experts, hived off from the hurly-burly of day-to-day activities, with time to think of the future and to consider how recent social and scientific theories could be put to work. He recognized that as practising politicians, he and his colleagues would tend to look to the next election and limit themselves to a four-year attention span. The planners, he believed, might have the freedom to look forward to the next generation.

On January 2, 1946, the day after Cadbury's appointment, the Economic Advisory and Planning Board came into being, with Tom McLeod designated as full-time secretary. The board was, in essence, a committee comprising the ministers holding economic portfolios, with Cadbury acting as chairman on the premier's behalf. Its staff quickly became established as the economic intelligence unit of the cabinet, a relationship that was cemented with the institution of annual cabinet-Planning Board meetings where the politicians and the bureaucrats engaged in wide-ranging and vigorous discussions of longer-range policies and programs.

Some CCF activists felt that the creation of the new board shut them out from the government's policy-making processes. The Legislative Advisory Committee, made up of backbench MLAs and party officers, recommended that the Planning Board should be open to submissions from consumers, farmers, and workers, and that perhaps private citizens should sit on the board. The cabinet rejected this suggestion, although some members of the public served from time to time on the board's subcommittees.

The Planning Board never achieved the Olympian heights that

Douglas had mused about before the election. For one thing, many of the levers of economic control—monetary policy, the income-tax system, trade policy, and so on—rested in the hands of the federal government. Just as important, the various ministers regularly borrowed the board's staff for fire-fighting duty when they needed research support in coping with immediate problems. Despite these limitations, the board managed to hold a position apart from, and in a sense above, the daily routine, and to maintain a long-term view. One of its early works was a four-year plan, which outlined where the government could get the best results for its economic development dollars. From its vantage point, the board could also observe the overall pattern of government activities, assess their effectiveness in the light of the cabinet's declared objectives, and speak before being spoken to.

The greatest temptation of the CCF's first term in office was to plunge into expensive social and educational programs, despite the government's shortage of cash. Douglas once quoted Jimmy Thomas, a British Labour cabinet minister: "The trouble with socialists is that they let their bleeding hearts go to their bloody heads." At the first of the cabinet-Planning Board meetings, Cadbury argued strongly for imposing restraint on social and educational spending. The government should invest more money, he said, in programs that would increase the productivity of the provincial economy.[9]

To some extent, too, the planners had concluded, the government should limit the creation of new state-owned businesses and offer more support to private industry. This caused great distress in some sections of the CCF, although it posed fewer problems for the premier. He had said in a pre-election radio broadcast that "The CCF does not want to own everything. In fact, we recognize that even if it were desirable, it would break down under the weight of bureaucracy and red tape."[10] Party president Carlyle King, however, confronted Cadbury and McLeod and accused them of betraying socialism.

Experience had shown that nationalization for the sake of nationalization was not a sound basis for public policy. Quite obviously, the government could not afford to provide all the capital that was needed for industry and meet its other growing commitments as well. It had become clear that the government should restrict its business investments to ventures which satisfied a compelling public interest—economic or social. On this basis, the cabinet set aside proposals that it nationalize breweries, coal mines, and petroleum exploration. In the 1947 legislative session the government brought forward a bill to create an Industrial Development Fund, which would offer low-cost loans to private companies wishing to invest in the province. On the floor of the House, one of the CCF MLAS, a veteran from George Williams's time, reminded Douglas that the Manifesto had committed the party to "the eradication of capitalism." The premier responded that the government would encourage private enterprise "whenever it did not interfere with the welfare of the people."[11]

The fund sat mostly dormant for several years. It appeared that the CCF could not attract investment even by giving money away. By 1957, though, activity had picked up. The fund had made loans totalling $2.5 million and helped to start up several small businesses ranging from a co-operative creamery to a wire and cable plant. A *Globe and Mail* reporter, looking at the Douglas government's efforts to attract oil companies, potash companies, and secondary industries, wrote that Saskatchewan was "now the biggest booster of free enterprise on the prairies."[12]

Douglas and the CCF faced a damned-if-you-do, damned-if-you-don't situation. The government's success in bringing private investment into the province gave rise to the criticism that the grants and loans made to private business were part of a political slush fund. When it entered a joint venture to open a steel plant in Regina, for example, the Liberals—who had raged against the low level of private investment in the province—levelled unfounded charges that Douglas was doing business with cronies.

The problem became most acute in the oil exploration program. The decision to open the way to private development turned a wave of speculators loose, including some operators whom a concerned provincial official called "the dregs of humanity."[13] The speculators travelled around the province purchasing mineral rights from farmers, often for a fraction of their value. The government had little choice but to go the private route—it lacked the capital to engage in high-risk oil exploration, and it would have had to fight its way into markets controlled by the multinational majors if it had started production. However, the speculators' activities caused the CCF, including the premier, some embarrassment.

In the Weyburn area, Charlie Broughton, the smooth-talking Englishman who had organized politically for Douglas for twenty years, emerged as a director of the Freeholders' Oil Company. Broughton and his associates put out a brochure which suggested that the company was a sort of co-operative, and that all the farmers who signed over their mineral rights would get a share of whatever oil was discovered. As a respected local CCFer, Broughton got a good response to his offer. When the farmers read the contracts they had signed, though, they found that Freeholders' was not a co-operative and that the company reserved the right to decide how much to pay them for oil found on their own land. Freeholders' folded up, in the end, without transacting any business, and Broughton never got rich. However, some farmers felt betrayed, and one member of the Weyburn CCF executive challenged Douglas to repudiate his long-time organizer. Douglas stayed loyal to Broughton, and the challenger resigned his position.*[14]

While the Douglas government made various efforts to court private industry after 1947, it continued to expand its own holdings, although

---

* In the late 1950s the government set up a mediation service and tried to encourage the speculators who had bought mineral rights to re-negotiate their contracts with the farmers.

on a more business-like basis than before. Cadbury set out the principles of a strict routine for creating enterprises, including feasibility studies and discussion by the full cabinet. Under this more rigorous regime, the government established a province-wide bus service, began the mining and sale of sodium sulphate, and gave Saskatchewan Power a monopoly on retail natural gas distribution. These companies lost money on some of their operations, but that was the result of a deliberate choice. For example, in the distribution of electric power and natural gas, and in the maintenance of some rural bus routes, the government provided service at rates which equalized charges to rural and urban users, to customers on isolated lines and those on heavy traffic lines. The economics of profit and loss was softened by a willingness to meet social needs.

At an early stage in their studies, the planners realized that they would have to give a lot of their attention to the problems of agriculture. Cadbury, at the Planning Board's first meeting with the cabinet, emphasized that farming was still the mainstay of the provincial economy, and he plumped for substantial increases in funding for agricultural programs—more money for education and research, better soil erosion and water conservation programs. In agreeing to this proposal, the cabinet put itself in a dilemma. Should it work for the highest level of efficiency in agriculture, or should it try to protect the small farm and keep the rural population at a high level?

The mythology of the family farm as a place of virtue and godliness had always been important to the CCF movement. Early in the life of the new government, a group of backbenchers led by John Wellbelove, the MLA for Kindersley, proposed that the government should put a limit on farm size as a means of preserving the family farm. Such a measure would have created political havoc, and the idea died. The planners looked at farming in terms of its productivity rather than as a lifestyle to be subsidized. They saw the small farm as an unproductive unit which provided a low level of income for the people who worked on it. They recommended against spending a lot of money to save small farms.

Old ways, however, die hard. Many citizens were genuinely attracted to rural life, and the CCF was definitely interested in the rural vote. Besides, the planners' calculations of efficiency were not the final word. Douglas believed that the government's accounting system should reflect social costs and social benefits as well as the costs and benefits recorded in the market place. The government set out, then, to improve life for all the residents of rural Saskatchewan. From his early days in Weyburn, Douglas had brooded over the living conditions of people in the villages, hamlets, and farmsteads, scattered over wide expanses and lacking many essential services. As premier, he assumed a personal responsibility for changing these circumstances.

With its earliest actions, the CCF government started to alter the character of rural Saskatchewan. It tackled the problems of redistributing health and educational services, in order to redress some of the inequalities experienced by rural people. It extended the road network, and offered help for home improvements and the provision of running water. Another enormous change began in 1949, with the government's commitment to bring electric power to 40,000 farms. There were delays in the start of the project, causing Joe Phelps to resign from the Power Corporation's Board of Directors. Douglas had to plead that the government had run short of capital funds and did not want to "bite off more than we can chew." Despite the delay, some Saskatchewan residents rated the rural electrification plan as the CCF's greatest achievement. More than any other program, it raised living standards in the country to the same level as those in the cities.[15]

Douglas continued to search for a better understanding of the dynamics of rural life in Saskatchewan, and of "the continued volatility of the rural economy."[16] In 1952 he sponsored the establishment of a Royal Commission on Rural Life, which set out to examine social and economic conditions on the farm. The commission's work had little visible impact on the government's farm policies. However, it broke new ground in the area of participatory democracy, serving as a forum for those who wanted to explore their communities' life and problems. To that extent, it created a new awareness of how the political process worked.

The work of the planners reached out to the field of economic development, but it also reached into the heart of the government, into the cabinet, the decision-making centre. The steps they took to streamline the flow of information—to insure that the cabinet remained up to date on what was going on, and could respond quickly to any hitches—were among the Planning Board's most important contributions to the province. Douglas and Fines not only accepted but promoted the recommendations for change. In doing so, each one sacrificed some of the traditional powers of his office for the good of the cabinet. The premier and the treasurer could no longer control events by keeping their colleagues in the dark, even if they had wanted to. Reports on the governnment's work and proposals for change now came to the cabinet as a whole.

The cabinet was surrounded by an array of specialized, professionally staffed agencies, each of them answerable from day to day to a cabinet committee. The Planning Board, as noted earlier, provided the overview of the provincial economy. The Government Finance Office watched over the crown corporations, while the Treasury Board advised cabinet on the annual budget. The Cabinet Secretariat pulled together the various streams of information and packaged them for the ministers. This high level of co-ordination and specialization marked a breakthrough in the art of government in Canada. Before this, most governments had been content to operate in a loosely structured, amateurish fashion, reacting to crises or to demands from pressure groups as they came up. The Patterson cabinet, like its counterparts across Canada, had kept no formal agenda and no record of proceedings beyond what might be contained in the premier's notes or in his colleagues' memories. With experience, the

Douglas cabinet system became highly sophisticated, and, with a few minor changes, is still in operation in Saskatchewan today.

The CCF method of organization served as a model for other provinces, and veterans of the Douglas years took senior positions in Ottawa when the Thatcher Liberals smashed the Saskatchewan civil service in 1964. Tommy Shoyama, a British Columbia-born economist who served as chairman of the Planning Board after Cadbury, rose to become deputy minister of finance in the Ottawa of the 1970s. Al Johnson, a Saskatchewan native who succeeded McLeod as deputy provincial treasurer, also became a deputy minister in Ottawa, and then head of the CBC. Other members of the "Saskatchewan Mafia" moved into senior jobs in the federal Privy Council Office and in federal departments. Don Tansley and Jim MacNeill became deputies, and Al Davidson, Del Lyngseth, and Art Wakabyashi, among others, became assistant deputy ministers. The Mafia left its footprint on the public service of Canada.

Fundamental changes in the machinery of government brought changes in the role of the premier, changes that, for the most part, were highly compatible with Douglas's style of leadership. He sought to lead rather than to direct, and he preferred holding joint deliberations to giving orders. His method was essentially Socratic. He deferred to the specialized knowledge of the experts, and did not pretend to have all the answers. He did, however, have a gift for asking the right questions. He also had a remarkable ability to relate expert advice to the facts of real life, and to the real needs of his constituents. Shoyama, a brilliant economist who sat at the centre of many conferences, spoke almost in awe of the premier's ability to direct the flow of a technical discussion, and, by questioning, keep the experts' feet on the ground.

In working with his professional staff, Douglas tried to instill a sense of the music of the English language. Johnson and Shoyama once laboured to put together a speech for the premier, only to have him throw it aside with some irritation. Pacing up and down, Douglas dictated a new version with only minutes to go before he had to deliver it. He said later of the first version, "There was no rhythm in it."

Few things roused Douglas's ire faster than an attempt to cover uncertainty with a blanket of words. Sooner or later, most of those who worked for him got the lecture on verbal obfuscation. The premier wanted direct reports delivered in sparse, understandable language.

Douglas once highlighted his dislike of bureaucratese by pulling an item from his morning mail. He had his secretary bring in a letter from a voter who was angry about the Saskatchewan Power Corporation's method of putting up its power lines. Between the signature and the salutation there was one sentence: "Some bugger bust my fence." "There it is," said Douglas. "Subject, 'bugger,' verb, 'bust,' object, 'fence.' Why can't you fellows write like that?"[17]

18

Minister of Co-operative Development

I N 1949, having brought profound changes to Saskatchewan's health-care system, Douglas shuffled himself out of the Public Health portfolio and into that of Co-operation and Co-operative Development. According to an official statement, the move reflected the government's desire to put more emphasis on economic development. More important, Douglas was shedding the burden of the most active government department to put more time into political work. The CCF had lost seats in the 1948 election, and this had prompted him to comment sourly, "That's the last time I'll ever campaign on my record."[1]

Douglas's interest in co-operation and the co-operative movement was by no means newly acquired. In his conception of the socialist society, the ideals of that movement played a central role. Co-operatives, he once told the House of Commons, are "the most important form of social ownership."[2] In his view, co-operation meant more than a new set of institutional arrangements. In its truest form, it was a system of human interrelationships based on the principle of mutual support. Mutual support—Christian brotherhood—was to be the essence of a socialist world.

Douglas regarded the rise of the unions and the co-operatives in the nineteenth century as "an attempt to apply in the realm of economics the teaching of all the great religions."[3] In greeting a convention of Co-op Women's Guilds in 1951 he said, "When we devote our time and energy to the building of the co-operative movement, we are doing more than working for ourselves; we are helping mankind along a road that leads to social justice and economic emancipation."[4] In another speech he made in the same year he contended somewhat extravagantly, "Just as Abraham Lincoln freed the blacks, so the co-operative movement is freeing the whites from economic slavery."[5]

Douglas had set up the Department of Co-operatives and Co-operative Development in 1944, in keeping with an election promise. Its first minister, Lauchlan McIntosh, was an American-born farmer, and had worked for many years on the field staff of the Wheat Pool. Although a generation or more removed from his roots, he remained the epitome of the canny Scot, interested more in practical problems than in ideology.

When the Douglas government took office, Saskatchewan's co-operatives already had a combined membership of more than 300,000. It is likely most of Saskatchewan's families, especially in the rural areas, belonged to some form of co-op. Many members in the CCF caucus in the legislature had participated in co-ops, either as members or as officers. By supporting the co-operative movement, the government could further the aims of the CCF and make political gains at the same time.

The well-established co-operatives continued to prosper and grow throughout the Douglas years, and their membership pushed past the half million mark. As Douglas sometimes pointed out, a whole range of Saskatchewan-based enterprises had sprung up in a single lifetime—grain, livestock, and dairy co-ops, retail and wholesale co-ops with an interest in refining, mining, and lumber mills, and a chain of credit unions.

As minister, Douglas spoke often at co-operative conventions and rallies, and delivered his message—partly inspirational, partly hard-nosed advice—with the brilliance that had earned him a national reputation as an orator. He was generous with his time, making himself available to any delegations of co-operators who wished to consult him. His presence in the portfolio brought the prestige of high office to the co-operative movement. As one co-operative leader put it, "The fact that the Premier has taken over the Ministry of Co-operatives is a sign the movement has come of age."[6] The movement had, in truth, achieved a cautious middle age, and this was a source of some disappointment to Douglas. Where the co-ops had once been a force for social and economic experimentation, they would now choose safe, steady growth.

The co-ops moved ahead vigorously after the CCF came to power. In his first days as premier, Douglas established contact with co-op organizations in the United Kingdom, notably the Scottish Wholesale Co-operative. Through this organization, Douglas set out to open up a flow of traffic between Scottish and Saskatchewan co-ops through the port of Churchill, Manitoba. The CCF would work for years to increase the rate of traffic through Churchill, the closest port to the prairies, but the federal government never gave its support to promoting or improving the Hudson Bay trade route.

In another early venture, Douglas talked the governments of Manitoba and Alberta into lending money to a co-operative farm machinery company in Winnipeg. Since the early days of settlement, the prairie farmer had been exposed to the price gouging of a small group of Ontario manufacturers. The problem had been investigated by countless official bodies, and an all-party committee of the Saskatchewan legislature had concluded in 1939 that "the true and permanent solution of the problem of farm implement prices is to be found in co-operative effort."[7] From this recommendation came a campaign within the co-operative movement, supported by the Patterson government, leading to the formation of Canadian Co-operative Implements Limited (CCIL). Wartime steel shortages, however, made it impossible for the new company to move into production.

By 1944 the end of the war was in sight, and Premier Douglas gave his attention to the situation as soon as he came into office. With Douglas getting the promise of financial support from the other prairie provinces, CCIL was able to expand its membership and purchased a small plant in Winnipeg. Here it began to produce some farm equipment in 1945. At the same time, it made an agreement with Cockshutt, a large eastern manufacturer, to distribute that company's farm machinery.

The venture was not a success, and, after struggling on for three decades, it folded. It suffered both from lack of capital and of experienced management. The risks of producing for the boom-and-bust farming industry were just too great. At the same time, other co-op enterprises in western Canada refused to share the risk, either through providing capital or by helping to distribute CCIL's products. One small company, standing alone, proved a poor competitor in a market where large corporations, most of them multinationals, could spread their risk among many enterprises.

Douglas and his cabinet would run into a similar set of problems in the 1950s when they tried to make room for the co-operatives in the oil exploration business. Saskatchewan's co-ops had set up a Co-Operative Refinery in Regina in the 1930s, and had succeeded in marketing their products to co-operatives across western Canada and the western United States. In the early 1940s the refinery organization created a small subsidiary to undertake oil exploration on its behalf. However, this small enterprise lacked the risk capital that was needed to finance a successful drilling program.

In the 1950s, when it became obvious that Saskatchewan had some rich oil deposits, the government opened the way to private development. The CCF cabinet—and Clarence Fines in particular—felt that the risk of coming up dry far outweighed the benefits of putting public money into oil and gas drilling. However, Douglas still hoped for some measure of public enterprise in this field, and took steps to reserve crown land in a promising area for the co-op oil company. His action brought a torrent of complaints and criticism from the private oil companies and their Liberal sympathizers. The co-ops, despite their favoured position, declined to put their capital into any drilling venture, and the premier's gesture went for naught.

Saskatchewan's co-operative farm movement, perhaps the most controversial attempt to bring about social change through co-operation, also failed after a promising start. The Douglas government initially decided that it should back the development of co-op farms, and won support for the idea both from its advisers and from its left-wing supporters. The co-op farm—which drew half a dozen or so families into a shared farming operation—was seen as an ideal way to settle young soldiers coming back from the war. It also promised to stop the long decline in population in rural Saskatchewan. The Economic Advisory and Planning Board expressed the view that co-operative farming "holds the answer to several key economic problems in the Province, and combines large-scale farming with resident ownership, so implementing two desirable policies at one time."[8] It recommended that $250,000 be set aside as an initial fund to support such developments.

By 1949 there were seventeen farm co-operatives with 181 members engaged in various types of farming. It was becoming evident that co-operative organization allowed for a more rational use of human effort and for such things as regular hours and annual holidays. The co-ops also provided some of the social benefits of the village or town. At least one of these farms, Matador, specializing in cattle production, became an international showpiece. Douglas's planners became even more enthusiastic and recommended the expansion of the development fund to $1 million.[9] However, the cabinet deferred the idea, since the interest in setting up new farms seemed to have declined. Then, one by one, the existing associations dissolved.

The provincial Liberals under Walter Tucker correctly identified the farm co-operatives as—potentially—one of the most important innovations of the period. Tucker held them up as proof that the CCF were simply Communists in disguise, intent on turning Saskatchewan into a copy of Soviet Russia. It is unlikely, however, that the Liberal campaign killed the co-op farm movement. It seems that, despite their tradition of co-operating in other areas, prairie farmers were simply not interested in sharing their land, their income, and their living space with other farmers on an equal basis. It is conceivable, perhaps, that if the CCF had conducted a huge educational effort to change the cultural expectations of Saskatchewan citizens, it might have enticed more people into starting co-operatives. However, the government's first efforts in mass socialist education, through its Adult Education branch, ran into fierce opposition even from within the party, and the idea was dropped after 1945.

The Department of Co-operatives did, however, carry on a more low-level educational program, sending out pamphlets on how to set up retail co-ops and community recreation centres, and providing follow-up help. Most of the projects that resulted were small scale, nurtured from the ground up, and they generated few headlines.

In northern Saskatchewan, the growth of the co-operative movement brought new opportunity. The fishing and hunting economy of the native people fit well with the self-help philosophy of the co-operative movement. The government also set up co-op trading and marketing agencies in the north, designed to protect northern communities against the predatory practices of private fur traders and fish buyers. In 1959 Douglas led a move to turn over two of the northern crown corporations, Saskatchewan Government Trading and the Saskatchewan Fish Marketing Service, to regional co-ops. This was in keeping with his belief that the ownership and management of public enterprises should be located close to the grass roots. The transition was successful.

In the mid-1950s, Douglas began to sense a waning of the dedication and enthusiasm within the co-operative movement. He warned the movement's leaders, and his colleagues, that they were too satisifed with the accomplishments of yesterday, and spent too little time talking of and planning for the challenges of the future. The movement, he said, had lost the kind of moral fibre that had produced the Wheat Pool and the Co-op Oil Refinery. In writing to the editor of the *Western Producer*, he said, "The spirit of self-sacrifice which put up the refinery in the first place isn't here in sufficient strength to do that kind of job today...I doubt if we have challenged the young people of this generation with the task that lies before them. We have acted as if all of the battles have been won."[10]

Through half a century of living in Manitoba and Saskatchewan, Douglas had grown to identify the co-operative movement with political fervour and self-sacrifice. In fact, though, there was no necessary connection between the economic motives of co-operators and socialist idealism. The situation resembled that of the trade union movement. Committed socialists tended to be committed co-operators, and often emerged as officers and leaders of the various associations and societies. But as with the trade unions, the opposite did not hold true—it did not follow that co-operators were necessarily socialists. Indeed, some viewed the co-operative movement as the appropriate alternative to socialism. To others, co-operation was nothing more than a useful device for improving their personal economic position, and it required no ideological commitment.

As Saskatchewan's co-operative societies grew, the old interpersonal bonds weakened, and the influence of hired managers and accountants increased. The co-ops became more concerned with imitating the private sector as the best means of competing with it, and the general membership of the associations became increasingly passive. As a young politician, Douglas had preached that co-operative ownership might transform society. When he left the Co-operative Development post in 1961 it was plain that the co-operative movement, as materially successful as it was, had not lived up to his expectations.

19

The Perils of Power

ONE DAY IN THE MID-1950s, Tommy Douglas received a letter from an old comrade. Lewie Lloyd worked for Douglas as a co-op organizer, driving from village to village, trying to help struggling consumer and producers' groups stay on their feet. In this letter Lloyd looked back to 1933, when he had attended the CCF's Regina convention with his friends and slept out under the stars at the Regina fairgrounds. Where was that spirit now, he wondered. Was the CCF's popular leader the party's only asset? He wrote, "I told Woodrow [his younger brother, the education minister], the old spirit is dead, we have some good ministers but say what you like I doubt if we could win an election without Tommy Douglas."¹ Douglas could only respond that the old days were gone for good. The party, he told Lewie, would have to learn to live in a different world.

There is no doubt that as the years went by, Douglas moderated his political message in response to the growing prosperity and increasing caution of Saskatchewan's voters. He came to power in the aftermath of a depression and in the midst of a war, pledged to work for social and economic transformation. In the end, he stood as a symbol of stability and economic growth. Before the 1944 election Douglas talked about smashing "the chains of our economic servitude."² Thirteen years later the CCF government had put most of its programs in place; the toughest choice facing the province, he told a party convention, was whether to implement daylight saving time.

Douglas maintained his rhetorical style and his vision for a future new society, and this obscured the changed substance of his party's program. He was still harshly critical of the big interests and a warm friend to working people. His opponents kept attacking him as a dangerous tyrant—Walter Tucker, the Liberal leader, compared him with Lenin and Hitler—but they had trouble making the charges stick.³ An American feature magazine captured a more typical image: Douglas on a bowling outing with his Sunday school class, wearing the striped wool socks that Irma had knit.[4]

By 1950 the push for profound social reform in Saskatchewan was spent. The CCF would venture no further experiments with land owner-ship or state-owned industries, and make no attempt to put a socialist curriculum into the schools. Saskatchewan was changing rapidly enough for most tastes. The building of highways, power lines, schools, and hospitals was reshaping the face of the province and the lives of its people. Douglas came to symbolize a government that was activist, rather than overtly socialist. His policies appealed to individual values: pride in one's province, a fair return for the farmer, opportunities for the children. Down the road, perhaps, the CCF would put the corporate monopolies in their place, but the battle would not be fought in Saskatchewan.

Though his party played on the image that he was universally loved, Douglas had his share of adversaries. Anti-CCF feeling was widespread in the business community, among professionals and ranchers, and within some ethnic groups. The media, almost uniformly pro-Liberal, echoed these sentiments. Still, Douglas won the allegiance of many rank-and-file reporters in and out of the Press Gallery. Chris Higginbotham, a freelance reporter, spent long Sunday afternoons in the premier's office taping the interviews which became the basis for a sympathetic book: *Off the Record: The CCF in Saskatchewan.* (The same interviews, edited later by Lewis Thomas, appeared as *The Making of a Socialist.*) A visiting reporter from the Vancouver *Sun,* Jack Scott, wrote about Douglas in such glowing tones that the CCF printed one column as campaign literature. Here, wrote Scott, was "a dreamer and a humanitarian, incorruptible, genuine and intellectually honest."[5]

The premier's private life remained unchanged on the surface. Joan, a second daughter, joined the Douglas family in 1945 and, although Irma sometimes officiated as honorary head of the Girl Guides or the Salvation Army appeal, she still focused her efforts on making a comfor-table home. Each summer the family took a holiday at Carlyle Lake, where Douglas played a few rounds of golf and the family picked ber-ries, rowed the boat, and visited with old friends from Weyburn. What was different now, according to Shirley Douglas, is that he made no new friends. Douglas, she said, avoided playing favourites among his cabinet, his caucus, or his officials. He cut himself off from the society of his colleagues, a tactic designed to strengthen his leadership as well as to give him more time to work. Thousands of people regarded Douglas as their friend; very few dined at his house or drank tea in his front room.

Unless he was on the road, Douglas usually spent between ten and twelve hours a day at the legislature, dictating letters, preparing speeches, meeting with other MLAs, and hearing delegations. His daily routine was simple. He took lunch in the basement cafeteria, lining up with the other government workers for his tomato juice, poached egg, and prunes. If he was hosting distinguished visitors from Princeton or Pakistan, the whole party might troop down to the cafeteria line-up, eat at the arborite tables, and afterwards return their trays and dishes to the racks.

Each afternoon at 5:30 Douglas walked or drove to his house on Angus Crescent, about six blocks from the legislature. Of this refuge, his daughter Joan Tulchinsky wrote, "Mom built him not only a castle, but almost a fortress. Nothing was allowed to disturb him at home, she organized everything from major repairs down to being sure his clothes were clean and ready whenever he wanted...With her energy and organizational skills, I'm sure she could have run General Motors, but it was all just for him."[6] When he got home, Shirley recalled, he was often "so tired that he could hardly speak." Irma took the phone off the hook and served dinner, and afterwards the premier went to his bedroom and collapsed into a deep sleep. At 7:15 Shirley roused him, and he returned to his office until about 11 o'clock.[7]

On Saturday, the premier and his staff worked a full morning on government affairs, and then he held meetings on CCF business in the afternoon. Saturday nights the Douglas family sometimes went out for dinner, often to the W. K. Chop Suey House on South Railway Avenue. His friendship with the Yees, the family that owned the restaurant, continued through his remaining years. On Sunday night he went alone to visit the sick in hospital.

To the public, especially to the party faithful, Douglas seemed indestructible. At fifty, he still stepped lightly, always ready with a smile or a joke. The people who worked for him saw another side—a driven man who constantly demanded more and better work from his staff and would not tolerate excuses. He was hardest of all on himself. Once almost every year his health collapsed—usually a flare-up of his childhood knee injury—and he spent a few days in hospital. While he played cards with the nurses, his friends worried about his recovery. "I always thought he was going to die," said Shirley. "There was this constant whirl about, he looks so tired, he is so tired."[8]

In the fall of 1949 Douglas tried to re-establish a personal link with his neighbours around the province through a series of "Fireside Chats," broadcast on the Moose Jaw and Prince Albert radio stations. Every Sunday evening in Weyburn, he said on his first program, young people from his church congregation had gathered in his living-room to read over their favourite poems, stories, and quotations together. He asked his listeners to send in their own selections, and then, with the orchestral music swelling underneath, he began:

God give me sympathy and sense,
And keep my courage high.
God give me calm and confidence,
And please—a twinkle in the eye!

On the same evening he read "A Soldiers' Prayer," a poem from Longfellow, Kipling's "If," and the 23rd Psalm. He closed with what became his sign-off through the series, a poem based on a text from St. Paul, "God keep watch 'twixt thee and me."

The Fireside Chats illustrate something of the culture of the CCF years. They show a strong, even sentimental attachment to Anglo-Canadian family values. They focus on themes like "Faith," "Friendship," and "The art of growing old gracefully." The premier favoured Victorian poets like Wordsworth, Tennyson, and Kipling, as well as popular American poets from his younger days. At the same time, he often appealed in his own words for tolerance and understanding among communities in Saskatchewan. In one program Douglas recalled his boyhood in Scotland—the ships on the Clyde, football crowds, Edinburgh Castle, and Loch Lomond; he also read from St. Paul in Scottish dialect. Another evening, he focused on Robert Burns, "The Poet of the Common Man." Here he combined Burns's lyric works, "Flow Gently Sweet Afton" and "To a Mountain Daisy," with the poet's statements of radical liberalism:

If I'm designed yon lordling's slave,
By nature's law designed,
Why was an independent wish
E'er planted in my mind?

The Fireside Chats often took a religious tone, but the premier explicitly rejected the narrow outlook of fundamentalist Christianity. "We can never all agree on what religion means—we can only know what it means for us...Judge not, that ye be not judged." Our highest responsibility, Douglas said in a talk on "Brotherhood," is to work for world peace, starting in our own back yards. "Our neighbours are no longer merely the people who live next door; they are the people of every race and every tongue and every creed." The premier closed his series on March 19, 1950, with a program called "Fight the Good Fight." "Mankind has always been led by those who have dreamed dreams and seen visions...Those who fight the good fight know that they may lose a battle but ultimately they will win the war. They may be worsted in a fight but at some time and somewhere the things for which they fought will become a reality."[9]

Douglas never again returned to the mass media as an outlet for his creative urges. He continued to preach a dozen or so sermons a year before religious congregations, and to lecture at colleges. From time to time he wrote articles for publication in newspapers, journals, or books. His beliefs were also set out in thousands of letters to Canadians in every region.

The premier's main work of inspiration, of course, was to fire up the CCF troops, and he conducted frequent public-speaking and organizing tours. In June 1947, a typical month, he spoke at ten meetings. During the next year's month-long election campaign he made forty public speeches. But the solo efforts of the leader were not enough. The 1948 election gave Douglas his largest-ever personal endorsation in Weyburn, more than 56 per cent of the votes cast in a two-way fight with the Liberals. Elsewhere, though, the CCF dropped fourteen seats, and lost two cabinet ministers. Douglas complained to M. J. Coldwell of the party's "deplorable" state of organization, its "complacency and over-confidence."[10]

Popular interest in the CCF movement was diminishing as its Utopian flavour ebbed. The leaders that had brought the Saskatchewan party to power—people like Douglas, Clarence Fines, and Jack Douglas—now spent their time running the government rather than the party. By late 1950 CCF membership had fallen to less than a third of its 1944 level. Douglas urged MLAS and council members to work harder on education and organization. It was already time to start working for the next election, he told Dr. Hugh MacLean. "I have pretty well decided that for the next eighteen months I must 'scorn delights and live laborious days.' "[11]

Douglas had many sources of information. If he wanted a reading on the mood of the voters or the party's readiness, he could consult his caucus in the House, Carlyle King and the provincial party, or CCF workers in Weyburn such as Charlie Broughton and Auburn Pepper. Unfortunately, the "yes disease" was running rampant among second-rank workers and others who held him in awe. Douglas was such a kind man, and he cared so deeply about the party; why burden him with bad news? In an effort to get an unbiased view, Douglas asked Graham Spry, his London agent-general, to report to him on public opinion in the province after a 1951 tour. Spry advised Douglas to stick to a business-like, moderate approach. The voters liked the expansion of government services and the signs of economic growth. Spry wrote that "a Douglas government" and "a government that does things" would win more votes than talk of the Co-operative Commonwealth.[12] Whether it was Spry's advice or Douglas's organizing or the Liberals' disarray, the CCF share of the vote rose to an all-time high of 54 per cent in the next election, giving the party its third victory.

The Saskatchewan CCF had saved itself at the polls, but in other provinces apathy and low morale sapped the movement. Coldwell was growing older, and there was no one in sight to succeed him as national leader. The rumour grew that Douglas would abandon his life in Regina and move to Ottawa. The premier denied it. A would-be prime minister, he told a reporter in 1957, should have both legal training and a command of French—both of which assets he lacked and which he knew David Lewis possessed. He might go to Ottawa "as a duty...but I would first try to persuade them to choose someone else."[13]

The Liberals, with their lack of unity and leadership, helped to make the CCF the voters' choice. For fifteen years they searched in vain for a leader who could meet Douglas head to head. The actions of the federal Liberals also hurt the provincial party. Ottawa's refusal to pay cash advances for grain in storage, its loss of overseas wheat markets, its stalling on the South Saskatchewan River dam—Douglas used them all to his advantage.

Still, while he berated the Liberals in season and out, he harboured no personal grudges. In fact, a journalist reported in the 1950s that three photographs adorned his office. The first showed James Woodsworth, the second Abraham Lincoln. He often used the American president's phrase "no nation can exist half slave and half free" in demanding that the Canadian people should control the economy as well as the electoral system. The third photo portrayed Mackenzie King, the former leader of the party that Douglas most despised.

King and Douglas had grown quite close in Ottawa. When the Saskatchewan CCF opened its first session of the legislature in 1944 King sent good wishes to the new premier, adding that he took "a special interest in the careers of younger men in the public life of our Dominion." This interest was especially strong in Douglas's case, King wrote. In 1948, when King announced that he would retire from public life, Douglas wrote a letter of appreciation in which he said, "I cannot help but feel that when you lay down the mantle you will be bringing to an end an important era in Canadian history that may one day be regarded as one of its greatest eras." He then asked for an autographed photo, "in order that we may pay our tribute to a good and great Canadian."[14] Douglas never spared Mackenzie King in his public attacks on the Liberal government, but he obviously respected the man who led the country for more than twenty years.

William Patterson, the scapegoat in the Liberals' 1944 loss, retired as provincial Liberal leader in 1946. His own party promptly abandoned him and it was Douglas who came to the rescue. Patterson had not used the premier's job for personal gain and he retired a poor man. His Liberal associates made no move to find him a job or an appointment. The former premier's bitter obstructionism in the legislature had earned him the dislike of the CCF side, but Douglas took special steps to secure him a pension. Douglas and Woodrow Lloyd also found a teaching job for another impoverished former premier, the Tory J. T. M. Anderson, a gesture that brought howls of protest from within the CCF.

Patterson's successor was Walter Tucker, a Saskatoon lawyer and the member of parliament for Rosthern. Douglas and Tucker had maintained a cordial relationship before 1944, but this soon changed. Tucker began with a reputation as a progressive, but he set out on a bombastic red-baiting campaign, certain that he could paint Douglas as a Stalinist dictator.

The two men were still friendly enough in the summer of 1947 to agree to a meeting before a joint CCF-Liberal picnic north of Yorkton. On this festive occasion at the Crystal Lake golf course, 3000 people ate 800 gallons of ice cream, swam, sang songs, and lined up for airplane rides. Late in the afternoon the party leaders climbed up to a platform trailer, and the crowd gathered round. The debate that followed pointed up the differences in style between Tucker and Douglas. The premier, wrote a reporter, seemed "a frisky young colt," while his older, larger opponent was "the plodding workhorse."

Douglas first laid out what the CCF had provided for the province: special funding for financially strapped school boards, grants for hospitals, protection against foreclosure for farmers, increased support for single mothers. Tucker protested that the Liberals had introduced mothers' allowances to Saskatchewan when the premier was "just a little fellow." "I am still a little fellow," said Douglas. "Mr. Tucker is big enough to swallow me, but if he did he would be the strangest man in the world. He would have more brains in his stomach than he does in his head."

Tucker, in response, charged that the CCF was hiring people to teach "communism and socialism" in the province. The real premier of Saskatchewan, he said, was not Douglas but the socialist bureaucrat George Cadbury (the CCF often said that the real Liberal leader was Jimmy Gardiner). Tucker drew the biggest boos of the day when he repeated his charge that Communists backed the CCF "financially and otherwise."[15]

The Liberals stuck to the anti-Communist theme over the next year, making "Tucker or Tyranny" their slogan in 1948. If Douglas was re-elected, Tucker warned, the CCF would gobble up land, confiscate savings, and restrict personal freedoms. The socialists, he said, "follow a direct line as laid down by Moscow."[16] The crusade failed on the surface, in that the Liberals lost the election. Tucker picked up seats, however, and several of Douglas's organizers across the province blamed the red scare for their losses. The setback reinforced the growing mood of caution within the CCF.

Perhaps Douglas should have ignored his opponent's barbs and kept to the issues, but in the course of the 1948 election campaign he became so angry that he attacked Tucker personally. Tucker, in turn, sued Douglas for $100,000 in damages. The Liberal leader had a stake in the Rosthern Investment Company, a potential liability in a province where many people still regarded mortgage dealers as pariahs. Douglas made a special campaign visit to Rosthern to provide details of how Tucker had collected up to 15 per cent interest on overdue loans, and how he had been "charged with fraud" in a deal with some illiterate immigrants. In fact, the family in question had prepared a civil case against Tucker but had not pressed it. There had been no "charges," and not even a hearing in court.[17]

Tucker's slander action against Douglas reached Court of Queen's Bench in the fall of 1948. The jury rejected Tucker's claim and the judge ordered the Liberal leader to pay the costs of the trial. Later, a Court of Appeal ordered a new trial, saying the first judge had misdirected the jury, but Tucker dropped the case. Tucker, said Douglas later, made "a major error" in launching the action in the first place; testimony only supported Douglas's main thesis that Tucker was a financier who preyed on weaker people.[18]

For the next five years Tucker worked to turn the tables on Douglas, searching always for evidence of corruption within the government. The teachers and farmers in the cabinet offered poor targets for surveillance, and the public ignored the news that some workers on the government payroll supported the CCF. However, the Liberals became convinced that Clarence Fines would provide the weak link they were looking for.

Fines was crucial to the CCF's success. He balanced the budget year after year, worked steadily at reducing the province's long-term debt, and won the tolerance, if not the applause, of big and small business. He persuaded moderate voters that the CCF governed well. At the same time, Fines held his own with party activists who wanted more funding for social services and education. But Fines also pursued a parallel career as a speculative investor, and it was here that Tucker hoped to trip him up, and, along with him, the government. Some of his investments exposed him to what would today be judged conflicts of interest.

In one highly publicized case Fines actually played up his dual identity as treasurer and private investor. When the CCF came to power in 1944, Saskatchewan's credit rating was extremely low on North American markets. To make things worse, the new government's critics were telling the world that the socialists would default on their debt. To demonstrate his faith in Saskatchewan's future, Fines went to his bank manager for a loan and then purchased $15,000 in provincial bonds. The Dow Jones wire took up the story, and soon the value of the bonds began to rise. The Liberals assailed him in the House, but Fines simply challenged them to follow his example. Ever afterwards, he took some personal credit for having strengthened the province's financial outlook. He also pocketed a $3000 profit the next year, a sum greater than the annual incomes of most of his constituents.[19]

Fines's bond investment was a calculated and perhaps defensible political display. His other dealings were more worrisome. He dabbled in the commodity markets, Saskatchewan resort properties, and Saskatchewan gold mines. Even if he did not have insider information in these deals, he had a privileged relationship with local investment dealers as minister responsible for the Securities Commission.

In 1950 Fines encouraged Douglas to join in a partnership which raised more questions about the treasurer's judgement. Morris Shumiatcher, the former government adviser, had opened a law practice, and from there entered into a variety of private ventures. Shumiatcher owned a share in the Sunset Drive-In Theatre at the corner of Pasqua Street and the Trans-Canada Highway in Regina. The principal shareholder was Phil Bodnoff, a Regina businessman. On October 15, Fines invested $1250 of his own money in the business, along with $500 from the premier.

When the media broke the story the next year, the fact that a Baptist minister had invested in a drive-in caused a minor sensation. Old Herman Danielson, a Liberal MLA from Arm River, dubbed the outdoor theatre "the P.P.P."—the Premier's Passion Pit. This attack added some spice to debate in the assembly, but it promised little political payoff. However, behind the quaint irony lay a more serious issue. Bodnoff, the Sunset Drive-In's owner, had obtained a $75,000 mortgage loan from the Saskatchewan Government Insurance Office in June 1950 to buy two movie theatres in Weyburn. Fines, as minister in charge of the SGIO, was a member of the board that approved the loan.

When the Liberals raised the matter in the early part of the 1952 session, Fines willingly allowed it to go before the legislature's Crown

Corporations Committee. In Liberal minds, the case was clear. First, it appeared the government was lending money to its friends. Second, it seemed the treasurer and the premier were trying to profit personally from the granting of such loans.

Fines protested that he had not known Bodnoff in June 1950, despite his investment in Bodnoff's drive-in three months later. He waved cancelled cheques before the committee to show that the SGIO loan had gone into Bodnoff's Weyburn properties and not into the Sunset Drive-In. Tucker said the cheques proved nothing. The committee, dominated by CCF members, ruled that there was no evidence of corruption. Douglas said that his own conscience was clear: "I make no apology for investing in any local venture that can be of assistance to the community," he told the committee.[20]

The next year, in 1953, the Liberals made a new and more sensational attempt to destroy Fines and the government. They chose as their weapon a sworn statement from Joseph Oliver Rawluk of Regina. Rawluk and his wife had been associated with Morris Shumiatcher in an insurance business, Financial Agencies Limited. The firm had sold Saskatchewan Government Insurance in Regina, but had folded in early 1952. Shumiatcher was the company's solicitor and a director; Phil Bodnoff was a shareholder and a director. Soon after the company's demise, Rawluk lodged a complaint that Fines was skimming money from Government Insurance offices across the province. The charges, when Tucker made them public, triggered an uproar in the House, and the public hearings that followed made front-page news for a month.

On the morning of March 10, 1953, Tucker rose in the Crown Corporations Committee to read out Rawluk's statement for the first time. It said that Fines and Mike Allore, the SGIO's managing director, were extorting money from the SGIO's independent agents as payment for granting the agents their franchises. Fines, in other words, was alleged to have guaranteed insurance business to CCF contacts and then demanded kickbacks.

Tucker refused to table the document, saying that Rawluk himself should explain his evidence, with the support of other witnesses. The Liberal leader was proposing to turn the Crown Corporations Committee into a self-appointed committee of inquiry—a job it had no mandate to perform. Strangely enough, the CCF went along. The committee should have at least returned to the legislature for instructions, but it did not. By chance, the government's expert on procedure, Committee Secretary George Stephen, had left the room. Fines, who was present and anxious to clear his name, agreed to Tucker's proposal. When Stephen returned, he was appalled at what had happened. He knew legislative committees to be poor instruments for settling points of law. He wanted Fines to withdraw his consent and ask for a judicial inquiry instead. However, Fines chose to let his own decision ride. Douglas knew that if and when the CCF-dominated committee cleared Fines, the Liberals would only accuse the government of covering up.

That same evening, the Committee on Crown Corporations convened again, moving from the committee room to the legislative chamber to accommodate the crowds. The *Leader-Post* and the *Star-Phoenix* probably lavished more ink on the ensuing hearings than on any other event in Saskatchewan's history, offering the full transcript of testimony from the key witnesses.

Unfortunately for the Liberals, Rawluk and his affidavit were suspect from the beginning. He had sworn out his statement in the law office of D. V. Heald, a member of the provincial Liberal executive, almost a year prior to Tucker's revelation. Rawluk had tried to sell the statement to Tory and Independent candidates during the 1952 election campaign, but had found no takers. He then gave the document to Tucker, who sat on it for the first month that the House was in session. Although Tucker insisted that he held damning evidence of corruption in high places, he was not ready to press any charges on his own behalf. He preferred to work through his unhappy mouthpiece. Tucker claimed that Rawluk was "anxious" to make the facts public. Rawluk said, "I am here against my will," and indicated that Tucker had forced him to proceed.[21] For the CCF, the issue became one of Walter Tucker's methods rather than the alleged misdeeds of Clarence Fines.

Rawluk could not back up any of his accusations, and the story that unfolded embarrassed the Liberals rather than the CCF. The committee established that he had written bad cheques on behalf of his company; that he had sold policies without registering them with SGIO; and, finally, that Government Insurance had stripped him of his franchise after suing successfully for $3000 in unpaid premiums.

It seemed that Rawluk had a personal grievance against Fines. However, he could not prove that he had met the treasurer on business more than once, when Fines had given him a ride before the 1952 election. He told the story that Fines had picked him up at a prearranged spot on 11th Avenue; when Rawluk climbed into the car, he placed $100 in tens and twenties on the driver's seat next to the treasurer. Neither Tucker nor Rawluk's lawyer took this account seriously enough to pursue it at the hearings. Douglas put out a call for other insurance agents to come forward and report any complaints. None did, although some wrote in support of Fines and Allore.

The Crown Corporations Committee reported to the legislature on April 11, 1953, after hearing twenty-six witnesses and recording 1700 pages of testimony. It found the charges against Fines and Allore "wholly unwarranted and unfounded" and stated that "Mr. Rawluk must be regarded as wholly unworthy of belief."[22] But as Douglas had feared, the Liberals now rejected the work of the committee and demanded a judicial inquiry.

In the assembly's debate on a motion to receive the report, Tucker and his associates labelled the document a "white-wash" and one that did not have the support of the opposition "in any way shape or form."[23] They moved an amendment proposing that the report be set aside and that the chief justice of Saskatchewan be requested to name a judge to "review the evidence, to re-hear witnesses and, if so inclined, to over-rule and reverse the findings of the Legislature's own committee." Attorney-General Corman, in a broadcast a month later, described this idea as "preposterous and undemocratic."[24] Douglas, in responding for the government, argued that no legislative inquiry, having completed its assignment, had ever asked for a retrial of its own work. And why did the Liberals want another inquiry, in any case? Tucker had held the affidavit for nine months before introducing it and had had plenty of time to consider his options. In the end he had chosen explicitly to bring the case to a legislative tribunal—probably, Douglas said, because that route offered greater political opportunities. With Douglas's intervention, the debate on the amendment ended, but there was more to come.

The opposition introduced a second amendment which, strictly speaking, was not an amendment at all. It demanded that the committee's report be struck down and replaced with a contrary 16,000-word report from the Liberals. It took J. W. Horsman from Wilkie almost two hours to read the minority report into the record; essentially, it argued that "the charges against Allore and Fines have not been disproved." Douglas knocked this ball right out of the park. As Corman later put it, "The debate for the Government was opened by Premier Douglas, but when he resumed his seat, not a single, solitary Liberal on the Opposition benches got up to reply. They permitted the Premier's summing up of the evidence to go unchallenged. The vote was taken without further debate."

Douglas's speech lasted two hours and fifty minutes. He hotly rejected the Liberal assertion that Rawluk's accusations had "not been disproved." The onus was on Rawluk and the Liberals to prove their case, and they had failed to do it. Did any Liberal actually believe the story of the pay-off to Fines? Douglas challenged them to stand up in the House if they did, crying, "Come out of the bushes and let's see the colour of your liver!"[25]

Not long after, Walter Tucker retired from the Legislature and from politics. Douglas withdrew from the Sunset Drive-In Theatre, and from his association with Shumiatcher. He wrote to Dr. MacLean that the cabinet's former legal adviser seemed to have "a penchant for selecting unreliable associates in his business enterprises."[26]

Fines had hoped to retire in 1956 to pursue his career as an investor, but after the Rawluk affair he felt that to resign would be a sign of weakness or guilt, and he stayed on for another four years. During this time, although he drove a medium-priced government car and lived in an unpretentious home, he enjoyed what passed for a mildly flamboyant lifestyle in a small provincial city, buying his wife a fur coat and keeping his basement bar well stocked. The rumour mill insisted that Fines had plundered the government coffers, and was sharing the loot with his friend the premier. Some of the worst of the gossip peddlers were members of the CCF. Douglas assured one supporter, "I have no income other than my salary and indemnity, and I think my bank balance at the end of last month showed I was overdrawn in the amount of $40.00. This would hardly warrant my being called a millionaire."[27]

Fines had accumulated his savings from his investments, not from the Treasury. As he travelled the continent on government business during the 1940s and 1950s he cultivated a growing circle of rich acquaintances. He had a keen sense of where to ask for investment advice and how to use it. His contacts were helpful to the province, to himself, and, since he was the leading CCF fund-raiser, to the party.

At times, the dividing lines between his responsibilities grew hazy. The office records Fines left to the people of Saskatchewan show that as minister responsible for the Liquor Board he intervened directly in the board's purchasing decisions; he accepted hospitality and small personal gifts such as clocks and wineglasses from liquor companies; he also collected at least one campaign donation from a distiller's agent. Some in the CCF believed that the party never accepted money from brewers and distillers, but there was no written policy. Douglas, it seems, was at least aware of where Fines stood on the issue. In July 1960, Fines deposited a $1500 gift from an agent of Alberta Distillers into account number 3100 at the Toronto General Trust branch in Regina. It was one of his last acts before retiring from politics. "If at any time in the future you have any problems concerning this account," Fines wrote to the trust company office, "please be good enough to discuss them with Mr. Douglas."[28]

Fines left the government and his wife in 1960, and moved to a prosperous retirement in Florida. Right to the end of his career in Saskatchewan, his party regarded him as a political asset. A delegation of left-wing and labour CCFers pleaded with him to stay on. One of this group said later, "He represented the right-of-centre point of view that we needed to win."[29] In later years, the gossips and cynics worked to blacken Clarence Fines's reputation. His legacy to his party and to Canada, however, is clear. For the CCF, Fines established a record of financial prudence. At the same time, in finding the money for a vastly expanded range of programs, he provided an example for other provincial governments to follow.

After Walter Tucker's departure, the Liberals remained leaderless until November 1954, when they chose Hamilton McDonald, a war veteran and a former Tory. The new leader gave the CCF its fourth election victory and then departed, to be rewarded later with a seat in the Senate. Douglas viewed McDonald as an honest man who understood nothing about politics, and he was able to work with him on a friendlier basis than with any other leader of the opposition.

Ross Thatcher, who succeeded McDonald in 1959, posed a much greater challenge. A former CCF member of Parliament, he strenuously applied the CCF's organizing methods to the Liberal party and matched the government promise for promise. At the same time, Thatcher pledged to provide lean, efficient government to replace what he viewed as the

Douglas administration's bureaucratic bungling. He was a tireless worker, a diabetic with a hypertension problem who kept his followers in line with his exemplary hatred for socialism and his occasional tantrums. "Canadian socialism was born here," he wrote in 1958. "It should be buried here."[30] In Thatcher's first provincial election, in 1960, the CCF share of the vote slipped to 40 per cent, but strong Tory and Socred showings blocked a Liberal breakthrough. In 1964, after Douglas's departure, Thatcher united right-wing voters and first-time voters and ended the CCF's twenty-year reign.

Douglas had met young Alderman Thatcher in Moose Jaw in the early 1940s and the two sometimes discussed CCF strategy in the cafés of Main Street. Thatcher served as a CCF MP after 1945, but he slowly emerged as a right-wing maverick, demanding lower corporate taxes, a restoration of the means test for pensioners, and cuts in public works spending. Some CCFers wanted him expelled from the party. Douglas, hoping to avoid a split in Saskatchewan, advised Coldwell to let him drift away at his own speed. Finally, in 1955, he crossed the floor in the Commons.

Thatcher's rise within the Liberal Party came partly because of a Douglas miscalculation. After his defection from the CCF, Thatcher gained prominence as a critic of Saskatchewan's crown corporations and the premier challenged him to a debate on the subject. In the spring of 1957, when Thatcher was contesting the Assiniboia federal seat for the Liberals, the two men squared off in the town of Mossbank, southwest of Moose Jaw. Nearly 1000 people crowded into the hall where the event took place, while many more sat in their cars outside in a heavy downpour and listened to the debate on the radio.

Douglas had nothing to gain from taking on a federal Liberal candidate. Once the debate began, moreover, he made critical mistakes. He underestimated his opponent's abilities, and opened in an almost light-hearted manner. When he was finished, Thatcher came out swinging, complaining about inefficiency, waste, and poor service to the public, and suggesting that the government had lied about the crown corporations' financial results. Then Douglas got badly bogged down in detail. He did not have Thatcher's background in business, and should not have carried the war into the enemy camp. He trotted out technical analyses of load factors and writeoffs, and tried to justify the crown corporations on the basis of their balance sheets rather than from the perspective of public need. Instead of relying on socialist principles, he used the criteria of the private sector.

Bob Moon, a *Leader-Post* columnist, observed the next day, "There was no clear winner officially, and it may be doubted if a single vote was changed." However, Thatcher had emerged as "a new factor in Saskatchewan politics," said the Calgary *Herald*, "not because he won but because he did not lose."[31] When Hazen Argue took the Assiniboia seat for the CCF, Thatcher moved to the provincial scene.

Douglas turned back the Thatcher challenge in 1960, but he did so partly, once again, by appealing to the capitalist values of stability and investor confidence. Thatcher had lamented the province's "economic stagnation"; Douglas pointed to the construction of two privately owned potash mines, a uranium mill, a steel plant, and other industries. Jack Scott, the Vancouver columnist, wrote, "No other province has so advanced a welfare program or is as eager to welcome the free-wheeling free-enterprise industrialist."[32] Douglas highlighted these points in a campaign debate against Thatcher at the Saskatoon Arena; per capita private investment, he said, was the second highest in Canada.

Thatcher tried to move the Liberals to the political centre, promising help for seniors, students, and farmers, but occasionally he blew his cover. In the arena debate he resorted to Commie-bashing, warning that socialism meant regimentation and tyranny, and the audience of farmers drowned him out with "a chorus of boos."[33] Douglas, the old pro, remained calm this time. He regarded Thatcher as a gifted politician who had decided to take the low road to power. Besides, he was satisfied with his own tactical position. The province was moving ahead. Electrical generating capacity had doubled since 1956, and natural gas use had quadrupled. Over the same period, the value of resource (oil, mineral, timber) production had doubled, to $240 million annually; work had started on a Saskatchewan River dam, a $200 million project; the province's share of education costs had risen from 31 per cent to 45 per cent; work had proceeded on seventy-two senior citizens' homes.[34]

The CCF was also preparing during the 1960 campaign to introduce medicare, its last great social reform. This, more than anything, caught the imagination of the voters. Graham Spry, on another fact-finding tour, found that the public questioned the aging government's vigour and was "cautious and dubious" about the proposed CCF merger with organized labour in a New Party.[35] But the promise of public health insurance worked strongly in the government's favour. The medical profession fought back against the health insurance proposal with a campaign of distortion, but election day gave the CCF a clear majority of seats. Afterwards, the premier wrote to several friends that it had been "the hardest fought campaign we have had to date...the result is little short of a political miracle. It justifies my faith that when great issues are at stake the ordinary citizen will rise to the occasion."[36]

20

Medicare

MEDICARE WAS THE GREATEST single achievement in the political career of Tommy Douglas. Perhaps more than any other event in Canadian history, the coming of state health insurance to Saskatchewan fulfilled the hopes of the social gospel reformers. It made high-quality health care available to everyone, regardless of their ability to pay.

Douglas shared this achievement with the other members of his cabinet, especially Woodrow Lloyd. Douglas set the machine in motion when he called the legislature together in the fall of 1961 to approve the Medical Insurance Act. He then moved to the federal scene, and Premier Lloyd took on the tough job of putting the plan into effect, along with his fellow ministers and his staff.

This was the CCF's last major initiative before its defeat at the hands of Ross Thatcher's Liberals in 1964. The medicare crisis strengthened the Liberals, while it does not appear to have attracted voters to the CCF banner. However, there are several reasons not related to medicare that might also explain the 1964 loss. Certainly the departure of Tommy Douglas, and the absence of any bold new plans, convinced some voters that the CCF's time was past.

The idea of state-run health insurance, to be financed out of general tax revenues, had been endorsed by the farm and labour movements and even by many Liberals as far back as the First World War. Medicare figured as a campaign promise for the CCF in 1944, but the cost of running other health services in the early years put it out of reach. The Saskatchewan hospital insurance program, for example, cost $7.6 million in 1947, or more than 15 per cent of the provincial budget. This rose to $29 million, or more than 20 per cent of the budget, by 1955.

Provincial CCF conventions repeatedly pressed for the introduction of a health insurance plan. Douglas, in turn, called on Ottawa to help

Saskatchewan with a pilot program, and to ignore the other provinces' foot-dragging. If Ottawa had agreed, the CCF would have gained an important ally in any dispute with its doctors. "There is no longer any cause for delay," Douglas told the St. Laurent Liberals in 1952, but the federal government shrugged off his pleas.[1]

Two developments in the late 1950s allowed the CCF to go it alone. First, the Saskatchewan government's revenues, especially from resources like oil and minerals, rose rapidly. Second, Paul Martin, the federal minister of health, convinced his Liberal cabinet colleagues and a majority of the provinces to agree to a national hospital insurance plan. Starting in July 1958, Ottawa paid half of the Douglas government's hospital operating costs. Some observers have suggested a third factor. After a decade of working on economic development, the premier wanted to take the CCF back to its roots as a party of social concern. Douglas believed, said Allan Blakeney later, that a good social issue would "energize the party."[2]

By 1960 more than half the province's population subscribed to private health insurance plans. As the Hall Royal Commission report would point out in 1964, many of these plans had serious flaws. Besides, some people could not afford private insurance. Others believed that they were healthy enough or financially secure enough not to need insurance, and often they were proved wrong. The doctors boasted that nobody was refused medical care for lack of funds. Instead, they hired agencies to collect their fees when the patient recovered—or from the patient's estate.

Douglas announced the cabinet's decision to proceed with medicare in April 1959, in a by-election speech at Birch Hills. Although he did not mention it, his senior officials were already at work on a draft bill for the legislature. In a radio broadcast in December he reaffirmed the government's intentions: "If we can do this—and I feel sure we can—then I would like to hazard the prophecy that before 1970 almost every other province in Canada will have followed the lead of Saskatchewan...Once more Saskatchewan has the opportunity to lead the way. Let us therefore have the vision and courage to take this step, believing that it is another advance toward a more just and humane society."[3] Douglas promised in this broadcast to appoint a special committee to give advice on what type of medicare plan would best suit Saskatchewan.

At the same time, he made it clear that the plan should conform to five basic principles:

• Under the scheme, medical bills would be prepaid. Patients would never see a doctor's bill.
• The plan must be universal. It must cover everyone, regardless of age or physical disability.
• The launching of medicare would go along with continuing improvements in all areas of health service. It would not siphon off money from other areas.

• The plan was to operate under public control. This was not to be a subsidy scheme for private insurance companies.
• Medicare legislation must be acceptable to both patients and doctors before it went into effect.

The fifth principle, unfortunately, would prove impossible to uphold. Saskatchewan's doctors could not support the creation of a state-controlled medical insurance plan.

The doctors had worked for years within government-sponsored systems of various kinds. However, rather than warming up to the idea of universal medicare, their opposition had grown more and more rigid. Starting in 1945, they provided free service to the poor and applied to the government for repayment. A committee of physicians worked zealously to check any abuse of this system by their colleagues. In this case, the doctors found it prudent to exchange the principle of freedom of practice for the guarantee that their high-risk accounts would be paid in full.

The doctors had worked, without apparent mishap, in the regional medicare scheme set up in Swift Current in 1946. However, when the government proposed to extend this scheme to the Assiniboia and Regina Rural health regions in 1955, the College of Physicians and Surgeons spoke out against it. The voters of both districts voted down the idea of paying regional health insurance taxes, perhaps giving the doctors confidence in their ability to sway public opinion. During the same period, the college pressured its members to stop working on salary for local governments, and the municipal doctor plans disappeared one by one.

Saskatchewan's doctors had staked out their position on health insurance in a statement issued in 1942, two years before the CCF government came to power. They agreed that they might go along with state-supported medicare, but only on two conditions. First, they demanded a fee-for-service system of payment. Second—and here was the sticking point—they wanted a measure of control over the program.

In 1945 Douglas wrote a letter to the College of Physicians which the doctors later claimed was a solemn promise that he would meet their terms. Any medicare plan, said the premier, would be run by a commission that was "free from political interference and influence." This commission was to include representatives from government, the public, and "those giving the service."[4] Ed Tollefson, in his review of the medicare crisis, has speculated that the views of the college and the government were close enough in 1945 that they might have reached an agreement on health insurance if they had tried. Over the years, though, the two sides moved apart. When the time came to put Douglas's words into action, it became obvious that they were open to more than one interpretation. In his view, participation by doctors could never be the same thing as control.

Through the 1950s, while governments stood still on the issue, the medical profession moved rapidly into the health insurance field. They built up two non-profit insurance companies in Saskatchewan, and whole municipalities purchased group coverage. The Association of Rural Municipalities appealed unsuccessfully to the CCF to extend local taxing powers to make such group participation easier. By 1960 these non-profit plans served a third of the people in the province, and the doctors felt the government should subsidize their insurance services rather than creating a new one.*

The growing commitment to private insurance went hand in hand with a general change of outlook on the part of Saskatchewan's doctors. Hundreds of physicians moved in from outside, and few of them knew or cared about the province's co-operative traditions. More than 200 of them—out of a total of fewer than 1000 physicians and surgeons in practice—came from Britain, often as refugees from the Labour government's National Health plan. The older, country doctors lost their influence within the College of Physicians, and the urban specialists took their place.

Given the widening gulf between the two sides, perhaps Douglas should have seen that any attempt to impose medicare would force a confrontation. But according to William Davies, who served as health minister during the 1962 doctors' strike, Douglas thought when he announced his plans that the doctors would bow to public opinion. He held to his rationalist conviction that with a little more time to get the facts across, he would induce his opponents to come over to his side. Most of the cabinet agreed with the premier and expected medicare to fall into place after some initial resistance, as with the 1947 hospital insurance program. Davies said that only he and Woodrow Lloyd warned that the doctors would go to the barricades for their cause.

After the premier's radio talk outlining the principles of medicare, the College of Physicians expressed dismay that he had not consulted with the profession. Douglas met with the college executive, and they agreed on terms of reference for a medicare advisory committee to be made up of doctors and lay people. A month later, however, the college changed its course. Its registrar, G. W. Peacock, demanded that the proposed committee survey "all the health needs of the public" and approach health insurance without regard to the premier's five principles. The college, replied the premier, was making it difficult to do business.[5]

The college warned, in its public statements, that the CCF aimed to put all doctors on salary. This was a step that Douglas had rejected many years before, even though his health planners had warned him during his first term in office that fee-for-service medicine is bad medicine. The fee system encourages the physician to see as many patients as possible, to diagnose and prescribe with assembly-line speed, and to put aside the counselling and education that might prevent further illness. The

---

* The CCF argued that this was a dead end, and events in Alberta proved them right. When the Social Credit government tried to subsidize private insurance plans in the 1960s, the resulting patchwork left many people unprotected. At the same time, the system cost the public more than medicare in Saskatchewan.

planners also warned that with fee for service, physicians and surgeons make the biggest profits by performing the costliest procedures, whether the patient needs them or not.

The doctors had countered with the argument that a salary system would reduce them to the level of state employees, discourage initiative, interfere with the hallowed doctor-patient relationship, and dilute the quality of medical care. This last contention was one which Douglas could never understand or accept. To the end of his life he maintained a burning interest in medicare, and he never believed that the profession was achieving the standards that were possible, that it too often ignored available technology and clung to the outmoded one-doctor practice. However, to the distress of his socialist supporters, Douglas declined to force the doctors on to a salary system in the mid-1940s because he wanted to get his health program for the poor off to a quick start. In doing so, he established a precedent that the CCF government never seriously questioned.

In April 1960, after months of delay, the government announced the composition of the Advisory Planning Committee on Medical Care. It was to include nominees from the College of Physicians, the government, business, and labour. The committee would be chaired by Dr. Walter P. Thompson, a distinguished scientist who had recently retired as president of the University of Saskatchewan. The government's timetable called for the committee to report by the end of December 1960. However, the doctors' representatives used every opportunity to delay the committee's work. This hijacking is crucial to the medicare story, since Douglas felt he could not put health insurance into law without an Advisory Committee report. And while the doctors delayed, the appointed day for the founding of the new national CCF-labour political party approached, as did the time for Douglas's exit from provincial politics.

The CCF decided to make medicare a key point in its 1960 provincial election strategy. When Douglas appeared on a Regina television forum in March 1960, a doctor asked him how he could pretend the Advisory Committee was really studying the issue when the government had already made up its mind. Douglas suggested that if the people wanted to avoid medicare, they should vote against the government. "The people of this province," he said, "will decide whether or not we want a Medical Care Program. The [committee] will determine the terms and conditions, the Schedule of Fees, and so on."[6]

When the Saskatchewan doctors realized that Douglas was prepared to stand or fall on the medicare issue, they took vigorous action. With the help of the Canadian Medical Association, they raised nearly $100,000 to spend on publicity during the election campaign, more than any of the political parties. The tone of their material was so extreme, though, that it played into the government's hands. Doctors would flee the province to avoid medicare, the advertisements warned, and the CCF would have to bring in "the garbage of Europe" to tend the sick. Medicare bureaucrats, they said, might commit women with menopausal problems to insane asylums.[7]

All four political parties promised improvements to the health insurance system. Only the CCF promised a single, universal plan. In June 1960 Douglas and his party won a solid majority of seats, and he took this support as a mandate to proceed with medicare. The doctors' campaign, he said after the election, had only hurt the medical profession. "Men and women who set up municipal doctor plans, union hospitals and anti-tuberculosis programs are not likely to be frightened by cries of 'state interference' and 'red medicine.' "[8]

Douglas remained convinced that before too long the profession would fall into line, even if he had to apply pressure. When the government had set up the Swift Current regional medicare plan in 1946 he had heard rumours that the college was advising Swift Current doctors not to co-operate. He had threatened to rob the College of Physicians of its powers to license doctors and give them to the university. In the 1960 campaign he again ordered the college not to harass doctors who were willing to co-operate with province-wide medicare. "What the legislature has given," he said, "the legislature can take away."[9] He underestimated the solidarity of the medical profession. Hardly a single doctor would support the government during the crisis.

For more than a year after the 1960 election, Thompson's advisory committee shuffled its papers. The group had not even started open hearings by November, and Thompson wrote to Douglas that he wanted to resign. Douglas replied with a reassuring letter, predicting that the committee would reach "some common understanding," perhaps after hearing from the public.[10]

For the most part, Douglas had no direct dealings with the College of Physicians and Surgeons during this period. He left the job of meeting with doctors to J. Walter Erb, whom he had appointed as his minister of public health in 1956. Erb, sadly, was the most incompetent cabinet minister in the history of the CCF. Clarence Fines recalled that Erb usually botched answers to questions in the House and frequently had to be rescued by other ministers. Davies, Erb's successor, said that Erb could not write a letter. Allan Blakeney, who joined the cabinet in 1960, said that Erb always gave both the government and the doctors the impression that the other side was ready to make concessions. When it was obvious that Erb was making no progress, several cabinet ministers urged Douglas to fire him as health minister. The premier, ever loyal to his subordinates, did not. "If Blakeney had been the health minister right from 1960, there would have been an understanding about what the government was going to do," said Robert Walker, the attorney-general at the time. "The doctors wouldn't have lost all the face they did by pulling off a strike...Erb was incapable of communicating a straight story to the doctors and he was incapable of giving us a straight report on what the doctors were saying to us."[11]

The spring of 1961 passed, and with it Douglas's last regular session in the Saskatchewan legislature. There was still no medicare bill from the government. In June, Douglas announced officially that he would stand for the leadership of the New Party at its founding convention that summer.

Some of the doctors now decided that the profession should make a deal with Douglas rather than wait for someone else to take over as premier. A breakaway group of them approached Walter Smishek, a labour representative on the Medical Care Advisory Committee. They asked him to go to Douglas and insist that Walter Erb be fired as minister of health. Perhaps a new minister who understood the issues could work out a compromise, they told Smishek, between the cabinet and the College of Physicians and Surgeons. Smishek went to Douglas, but Douglas said it was a bad time to make cabinet changes. The college, satisfied with the lack of progress, continued its occasional exchange of letters with Erb.

Douglas took the federal leadership of the New Democratic Party in early August. He had already instructed officials to polish up the draft medicare bill. Now the cabinet asked Thompson's committee for an interim report that would contain "at least the broad outlines" of their recommendations.[12] The Advisory Committee reported at the end of September. Thompson told the cabinet that the document was the best he could do, given the college nominees' lack of co-operation. It called for the establishment of a universal health insurance program to be run by a government-appointed commission. The doctors, it said, should be paid on a fee-for-service basis.

Almost immediately, Douglas called the legislature together to approve a Medical Care Insurance Act. The special session opened with a short Throne Speech and a debate, which gave the Liberals a chance to rag Douglas about his impending departure from the province and about the trade unions' role in the new NDP. Ross Thatcher, the Liberal leader, also criticized the medicare proposal. He did not reject health insurance per se, but he demanded that Saskatchewan voters should have a chance to make their views known in a plebiscite.

Douglas used the Throne Speech debate to say farewell to the legislature as well as to extol the virtues of medicare. Once again, he spoke of his pride that Saskatchewan was taking the first step: "I believe, Mr. Speaker, that if this medical care program is successful, and I think it will be, it will prove to be the forerunner of a national medical insurance plan. It will become the nucleus around which Canada will ultimately build a comprehensive health insurance program which will cover all health services—not just hospitalization and medical care—but eventually dental care, optometric care, drugs and all other services which people receive. I believe that such a plan operated by the federal and provincial governments jointly will ultimately come to Canada. But I don't think it will come unless we lead the way."[13]

The Medical Care Insurance Act, as Walter Erb put it before the House a few days later, contained one important change from earlier drafts.

Patients would not pay any premiums, and the entire program would be funded from general tax revenues. Douglas had told a reporter as late as September that premiums might pay for a third of the cost of the insurance plan. He was a strong supporter of the idea that there should be a direct medicare tax, said Bill Davies later: "He felt that if everyone paid something, they would value the plan more."[14] However, Davies said, others in the cabinet opposed the collecting of premiums.

The College of Physicians and Surgeons took a bleak view of the government's action in the House. The doctors' spokesmen protested that Erb had not warned them about the special session and had not given them a look at the bill before it was introduced. At an emergency general meeting on October 13—the same day that Douglas addressed the House—they voted 295 to 5 against co-operating with the medicare plan.

Some analysts have called the government's failure to consult with the doctors "a grave mistake."[15] However, it is hard to see what Douglas would have gained by inviting the College of Physicians to look at his bill in advance. The college's appointees, along with a Chamber of Commerce member, had refused to sign Thompson's interim report. They had handed in a minority report proposing their own plan. As Al Johnson has written, "It was not universal, it was not compulsory, it was not to be administered by a public body, it was not to be financed on the basis of ability to pay, it involved unconditional government subsidy to private bodies and it involved a means test."[16]

On November 1, 1961, Tommy Douglas stepped down as premier. Cabinet and caucus chose Woodrow Lloyd to replace him. A few days later the medicare bill passed in the legislature with the support of the Liberals. Lloyd set April 1 as the start-up date for the insurance program and appointed William Davies as health minister, moving Walter Erb to public works. Erb resented his demotion and, in May 1962, with the government under siege, he deserted the CCF for the Liberal Party.

The Medical Care Insurance Act was now law. There had been no legislative committee hearings and no briefs. The CCF's critics, and some of its members, believed that Douglas had forced the pace so he could take credit for the measure when he moved to Ottawa. Douglas later denied having this motive. "I was convinced that unless we got medicare going in 1962, it wasn't going to have a chance to get the wrinkles ironed out and be operating with relative smoothness by the time we came to the election in 1964."[17]

Lloyd and Davies worked unsuccessfully over the winter to set up a medical insurance plan that would be acceptable to the College of Physicians. Davies approached several popular doctors to serve on the board of the new Insurance Commission, but they told him that the college would come down on them "like a ton of bricks" if they agreed to work with the CCF.[18] In March 1962 the government reopened talks with the college on possible amendments to the Medical Care Insurance Act, and postponed the start-up for medicare from April to July 1. Douglas later described this delay as crucial in giving the doctors the confidence to go ahead with their strike. Davies said, however, that the Insurance Commission, the agency that was to run medicare, was simply not ready to function on April 1.

The talks with the college broke down and the doctors and their supporters mobilized. Across the province, opponents of the health insurance plan formed Keep Our Doctors committees—a response to the doctors' warnings that they would leave Saskatchewan en masse when medicare came into effect. Some of the activists were citizens who had been frightened by the doctors' statements, and some were veteran Liberals. As a reporter was to write during the ensuing strike, "The same people, wearing a succession of different hats, act in the names of the local boards of trade, of municipal councils, of the Keep our Doctors committees, and even of the hospital boards of many small communities."[19]

While the anti-medicare groups grew in strength, Prime Minister Diefenbaker called a federal election. Douglas ran in Regina, and his campaign encountered bitter hostility, vandalism, and threats. The race would have been an uphill struggle even without the KOD, but the medicare crisis made the 1962 federal election perhaps the most unpleasant in Douglas's career. On election day in early June, he went down to defeat.

Rumours persisted that Douglas was meddling in the talks between Lloyd and the doctors, that he had ordered Lloyd to take a hard line and had sabotaged a near agreement. Douglas and Davies both denied this allegation. As the doctors' strike began in early July, the Toronto *Star* found the former premier at his cabin at Carlyle having a "friendly chat" with some local doctors. "It would be the height of impertinence for me to advise the government," he said. "Mr. Lloyd is coping with the situation. He doesn't need my help."[20]

Essentially, the strike signalled the doctors' defiance of the idea that the legislature should make the law. A nameless editor at the Regina *Leader-Post*, in egging on the doctors and the KOD groups, attacked the parliamentary system: "The people of Saskatchewan have devoted an immense amount of energy in fighting the tyranny of determined men who are obsessed with the notion that support of the majority of members of the legislature justifies the use of this power in the name of allegedly democratic majority rule to foist their own will on the people."[21]

The strike soon lost steam. The government flew in replacement doctors, many of them from Britain. Public opinion across Canada crystallized on the side of the CCF. The Liberals called for an emergency debate, and Ross Thatcher got his picture in the papers for kicking the front door of the Legislative Chamber. By the end of July, however, the college and the government had reached agreement with the help of a mediator, and the doctors returned to work.

Medicare, despite all the ruckus, made life easier for Saskatchewan's doctors, ensuring that all their bills would be paid. They now had to bargain collectively if they wanted to raise their fees, but, otherwise, they kept control of their profession. The Medical Care Insurance Commission issued all payments directly to doctors; community-run clinics could not collect the fees and put their doctors on salary. The College of Physicians retained its control over licensing and discipline.

In the spring of 1964 the Saskatchewan CCF under Woodrow Lloyd narrowly lost a general election to the Liberals. Douglas, like some other observers, blamed the medicare crisis for the loss—as well as the fact that Lloyd chose muddy April, and not the traditional June date, for the vote. "I think if I had stayed I would have won the '64 election," Douglas said in a 1980 interview. The Lloyd government, he explained, made a mistake in postponing the start of medicare from April to July 1962 and allowing the doctors time to plan their strike. "The moment [the doctors] saw that the government was prepared to give way for three months, that gave them the idea that they could get it postponed a year or two years or three years. And I wouldn't have budged, because I dealt with the medical profession while I was minister of Health and I knew that if you ever gave an inch, you were through."[22]

However, if Lloyd erred in delaying the start-up of medicare, then Douglas's previous mistakes in timing were even more serious. Perhaps he should have brought down his Medical Care Insurance Bill early in 1961, and put the plan into effect by April or May of that year. Instead, he waited for the Thompson report, so he could show he had consulted the doctors and the public. The report, though, proved to be a useless tool for placating the critics. The college doctors did not sign it, and the government could not pretend to have studied it before presenting a Medical Insurance Act a few weeks later.

The medicare crisis gave Thatcher prominence as the most effective anti-CCF leader, and the Liberals emerged as the best-organized alternative to the CCF. However, Thatcher did not, in 1964, propose changes to the health insurance plan, and a survey of Saskatchewan doctors taken in 1965 showed that most were satisfied with medicare in practice. Accounts of the period have given the doctors' strike too big a part in the Liberals' 1964 victory.

The Saskatchewan CCF government died, above all, of old age. The province had reached a new height of prosperity, and Premier Lloyd promised further economic development. But the Liberals, whose candidates were younger and hungrier than the CCF's, promised to do the same things—and to do them better. The slump in oil exploration, the stagnant population levels, the government's failure to attract secondary manufacturing—the Liberals, as a party of business, promised to cure these ills. In one remarkable blunder in 1963, Lloyd's government extended full financial support to the Roman Catholic high schools—without consulting any of the public school boards. The move awakened the latent anti-Catholic feelings of many Saskatchewan Protestants, and may have hurt the CCF more than medicare had.

The chance nature of the electoral system also played a part. The

Liberals and the CCF drew almost an equal number of votes in the 1964 election. If the CCF had taken 240 more votes in the right areas, they would have won. Of course, if the Liberals had taken a few hundred more votes, they might have greatly increased their majority in the House.

For Douglas, leading the struggling federal NDP, the loss of Saskatchewan was a heavy blow. To his credit, he did not break stride. He respected the right of the voters to change governments, to blow the cobwebs out. He realized that the party had not worked hard enough to offer fresh ideas to first-time voters.

Democratic socialists, he told the 1964 Saskatchewan CCF convention, must take the long-term view. There were still great breakthroughs to come, he said. Canada remained a selfish society, with enough repair shops for its Cadillacs but not enough hospitals for its people. It was true that the organized left, after more than thirty years under a party umbrella, had failed to get its message to most Canadians. Take heart, he said; Sweden's Social Democrats had worked for seventy-one unbroken years in opposition; Germany's had waited 102 years:

> You know, there's a passage in the Acts of the Apostles that tells about the early Christian church when it was located in Jerusalem. They used to keep together by having little meetings, talking about the great days of the past, and what a wonderful thing it had been to have the privilege of working with the founder of their religion. And then a terrible thing happened. The Church was persecuted. Some of them were put to death and some were imprisoned, and the Bible says, "and they were scattered abroad teaching the Gospel."
>
> In other words, what looked like a terrible tragedy scattered them out over the world of that day. Instead of sitting around and holding hands with each other and saying what a wonderful group they were, they were forced to go out and talk to other people.
>
> That is exactly what the 22nd of April last may do for us.[23]

21

New Start,
False Start?

EVEN BEFORE its twentieth birthday the CCF's hopes for someday forming a national government were diminishing fast. The
party's wartime popularity had faded. Its leaders' predictions
of a postwar depression had proved false, and Canada was enjoying an
economic boom. Coldwell's caucus shrank to a mere thirteen members
after the election of 1949. To many observers the CCF looked irrelevant,
"for it appeared the Liberals could do almost as much in the field of
welfare and were probably better equipped to manage a mixed
economy."[1] The party tried self-renewal, but its fortunes slid further.
Finally, its leaders agreed to end its existence, and moved to design a
new party that would have a broader appeal.

Tommy Douglas lent his name to the national committee that formed
this New Party, and agreed to serve as first national leader when an
alliance of the CCF and organized labour took the name New Democratic
Party at its first convention in 1961. All the same, he said good-bye to
the CCF with doubt and regret.

The CCF tried hard, in its last decade, to make its message more appropriate to an era of full employment and economic growth. Frank Scott, the
national CCF president, called in 1950 for a new statement of basic objectives. After years of haggling by various committees, the party ratified the
Winnipeg Declaration of Principles in 1956. This declaration failed to win
votes, and at the same time it disappointed party militants. The media condemned it as a shift towards the crowded political centre; *Maclean's* magazine pronounced itself "dismayed" that the party had "given up most of its
reason for being."[2] The document touched on the familiar CCF hopes for
pensions, health care, and world peace, but it was, in its economic outlook,
much more cautious than the Regina Manifesto. It drew a less absolute contrast between the prevailing market economy and the planned economy
of the future, and, avoiding the manifesto's cry for nationalization, it made
clear that private industry should always have a place in society.

Douglas defended the Winnipeg declaration in his speeches and in a series of radio broadcasts. He insisted that the CCF still opposed the capitalist system, the system where a small corporate elite holds great political power. Social and economic decisions, he said, must be based on human need, and not on the desire for profit. The CCF still wanted a planned economy, where public bodies would channel investment to useful ends. On the subject of government ownership he quoted Woodsworth and his own early speeches: the party wanted to take over monopolies, but had always left room in its thinking for competitive private business.[3]

George Cadbury, his former senior adviser, wrote to Douglas that the national CCF had learned a "sane wisdom" from the experience of governing Saskatchewan. "I see rather the reflection at a national level of the arguments that Tommy McLeod and I had with Carlyle King in 1946, when, as you will remember, he summoned us to his office to tell us that we were no Socialists because we said there was a place for the private enterprise sector."[4]

But the declaration's "sane wisdom" left the the majority of voters indifferent. The CCF continued to stagnate at the federal level and in most of the provinces. It was now apparent that the movement would have to rebuild itself through structural change, not internal debate.

The New Democratic Party is the product of this structural change. To a great extent the party is the work of David Lewis, who became national president of the CCF in 1954. As a university student at Oxford, Lewis had come to know several influential Labour Party politicians. He had been deeply impressed by that party's formula for making labour a political power and by its success. For a quarter of a century he advocated a similar structure for Canada's political left. As a party official and a leading labour lawyer, he was able to persuade both the CCF and organized labour to study the idea of joint political action.

The divided Canadian labour movement had largely avoided formal ties with the CCF, and most unions remained politically independent. Nonetheless, the industrial union congress had declared in 1943 that the party should be its "political arm," and several prominent labour leaders from the Steelworkers, the Auto Workers, and the Packinghouse union had worked hard for the CCF cause. These now joined David Lewis in seeking a way to bring organized labour into politics.

The task was made simpler for Lewis and his allies when, in 1956, the Canadian Congress of Labour and the Trades and Labour Congress ended their years of feuding and joined to form the Canadian Labour Congress. Lewis hoped that the more politically active industrial body, the CCL, would draw the more aloof, conservative, craft-based TLC into an active political role. His hopes seemed to be fulfilled when Claude Jodoin, drawn from the ranks of the TLC as first president of the new congress, agreed to work with Lewis towards a new political arrangement.

The March 1958 disaster at the polls gave the national CCF more evidence, if it needed more, that it must reorganize or die. In the federal election of that year John Diefenbaker's federal Conservatives crushed their opponents, reducing the CCF representation in the House to eight seats. M. J. Coldwell, the national leader, suffered his first defeat in twenty-three years. The setback finished him as a national force. The CCF House leader, Stanley Knowles, lost the seat that Woodsworth had first taken in 1921. After this, Lewis wrote later, the party had no choice but to turn to labour for help.[5] Within a few weeks Knowles found a job in the Canadian Labour Congress as the vice-president in charge of developing the New Party.

The Labour Congress had already been preparing, even before the disastrous election, to sound a mating call. Lewis, along with Eamon Park of the Steelworkers, had drafted a resolution that went before the Congress executive in February; it spoke of the need for "a fundamental realignment of political forces in Canada...[and]....the need for a broadly-based people's political movement which embraces the CCF, the Labour movement, farm organizations, professional people, and other liberally-minded persons interested in basic social reform."[6] The spring convention of the Congress approved the resolution and assigned ten delegates to a national committee to set up a New Party. The CCF convention in July gave the resolution unanimous support and named ten more members to the committee, including Lewis and Coldwell. Douglas allowed his name to be added to the list, but party records suggest that he attended only three meetings in the next three years. After mid-1959 Woodrow Lloyd became Douglas's official proxy.[7]

On paper, the New Party would differ only slightly from the CCF. In the CCF, members and affiliated groups joined provincial sections. In the NDP, the national organization seeks links with other groups. Theoretically, farm organizations, co-ops, and professional bodies have all been free to work out terms of affiliation with the federal NDP. In practice, only labour unions have done so.

Sceptics have suggested that had they cared to, the unions could have affiliated with the CCF's provincial bodies, and that the whole New Party process was a waste of time. Defenders of the New Party insist that the building process itself, the meetings, the debate, the socializing, drew many new faces into the movement between 1958 and 1961. The NDP's contacts in the middle levels of trade union leadership paid off in the 1960s, when labour became an important source of money and organizing talent. However, there is little evidence of the grass-roots initiative and enthusiasm that had spawned the CCF a quarter of a century earlier.

The operation was controlled from the national offices of the party and the unions. The New Party Committee spent little time with political ideas. Its aim was to get the various unions and union federations to pledge support for the New Party. These unions, it was hoped, would then persuade their members to become active at the local level. The decision to "move faster at the top than at the bottom" with a union-based campaign worried Douglas from the outset, and it added to the disadvantages he faced when he set out to bring the organized farmers' movements into the fold.[8] It is hard, in fact, to point to anyone outside the Lewis-Knowles circles who voiced real enthusiasm about the process, despite the CCF's unanimous support at the 1958 convention. Knowles wrote a euphoric book which forecast a rising tide of labour support for the New Party; but even Donald MacDonald, the leader of the CCF in labour's Ontario heartland, wrote to Knowles, "we must lean over backwards to assure the genuinely liberal-minded people that this new political party is their political home and that they will not be squeezed out by labour domination."[9]

Many others from the CCF were more vocal in their criticisms. Douglas Fisher and Arnold Peters, both northern Ontario MPs, publicly questioned changing the party's name. The CCF in Fisher's riding had already enlisted urban liberals and labour. He wondered, "what are we cutting ourselves off from J. S. Woodsworth for?"[10] But the opinions of the CCF's eight members of Parliament carried little weight either with its own National Executive or with the New Party Committee. The *Financial Post* predicted that the international unions would run the NDP and "take their orders from the U.S. 'head offices.' "[11] Two rising activists in the Manitoba CCF, Al Mackling and Howard Pawley, echoed this concern, warning of "union control without union responsibility."[12]

In Saskatchewan, Douglas faced a perplexing problem. As a member of the National Committee he was expected to promote the New Party idea in his home province, but he could not pretend to his supporters that the Saskatchewan CCF was a failure. Several of his closest friends and advisers were lukewarm to the idea of abandoning the CCF for the sake of a gamble in Ontario. His deputy, Clarence Fines, a senior statesman who had chaired the CCF organizing convention of 1932, expressed pessimism. Fines, on the verge of retirement, wrote to Coldwell, "If any change were brought about in the immediate future, it would be the beginning of the end in Saskatchewan, where our farmers are still very much afraid of any organization dominated by the trade union movement."[13] Coldwell, who had brought both Fines and Douglas into politics, wrote "I've never been enthusiastic about a CCF-Labour alliance. It may work out, but labour has been for us 'a weak reed.' "[14] Woodrow Lloyd also wrote to Coldwell: "The Committee to date has had an almost complete preoccupation with structure, without attempting to answer the question: structure for what?"[15]

Jack Corman, one of Douglas's most trusted strategists, resigned himself to the death of the CCF name, but, he wrote, "the success of the new party will depend on the extent to which basic CCF principles are incorporated in the new party program, and the extent to which the constitution guarantees the CCF equal voice with labour in future council and convention decisions...The CCF, despite its inability to poll the votes to form a national government, has won the esteem and respect of Canadians for its inspired unselfishness, progressive leadership and its dogged advocacy of humanitarian reform...the CCF has not been a failure, but a glorious success."[16]

In this climate of conflict, faced with a mixed set of loyalties, Douglas was forced to sort out his own thoughts. It is small wonder that for some time he showed ambivalence to the New Party effort.

Douglas had always preached that the economic salvation of the farmer and the worker lay in uniting their forces against the common foe—big business. The New Party project was dedicated to such a union. Furthermore, it was led by two of Douglas's strongest allies on the national scene, Stanley Knowles and David Lewis. At the same time, he had to listen to the warnings of his long-time associates in Saskatchewan. He did not accept the view that a marriage of lobby groups would automatically change voting behaviour at election time. As he said in 1985, "The longer one has to do with politics, the longer one is impressed with the fact that if democracy means anything, you've got to convince the people, and you don't just convince people by saying a certain organization of which you're a nominal member is going to join us. There's no guarantee that they're going to work for you or vote for you, or that they will understand the program you're trying to put in...If I had the power tomorrow to put all the trade unionists and all the farmers into the NDP en masse, I wouldn't do it. Because, it's like marching in a captive army and thinking they'll defend your city, and when the pressure comes they're found down in the basement somewhere."[17]

In his public statements, in his letters to citizens, Douglas supported the New Party concept. It promised, he said, to become "a broad based political party representing the great majority of those who work to earn their daily bread."[18] Farmers, he said, should seize the opportunity: "My own feeling is that if the prairie farmers are going to get their fair share of the national income, they must seek allies in their fight for economic justice."[19] Douglas wished to avoid discord in his party; he knew that "union makes us strong" and factionalism destroys left-wing causes. He decided, however reluctantly, to go along with what looked like the main wave within the Canadian movement.

Privately, he vacillated. In mid-1959 he wrote to Carl Hamilton, "I am not prepared to submerge the identity of the CCF unless I know what we are joining, and with whom." He disliked the New Party Club idea, which created a third force in the New Party outside labour and the CCF. The clubs were meant as an entry point for the "liberally-minded," but Douglas feared they would bring an invasion of the unwashed—"communists, Trotskyites, neo-fascists or funny-money theorists."[20]

He disliked the "structure first, principles later" approach that Lewis was taking; at best, he feared it would produce a well-organized party with no policies. He wrote to Knowles, "It seems to me that we need to set forth some clear-cut concept of where we are going."[21] For all the talk of labour domination, the National Committee was making sluggish progress in winning labour over. The rank and file in the trade unions, he said, appeared to be apathetic towards the whole process. He counselled delay: "There ought to be as little publicity as possible on a national scale...we should let this movement evolve naturally at the constituency and provincial levels."[22] The year 1960, he told Lewis, was far too soon for "a final and effective decision on winding up the affairs of the CCF."[23]

Perhaps Douglas's web of memories about the grass-roots origins of the CCF was too nostalgic. It was true that in earlier days the CCF faithful in Saskatchewan flocked to study sessions in their neighbours' homes and to public meetings at country schoolhouses. All the same, the movement had not "evolved naturally"; a few dozen labour, co-op, and farm leaders had worked hard to make the CCF something more than a debating society. The early CCF was a people's movement, but it was led, like the embryonic New Party, by a coalition of notables.

Some CCF radicals on the prairies and the West Coast worried that the New Party would abandon the movement's most important goal— the establishment of a socialist economy. For many veterans, socialism meant the nationalization of industry, together with central control by state planners. William Irvine, the old lion of Alberta, wrote that "to refuse to state our objectives unequivocally will inspire mistrust, confuse our following and reveal both intellectual and moral weakness."[24] In early 1960 a series of working papers on the New Party's policy choices avoided the term socialism, as did the draft constitution and party program issued later in the year. The British Columbia CCF insisted that this should be corrected. Its leading radical, Colin Cameron, blamed Douglas for the decision to soft-pedal the movement's socialist roots: "Tommy Douglas quite clearly disassociated the New Party from any socialist program when he spoke in Victoria recently."[25]

Cameron was right in supposing that Douglas could no longer support his old-time socialism, but he had clearly missed the drift of recent CCF thinking. In the days of the manifesto, left-wing CCFers like William Irvine had believed that a panel of public servants, properly organized, could manipulate a state-owned economy for the benefit of all. The years since had dampened the CCF mainstream's appetite for nationalizing industry, and increased its desire to control economic life by other means. Perhaps Douglas can be faulted for not making this clearer in his defence of the Winnipeg declaration. In the promised land of the late CCF—and the NDP—private companies would not be kept out of sight like unwanted children. They would share in the economic planning process, even if only as junior partners. The resulting system might be termed democratic socialism by some, but it would not be the socialism of the manifesto.

Douglas believed that many trade union leaders supported the New Party process, even if the rank and file were apathetic. Among Canada's farmers, however, even the leadership appeared indifferent to the fate of the proposed New Party. This became a great source of agitation for the premier. He wrote to Knowles, "I am very disturbed by the way the whole thing has been handled... Most alarming of all is the fact that the CCF and CLC seem to be pushing ahead without the farm groups who, in my opinion, are indispensable to such an alignment."[26]

Douglas feared that in neglecting to build farm support, the movement would sacrifice its position in Saskatchewan. Like his colleagues, he worried that the CCF would exchange its prairie base for some vague promises of future labour support in Ontario. While he could see that the national CCF was in danger of fading from the political scene, he could never concede that the party had failed in Saskatchewan, where it was firmly rooted in the province's political life. It seemed that the New Party, intended as the CCF's salvation, might threaten everything he and his comrades had achieved over twenty-five years.

The one important mission Douglas undertook for the New Party Committee—along with Hazen Argue, the Saskatchewan MP and CCF House leader, and Donald MacDonald of Ontario—was to court the organized farm movements. The effort failed completely. Ontario farmers, said MacDonald, had "had their fingers burned" in their association with the do-nothing United Farmers government of 1919, and had no desire to join the New Party as a group.[27] In the West, farm groups felt the same way. The first New Party seminar in Manitoba, in the summer of 1959, attracted 300 people, but only thirty were farm representatives.

Douglas tried to reassure Saskatchewan farmers and their organizations by bringing farm and labour leaders together. Over the winter of 1958-59 he organized a series of "week-end institutes," and in May he led a joint session of the Saskatchewan Farmers' Union and the Saskatchewan Federation of Labour. The Farmers' Union leaders expressed sympathy for the CCF premier; however, they could not join an organization they knew nothing about, "a synthetic coalition which doesn't exist except on paper, and that on a national level."[28] In mid-summer 1959 Douglas met with Argue and MacDonald. Recognizing the mood of the Canadian farm organizations, they concluded that the New Party would have to draw its farm support from individual farmers, just as the CCF had since the late 1930s.

The farm groups clearly wished to keep their contacts open with all political parties. On the prairies especially, farmers were happy with the work of John Diefenbaker's new federal government, which promised to find vast new markets for Canadian wheat. At the same time, the self-image of farmers had changed since Coldwell and Williams had worked to form the Farmer Labour Party in 1932. With the disappearance of the small farm, and growing prosperity for those that survived, farmers saw themselves more and more as entrepreneurs and less as victims of capitalism. Even in Saskatchewan, where the CCF party and government had worked to bring the two sides into harmony, hostility towards organized labour remained uncomfortably close to the surface. Saskatchewan unions were a known quantity, part of the fabric of local political life, but Douglas was asking the farmers to join with eastern labour. The farm organizations saw the CLC and its big eastern locals as creatures of the international unions, or perhaps as allies of central Canadian business on issues such as tariffs, freight rates, and farm subsidies. They could not be seen as prospective political bed-mates.

Despite the warnings from Douglas and Argue that they needed more time to secure grass-roots support, especially from the farming community, the New Party organizers pressed for an early founding convention. They worried that the New Party was "marking time," that it was "all dressed up with nowhere to go," and that it might lose momentum.[29]

Douglas and the eastern leadership also differed on the site for the proposed founding convention. Douglas felt that it should be held in Winnipeg, to avoid the appearance of an eastern takeover. Delegate representation, he added, should be split equally between the unions and the CCF. He contended that CCFers "will be hurt and offended if they get the impression that the CCF has been tricked into a founding convention at which they can be outnumbered and outvoted."[30]

In late February 1960 Lewis and Knowles visited Douglas and his colleagues in Regina. They considered and then rejected his ideas for the convention. The views of the prairie farm community, and of the one group of CCF politicians with a winning record, would not figure in the countdown to the New Party's formation. The committee ruled that the founding convention would be held in Ottawa in July 1961, in order to attract delegates from Quebec, and that there should be no limit on the number of union delegates.*

At this point, as the 1960 provincial election approached, Douglas moved to distance the Saskatchewan CCF from the New Party effort. His caucus had asked for such a step, and his provincial party had demanded it. The CCF's doubts had trapped it in a schizophrenic bind. The party wanted renewal, but it wanted to hang on to the old ways. It wanted to bring other Canadians into a democratic partnership, but it wanted to control the process. In a statement to the legislature on March 9, 1960, Douglas came close to disavowing the party that he would lead after 1961. The Liberal press and opposition jumped eagerly on the contradiction.

> Any new national party...will not in any way affect the status of the Saskatchewan CCF. We are now affiliated with the national CCF organization. The annual convention of the Saskatchewan CCF will decide whether or not to affiliate with the new party if and when it is formed.
> If it decides to affiliate with the new party, the position of the Saskatchewan CCF will remain unaltered. This will not affect the provincial autonomy we now enjoy under our constitution, and our policy will continue to be set by our annual constituency and provincial conventions.[31]

Douglas won the 1960 Saskatchewan election with a solid majority. It was the CCF's last victory on the prairies. Many of the veterans—people like John Brockelbank, Woodrow Lloyd, Sandy Nicholson—would soldier on for the cause of the NDP. But public support would ebb away. Despite Douglas's leadership in Ottawa, the New Party would suffer a prolonged drought in Saskatchewan.

---

* The CCF was outvoted at the New Party's founding meeting. About 45 per cent of delegates came from the CCF, 30 per cent from organized labour, and 25 per cent from the New Party clubs.

On August 9, 1960, at the largest national convention in its history, the CCF agreed to yield its future to the New Party. There were, however, internal rumblings of discontent. The Saskatchewan delegates were negative enough in their comments to gain the attention of the press. They spoke loudly of Saskatchewan's right of self-determination and the need to keep the CCF name.[32] On another front, the party establishment lost a decision to the membership on the issue of interim leadership. Against the advice of their national council, CCF delegates chose Hazen Argue, a heavyset, good-natured farmer from west of Weyburn, to guide them through their last year.

22

High Noon

THE LEADERSHIP ISSUE plagued the Canadian left from the beginning of the 1950s. With M. J. Coldwell's defeat in the 1958 election, the CCF's lack of rising young leaders became obvious to the whole country. Year after year the same names had appeared on the CCF executive roster: David Lewis, Stanley Knowles, Frank Scott, Thérèse Casgrain; all of them worked faithfully within their well-defined spheres, and none challenged Coldwell. In 1960, when labour and the CCF finished their plans to launch their new venture, only one candidate, Hazen Argue, stepped forward to claim the leadership. Douglas had denied for years that he would ever head a federal party, but he felt he had to stop Argue. At the founding convention of the NDP in the summer of 1961 the fifty-six-year-old premier swept to an easy victory.

Voices inside and outside the federal caucus had long suggested that Douglas would succeed Coldwell. The older man, worn down by electoral losses and by his wife's long illness and death, had lost his grip on his federal caucus in the mid-1950s. After an embarrassing revolt over foreign policy he tried to resign, but his caucus had rejected his resignation. Douglas, said one reporter, was the only person who could replace Coldwell and project the "appealing and memorable image" that the party needed.[1] Coldwell himself, from the beginning, regarded Douglas as his natural heir.

In mid-December 1957 David Lewis, the national CCF president, wrote what was perhaps his first firm leadership proposal to Douglas, asking the premier to take over the national party at its 1958 convention.[2] Douglas declined, saying that he wished to fight one more election in Saskatchewan. In a 1958 interview he said, "The province deserves everything I and others can give it for the next twenty years."[3] Coldwell's health was bad; the CCF took a pounding in 1958 and Coldwell lost his seat; but in the absence of any alternative candidates, M. J. remained as nominal leader. After a meeting or two with the party's caucus of eight MPs, he chose not to return to Parliament Hill and the party slid further into disrepair.

One day soon, CCFers believed, Douglas must step forward to pick up the pieces. Carl Hamilton, then the CCF national secretary, said, "I don't remember anybody ever talking seriously about anybody as successor except Tommy Douglas at the early stages. Of course, David's name came up, but he always made it abundantly clear that he was not available."[4] It is not surprising that Douglas developed the idea that he was wanted. The most prominent figures in the party were pushing him to lead, and they would continue to push until he gave in.

The eight-member CCF parliamentary caucus of 1940 had included some excellent members, including Douglas, Coldwell in his prime, and Angus MacInnis; the ragged caucus of 1958 was made up of mavericks and eccentrics. David Lewis, as CCF chairman, sat in when the caucus chose its leader; his preference, Hazen Argue of Saskatchewan, defeated two other candidates in an absurd 3-2-2 vote. From that point on, the caucus followed its own course and had almost no contact with either the national executive or with Coldwell. Argue's closest colleagues—Douglas Fisher and Arnold Peters from northern Ontario and Frank Howard from northern B.C.—began to develop the anti-establishment complex that would guide their conduct during the coming leadership contest.

Hazen Robert Argue was something of a boy wonder in the CCF. Graduating in agricultural economics from the University of Saskatchewan in 1944, he went to Parliament in 1945 from the riding of Wood Mountain. He was twenty-four years of age, a farmer's son from Kayville who had never travelled further than Calgary. Nonetheless, he showed great self-confidence and could soon hold his own in the debates on freight rates, pork prices, and other farm issues. He worked hard on constituency matters, and his riding stood by him when most CCF MPs went down before the Diefenbaker tide. A few weeks after the 1958 election, Argue became the CCF's federal House leader, a job that greatly raised his public profile. He was now one of the logical candidates to succeed Coldwell when the old leader retired—as it appeared he would do at the 1960 CCF national convention.

More than anything, said Fisher, Argue could please the crowds. He had "a great ability to stand up there and roll it. He was a marvellous bullshitter." Fisher continued, "Tommy told me about the time they campaigned together. At the beginning of the campaign, Hazen's speeches would be very short, and Tommy's would be long. By the end of the campaign, Tommy's speeches were getting shorter because Hazen was stealing all of his best material."[5]

The long-time members of the executive had little time for Argue. They saw him as a stopgap House leader with a regional appeal, and no knowledge of any issue outside the farming business. They knew that if Argue took the national CCF leadership on Coldwell's retirement, the MP from Kayville might walk into the New Party leader's job by default in 1961. The old guard decided, therefore, that he could not have Coldwell's job. They would take the risk of leaving the party leaderless for a year, and hope that Diefenbaker did not call an election. A few weeks before the 1960 convention they extracted a promise from Argue that he would not seek the leadership.

One of the inner circle, Andrew Brewin, tried to justify this decision in a public reply to a 1966 newspaper column by Doug Fisher. The CCF executive, he wrote, had not wanted to "prejudge the choice of leader" for the New Party.[6] This self-contradictory letter made it clear, though, that the CCF big guns were determined, in the spring of 1960, to leave the way clear for Tommy Douglas.

When the caucus militants heard about the executive decision to keep the national leader's chair vacant, they were outraged. Fisher, Peters, and Howard had no illusions about Argue—they rated him as only a passable and sometimes lazy House leader—but they were angry that nobody had consulted them about this important turn in party strategy. Douglas, fighting in a provincial campaign, was denying that he had any plans to move to the federal scene. The Lewis clique's attempt to keep the leadership open for Douglas seemed inexplicable.

The MPs mounted a pro-Argue campaign. Four of them issued a bulletin to party members deploring the actions taken by "a certain group" to ensure that the party was left leaderless. The statement said, "There is near unanimity that Premier Douglas would be the perfect CCF National Leader," but in his absence, "we have urged our present House Leader, Hazen Argue, MP, to run for leader at next week's convention. (Hazen, of course, has always been a stong supporter of Tommy Douglas.)"[7]

The CCF held its last national convention in Regina in July 1960. Douglas stayed aloof from the manoeuvring over leadership. He avoided the backroom meeting where the executive called in Argue to confirm that he was not a candidate. After this meeting, Fisher arrived in Regina and began to bully Argue into changing his mind. Fisher placed a call to Ottawa and watched as Argue spoke with caucus members Frank Howard and Arnold Peters. They told him not to show his face on Parliament Hill again unless he followed Fisher's orders: he should read to the convention the speech which Fisher had prepared for him. Then, as Peters told it afterwards, Argue arranged a meeting with the executive; while Fisher "held him up by the friggin' coat," Argue announced he would reject the official strategy and stand for the leadership.[8]

When the matter came to the convention floor, several respected party members, including Angus MacInnis, spoke out against the plan to leave the leadership open. Some delegates raised the hope that Premier Douglas might take the job, but he stated that "he had a responsibility to the people of Saskatchewan who had elected his government, and...he was not available for the national leadership." The rank and file then acclaimed Hazen Argue as the party's last national leader, successor to

Woodsworth and Coldwell. Under the heading, UNANIMOUS SUPPORT FOR ARGUE, the Saskatchewan party paper, *The Commonwealth*, reported that Argue's victory was greeted with a standing ovation and thunderous applause.[9]

Argue was now installed as the national leader of a political party that was in the process of dissolving itself. He was the only CCF or NDP leader ever elected without the blessing of the party brass. In fact, he had sabotaged the plans of the executive group, and from now on every other member of the National Committee for a New Party would oppose him. He had "committed the cardinal sin of breaking his solemn word."[10]

The stage was now set for the founding of the New Party and the selection of its leader. Observers still tagged Tommy Douglas as the obvious choice, although Douglas felt that either David Lewis or Stanley Knowles should take the job. Fisher and friends wanted Hazen Argue to give it a try; left to himself, some of them said later, Argue might have backed out. One informed observer suggested that "Hazen was a device, a tool for some people to express their problems...I never had any sense that Hazen was being supported for his intrinsic capabilities."[11]

But if Douglas's persistent refusals were genuine, reasoned Fisher, Argue might emerge as the front runner. Even if the Saskatchewan premier decided to seek the federal leadership, someone should challenge him for the sake of drawing national attention to the New Party. "There would have to be a contest," said Fisher later. "It couldn't just be an affirmation."[12] Argue and Fisher launched a campaign, and Argue remained for some time the only declared candidate.

If the process of forming the New Party had been smoother, if the CCF chapters had expressed less anti-labour hostility, David Lewis might have emerged as the man of the hour in late 1960. Lewis was gifted with many talents, and after twenty-five years as the key party organizer he knew both the national CCF and the labour movement better than Tommy Douglas. He was bilingual, a Rhodes scholar, a distinguished lawyer; Douglas wanted him to stand for the leadership, and his son Stephen has said that his father yearned for the job. Lewis chose, though, to remove himself from consideration. According to Stephen, he saw Douglas as the only realistic choice. Only Douglas could bridge the CCF-labour split in the new party. Lewis said that his own status as a Toronto labour lawyer eliminated him from the running; he told his family that he did not think Canada was ready for a Jewish party leader in any case.[13] From 1957 on David Lewis waged a campaign for Douglas within the party, and his opinion carried a great deal of weight in the CCF.

Stanley Knowles, a member of Parliament since 1942, had won a national reputation as a parliamentarian and a defender of working people and the poor. He had helped to create the New Party from his post at the Canadian Labour Congress. However, Knowles (unknown to the world) suffered from multiple sclerosis and felt he could not run for the leadership. In fact, he once told Douglas he was "desperately afraid" that fate might force him into the leader's job.[14] Knowles, too, was a Douglas supporter.

Throughout the late 1950s, rumours had persisted that Douglas would move to the federal scene after the 1960 provincial election. The election came, the CCF won, and Douglas stayed put in Saskatchewan. "I am not available for this office," he told a supporter. "I don't think public men can play fast and loose with the electorate. Last June I accepted an office from the voters of Saskatchewan, and I feel that my first responsibility is to carry out the task which they assigned to me."[15] In the fall of 1960 he wrote to Andrew Brewin, "I spent nine years in Ottawa and at times I was almost overcome with the frustration and futility of being a voice crying in the wilderness...I feel that my first duty is to stay here and get this [medicare] plan operating on a strong basis."[16]

Douglas was comfortable in Saskatchewan; he was popular, and he exercised real power. We have uncovered no evidence that would suggest that he actively sought the federal leadership. In fact, he wrote that "the job ought to seek the man rather than the man seeking the job." As it happened, the job ended up on his doorstep.[17]

Some have insisted that Douglas knew all along that the job would fall into his lap, and that he eased himself into the leadership contest through a protracted series of half-deceits. It seems more straightforward to assume that Douglas led the Saskatchewan CCF through the 1960 provincial election believing that he would stay in the province; that his repeated statements promoting Lewis as "the logical person to head the New Party" were meant seriously; and that he agreed to run federally only when it became clear that Hazen Argue might win a disastrous acclamation.[18] His letters and statements on the leadership through 1960 and 1961 highlight his sense of duty, and his calculations about what was good for the party, rather than his personal goals.

Douglas showed signs of yielding in letters he wrote near the end of 1960, when it became clear that Lewis and Knowles had bowed out. He liked Argue personally, but he did not want him acclaimed to the leadership. Argue, he said later, "had a good farm background, but little experience of urban problems or foreign affairs."[19]

In early 1961 the leaders of the New Party committee made their feelings public. At a news conference at the National Press Club theatre in Ottawa, Lewis, Knowles, and Claude Jodoin of the CLC all pledged their support for Douglas. Argue hovered at the back of the room, and repeated the premier's assurance that he would not run. The New Party organizers also orchestrated a letter campaign. Petitions poured into Douglas's office from across Canada, begging him to accept the federal leadership. To those who protested that Lewis should not take sides, the CCF chairman replied that he had "no apologies...Tommy Douglas is the best political leader of any political party in Canada."[20]

In Saskatchewan, citizens and colleagues offered Douglas conflicting advice. Constituency organizations passed resolutions, some encouraging him to go, some asking him to stay; the feelings in the caucus reflected this split. Many admirers implored him to remain and protect the one beachhead of Humanity First. A woman wrote, "I figure you belong to the people who stood by you years ago with their nickels and dimes, yes—even their *love*. I know this means a lot to you, surely they can find someone else to lead the New Party."[21] His closest companion, Irma, leaned towards taking the Ottawa job; while she did not want to leave Saskatchewan, she felt that her husband "had a real responsibility" to the national movement.[22]

Argue, meanwhile, was building on support from dissident unionists, far leftists, anti-labour CCFers, even some people who only wanted to keep Douglas in Saskatchewan—"all the people who had a grudge against the whole process."[23] Argue was developing some grudges of his own; he complained that he got no co-operation from the national office, that big union halls were closed to him, and that he was not getting the same opportunity as Douglas to address New Party rallies. He was further frustrated, he said later, in his attempts to canvass the delegates to the upcoming New Party convention. "I was the national leader of the CCF, and I couldn't get the delegate list. Christ." Argue got the distinct feeling that by opposing Douglas, he was breaking the club rules.[24]

For his part, Douglas did nothing to help or to criticize his rival. His close supporters felt that Argue was exploiting every division in the party to win support, taking a radical labour line in Ontario and an anti-labour line in the West. A pro-Douglas MP wrote, "Tommy is aware of what is going on, but refuses absolutely to become involved. I think he is wise in this respect, as long as the rest of us...carry the ball for him."[25]

In late March, Douglas's cabinet associates agreed that each would write him a note of advice. One or two begged him to stay until after the next election; most concluded that the premier must move to the national stage. After the electoral disaster of 1958, and three years without solid leadership, the national movement was "approaching the abyss. Unless the New Party makes some significant impact at the next election, we are facing slow strangulation."[26] Douglas replied to all that he had suffered "many sleepless nights...we have been friends bound together by a common loyalty to certain ideals and goals of achievement." His chief confidant seems to have been John Brockelbank, now the elder statesman of the provincial party and the only member to have sat in the legislature since 1938. He wrote to Brockelbank:

> Frankly, I'm not keen about entering the Federal field. My colleagues here have been so pleasant to work with, and the job is so fascinating, I'd like nothing better than staying here in Saskatchewan...I have no illusions about our achieving government in Canada in my lifetime. But if I can help lay the foundations for a movement that will ultimately establish economic democracy in Canada, that would be a worthwhile contribution.
>
> I have no fears about Saskatchewan...Indeed it may help to have a change of voice and face...It may be that my greatest contribution to Saskatchewan would be to help to win 30 or 40 seats for the New Party in 1962.

If Douglas was to leave Saskatchewan, he wanted the party to take the responsibility. He declared his refusal to campaign for the leadership; further, he would not leave unless the Provincial Council released him from his provincial job, and he would not approach the council for his release. "It will take a little time to persuade our people that this is a wise move," he told Brockelbank. "This is something I must leave to you and my other friends."[27] Nothing in all of this suggests a man driven towards the national leadership by a burning ambition.

In April Douglas wrote a letter that brought "great happiness" to David Lewis. He said he was willing, finally, to stand for the leadership—but only if his Provincial Council agreed, and only if he noticed "substantial signals" of support. He wrote, "I have become convinced that nothing is more important for the future of Canada and its people than the success of the New Party in the next election."[28] Perhaps in violation of his no-campaigning pledge, he made a short speaking tour in Ontario.

Although his letter to Lewis was leaked to the press, he did not formally announce his plans until well after the Provincial Council voted 36-16 to release him. In late June, only a month before the founding convention, he called reporters together at his office in the legislature. His central concern, he told them, was that the New Party should be strong enough to help shape the future—to "end economic stagnation in Canada and encourage peace throughout the world."[29] "We must either break through," he wrote to an old comrade, "or lose the beachhead...the time has come to go for broke."[30]

The *Globe and Mail* suggested that Douglas was throwing away the party's base of power. An anonymous editor wrote, "Without Mr. Douglas, the prospects of the Saskatchewan CCF would be distinctly cloudy...It would not be too much to say that he has been the CCF for the past seventeen years."[31]

In part, Douglas's final decision grew from a growing concern over what he saw as a drift to the right in Canadian politics. He wanted to offer voters across the country "a genuine choice between progressive and reactionary policies."[32] The New Party had not provided a clear direction, so Douglas set out to restate the priorities he had laid down a quarter of a century earlier. Speaking to the New Party's first meeting in Toronto, and at the Château Laurier in Ottawa, he called for measures to create purchasing power, for a proper system of health care and pensions, and for a foreign policy that would extricate Canada from the cold war between the superpowers.

Capitalism had outlived the CCF; but Douglas, at least, would carry some of the Christian idealism of the old party into the new one. Despite the new logo and the new stationery, his message was one of continuity. The old fight would go on. He was convinced that the country was "in a mood to respond to an appeal for emphasizing the things of the mind and the spirit in our national life."[33]

The founding convention took place in mid-summer 1961 in the sweltering heat of Ottawa's Lansdowne Park Coliseum. The National Committee's mating dances had brought 1800 delegates to Ottawa, four times as many as had attended the biggest CCF national convention in history. CCF party delegates were in the minority, although many of the trade unionists present had long ties to the party. More than 500 New Party Club members turned up, many from provinces with shallow CCF roots such as Alberta and Quebec.

For a moment, at the very start, the euphoria faltered, when a delegate asked that Hazen Argue address the convention. But Argue was to be heard only as a leadership candidate, and would not deliver a report as national CCF leader. The floor went instead to the founder of the feast, David Lewis, who delivered a stirring keynote address, attacking the "shabby values" of the consumer society.

Much of the convention was spent debating and approving a party program. As with the Regina Manifesto, many proposals from this founding document have since been written into Canadian law—medicare, some consumer protection, an effort at regional development, and (during the 1970s, at least) some controls on foreign investment. Like the Regina Manifesto, too, the program called for centralized economic planning— and as with the CCF, Douglas and the NDP were never to make clear how this planning would be applied.

On Friday night, August 1, the night before the leadership vote, Arnold Peters advised Argue to pull out of the race; that way, he reasoned, the exact extent of Argue's support would remain unknown and Argue would hold more clout in the party. In Peters's opinion, "everybody had their mind made up before they went there"; even if Argue drew a last-minute underdog vote, it was unlikely that he would draw more than 30 per cent, with Douglas taking the other 70 per cent. "There was no animosity between the two men," said Peters, and Argue did not oppose the idea of withdrawing. However, Jeannie, Argue's wife, was incensed by Douglas's remark that "the job should seek the man rather than the man seeking the job." She took it as evidence that Douglas saw himself as the anointed one. Supported by Argue's other advisers, she insisted that he stay in the race.[34]

The voting went nearly as expected. Douglas took three-quarters of the ballots cast. Lewis and Claude Jodoin hoisted Douglas on to their shoulders as the crowd cheered. Many of those present felt certain that this was a turning point in Canadian political history.

Douglas opened his victory speech with two minutes of unsteady French, pleading for national unity; switching to English, he heaped praise on his opponent, Hazen Argue. "Few men in this country," he said, "have a greater contribution to make." Douglas pledged his loyalty to the party, as Argue had a few minutes before. "God helping me, I will do everything possible to justify the trust which you have placed in me. But any success which I may achieve will be entirely dependent on having you behind me—and not too far behind me."

The common people, he said, must come together to remake the

North American economy, to redirect capital for economic growth and provide purchasing power for workers, farmers, fishermen, and pensioners. "But the only value in developing our economic resources is to give us the wherewithal to enjoy the good life: this means the right to enjoy good health and the things of the mind and the spirit."

If Canada could discover a sense of national purpose, many things were possible: public health insurance, a public pension plan, education for all, a redirection of effort towards international development, a new effort to bring about world peace. He closed with the verse that had become a hymn for the British Labour Party:

> I shall not cease from mental strife,
> Nor shall my sword sleep in my hand,
> Till we have built Jerusalem
> In this green and pleasant land.[35]

In the weeks that followed the convention, the man with the ready smile and light-footed stride became the emblem of the New Democratic Party. His photos appeared in party newspapers and pamphlets; at the founding convention of the Ontario party, a portrait of heroic size beamed down on the delegates. Local associations cried out for his magic touch. As a jaded Hazen Argue remembered it, party members projected all their hopes onto Douglas: "Marjorie Cooper thought, Christ, he's going to save the world from war, he and Nehru, just sit down over coffee at the United Nations and they'd get it all patched up."[36] In fact, the end of the convention left Douglas almost alone, facing the enormous job of breathing life into the New Party's resolutions. At the time of the convention, despite all its hoopla, the Gallup Poll gave the NDP only 12 per cent of the decided vote. By maintaining a killing pace, Douglas worked this up to 13.5 per cent over the next year.

Until November 1, 1961, Douglas carried a full load as premier of Saskatchewan, steering the Medical Care Act through the legislature. As he handed over the premier's chair to Woodrow Lloyd, the partisan *Leader-Post* praised him, for once, as "an indefatigable worker, a zealous crusader, and an inspired and inspiring leader."[37] From the high-ceilinged office with the big windows overlooking the legislative grounds, Douglas moved to a gloomy cubicle below the River Heights Shopping Centre, within earshot of Regina's airport. Eleanor McKinnon, who had run the premier's outer office for seventeen years with firmness, efficiency, and grace, also moved to the basement suite next to the barber shop.

Douglas spent much of his time on the road, accompanied by a single adviser, Tommy Shoyama. During this winter of 1961-62, Shoyama served as roving theoretician, baggage handler, and press aide. When Douglas got sick on the road, Shoyama supplied the chicken soup. Shoyama recalled, "We'd go any place there was some possibility or expression of interest—like Truro, Nova Scotia. How come? Because who was there but a United Church minister, who had come of course from Saskatchewan. Same thing in Hawkesbury, Ontario."[38]

While Douglas tried to push back the boundaries of the party geographically, there was a vacuum at the centre. The National Committee for a New Party had folded, and so did the New Party clubs. The new executive struggled for consensus, and had little contact with the caucus in Parliament. The labour movement backed away, fearing to contaminate the party's image; this sudden fit of decorum only robbed the NDP of organizing strength. National Secretary Carl Hamilton, abandoned in Ottawa with only a green assistant and a researcher to back him up, slipped towards a breakdown.

Douglas tried to fill the organizational gap by travelling further, faster, although in retrospect he doubted the wisdom of this course. "I think we made some very serious mistakes both as to strategy and to our approach," he said. "On policy matters, fine...But at the very time when we should be holding on to what we had, we were trying to break new ground."[39] He took too much on himself, and the party sometimes seemed to be a one-man team. One party staff member wrote in a memo, "Tommy often appears travel-weary and haggard on his television broadcasts, and I think that this is at least in part attributable to his arriving in town, grabbing a taxi, and taping a broadcast without even having time to catch his breath."[40] When a supporter recorded a song called "A Douglas For Me," the party held the official presentation ceremony at Toronto Airport so the leader could catch a plane.

Like the first leaders of the CCF, Douglas tried to bridge the gap between farmers and labour, to explain to both sides that they needed each other. In his last appearance as premier on Saskatchewan television he responded to charges that he had sold out to the CLC: "I went into politics twenty-six years ago," he said, "because I was convinced the farmer was the most exploited group in society."[41] He promised to bring the same conviction to his new job as federal leader. Farmers and labour must work together, he often said, against the common enemy, the corporate elite, a group that "you could put in the corner of a room."[42]

But within the Saskatchewan CCF there was still grumbling about labour domination in the new party. In fact, the Saskatchewan party would refuse to change its name to "New Democratic Party" until 1967, and clung, meanwhile, to the old CCF label. A month after Douglas left the legislature one of his old associates from the Young Fellows' Club of the 1930s, Jun Stavely, captured the Weyburn provincial seat for the Liberals. The CCF's senior organizer, Jack Douglas, managed the campaign, and Douglas spoke eight times in the riding, but even the Weyburn Hospital workers deserted the party. The result reflected Stavely's popularity and the CCF candidate's inexperience, but it was also a slap at Tommy Douglas. The *Leader-Post* crowed that the by-election had tarnished the Douglas "halo of invincibility."[43]

The loss of the Weyburn seat was, of course, a shock; with the turn of the year, a greater one lay in store. On February 18, 1962, the rumours that had surrounded Hazen Argue became a reality. Under the blandishments of Ross Thatcher, the Saskatchewan Liberal leader, Argue announced his departure from the party. He had returned to his farm after the founding convention, and brooded on his loss. None of the leaders of the NDP had telephoned to ask his advice over the winter, and he felt ostracized. Throughout his leadership campaign, Argue had courted union support and accepted union money; now he charged that the CCF had sold its soul to a clutch of eastern labour bosses.

On Friday, February 16, Argue attended a CCF banquet in Regina. On Saturday he met with Douglas to plan for some upcoming radio broadcasts. On Sunday he delivered himself up to Thatcher, his old office mate, the man he had scourged in earlier times for betraying the CCF and joining the Liberals. They drove together to a news conference, where Argue announced his decision. "The NDP has now become the tool of a small labour clique," he said, "and is effectively under their domination and control. The NDP has come more and more under the control of a few labour leaders, mainly within a few large and powerful international unions...Class control of a national political party, now acquired within the CCF, constitutes a dark and sinister threat to democratic government in Canada. The challenge to freedom is real." Two days later he repeated his statement in the Commons, and formally resigned from the NDP caucus.

Douglas had been blind-sided by his own House leader. On the Sunday of Argue's announcement he stated that he was "surprised and disappointed." In a press statement the following day he described Argue's move as "abject betrayal...Mr. Argue saw no labor bogeyman in the NDP organization until he was beaten by me in the leadership contest."[44] After this early flurry, Douglas rarely mentioned Argue. When the two met on an aircraft a few days later, they did not speak.

In looking back on this desertion, Douglas reflected, "Argue was in my opinion a straight opportunist. He would go wherever it best suited him, wherever the returns, whether the returns were financial or political, might be...Argue wasn't fighting on any basic principle. He was fighting on whether or not he would win."[45] There have been other defectors from the CCF/NDP, including elected members, and even some of those who drafted the Regina Manifesto. None, with the possible exception of Ross Thatcher, have endured as much derision as Argue. On the sixth floor of the Centre Block in Ottawa, near Woodsworth's old office, portraits of former national CCF and NDP leaders line a wall. Hazen Argue's photograph is absent.

Argue turned in an eloquent series of performances for the news media and in the House of Commons. His words reinforced the complaints of those in Saskatchewan who felt that the barons of labour had snatched away their party. They hurt the NDP badly in southern Ontario, where Donald MacDonald had worked for years to build up a rural following, always facing a suspicion that he represented a trade union party. In snaring the MP from Kayville, the Liberals had made a good start at obliterating the New Party's chances in its first federal election.

23

The Bitter Taste

ON THE NIGHT of the worst election defeat of his life, Tommy Douglas stepped out from his empty downtown committee rooms and walked with Irma into the summer night. A train rumbled along the tracks a block away. The streets of Regina were still. The Douglases climbed into the Pontiac that their supporters had given them a year before and drove east through the old ethnic neighbourhoods to a television station on the edge of the city. There, Douglas told the country that he was saddened by his loss and quoted an old ballad: "I'll lay me down and bleed a while, and then I'll rise and fight again."

They returned to their house on Angus Crescent, where they sat with campaign manager Ed Whelan and his wife Pemrose, drinking tea and eating raisin toast. The phone was silent, except for a call from Stanley Knowles and another from the telegraph office. A weeping supporter appeared briefly at the door. "Then Tommy and Irma presented Ed with some gold cufflinks," Pemrose recalled, "and then we called it a pleasant little evening, about as subdued as anyone could be."[1]

Ten months after the triumph and celebration of the New Democratic Party's founding convention, Douglas led his poorly financed and organized troops into an electoral massacre. In Ontario, all but a handful of his candidates went down before the revived Liberal Party. On the prairies, John Diefenbaker and his Tories buried the NDP, just as they had decimated the CCF in 1958. Even the new NDP leader, running in Regina, suffered a humiliating rejection.

As prime minister, Diefenbaker had insulted his French-speaking colleagues and muffed his chance to consolidate his hold on Quebec. His strength was waning in Ontario, too, as Pearson's Liberals showed a new interest in pensions and social issues. On the prairies, though, his appeal remained unchallenged. He was still "The Chief," and his combination of bombast and populism generated a mood of adoration that kept most constituencies under his control. With western Canada's help, Diefenbaker formed a last, shaky minority government.

Besides having to fight Diefenbaker on his home turf, the federal NDP in Saskatchewan was hurt by the poisonous spirit of the medicare crisis. The Medicare Act that Douglas had so proudly ushered through the assembly had been proclaimed, and Premier Lloyd had set July 1, 1962, as the start-up date for the new program. The doctors, however, insisted that they would not work under the new law.

Through April and May, the province entered a period of political disruption unparalleled in its history. The organized medical profession convinced many sick people and their families that all of Saskatchewan's doctors would soon leave the province; these frightened people, together with the long-time foes of the CCF, formed the KOD, the Keep Our Doctors movement. A miasma of hatred settled over the capital city, most of it directed towards Woodrow Lloyd and Tommy Douglas. KOD spokesmen, unknown callers, the graffiti on the walls threatened violence, even death. Whelan, the campaign manager, got phone calls at home from the same man, night after night; the man said, "I'll shoot you, you Red bastard!"

The low point of the campaign came late in May when a Douglas motorcade passed through the west side of Regina. CCF supporters turned out in force, but so did the KOD, booing and holding picket signs aloft. Some homeowners placed coffins on their front lawns. Occasionally a spectator dashed out to hammer at, spit at, or throw stones at the Douglas car.

Even if NDP workers in Regina had been able to ignore the medicare dispute, they could not ignore the weaknesses in their own organization. Some longtime CCF supporters remained unhappy about labour's new influence, and chose not to campaign. There was squabbling and intrigue at campaign headquarters, and Douglas's long absences hurt his chances further. As the leader of a national party fighting its first battle he was, unfortunately, needed everywhere.

Why did Douglas run in Regina in the first place? He had trouble explaining the choice himself, admitting, "It was a complete misreading of the political situation to think we could go in there and win."[2] Regina had elected a couple of CCF members of Parliament in the 1940s and early 1950s, but had rejected both Coldwell and Dr. Hugh MacLean in earlier days. Certainly, it was not a safe seat in 1962. He might have challenged Hazen Argue in his old federal riding, now renamed Assiniboia, but he feared this would seem "an act of vindictiveness" against the turncoat.[3] The best idea, perhaps, would have been to run in an industrial seat in Ontario or British Columbia. Instead, he chose Regina, but Regina did not choose him.

The election results on the night of June 18, 1962, showed that Douglas had lost to his Conservative rival Ken More by more than 9500 votes. The five-term premier had received only 29 per cent of the popular vote. Regina voters did not, however, single Douglas out for any special

The Hon. T. C. Douglas

All illustrations are from the Douglas family album, unless otherwise noted.

Tommy and M. J. Coldwell, 1971
CAPITAL PRESS, DUNCAN CAMERON
PHOTO

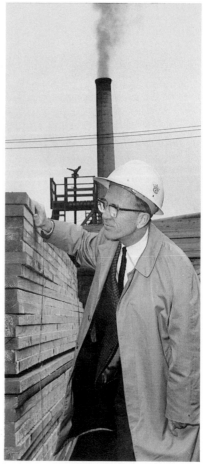

Lost in the lumber pile COLUMBIAN
PHOTO, NEW WESTMINSTER, B.C.

Talking to the union STAN
TURNBULL PHOTO

Three generations of leadership:
David Lewis, Ed Broadbent,
T. C. Douglas

Tommy at the podium PHOTO
FEATURES LTD, MURRAY MOSHER
PHOTO

Two Saskatchewan premiers,
T. C. Douglas and Allan Blakeney,
1969

Election victory, Nanaimo-
Cowichan-The Islands, 1969
VANCOUVER PROVINCE, PHOTO

At the Chinese Embassy

Tommy and constituency visitors at
Rideau Hall, 1973

The party veterans: Tommy, Grace
MacInnis, Stanley Knowles

Tommy at the University of Regina

Sod-turning at Brandon University:
Tommy (second from left), Stanley
Knowles, Dr. E. J. Tyler

Shirley and family: Kiefer, Tom, and
Rachel

The proud grandfather: Tommy
with the Tulchinskys

punishment; New Democrats running elsewhere in Saskatchewan got an even smaller share of the vote. The defector Argue, running for the Liberals, was the only candidate to break the Diefenbaker spell over Saskatchewan. *

It was no comfort to Douglas to know that most other NDP candidates shared his fate. He had hoped for a forty- or fifty-member caucus in the House of Commons, but only nineteen party members won in their ridings. David Lewis was elected to Parliament for the first time, and Stanley Knowles re-entered the Commons from his Winnipeg fiefdom, but many promising newcomers lost their deposits.

The party ran a record number of candidates, and spent $116,000—six times as much money as the CCF had spent in 1958, although a pitiful amount compared to the expenditures of the Liberals or Tories. Still, in spite of Stanley Knowles's pre-convention visions of a rising tide of labour support, the union rank and file did not come through—only 23 per cent of their votes went to New Democrats, compared with 25 per cent to the Tories, and 38 per cent to the Liberals. The labour power that was to give the new party its thrust failed at take-off.

Douglas, with his tiny staff and his economy-class travel budget, could not begin to solve the party's financial, structural, and personal problems. Inevitably, though, some in the flock still hoped before the election that their new Moses would lead them out of the political wilderness. Expectations for a breakthrough ran high; in the end, the NDP's share of the popular vote in 1962 was about the same as the CCF's had been in the setback of 1949. In looking back on the muddled state of the federal NDP before the 1962 vote, Terry Grier, former national secretary and NDP member of Parliament said:

> I think we all had a hard time getting our act together, and Tommy must have found the adjustment process even more difficult...The party was not in a position to fly people back and forth (to national executive meetings), so I don't think Tommy led the party in any strategic sense...
>
> Tommy must have found it difficult to move from the arena of Saskatchewan politics to the arena of national issues. What he was doing was being the party's principal speech-maker, and that was I guess the extent of his leadership. He travelled wherever we asked him to go, he rallied the troops, he made these incredibly eloquent speeches, with the mixture of humour, analysis and uplift that one has come to associate with Tommy, and nobody could touch him from that perspective. But in terms of pulling the party together, no. Tommy didn't do it, and I don't think frankly that anybody did it.[4]

Douglas had trouble fitting into his new role, probably because he was expected to organize the party as well as lead it. The climate in which he had worked in Saskatchewan had spoiled him. Douglas was a team

---

* Douglas and many of his followers complained for years that Regina's Liberals threw their support to the Tories in 1962. In fact, the Liberals ran a prominent candidate and finished a very close third behind Douglas.

player, used to working in a climate of mutual trust with his cabinet colleagues. Here it was not clear who was on the team, or what direction they wanted to follow. The party executive had regional balance and trade union representation, both admirable characteristics, but it barely functioned.

For seventeen years he had worked with professional, highly motivated staffs, and it had left him free of administrative concerns. Leadership had meant working out new policies and putting them before the public, such as when he had introduced the people of Saskatchewan to the rural power scheme or to medicare. He had consciously left fundraising and membership problems to his lieutenants, especially Fines. Now, it seemed, the NDP needed a general manager, and expected to find one in their political leader, ignoring the fact that the requirements for the two jobs may be poles apart.

Douglas tried to give ideological leadership, and stretched himself to cover a wide range of national concerns. The founding convention had left some areas of policy vague, and Douglas found himself making up the party position on the fly. In January he spoke to the Osgoode Hall Legal and Literary Society on "Canadian Unity and the Constitution." In making his pitch for constitutional reform, he recycled many of the ideas he had put forward as a provincial premier:

> There will never be unity in Canada as long as citizens of one area are compelled to accept lower standards of health, education and welfare than their fellow Canadians in some other part of Canada.
> Canada is not a collection of sovereign states pieced together in a loose federation. Canada can make co-operative federalism work. We have two nations of people of different language, culture and outlook. Our task is to preserve these distinctive differences and at the same time devise a constitution that will satisfy human needs and advance the economic welfare of all Canadians.

In the same speech he advocated a Bill of Rights that would guarantee "the basic freedoms of religion, speech, assembly, press and association."[5]

In February, on a "Nation's Business" telecast, he stated his case for a national health scheme that would be comprehensive and universal in its coverage. During the same month he appeared at a news conference with Romeo Mathieu, a federal party vice-president from Quebec, to propose the creation of a commission on bilingualism and biculturalism.

Douglas also spoke to the Indian-Eskimo Association of Canada, pledging, among other things, "ample capital investment funds for on reserve schemes for economic development and community development and...introduction of self-government on reserves." In other appearances, he proposed a Canadian youth service that would be sponsored by the Government of Canada and serve in the work of the U.N. agencies. He also called for a ten-fold increase in Canada's aid to underdeveloped countries, saying that even if this meant sacrifices, "The Canadian people would make those sacrifices gladly."[6]

The closing days of the campaign found Douglas far from home. On June 11, a week before the election, he was speaking in Montreal, promising a bilingual civil service, a department of federal-provincial relations, and a new tax deal with the provinces. On the 14th he enjoyed a rousing reception in Winnipeg, proposed a form of public ownership of the food monopolies, and advocated recognition of Red China and its admission to the United Nations.

These forays hardly suggest a leader unaware of the key national issues. But the adulation of audiences in the big cities could not be translated into support in Regina. Three days before the election the Regina NDP organized a final rally, and the KOD staged a counter-rally. The campaign of hostility continued to the end.

Douglas's formal post-election statement ended with the quotation of 2 Corinthians, 4: 8-9: "We are troubled on every side, yet not distressed; we are perplexed, but not in despair; persecuted but not foresaken; cut down but not destroyed."[7] A few old friends sent him letters expressing their confidence in him and praising his dignity in defeat. Jack Douglas wrote in bewilderment that Saskatchewan had deserted its former premier for Diefenbaker, "the greatest phony that ever headed a Canadian government." The leader of the federal NDP, now without a political home, replied to all, "I think it was Victor Hugo who said, 'nothing is so irresistible as an idea whose time has come.' " To Jack Douglas, his old comrade-in-arms, he added in sympathy, "I'm going fishing too."[8]

Douglas had traded in a career as a successful provincial leader, and many thought he had traded down. He now stood on the margins of Canadian politics. Towards the end of his life he reflected, "I think a lot of people, and they may have been right, a lot of people thought I should have stayed. I had a nice, comfortable set up, I was a Premier, had a very popular cabinet...and why in heaven's name should we be worrying about the socialist movement in Canada as a whole? What we were going to do, trying to make the party come alive, just didn't interest them. Maybe they were right, too. Maybe we were trying to push the thing too fast. Maybe we were trying to jump the gun, but I suppose to some of us of my age group, there was always the haunting recollection of what had happened to the Progressive Party...which had just died out from lack of steam, from a lack of objectives, from being so satisfied with themselves."[9]

A side-light on the character of this defeated candidate is shown in an exchange of correspondence twenty years later between Douglas and the daughter of the man who crushed him in Regina in 1962. Morinne More was planning a scrapbook to present to her parents at the time of their golden wedding anniversary, and she asked Douglas for a contribution. Douglas provided his recollections of a tour of Russia that he and Ken More undertook in the mid-1960s along with some other members of Parliament. More was stricken with what looked like a serious illness and entered hospital in Moscow the day before the delegation was to leave that city. Douglas volunteered to stay behind while the others continued their tour. He wrote to Morinne:

> All night I worried about poor Ken, all alone in a foreign city, being cared for by people with whom he could not communicate. I arose early and had a hasty breakfast before hurrying to the hospital to see my ailing friend. I was prepared for a wan and depressed Ken, fearfully accepting the ministrations of some strapping Russian nurses who would probably bully him because of their inability to communicate with this foreigner from a distant land.
>
> Imagine my amazement when I entered the private room allotted to him. Ken was the centre of a bevy of pretty nurses, each competing with the others to serve the visitor from far-off Canada. Sitting in the midst of this flock of femininity was Ken with a grin on his face that stretched from ear to ear. Far from being homesick, as I had feared, he was in his element. His desire to catch up on our departed colleagues had cooled considerably...I found that any difficulty I had experienced in persuading him to go to the hospital was nothing compared to the task of getting him to leave it![10]

Saskatchewan swung back to the NDP in 1968, giving the party six seats in the year the rest of the country went wild for Pierre Trudeau. Douglas learned of the new mood of success one evening during the campaign when he landed at the Regina airport and climbed into a car with Ed Whelan. He was irritated, dishevelled, in the midst of his party's fourth losing campaign in seven years, and he snapped at Whelan, "Why did you get the Armouries? You can't fill the Armouries."

"Well," said Whelan, "they're waiting for you."

All the way into town, Douglas complained of his fatigue and repeatedly ordered Whelan to keep a cab standing by so he could get to his hotel quickly after the meeting. When they entered the Armouries the people were packed together, singing "Tommy is our leader," and when he spoke they cheered everything he said. There was even a delegation from Weyburn, including some of the Oxelgren boys who had saved Douglas from hooligans at a schoolhouse meeting in 1935. After the rally, when Whelan reminded Douglas that his cab was ready, he replied, "Look, some of these people came all the way in from Weyburn. I'm not leaving yet." Finally, when the crowd had dispersed, Douglas stepped out into the autumn air.[11]

24

A Minor Party

DOUGLAS HAD ONLY a few days to "lay down and bleed awhile" after his defeat in Regina. A New Democrat MP in British Columbia unexpectedly resigned his seat, and Douglas was soon campaigning in a by-election on the west coast. By mid-October he was back in the House of Commons after an eighteen-year absence.

The Burnaby-Coquitlam riding, just east of Vancouver, housed plant, mill, and dock workers, teachers and tradesmen, and retired people. Some of them had supported the CCF since the mid-1930s, when Ernie Winch had led the provincial party from his Burnaby base. In the June 1962 federal election, Burnaby-Coquitlam elected Erhart Regier, the NDP candidate, for the fourth time in a row. Regier was a transplanted Saskatchewan native, with a deep and sentimental loyalty to Tommy Douglas. Distraught over Douglas's loss in Regina, he phoned the leader and offered to resign from the Commons. Douglas ordered him to sober up. A day or two later, Douglas read in a newspaper that Regier had asked the Speaker of the Commons to declare his seat vacant.[1]

The thirty-member NDP executive in Burnaby-Coquitlam, lacking a strong local replacement, acted according to Regier's wishes and invited the former premier of Saskatchewan to become their candidate. With the help of reinforcements from Ontario, the NDP took more than half the votes in the October by-election.

The Douglases rented an apartment near Burnaby Park, a few blocks from the New Westminster city line. Bert Hill, a member of the riding executive, lived nearby, and he built Douglas a private office in the basement of the Hill house. From the first, said Hill, Douglas won the allegiance of the local NDP. "When he started to speak, you couldn't hear anything else, he would just draw the people to him. He was one of the greatest guys that ever was."[2]

Douglas also took an apartment in Ottawa's west end, and returned to the same sixth-floor offices on Parliament Hill where he had begun his political career alongside Woodsworth and Coldwell. He would now try to bring vision and direction to a small caucus and to a national movement that had been demoralized, like Woodsworth's party in 1935, by a disappointing start.

Was the NDP to be a trade union party? Or should it be a party for everyone who considered themselves to be politically left of centre? Perhaps, as Douglas told his shell-shocked troops at the 1963 party convention, the NDP should try to attract everyone who had made a moral commitment to social reform. "This is not the time for the fair weather friend or the sunshine soldier," he said. "I do not offer you easy victories or personal gain. I offer you only the chance to serve your day and generation. I offer you the comradeship of being a partner in the great crusade for the uplift of humanity."[3]

He was entering perhaps the most arduous and thankless time of his career. Where Douglas had headed a government for seventeen years, he now led a minor party—fourth in numbers in the House, with fewer seats than Social Credit. Where he had enjoyed the overwhelming support of his associates, he now heard whispers that he was the wrong man for the job. The party's dreams of electoral success got rough treatment from the voters. Many New Democrats, looking at Douglas's five victories in Saskatchewan, expected him to work miracles on the federal scene. Leading a party that was poorly organized, chronically short of funds, and often ignored by the media, he had no miracles left in his kit. Never, during his career as federal leader, did Canadian voters give the NDP more than two dozen of the 265 seats in the House of Commons. The cheering and the handshakes still followed him wherever he went, but too often people turned aside and said, "I admire him—but I could never vote for him."

With each of the elections that followed in rapid succession through the 1960s, the membership of his caucus changed. His colleagues' most consistent characteristic was their habit of riding off in all directions. In the words of one member, the NDP in Parliament was "the last stronghold of free enterprise."[4] Douglas was reluctant to criticize his fellow MPs in later years, but clearly they did not behave as a team. On questions such as medicare and capital punishment there was general agreement, but in many other areas, members had personal agendas and ignored the party's priorities.

Douglas had worked in government with people who shared a common vision and a sense of discipline. He found that life was different for the leader of a rump minority in opposition. In the words of Cliff Scotton, a Douglas adviser, "When you're the premier, when you have the disposition of portfolios, the person who makes the decisions is the guy who sits in the glorious leader's chair...But when you get a group of people in [an opposition] caucus, they say, well, screw him, I got elected in Okanagan South because I'm good looking and brilliant."[5] Further, this was more than the usual opposition caucus. It was a gathering of the Canadian left, always a haven for prima donnas and free spirits.

Colin Cameron, a fiery Scotsman from Vancouver Island, bucked the party leader constantly on NATO and foreign policy. Bert Herridge, a B.C. farmer with anti-Semitic leanings, specialized in leaking caucus decisions to news reporters. Fisher, Howard, and Peters, the anti-establishment junta of the Argue leadership campaign, continued under Douglas's leadership as a formidable bloc. One day, when Peters and Reid Scott, another New Democrat, had to talk out a bill in the House, they decided to kill the time by attacking each other. Douglas came to Peters to complain, but Peters turned on him: "Where the hell were you? Where was your twenty minutes? You've got no goddamn business talking to me about it."[6]

Above all of this contention was the shadow of David Lewis, a shadow that lengthened over the years. Lewis had built up great influence as a longtime leader of the party executive, and had scored his first electoral win in 1962. In the hiatus caused by Douglas's defeat in Regina, Lewis acted as the NDP's parliamentary leader. It became apparent that he regretted his earlier decision not to accept the leadership at the founding of the New Party. "David Lewis, in my view, had ambitions from very early on," said Cliff Scotton. "I suspect he thought he would be superior to Tommy in an intellectual sense."[7] As Douglas Fisher put it, "Lewis realized that he had greater talents as a party leader than Douglas had—I'm speaking nationally...There was a realization that Douglas was archaic, his vocabulary was of the thirties. There was a frustration on David Lewis's part with Tommy Douglas as a national leader. I don't mean there was disloyalty—that couldn't be possible—but there was discomfort."[8]

Lewis would wait almost another decade for the leadership. He remained second in command, although between 1963 and 1965 he was out of the Commons. He was a mastermind on questions of caucus and party strategy, and on relations with labour.

The personal relationship between Douglas and Lewis remained outwardly impeccable until Lewis died in 1981. Some observers claimed they saw affection beneath the surface, some animosity. Stephen Lewis noticed a "slight strain" which got worse as time went on.[9] After 1968, when Stephen boldly advised him to step down, Douglas may have suspected that the elder Lewis was campaigning against him. But the two small, combative men, rivals in some ways, worked together in a businesslike fashion. They differed in their method of handling people, but they agreed on most issues, and they resolved as professionals to get along.

To oversimplify their difference in style, Douglas listened and Lewis talked. Douglas, after presenting his leader's report to a caucus or party council meeting, would hang back from debate. Lewis, when he chaired a meeting, spoke frequently and forcefully. Both approaches brought a share of criticism. As Grace MacInnis, who worked with both men over more than forty years, concluded:

Lewis wasn't a democratic person in his instincts. Tommy has been a democratic person, thoroughly democratic in his way of procedure. But Lewis always felt, organizationally, Papa knows best.

I think Douglas always believed that two heads were better than one...I think he always believed genuinely in co-operation, and I think he lived that way, and that's why people loved him.

Lewis would listen while everybody talked and then he would sum up the discussion, and the summing up often didn't have any relation to what had been said. But it was so brilliant and so well done. I think it was his very brilliance that made us a little discouraged at times.[10]

Douglas had cautioned before 1961 that the making of the New Party was largely an administrative exercise and did not reflect a broad popular desire for change. His experiences as party leader confirmed these early fears. The unions of the Canadian Labour Congress, which Lewis had seen as a key source of potential new support, could not deliver the votes of their two million members. There was little sense, in the media or among the public, that Canada's working people were anxious to make use of their new voice in Parliament or to help it define new public issues.

Douglas was restricted to playing much the same part in Parliament as the earlier leaders of the CCF had done, acting as a prophet at the gates rather than as a counsellor in the palace. He called on those in government to honour their promises and to uphold the democratic and civilized values that all parties held in common. But like any opposition leader, he found it extremely difficult to establish a record of accomplishment and campaign on it. During his tenure as party leader, the NDP never had sufficient parliamentary strength to force the hand of Liberal governments.

He was a critic of government policy and occasionally an advocate of new ideas. In lending his voice to nationalist and anti-war movements, he gave them greater stature and broadened the spectrum of political thought in Canada. Often, though, the other parties wrote him off as a minor figure in political life. Prominent Liberals such as Pearson, Walter Gordon, Judy LaMarsh, and Jean Chrétien have virtually ignored the NDP in their memoirs. But then, it has not been characteristic of politicians of any stripe to give credit to others whose ideas they may have "borrowed."

Douglas often argued after he retired that the NDP scared or shamed the Liberals into introducing their reforms of the 1960s. When he stepped down as leader in 1971, Douglas reminded the party that the NDP had fought for national medicare, a Canada Pension Plan, and federal housing programs. The Pearson Liberals had even moved in the area of economic planning, with the founding of the Economic Council of Canada and the creation of a regional industrial grant system.

This idea, that the NDP developed new policies during the 1960s and the Liberals put them into practice, was widely shared, although it seems impossible to prove. The Tory *Globe and Mail* once said that Pearson "put on the cloak of Mr. T. C. Douglas" in order to defeat Diefenbaker.[11] Professor Saywell's *Canadian Annual Review* called the New Democrats' greatest problem "having to watch the Liberals pursue their historic policy of stealing NDP policies."[12] Charles Lynch, a conservative columnist, wrote at the end of Douglas's life, "As much as any man, it was Douglas who turned Canada into the most highly socialized country in the Western world, without anybody really noticing what was happening."[13]

When Douglas entered the Commons in November 1962, Diefenbaker's career as prime minister was drawing to a close. Douglas respected Diefenbaker as a good westerner, and he knew the Chief was popular even among Saskatchewan voters who liked the CCF provincially. But three months after returning to Ottawa, Douglas helped to topple Diefenbaker, opening the way for sixteen unbroken years of Liberal government. He felt compelled to support a non-confidence motion from Lester Pearson, the leader of the opposition, who charged that the Tories were divided on defence policy, unable to produce a budget, and unsure of what to put before Parliament.

Douglas faced some resistance on the non-confidence motion from within his own caucus. Douglas Fisher and his allies argued that the wording of the motion was irrelevant. The Liberals were the long-term enemy, and should not be handed a chance to govern.* The NDP, moreover, had used up its funds and some of the goodwill of its workers in a recent election, and was not ready to face another one. In retrospect, Douglas could see the force of this argument. "From the standpoint of political strategy, it would have been wise to keep the government in power," he said. "But you just couldn't do it. We were really into bureaucratic chaos, and more and more the country was being run by the civil service."[14]

Diefenbaker was a hardworking public servant and a skilled debater. His government's successes had helped Saskatchewan probably more than any other province—putting national hospital insurance into place, building the dam, selling wheat to China. But Diefenbaker, said Douglas, was also a lone wolf, a man who veered erratically from suspicion to surrender. If the NDP had not helped defeat Diefenbaker, his cabinet would have blown itself to shreds anyway. The raggedness of the NDP was nothing compared with the plotting and factionalism in the Tory inner circle.

On the morning of the scheduled non-confidence vote, February 5, 1963, Douglas received a telephone call from Senator Wallace McCutcheon, a minister without portfolio from Bay Street. Douglas Harkness, the minister of defence, had resigned two days before, and the cabinet was split in two on the issue of whether Canada should accept American nuclear warheads. McCutcheon now asked Douglas and the NDP to vote with the Conservatives. Within a few days, he promised, the cabinet would get rid of Diefenbaker, and George Nowlan of Nova Scotia would take his place as prime minister.

Douglas grew impatient as McCutcheon droned on. "There's no use talking about the vote tonight," he said at last. "You haven't produced

---

* Premier Lloyd of Saskatchewan also objected to bringing down the Diefenbaker government. He feared that any perception of a Douglas-Pearson alliance would cause Saskatchewan voters to turn against the NDP and jump to the provincial Liberals.

a budget in eighteen months, the government is disintegrating. Three ministers have issued different statements openly contradicting each other, openly quarreling about the Bomarc missile."

"If you see us through this, Tommy," said the senator, "I promise you we'll have him out in forty-eight hours. He's going to be Chief Justice."

"We're not interested in getting rid of Mr. Diefenbaker," said Douglas, "and least of all in replacing him with you and your friends from Toronto. We're not voting against Mr. Diefenbaker. We're voting against the fact that the government has been unable to govern."[15]

In the vote that evening, Cameron and Herridge of the NDP sided with the government. The rest of the caucus tipped the balance against the Tories, making the final count 142-111.

In the election campaign that followed—the third for Douglas in ten months—the NDP leader campaigned on the issues of jobs, peace, and medicare. He hoped at least to gain the balance of power. Minority parliaments, he told his audiences, have produced some great reforms. "We will not enter into a coalition," he said, "but I am prepared to sit down with the leader of the largest group and work out the necessary arrangements by which the government should tackle our social and economic problems."[16]

Pearson campaigned for stable government. Only a Liberal majority, he said, could bring about the reforms the country needed. "We had a Liberal government for twenty-two years," Douglas told a rally in Vancouver. "They were so stable they never moved. They not only looked like a stable, there were times when they smelled like a stable."[17]

Working with a paltry $70,000 federal campaign budget, the NDP drew crowds in the thousands to Douglas rallies in the major cities. When voting day came the party barely held its million votes from the year before. Douglas, running against Liberal strategist Tom Kent in Burnaby, watched his margin of victory cut to fewer than 5000 votes, down from more than 8000 a few months before. Across Canada, the NDP dropped two seats to finish with a total of nineteen. The Liberals fell short of a majority, but support from either of the two minor parties on any measure would keep them in business.

The New Party had made no significant inroads with the farmers in the 1963 vote, nor with the "liberally minded," the urban middle class which it had set out to attract. The Liberal Party, after shifting its policies leftwards, was taking an increasing share of the growing white-collar vote. There was some talk—at least in the Toronto papers—that the two parties should merge. Douglas Fisher, now promoted to deputy House leader, began to push the idea of making a deal with the Liberals. Why not offer Pearson support in the Commons in return for a package of reform legislation? The party executive agreed.

It is unlikely that Douglas expected much from a secret meeting with Pearson. He found the country preacher's son affable, but indecisive as a leader. If Pearson promised a deal, he might change his mind the next day. "The last person to talk to him," said Douglas, "usually had the greatest influence."[18] However, he agreed to go along with Fisher to present a shopping list. One Sunday afternoon in October 1963 the two met with Keith Davey, a Pearson aide, and Walter Gordon, the minister of finance, at Gordon's apartment a few blocks from Parliament Hill. Soon after Douglas arrived, Pearson telephoned his regrets, saying he had a cold. In Douglas's memory David Lewis was also present; in Fisher's he was not.

The conversation soon bogged down. Douglas proposed old-age pension increases, swift adoption of the new contributory pension plan, a Canada Development Corporation, and tax reform to benefit moderate-income people. Gordon tried to interest the NDP in a short list of tax changes. Davey and Fisher, by Douglas's account, then began to shoot the breeze about the party merger rumours, and Gordon shooed them all out into the rain.

Within a few weeks, word of the meeting had leaked out. To make things more awkward, some Ontario New Democrats had also met secretly with Liberals in Toronto to discuss co-operation. The media reported that Fisher was busy with an association for Liberal and NDP thinkers called "The Exchange for Political Ideas in Canada," which he viewed privately as a device for snaring restless Liberals. The speculation on a fusion of the two parties persisted for months, despite Douglas's denials. He would resign, he said, if the NDP even considered a merger. When party members wrote to express their concern, he assured them that the merger talk was calculated simply to divide and demoralize the movement.

Pearson and Gordon had figured correctly that the NDP was too weak to assert itself in the House. They offered Douglas no promises on legislation. He would challenge them on a wide range of issues, from agriculture and pensions to Vietnam, but he would not try to defeat the government. "We are not a major political party at this time, and we must recognize this fact," he told Woodrow Lloyd. "Our job is to play for sufficient time so that when an election comes in two or three years we are an effective political force in Canada."[19]

It would be irresponsible, he said, for the NDP to support any motion of non-confidence against the Liberals when there was no alternative government in sight. Soon after the meeting at Gordon's apartment, the Tories introduced a motion before the Commons which condemned the Liberals for not consulting with the provinces. A Douglas amendment made the motion so innocuous—"this House urged the government to carry out the spirit of co-operative federalism"—that all parties voted for it.[20]

In any case, the NDP caucus found it easy to support much of what the government was doing. Left-wing Liberals such as Tom Kent and Walter Gordon had reached the peak of their influence, backed by an activist core of civil servants and a swelling federal treasury. They often stumbled, especially during what Douglas called the "60 Days of Derision"[21] at the beginning of Pearson's first term, but they made some important changes—offering federal help for provincial welfare programs, making old-age pensions universal, designing new consumer protection laws. The government introduced a new contributory pension scheme in 1963, and Pearson steered the idea past the provinces after an initial squabble. The NDP claimed credit for this idea, as did the Conservatives, but Douglas later praised Pearson's work. "A man might have been more forthright," he said, "but would he have got the Canada Pension Plan?"[22]

In the area of medicare, all federal parties moved towards a position of support for a national, state-run plan. NDP members in Parliament pointed to the success of the pioneering scheme in Saskatchewan, and urged the Liberals to move quickly and put a national plan into effect. How much direct influence they exerted is open to debate. The Liberals had been promising medicare since 1919, and now the Saskatchewan CCF had proved that the idea was popular and workable and would not be sabotaged by the medical profession. Even the Thatcher Liberals in Saskatchewan, an aggressively right-wing crowd, pledged to preserve the provincial plan when they came into office in 1964.

Many Conservatives also supported medicare. The Hall Commission, set up by Diefenbaker in 1960, reported in 1964 with a recommendation in favour of national health insurance. Mr. Justice Emmett Hall, the author of the report, was a former Tory with long experience on Saskatchewan's Catholic hospital boards. He had watched the flowering of the health-care system under the Douglas government and wrote favourably of the CCF's successes. Douglas called Hall's report "the finest statement on medicare that has ever been published in the English language."[23] (Mr. Justice Hall was often introduced in later years as "the father of medicare." He and Douglas maintained a warm relationship, and did not quibble about the paternity.)

Douglas introduced two non-confidence motions based on the government's lack of action on medicare, in 1964 and 1965. The motions attracted some support from the Tories, but were turned back by the Liberals and Social Credit. The NDP chose not to tie up the House on the issue. In 1966, under pressure from its left wing, Pearson's government introduced a bill to subsidize provincial health insurance plans—provided they were universal and state run.

For a short time it appeared the Canadian Medical Association and its business allies might gear up for a Saskatchewan-style confrontation. One Saskatchewan Tory MP—a medical doctor who had gone on strike in 1962—warned the Commons of "the ever-increasing demands on doctors' services, the over-utilization, the ever-increasing costs" that would accompany medicare, and he spoke of a "rough road" ahead. Douglas scoffed at these claims: "Medicare only had a long, rough road in Saskatchewan because there were mossbacks like the member for Saskatoon who fought against its introduction."[24] As it turned out, the Commons approved the medicare bill by a vote of 177 to 2. Liberal threats to delay the program's introduction brought a flood of mail to Douglas's desk, but the government changed its mind and began to subsidize provincial medicare programs on July 1, 1968.

Among the NDP's central principles, several were adopted into the political mainstream within a few years. Liberal governments built a comprehensive social security system, so that most Canadians were assured of food, shelter, and medical care. Ottawa also adopted a more interventionist role in the economy through public ownership and increased subsidies for private business. However, the principle that there should be justice for each worker in the workplace, one of the mainsprings of the socialist movement, was advanced only modestly during the Douglas period. There were some important changes in federal labour laws in the 1960s, but the status of working people in industry did not become a more important social priority generally. Douglas and Canadian union leaders continued to argue, as they had before, for the right of workers to organize and protect themselves. They failed to move the public. More important, they did not work together to develop new strategies for working people, either inside or outside Parliament.

Despite the improved labour laws, many workers remained vulnerable to routine abuse from their employers. On paper, they enjoyed the right to bargain collectively, but federally chartered employers such as banks and broadcasters flaunted their anti-union policies. The Canadian public remained hostile to unions, often viewing them as socially irresponsible and destructive. The unions, suspicious of each other, of the government, and of certain sections within the NDP, were wedded to the methods that had worked for them in the past. The NDP, constantly fighting elections, initiated few new policies of any kind. Neither the NDP nor the CLC could muster the resources to run an educational campaign.

The Pearson Liberals passed two major labour bills. The Labour Standards Act of 1964 fulfilled a Mackenzie King promise of 1919, extending a minimum wage and paid holidays to unorganized workers in federal jurisdictions. In 1966 Pearson brought in a bill to give federal public servants the right to form unions. Both measures passed the Commons without a dissenting vote. Apparently the Liberals and Tories saw no contradiction between granting government workers the right to organize and watching their friends in the private sector smash unions. At the end of the exercise, the Liberals had succeeded in bringing federal labour laws up to about the standard that Saskatchewan had reached in 1944.

Douglas and his labour spokesmen—Lewis, Knowles, Andrew Brewin—held to the traditional CCF positions on labour. The federal government should work out a national labour code with the provinces, so that provincial governments could not use workers in bidding wars to attract industry. Ottawa should also standardize and improve the rules governing private pension plans. On the basic issue, the relative power of workers and management, Douglas outlined his views in a 1970 article called "Labour in a Free Society": "The essence of industrial relations is conflict...Hence I would contend that the legislator has two roles to fill: first, to ensure, as far as possible, that the worker is able to bargain on fairly equal terms with the employer, and second, to prevent industrial conflict from doing irreparable damage to society as a whole."[25]

This passage is notable on two counts. First, it could have come from the pen of Mackenzie King during his term as federal labour minister before 1910. Second, it still went further than most Canadians were prepared to go. For workers to bargain on "fairly equal terms," they would require, as a first step, the unconditional right to form bargaining units, with severe penalties for employers who violated this right. No jurisdiction, Liberal, Tory, or NDP, moved to offer such protection during Douglas's lifetime.

Even members of the NDP shared in the generalized anti-union prejudice. Many veterans of the CCF resented the New Party alliance with labour, and this mood helped to torpedo Douglas in Regina in 1962. The NDP suffered the worst of two worlds: while it shied away from forging a strong and effective bond with the unions, it remained uncontestably a party of labour in the eyes of the public.

Much of the direct contact between the CLC and the New Democrat caucus was through David Lewis, and Douglas rarely received officials from the congress at his office. He concerned himself more with trying to raise a sense of solidarity among the rank and file. If active trade unionists did not speak out in their own defence, no one else would. He appeared frequently at union conventions and he urged labour to take a hand in the NDP. Government decisions on taxes, interest rates, and pensions, he said, could cancel any gains made at the bargaining table. "After all, we are not asking you to do us a favour," he told a Woodworkers' meeting. "The Party is your Party. It is in your interest to see that it operates effectively."[26]

The unions responded to these appeals and extended increasing support to the party. In the mid-1960s they were donating more than 40 per cent of the NDP's annual budget, and they helped to push the 1965 campaign fund to over a million dollars, fifteen times the total for 1963. In Burnaby the Woodworkers and the B.C. Federation of Labour sent in organizers, office equipment, and office furniture for the Douglas campaign.

The NDP picked up a third of a million new votes in 1965, and Douglas got 53 per cent of the vote in his riding, but the party still took only twenty-one seats across Canada. It was obvious that the New Democrats and their labour allies would have to do more work in the ridings and the union locals between elections. At the same time, the major labour issues—protection for the unorganized, the right to form unions and to bargain, the future of the workplace—formed only a small part of the NDP program.

If the NDP failed to advance the cause of Canadian workers, part of the cause lay within the labour movement. Top union leaders argued, simply, that the party had no ongoing role in the area of labour relations.

Once governments set up a legal framework, the unions claimed the right to police the turf. Any further political intrusion—into a union organizing struggle, a strike, or a health and safety problem—threatened the principle of free collective bargaining, and might prepare the way for a system of compulsory arbitration or other controls.

Clifford Scotton, who watched party-union relations from both sides, illustrated this point with an old Douglas story. A man was telling a stranger about how he and his wife divided their responsibilities. "The wife buys the clothes for the kids, and sends them to school," said the husband. "She looks after the car, and makes the payments on the house."

"But what does that leave for you?" asked the stranger.

"Well, I make the important decisions," the husband said, "like whether we should recognize Red China or drop the atomic bomb."

In Scotton's view, the labour unions claimed responsibility for the basic issues affecting Canadian workers, leaving Douglas and the NDP to worry about China and the bomb.[27]

One result of leaving a weak and fragmented labour movement to speak for all workers, unfortunately, was that unorganized workers, and even some organized workers, remained defenceless. The labour movement made gains for a minority of the well-organized in the 1960s, but left more disadvantaged groups behind, a trend that the leader of the federal NDP regarded as dangerous.

Douglas supported the autonomy of unions, and upheld the right to strike for workers in both the private and public sector. He remembered going on strike himself in the early 1920s, walking a picket line during a Winnipeg winter with a hole in his shoe, and he did not want to jump on the anti-union bandwagon.[28] At the same time, he understood that organized workers must be seen to share the benefits of their position. As a start, he suggested that labour should lobby more openly for the poor and sponsor community services such as health clinics and senior citizens' homes. "If trade unionists are not to become the aristocrats of labour," he wrote, "they must use some of their influence and economic muscle to raise the living standards of the underprivileged and forgotten groups in our nation."[29]

In the late 1960s the NDP passed through a period of self-analysis, and one result was that labour issues emerged briefly on the party's agenda. The study of "industrial democracy" was becoming fashionable in all of the developed nations. Young academics and politicians insisted that workers must look beyond the right to earn a minimum wage, and past the collective bargaining scene, to the day when workers would control offices and factories. Ed Broadbent, a political scientist who was elected to the Commons from Oshawa in 1968, put many of the new ideas before the NDP caucus. He believed that by taking more responsibility on the jobsite, Canadian workers could open up a new front in the socialist struggle—"chipping away at the capitalist right of property ownership."[30]

To some extent this discussion recalled some of the proposals of the early CCF. Douglas had written in 1935 that employers, with the help of the state, should set up works councils to give workers "a share in the control of industry."[31] As premier, however, Douglas had put aside his enthusiasm for worker participation. He raised the status of labour by naming workers' representatives to boards and agencies; but because he headed a government that was trying to make its businesses pay, he sometimes dealt with unions as adversaries. His advisers, especially Cadbury and McLeod, had argued that public enterprises should be managed in the interests of the entire public, and not for the benefit of one group. More important, the Saskatchewan unions had not responded to the early suggestions that they should help to run crown corporations.

Despite the failure of industrial democracy to take hold in Saskatchewan, Douglas still saw some possibilities. As NDP leader, he argued that technological change raised questions about job security and retraining, and that workers should have some control over how quickly change took place. He saw a role for workers on company boards of directors, in influencing corporate policies in such areas as advertising and the environment. Broadbent has said that Douglas was sympathetic to his work in the area of industrial democracy after 1968. But although the young MP talked Douglas and Stanley Knowles into forming a caucus subcommittee with him, the effort ran out of steam after only one or two meetings.

Broadbent continued to pursue his interest and produced a "Labour Bill of Rights," which was adopted at the party's 1971 convention. The NDP, it said, recognized the value of experiments in worker management, and an NDP government would encourage workers at crown corporations to negotiate a degree of control over the company.[32] Soon after this, the industrial democracy idea died within the NDP. Leading trade unionists feared that if labour activists joined management committees they would lose their adversarial edge, and independent trade unions would become company unions.

By the end of Douglas's years as party leader, the Canadian labour movement had grown larger and fatter, especially through an influx of public service workers. The NDP and the CLC, however, remained marginal entities on the fringes of power. They appear to have carried less weight with Prime Minister Trudeau and his suite than they had with Pearson. Most workers remained unorganized. Governments continued to restrict the powers of unions. The NDP and the CLC had reached no agreement on a new political approach to the rights of labour.

Douglas was greatly encouraged by one trend which gathered momentum after he retired. Through the late 1970s organized labour took his advice on using its muscle to help the defenceless, as the CLC entered into a network of coalitions with the mainline churches. These committees lobbied governments and educated the public on a wide range of issues, from medical care and native rights to Latin America. They testified to the continued potential of workers' organizations to win allies and to agitate for change.

25

In the Eagle's Claws

I believe in Canada. I have faith in its future, and am dedicated to its destiny. I believe that this country has the potential for greatness, not only in material terms, but in the things of the mind and the spirit. I believe that the ingenuity of our minds and the labour of our hands applied to our great resources can give Canada a standard of living and a quality of life far beyond our fondest dreams.[1]

A S A COLLEGE STUDENT, Tommy Douglas learned to respect the vitality of American politics and culture. The writings of American theologians such as Walter Rauschenbusch and Harry Emerson Fosdick broadened his understanding of the social gospel. He absorbed the optimism of American social science while studying at the University of Chicago. He made Franklin D. Roosevelt, the architect of the New Deal, one of his political role models.

In the 1960s, his critics—especially the newspaper editors—repeatedly attacked Douglas for holding anti-American views on foreign investment and the Vietnam war. He was the victim, they said, of a "deep, almost religious antagonism to the United States."[2] The critics were terrified, it seems, of stepping on American toes. People who fearlessly debated Canadian issues argued that it was improper to mention American actions—even when they determined the course of events in Canada.

Douglas, it is true, never shied away from criticizing the Americans. More often, though, he prodded Liberal and Tory politicians to take a more pro-Canadian stand. "I like the Americans," he once told an election rally. "I have relatives who are Americans. I like my relatives, but I don't want them moving into my house and taking over every room until I have to sleep in the basement."[3]

At the time the NDP was formed, the issue of Canadian independence lay outside the mainstream of political debate. The country had put John Diefenbaker into power partly because of the continentalism of the previous Liberal regime, but Diefenbaker had failed to give his "Northern

Vision" concrete form. Then, just as Douglas entered Parliament in 1962, the question of whether Canada should change its defence policy to suit the Americans began to tear the Conservative government apart.

The Tories had agreed in 1959 to accept the Bomarc, an American missile designed to take nuclear warheads, and to station it on Canadian military bases. The cabinet, however, delayed the logical next step, the installation of the warheads themselves. By late 1962 the ministers of defence and external affairs, Douglas Harkness and Howard Green, were disagreeing openly on whether to let the warheads into the country, while Diefenbaker tried to appeal to both sides. The Kennedy administration in Washington, meanwhile, was losing patience.

The leader of the opposition, Lester Pearson, urged the government to keep Canada free from nuclear weapons. As late as the end of November, he told an audience in Saskatoon that he was "completely opposed to the acquisition of nuclear arms by Canada."[4] A month and a half later he announced that he had changed his mind. Canada must meet its obligations to the Americans, he said, and equip the Bomarcs with nuclear weapons, to be maintained under "joint control."[5]

Pearson's announcement shocked many Liberals. In a major foreign policy debate in the Commons in late January 1963, the lead-off speakers for the major parties avoided any mention of nuclear arms. Douglas declared himself puzzled by the silence. He judged the prevention of nuclear war to be the world community's highest priority. He slammed the Conservatives for their confusion and the Liberals for their flip-flop. Both parties, he said, should return to a straight anti-nuclear position.

Less than a week later, on January 30, nameless officials at the U.S. State Department threw the Commons into pandemonium. Without consulting the Canadian government, they released an unsigned memorandum on nuclear weapons which appeared to favour Pearson against Diefenbaker. Canada, they wrote, would not really be joining the nuclear club by accepting warheads for the Bomarc. "As is the case with other allies, custody of the United States nuclear weapons would remain with the United States."[6] This blow against the tottering Diefenbaker government provoked intense excitement on Parliament Hill. When the House met the next day the prime minister thundered that Canada would "not be pushed around or accept external domination," and implied that Pearson was taking orders from the Pentagon.

Tommy Douglas branded the State Department message "an unwarranted and unprecedented intrusion" into Canadian affairs. The United States should not confuse Canada with Guatemala or Cuba, he warned, and he took the opportunity to denounce the American campaign against Castro's Cuba, specifically the abortive CIA-backed invasion at the Bay of Pigs. "This was an inexcusable intervention in the affairs of another member of the OAS," he said, "for no other purpose than to make the world safe for the United Fruit Company and Standard Oil." Canadians had a right to set their own course without outside interference. The Conservatives, however, had put themselves in an impossible position. "The government has to come down on the side of Mr. Green, who is against nuclear weapons, or Mr. Harkness, who is for nuclear weapons. Any government which tries to ride two horses going in opposite directions is going to find itself sitting in a most undignified position."[7]

A few days later the NDP helped to bring down the Diefenbaker government by supporting Pearson's catch-all motion of no confidence. It was clear that the Conservatives could no longer run the country.

The NDP's course of action during this period provoked complaints from both friends and opponents. Some party supporters complained that in backing Pearson, Douglas had helped to pave the way for a military and economic sell-out to the United States. Critics on the right, meanwhile, dismissed Douglas's worries about nuclear arms. The *Globe and Mail* called it a "phony issue" because nuclear policy was "a matter involving high emotions which has nothing whatever to do with the future welfare of this country."[8] Others felt that babysitting American nuclear weapons did not make Canada a nuclear power, and that Douglas should stop worrying.

Editorials like this confirmed the conclusions of an NDP researcher, Harry Pope, who had told Douglas before Christmas that Canadians liked President John F. Kennedy's cold war politics. During the Cuban crisis in the fall of 1962, when the United States and the Soviet Union had reached the brink of atomic war, the Americans had given Canada an hour and a half to put the joint Air Defence Command on alert. Douglas had complained about this, but Pope cautioned, "Canadians wanted to rally round the flag—America's flag." Criticism of the United States, he suggested, might be construed as pro-Soviet. The NDP, said Pope, must do more to show that "we are irrevocably committed to preventing the spread of communism."[9]

In April 1963 Canadians elected a minority Liberal government, and Lester Pearson moved into the prime minister's office. In the Throne Speech debate that opened the new Parliament, Douglas protested that the Liberal plan to let nuclear arms into Canada would increase the danger of nuclear war. He proposed an amendment to a Conservative no-confidence motion, and drew solid Tory support. The Liberals narrowly turned it back, 124-111. Douglas would have been shocked if it had carried. He confessed to one anti-nuclear supporter that the exhausted and penniless NDP was "not prepared to throw the government out."[10]

The 1960s witnessed the growth of a new national confidence in Canada. From sport to science to the arts, Canadians established a new international presence. They also took a fresh look at their history and their economy, and discovered, to their unease, that they had mortgaged many of their assets to outsiders.

The pattern of foreign economic domination was as old as the fur trade, and there was little evidence to suggest that the degree of control had changed. A 1966 study concluded that Americans owned about 27 per cent of Canadian industry, with higher concentrations in some areas, but it said that figure had remained stable for several years.[11] There is no doubt, however, that Canadian perceptions of the problem changed during this decade. Perhaps the barrage of American television, including the nightly reports from Vietnam, provoked Canadians into re-examining the benefits of depending on the Americans for culture, investment capital, and defence.

The New Democrats proposed a program of government economic intervention, one that would give Canadians control of new industries, but the Liberals declined to act. The Pearson government, said Douglas during the 1964 flag debate, was missing a chance at a fresh start. "A symbol of national independence will have little meaning," he said, "if, in the meantime, Canada has become an economic satellite of the United States. In that case, we shall be able to choose for a flag an American eagle with a beaver clutched in its claws."[12]

In earlier days, the CCF had not made an issue of foreign investment. Woodsworth had told the founding convention in Regina that "we do not advocate 'economic nationalism.' National isolation—if this is possible—means lowered standards of living; possibly a reversal to barbarism."[13] The CCF brain trust had shared this view. The authors of *Social Planning* wrote that "even a socialist Canada will probably have to give preferential treatment to the foreign investor."[14]

The CCF in Saskatchewan had also taken the view that capital has no national loyalties, and had welcomed American corporations looking for oil and potash. On one issue, though, Premier Douglas took a strongly nationalist stance. When the federal Liberals proposed to lend money to an American consortium to build a TransCanada pipeline, Douglas urged Prime Minister St. Laurent to reconsider. The pipeline would be the sole source of natural gas for Ontario, and Douglas worried that "the control of a vital natural resource is destined to fall into the hands of financial interests outside Canada." He urged, in vain, that Ottawa and the provinces should construct the new line jointly as a public utility.[15] Douglas argued here that Canadians should use public ownership to gain control over their economy, an argument he would often make during the 1960s.

The 1961 founding convention of the NDP agreed that Canadians should own more of their own economy. An NDP government, the meeting decided, should buy back selected industries from foreign owners and should set up a Development Corporation that would use capital pools, such as pension funds, to create new enterprises. One of the goals of this strategy was to increase the amount of processing and manufacturing done in Canada. As Douglas told an interviewer in the mid-1960s: "In Western Canada, and particularly in B.C., they stand every day and watch the logs with bark still on being put onto ships...and then go down and watch plywood coming back. They see pulp going out, and us buying back paper. They see iron ore and moly and coal going out and we buy back steel. They see copper ore going out and we buy back wire and cable and electrical appliances. And it has dawned on them over the past 10 or 20 years that what we're exporting are jobs."[16]

Douglas's speeches on economic planning borrowed heavily from John Kenneth Galbraith's *The New Industrial State*. The big corporations, he said, had already adopted planning principles, and made long-term decisions which greatly affected the employment and capital markets, but they did not take the public good into account. He proposed the creation of an array of new institutions to act as a check on corporate control. At Laval University he spoke of a planning and development council to co-ordinate federal and provincial actions, as well as an economic advisory council to look at the whole economic picture.

The idea of over-centralization, he wrote elsewhere, was "repugnant" to New Democrats. The provinces and the private sector could work with the federal government, as in Sweden, where decisions on plant location and the issuing of corporate bonds were taken by joint public/private boards. Through economic planning, Ottawa could direct corporate investments into "socially useful channels," nationalize some monopolies, and create "special agencies like the proposed Canada Development Corporation."[17]

Douglas spoke several times against trying to drive American investors out. Canada should assert control over its economy through new development, he said, not with "artificial barriers against foreign capital, or in discrimination against foreign firms." "Canadian economic growth," he pointed out, "particularly in the years 1945 to 1955, would probably have been much slower without the assistance of foreign capital."[18]

The proposed Canada Development Corporation became the symbol of Douglas's hopes for a new, Canadian-controlled economy. If it had been set up according to his wishes, it would have been the largest and most important corporation in the history of Canada. The corporate structure that Douglas proposed is hard to pin down; like a legendary beast from the ancient world, the CDC's characteristics changed each time it was described. The new corporation would help the private sector, the co-ops, and the provincial governments to invest in both resource development and in secondary processing. It would be "very large." In fact, it would "mobilize all Canadian savings." It would "go into the underdeveloped regions of Canada where the risk is high," and it would help in "developing a Canadian identity."[19]

The Liberals' new economic spokesman, Walter Gordon, picked up the CDC idea, and it figured high on his list of priorities when he became minister of finance in 1963. Gordon had played an important part in making foreign ownership a public concern with his Royal Commission on the Economy in the late 1950s, and now he had a chance to act. Unhappily, Gordon's career as a senior minister ended almost before it began. The Bay Street accountant hired some young consultants to help prepare his first budget, and to the Finance Department mandarins who were bypassed, Douglas said later, this was like "spitting in church."[20] The NDP had fun with the story in the House, but it marked the start of a long series of blunders and retreats for Gordon—in Douglas's view, a well-intentioned but inept politician.

The continentalists gradually took the upper hand in the Pearson cabinet, and the Canada Development Corporation proposal went astray in the shuffle. It reappeared fleetingly from time to time over the next eight years—in a reporter's phrase, "the jilted bride of the Liberal government."[21]

The Liberals did create an Economic Council to make a start on economic planning, and when Pearson brought in the legislation, he sounded as if he had hired Tommy Douglas to write his speech. Great corporations and provinces already planned their activities, he said, but "at present all this partial planning within our economy is not related; it is not co-ordinated." The new council, said Pearson, would bring government together with leaders of "our great industries, of trade unions, our farm organizations, so that together they can take an understanding and far-sighted view."[22] Douglas voted for the bill, but he wondered what the council's studying and recommending would amount to if the government had no will to intervene in the economy.

Douglas continued to pursue the foreign investment theme in Parliament and at NDP conventions through the 1960s. Slowly more Canadians came to agree with him that Canada was "like a farmer who tries to meet his debts by selling a piece of the farm each year."[23] One day in 1965, while Douglas was waiting for a plane, he wrote down the "Canadian Credo" that is quoted from at the beginning of this chapter. He delivered it to the Canadian Club in Victoria, and this time the editorial bullpen at the *Globe* applauded. The credo should be "read throughout the country," said the Toronto newspaper, because it warned that Canada might be absorbed, culturally and economically, into the United States.[24]

Other prominent Canadians spoke out with the same message. Walter Gordon published *A Choice for Canada*, conservative thinker George Grant wrote *Lament for a Nation*. In 1968 a federal task force headed by Mel Watkins, a Toronto economist, restated many of the ideas of Douglas and his NDP colleagues, backing them up with extensive new economic data.

The Liberals in Ottawa, after a long delay, responded to the increasing nationalist sentiment with two modest measures. In 1971 they set up a Canada Development Corporation to promote Canadian ownership of industry. In 1972 they created a Foreign Investment Review Agency to examine proposed foreign takeovers of Canadian companies.

To the New Democrats, the Trudeau government's CDC proposal was a step backwards. Its stated goal was to generate a high profit, and not to create jobs or stimulate regional economies. Ottawa would put up some capital—a maximum of $250 million—so that the CDC could buy shares in existing companies. The private sector, however, would hold a majority of the shares and most of the directors' seats. Douglas attacked the bill as a "legislative monstrosity." The Canadian people, he said, would take the financial risks in setting up the new company, and reap almost none of the benefits. The creation of the CDC would not solve the country's problems, or stop the "rapid acceleration in the takeover of Canadian businesses."[25]

To be realistic, no single corporation could have lived up to all of Douglas's expectations. First of all, there would have been a conflict between providing a fair rate of return for pension funds and the like and, at the same time, investing in socially useful projects. Second, and more important, Douglas and the NDP never agreed among themselves on a definition for "socially useful."

Douglas had often described the CDC as an operation that would bring new life to economically depressed regions such as Cape Breton, the Gaspé, and northern Ontario. The other economic spokesmen in the NDP caucus, Colin Cameron and Max Saltsman, promoted the idea that a Canada Development Corporation should "rationalize" Canadian industry and invest in the industrial heartland. If the Canadian economy were to grow up, they wrote in a 1967 study, it must put together firms that were large enough to sell on international markets at competitive prices. The CDC would clear up the existing "jungle of inefficient productive units" in the Canadian economy.[26] As Saltsman said later, "the CDC would make a judgement that the electronics industry [for example] was a good thing to get into, and buy up all the little electronics industries that came on the market, provide them with better financing, better management, better marketing advice, and then go out in the world. In other words, create giants of our own." Saltsman pointed out that Petro-Canada later played this function in organizing frontier drilling plays and energy industry supply ventures.[27]

The 1968 Watkins Task Force repeated the advice of Saltsman and Cameron. A news release from the NDP leader's office enthused that Watkins's report "confirms New Democratic policies to rationalize industry and to introduce much greater specialization."[28] But Douglas continued to insist, at the same time, that the CDC would work in the regions—that it should help to prop up Canada's poor provinces and failing one-industry towns by paying businesses to scatter themselves across the country.

The confusion became absolute in Douglas's 1971 Commons speech on the CDC bill, when he said the corporation "should be designed to reduce the disparities which are tearing the country apart...A properly constituted CDC could speed up the whole process of rationalization of industry in this country, something which is badly needed."[29]

The ambiguity over how to proceed with a nationalist economic plan was not restricted to Douglas alone. David Lewis and Ed Broadbent, his successors as party leaders, continued to call for a Canadian industrial strategy. Neither, however, could spell out what he meant.

Would an NDP government want to maximize the national income, or preserve the lifestyles of Canada's regions? Does it want to maintain people in their home towns, where there may be no jobs, or see them move to the big city, where there may be no housing or social support?

Is it better to spend money on small, high-risk factories in Baie Comeau and Moose Jaw, far from markets? Or should we commit funds to megaprojects, and risk colossal failures like the CANDU program and the Beaufort Sea drilling program?

Allan Blakeney, who served both as a federal NDP president under Douglas and as premier of Saskatchewan, said in 1985 that the party has never reached a consensus. Even if party leaders could agree on a program of hardnosed socialist planning aimed at building on Canada's perceived strengths, it is not clear where they would get the political support to put it into effect. "The party in opposition didn't want to get too detailed—the winners are in the future, and the losers are today," Blakeney said. "It doesn't help any to say that the textile industry will be eliminated in Louiseville, Quebec, but there'll be twice as many jobs and they'll be in Hamilton."[30]

Douglas's political adviser, Clifford Scotton, said his leader played on the economic planning theme as a symbol of the differences between the NDP and the old parties. Politically, however, it proved impossible for Douglas to come down to specifics: "And when people would say, how's it going to affect me, I work in a textile mill in Valleyfield, we'd say let's just get the fundamentals in place first and then we'll address those minor technical points. Well, those minor technical points might include whether the guy starved or ate...I think that tended to enhance the perception that people had that we were sort of impractical dreamers."[31]

In 1972 the Liberals announced a second nationalist measure, the creation of the Foreign Investment Review Agency to screen takeover proposals from foreign-based investors. In Douglas's view, the government was taking a negative approach, in that FIRA would not promote Canadian enterprise. And while the new agency might block some unwanted takeovers, it would do so only on a hit or miss basis. When the Liberals introduced their bill, Douglas said: "Even if a foreign corporation were refused permission to take over a Canadian company there is nothing to prevent it from setting up a company in Canada and driving the Canadian company out of business."[32]

Both the CDC and FIRA failed to achieve their stated purpose. FIRA had little impact beyond irritating foreign capitalists, and the Liberals began to dismantle it within a decade. The Mulroney Tories sold most of the shares of the CDC in 1986. The idea of paying private companies to locate in depressed areas, however, proved politically irresistible. The Liberals depended heavily on regional industrial subsidies to shore up their support in Atlantic Canada and Quebec, and under the Tories these payments to business were the only signs of a national industrial strategy.

Until Canada gained control of its economic life, Douglas believed, it could never take an independent stand on foreign affairs. One of his greatest concerns during the mid- and late 1960s was that Canada was remaining silent on American actions in Vietnam. But while Lester Pearson and his colleagues showed sympathy with the NDP's opposition to the war in Southeast Asia, they chose quiet diplomacy over public protests.

"The United States," Douglas told a 1967 convention of B.C. New Democrats, "is seeking to foist on the people of South Vietnam a government of rapacious landlords, military dictators, and former collaborators of a colonial regime...I can't think of any better way to spread communism." The Canadian government declined to speak out on the war, he said, because "we are not masters in our own house. We are becoming an economic colony of the United States, and our capacity for independent action in world affairs is being reduced to zero."[33]

A statement from Prime Minister Pearson during the same month suggested that Douglas was right. "A first result of any open breach with the United States," Pearson said, "would be a more critical examination by Washington of certain aspects of our relationships."[34]

Douglas belonged to a generation of North Americans who had held out great hopes for the United States as a bulwark of democracy in the postwar world. He had praised the Americans for their role in setting up the United Nations, and he was strongly pro-Zionist. NATO, he had believed in the late 1940s, would function as a bloc within the United Nations, an economic and military alliance of liberal states, and could lead the way in helping developing nations. By the mid-1950s, he had grown disillusioned with the neighbouring superpower; the United States, he told M. J. Coldwell, had "allied itself with dictatorships and every form of reaction." The hopes for economic co-operation within NATO were fading as the Americans carried out a "mad rush to build up military might."[35]

In public, Douglas favoured Canada's membership in NATO. Canada, he said, could argue its case for disarmament better from within the alliance. Holding to this position kept him on good terms with the NDP's other senior foreign policy spokesmen, Andrew Brewin and David Lewis, who were both more rigidly anti-Communist than Douglas and more reluctant to endure red-baiting. At the 1961 NDP convention Douglas spoke for the pro-NATO side, and helped to reverse the stand taken at the CCF's last meeting a year earlier. However, if NATO did not begin to function as an economic zone within the United Nations, Canada should eventually get out, he said.

With Vietnam, it seemed to Douglas, the United States made a decision to ignore its allies, world opinion, and international law. The Americans maintained a puppet regime in the southern half of Vietnam, in violation of the 1954 Geneva Agreement's provision for free elections for the whole country. A rebel force supported by the Communists fought back and by late 1964 controlled half the southern zone. The Americans, who had acted as military and secret police advisers, began to bomb the Communist north and to move thousands of American soldiers into the south. The hundreds of thousands of Americans who protested the growing conflict were called unpatriotic. Their friends in other countries won the label "anti-American." A Canadian editorial branded one of

Douglas's first statements on the war "an outrageous and irrational attack on the U.S."[36]

The Canadian Parliament held its first debate on Vietnam in May 1965, and Douglas appears to have surprised the other parties by calling for a complete American withdrawal. The Americans had no more business in a Vietnamese civil war than they would in Luxembourg, he said: "We do not want some new form of colonialism masquerading as an anti-communist crusade." The Americans, he said, should drop their conditions for opening peace talks. They should agree to meet with the southern rebels, the National Liberation Front, whom he said represented "a broad coalition" of anti-rightists. The Americans must face the fact that the Vietnamese might choose to reunite their country under Communist leadership. World Communism was not a monolith, he added. The West might very well establish relations with a Communist Vietnam, as it had with Yugoslavia. As the Americans withdrew, he said, an international peacekeeping force should move into Vietnam until free elections were held. At the same time, Western nations could begin a development program for rural South Vietnam.[37]

The NDP's proposals got a cold reception in the Commons. At least one Tory suggested that Douglas had returned to the days of 1938, when the CCF had tried to turn its back on Hitler.[38] Pearson and his external affairs minister, Paul Martin, had both apprenticed under Mackenzie King, and they took a more subtle line. They spoke in carefully shaded phrases about how they regretted the escalating war and hoped for a peaceful settlement. Clearly, though, they supported the American action.

Through 1965 and 1966, opinion in the United States and Europe grew increasingly critical of the Americans' Vietnam adventure. In a debate in the Commons in February 1967, Martin laid out the Douglas proposals of 1965 as official Canadian policy, virtually point for point. But while he encouraged the member for Burnaby-Coquitlam to speak out, he refused to introduce any parliamentary resolution on Vietnam or to rebuke the United States in public. Canada must remain neutral, he said, because of its membership on the International Control Commission—an ineffectual body set up to police the 1954 Geneva accords.

Douglas complimented Martin for his change of views, but he grew hot as he addressed the question of Canada's alleged neutrality. Canada, he said, was providing direct support to the Americans, in the form of $300 million worth of arms sales every year. Unless Canada could be sure that these arms were not going to Vietnam, we should scrap the Defence Production Sharing Agreement. He accused Martin of sounding like Pontius Pilate, washing his hands of all responsibility: "What is happening in Vietnam is shocking the conscience of the world more than anything that has happened since Hitler tried to exterminate the Jews in Europe. The bombing not only of military targets but of civilians, now proven beyond a shadow of a doubt, has caused millions of people in the world to question this disastrous military conflict."

Unfortunately, as the Liberals realized, there was probably nothing Canada could do to influence the Americans' course of action. Pearson and Martin chose to work through diplomatic courier, while Douglas called on the Canadian leaders to turn on the heat in public. He could not suggest how this might restrain the Americans, except that it might cause them to "pause and think."[39]

Douglas's position on Vietnam delighted the young militants of the party. Other New Democrats like David Lewis often emphasized the role of the Chinese and the Soviets in Vietnam, but Lewis appeared to some radicals to be looking for excuses for the Americans. Douglas spoke out against the Soviet invasion of Czechoslovakia, but in his speeches on Vietnam he was uncompromising in his opposition to American policy. Douglas became a figurehead for a Canadian youth movement that brought together leftists and nationalists. He was routinely invited to address anti-war rallies across Canada; he was listed on posters as a sponsor of the "Take Vietnam to Expo" protest of July 1, 1967, along with academics such as Northrop Frye and Edward Broadbent.[40] Douglas's whole philosophy, complained a Liberal backbencher, was to pull together anti-American groups. His supporters were "beatniks" or perhaps "Vietniks."[41] When he joined with other prominent Canadians—George Grant, René Lévesque, Farley Mowat—on a committee to send medical supplies to North Vietnam, editors complained that he was eroding Canada's neutral position in the war by extending partisan aid.

For Douglas, it was a return to the days of common fronts and the "daily struggle" of the 1930s. And as in the Depression, some members of his caucus questioned his decision to work with Communists. He agreed to see members of South Vietnam's National Liberation Front in his office and, as one aide said, he walked "arm in arm with folks that would have made David Lewis's hair curl."[42] Some party members also worried that the anti-war demonstrations would be seen as Communist-directed. Douglas replied, "In my opinion what we have to do is to attend in such numbers that it becomes our rally rather than theirs."[43]

On one occasion, the rivalry with the Reds descended to the level of street brawling. A gang of thugs, members of the Communist Party of Canada (Marxist-Leninist), set out to break up a rally on Parliament Hill in early 1970. When one of them began to swing a two-by-four at a young woman, Douglas disarmed him from behind, and then stepped in front of another man who was preparing to strike. Douglas's young supporters pulled him out of the way, and stood around him in a cordon while he delivered his speech.[44]

Some of Douglas's critics had called him archaic, a man of the past, but he had no trouble sympathizing with the most radical causes of the late 1960s. He demonstrated his openness, and his disagreement with mainstream political opinion, after the arrest of his daughter Shirley, who worked as an actress in California. She had helped the Black Panthers, a group feared by most middle-aged North Americans as the spawn of

Satan, and the police said she had been storing bombs in her home. Douglas announced immediately that he was proud of Shirley, and would stand with her.

Early on the morning of October 2, 1969, ten police officers entered the home of Shirley Douglas and her husband, actor Donald Sutherland, in Beverley Hills. While the police searched the house, she and her ten-year-old son stood against a wall. Two younger children sat in a bedroom and cried. Although the police found nothing, they charged Shirley with conspiracy to obtain a destructive device.

Shirley had taken a small part in fund-raising for the Friends of the Black Panthers, a group that helped the radical black group with a free breakfast program for poor children. The Panthers at this time were in a virtual shooting war with major police departments across the United States, and two of them had been arrested at Shirley's home when she gave her keys to friends for a weekend.

Rather than shrinking from the publicity, Douglas called a news conference at the National Press Theatre in Ottawa three days after the arrest. He announced his faith in Shirley's innocence. "I am proud of the fact that my daughter believes, as I do, that hungry children should be fed whether they are Black Panthers or White Republicans."[45] The next day, he flew to Los Angeles to be with his daughter.

A squad of Los Angeles news reporters turned out to meet Douglas at the airport, after getting word that the head of the Canadian Communists was coming to town. A news clip that was later played in his television obituaries shows the small, neatly dressed Douglas trying to peer around some beefy men carrying tape recorders. "She's not here, sir," says one of the reporters, "are you disappointed?" Douglas says firmly, "Who says she's not?" and a moment later Shirley walks into his arms. After this visit, Douglas wrote to Woodrow Lloyd, "Before going to Los Angeles I thought that American society was sick. After being there I feel that it is nigh unto death."[46]

The charges against Shirley came to trial in February 1970 and the judge threw them out of court. Almost two years later the U.S. Justice Department announced that it had closed the case. Later, newspaper reports made a strong case that the Los Angeles police had tried to frame Shirley, as a warning to other middle-class radicals, but had botched the job. Despite her innocence, however, American immigration officials began a campaign to deport her. After a long series of legal battles, Shirley returned to Canada in 1978 and was barred from working again in the United States.

Throughout the 1960s, friends and critics of Douglas's party complained that they had trouble telling the NDP from the Liberals. On issues such as housing, regional development, and consumer affairs the Liberals digested NDP ideas without any discomfort—or, as a Liberal might argue, the NDP raced to stay just slightly ahead. It was on the issue of Canadian independence that Douglas was most successful in establishing his distance from the Liberals. On the questions of Canadian complicity in the Vietnam war, and foreign investment, the NDP worked to inform the conscience of Canada, and won its place as an indispensable addition to the Canadian political scene.

Douglas became a member in good standing of the loosely structured Canadian nationalist movement, an alliance of academics, artists, politicians, and business people, all of whom supported some form of action to assert Canadian independence. But to many of the younger converts to the left, this moderate alliance was a waste of time. The radicals asked the question: Why set up a miniature replica of the American state?

Starting in 1969, these radicals made a determined effort to steer the NDP to the left, where the party would identify independence with classic socialism. This challenge provided the opportunity for a productive debate, and for the resolution of some of the fuzzier aspects of NDP policy. Instead, however, the appearance of the Waffle caucus provoked hostility and a long interparty struggle.

26
Rights and Powers

DURING ITS QUARTER CENTURY of existence, the CCF established a reputation as a party of constitutional reform. Its leaders, including Tommy Douglas, argued that the powers of the central government should be strengthened, so that Ottawa could regulate the way businesses operated within the community. At the same time, the CCF wanted a Bill of Rights to protect individual citizens.

The Quiet Revolution in Quebec provided a new momentum for constitutional reform, but not in the direction which the CCF had anticipated. The generation that took power in Quebec in 1960 demanded a strengthening of provincial powers and a special place for their province as the senior partner in Confederation. Douglas and the New Democrats, heirs to an English-speaking, centralist tradition, had to adjust their ways of thinking considerably. Before long, the NDP was supporting Quebec's call for special status. But while Douglas won some personal respect in Quebec, his shifting of position did not win many votes in either French or English Canada.

The young Douglas had first approached constitutional change as a civil libertarian in the 1930s, at a time when provincial governments were making free use of their police powers to repress organized labour and the left. As an MP and later as a provincial premier, he argued that if a strong central government had a constitutional Bill of Rights to work with, it could protect Canadians from such arbitrary provincial measures as Quebec's 1938 Padlock Law. The Douglas government in Saskatchewan adopted Canada's first provincial Bill of Rights in 1947. This measure, as it turned out, had little force in law, but it helped to reinforce the social conventions against discrimination in such areas as employment and housing.

At a first ministers' conference in 1950, Douglas proposed the idea of a constitutional Bill of Rights for Canada. Frank Scott, the CCF's constitutional adviser, had often said that Canadian governments had the power to suspend basic freedoms whenever they wanted to. In Scott's view, a Bill of Rights would entrench basic civil liberties in the constitution. All provinces would have to agree to any amendments, and no single group of legislators could tamper with it. This anticipated loss of provincial control caused the premiers to shoot down the idea when Douglas put it forward at Quebec. The conference minutes suggest that the premiers, for whatever reason, did not want to extend full civil rights to everyone. One remarked that "we have to avoid protecting disloyal people."[1]

The CCF believed that a strengthened central government would have the power to impose an overall plan on the Canadian economy, as well as protect the rights of working people. If there were uniform national standards in such areas as labour and environmental law, large corporations would be prevented from playing provinces off against each other. Scott wrote in 1951 that all the provinces should surrender some of their powers to the Government of Canada for the common good: "Laws dealing with corporations, workmen's compensation, minimum wages, hours of labour, industrial standards, pensions, public health, traffic regulations, collective bargaining, rent control, and so forth, have a common content throughout Canada because they confront a common social and economic situation. The more Quebec becomes industrialized, the more this will be true."[2]

The CCF's ideas for constitutional change were never implemented. Douglas worried in the mid-1960s that the federal structure had become less effective over the years. The major social programs—pensions, unemployment insurance, hospital care, medicare—had come only after long periods of federal-provincial bickering and public agitation.

As NDP leader, Douglas still spoke sometimes of constitutional change, but it was not always clear what he had in mind. Sometimes he spoke of strengthening federal powers. In 1969, for example, he complained that Prime Minister Trudeau was sticking to a "narrow interpretation of federalism,"[3] and demanded that Ottawa show leadership in the areas of housing, job creation, price controls, and pollution standards. Quebec, however, was to set its own course, in a manner that Douglas and the NDP never defined.

From its first days, the CCF attracted only fringe support in the province of Quebec. The party was seen as radical, Protestant, and English-speaking. Quebec voters had grounds to believe that under a CCF government, their province would be submerged in a centrally controlled federation dominated by English Canadians. Even Frank Scott, a Montrealer and a translator of Quebec literature, rejected the idea of granting extensive special powers to Quebec under the constitution.

The behaviour of the CCF in Parliament during the 1950s offended the leaders of the Quebec CCF. Harold Winch questioned the use of French in the Commons. Ernie Regier, in rejecting the idea of a bilingual country, called French Canada the "sore spot" in Confederation, which was translated in the French-language press as "running sore."[4] In the controversy that followed, Coldwell wrote that he supported the use of French in Parliament, the federal courts, and within Quebec, but stopped there. "The Bill of Rights which I proposed in the House," Coldwell wrote, "does not give support to the idea that bilingualism is established in Canada."[5]

Tommy Douglas, like Coldwell, saw the Quebec government using its position as the protector of the French language to press forward its economic and political claims. In his view, Premier Duplessis and the Catholic bishops hid behind Quebec nationalism as a way to beat back Ottawa, the unions, and social progress. For years, the CCF tried without success to convince the Québécois that their interests lay in allying themselves with working people across Canada. As late as 1969 Douglas voiced the same thought. "The fundamental problems of Quebec are not basically language and culture," he told a television forum, "they are economic and social."[6] In a later interview he concluded: "One thing I've always differed with Quebec on, no matter who was their leader, or what government was in office: that Quebec is part of Canada...They must have certain rights and privileges that are safeguarded, but on general legislation, we have to be a nation."[7]

The founding of the New Democratic Party in 1961 gave English-speaking social democrats a fresh opportunity to form ties with Quebec. During Douglas's years as NDP leader, however, this effort failed. According to John Harney, the NDP's Quebec leader in the mid-1980s, the party moved far enough at the start to alienate many voters in English Canada but not far enough to attract the French-speaking left in Quebec.

At its founding convention the NDP embraced the idea that Canada had been founded by two nations, French and English. Eugene Forsey, a CCF pioneer and a constitutional expert, left the movement when the convention put the phrase "the national identity of French Canadians" into the party program.[8] From supporting a "national identity" for French Canada—an ambiguous term that applied, perhaps, only to language and culture—the NDP would move steadily down the road to the idea of "special status" for Quebec. Pearson's Liberals muddled along in the same direction. For Douglas to have publicly fought this trend would have aligned him with the right wing of Diefenbaker's party; and even the Tories, after the Chief's fall, made the same choice as Douglas.

Douglas faced a dilemma in Quebec. On one side, the French-speaking nationalists waited for him to produce policies based on the principle of *deux nations*. But many of the English-speaking Montrealers—historically the most influential group in the Quebec CCF—resisted any drift to special status. In Harney's words, the Anglo faction always presented "either a denial of the original position, or an attempt to shunt it, saying, yes, it's important, but only theoretically."[9] Faced with this uncertainty, organized labour in Quebec withdrew the support it had promised the New Party.

Douglas had warned before 1960 that the leader of the New Party should be someone who spoke fluent French. He spoke almost none. Despite his sympathies with the emerging French-Canadian left, he could only look in on the Quebec scene as an outsider. Nonetheless, he tried to convince Quebec of his belief in the importance of French language and culture to Canada. In a 1962 election speech he called for a bilingual civil service to serve French Canada and offer wider job opportunities for French-speaking Canadians, and for a better tax deal for all provinces. Generally, however, the NDP leader returned to his more centralist ideas: certain powers should be transferred to Ottawa, and under no circumstances should Quebec (or any province) hold a blanket veto over constitutional change.

In February 1962 Douglas made a major proposal for the improvement of French-English relations. He and a Quebec member of the federal executive, Romeo Mathieu, jointly proposed the creation of a commission on bilingualism and biculturalism, a "rethinking of the relations between the two nations."[10] They put forward a list of possible commissioners, including Frank Scott, Pierre Trudeau of the Université de Montréal, and André Laurendeau, the editor of *Le Devoir*.

Pearson took up the idea, and when he became prime minister he appointed Laurendeau and Davidson Dunton of Carleton University to co-chair an inquiry. Their final report marked a milestone in presenting French Canada's case to the rest of the country. Certainly it influenced Douglas. He wrote glowingly in 1967 of a future when "the constitution will guarantee the right to an education in English or French to every Canadian in any part of Canada."[11]

Quebec enjoyed a re-awakening in the early 1960s, a period of cultural activity and social reform, but it took several years before there was any change in the balance of power in Parliament. Diefenbaker's government made little use of its Quebec members. When in opposition, the Tories kept the names of French-speaking cabinet ministers before the public, but only in connection with bribery and scandal. Pearson retaliated at one point by leaking a secret file linking former Conservative ministers—including one from Quebec—to a hooker named Gerda Munsinger. This move disgusted Douglas and made him wonder what other information Pearson might use against his opponents.[12]

It was in this unhappy climate that Pearson's government moved to promote national unity by introducing a new, and non-British, national flag. In doing so, the Liberals provoked one of the most acrimonious debates in Parliament's history. Douglas later admitted he could have lived with the Union Jack, but he respected his caucus' wish to support the change. Diefenbaker, however, derided the "Pearson pennant," and led one of the longest filibusters in modern parliamentary history. Neither of the old party leaders would give ground. They reminded Douglas of "two old bulls out on the prairie bashing their heads together."[13]

When the flag debate began on June 16, 1964, Douglas spoke in favour of Pearson's design—three maple leaves on a white background, with blue borders—although he said that one maple leaf, rather than three, would best symbolize a unified nation. Beyond that, he questioned the timing of the government's move. Canada needed action, he said, on jobs and medicare. Where was the Canada Development Corporation the government had promised?[14]

Douglas watched in disbelief for five weeks as Tory after Tory stood to decry the new flag as an attack on Canada's traditions, on the war dead, and on Christian values. When he next spoke in the Commons, he chided the Conservatives for wasting time; the best way to preserve the British legacy in Canada, he said, was to make Parliament work.

Douglas remained a monarchist. In a form letter that he sent to voters who asked him about his stand, he spoke of the Queen as the centre of "an invisible bond of loyalty" across the Commonwealth, a symbol of stability, continuity, and democratic values. But he saw nothing sacred about the Union Jack. "There comes a time," he told the Commons, "when any independent nation must cut the umbilical cord and step out on its own." He especially rejected the notion that the flag was a sop to Quebec; it would symbolize, instead, "a united people who are seeking to establish a Canadian identity on the North American continent."[15]

In September 1964 Douglas suggested an obvious step—that study of the flag should go to a special parliamentary committee, which would then report back to the party leaders. Pearson, who had wanted to ram his resolution through, and Diefenbaker, who had sought to block it, could hardly disagree. At a leaders' meeting two days later they set up the committee which produced the final design for a red and white flag.

However, the Tories resumed their blockade when the committee reported back. Just before Christmas, the government forced a final vote in the Commons. In Douglas's opinion, this was a clumsy move. All in all, he said just before the final vote, the flag debate was a "childish exhibition that has done the country no good."[16]

The nationalist tide was rising in Quebec, and the NDP tried to respond. Pearson had started to hand over control of some federal programs—for example, the new Pension Plan—to the province. This raised the question, as Canadians speculated about a new constitution, as to whether Quebec should acquire permanent powers in these areas.

An NDP Federal Council statement in late 1964 saw the party moving in two directions at once, attempting to appeal to both centralist and pro-Quebec feelings. Ottawa, the statement said, should have responsibility for social security, medicare, agricultural marketing, and housing—all provincial areas under the BNA Act—but Quebec should have "special consideration," even the right to self-determination.[17] At his nominating meeting in Burnaby a year later, Douglas claimed that the NDP, more than any other party, was in tune with the Quiet Revolution.[18]

The NDP increased its share of the vote in Quebec to 12 per cent in the federal election of 1965, and for the first time it found a high-profile Quebec leader. But Robert Cliche, a lawyer from Laval University, took charge of an organization that lay in bits and pieces. In one observer's words, "he was like a great actor without a production to carry him."[19] Soon after Cliche took office, three of the sparkplugs of the Quiet Revolution—Trudeau, Marchand, and Pelletier—enlisted with the Liberals.

Douglas's keynote speech to the federal NDP convention of 1967 reflected his party's willingness to break with its past. "If Ottawa is going to take the initiative in grappling with marketing, housing, town planning and higher education, it will find Quebec concerned about an infringement of its cultural rights." Therefore, he said, Quebec must have a "particular status."[20] Douglas was proposing a new form of federal-provincial co-operation, but according to whose rules? He had always been willing to let any province, Quebec included, sit on the political sidelines if it chose; but was the rest of Canada now going to pay Quebec compensation for opting out of national programs?

The nationalist premier of Quebec, Daniel Johnson, took the "special status" plea to a federal-provincial conference in February 1968, and met his match in the rising star of the Pearson cabinet, Justice Minister Pierre Trudeau. In a written commentary, Douglas appeared to side with Duplessis's heir against Frank Scott's former student. Ottawa should acquire more powers, he wrote, but Quebec should have "a different arrangement...This doesn't hurt the rest of us, and it gives Quebec a feeling of cultural security."[21] Douglas repeated these arguments in his television debate with Trudeau in the spring, but the new prime minister insisted that Quebec must be a province like the others, or renounce its claim to equal treatment within Confederation.

In 1978, when it appeared that Quebec was about to leave Canada, Douglas wrote that Trudeau had missed a "golden opportunity"[22] by ignoring the idea of special status in the late 1960s. However, the depth of the NDP's commitment to meaningful special status remained ambiguous.

After the departure of Cliche from the Quebec NDP in the late 1960s, the provincial party moved to a separatist position little different from René Lévesque's. Douglas, as an outgoing leader in a party already facing a split over the Waffle, avoided a confrontation. In the election of 1972, however, David Lewis repudiated the NDP literature produced in Quebec. Douglas remained personally popular in Quebec, but in John Harney's view, the NDP did not convince voters that it was serious about special status. Pierre Trudeau and René Lévesque had marked out clearly defined alternatives for Canada's future. The NDP wavered somewhere in the middle, unsure of how to fit its social democratic economics together with its constitutional statements.

Douglas's views on the place of Quebec under a new constitution were, to some extent, a puzzle in shifts and contradictions. His commitment to a constitutional Bill of Rights, however, never wavered. He had seen the Mounted Police fire on the crowd near the Grain Exchange in 1919, and had seen the wounded workers brought to Weyburn from the 1931 police riot at Estevan. He had watched the brownshirts troop through the cobbled streets of the Reich. In a sense, Douglas was a man who heard voices. He kept an ear out, where no one else might notice, for rumours from the world of secret arrests and midnight trials. "We may wake up some day to realize that that's not impossible on this North American continent," he said in 1985," where financial power is so highly concentrated in so few hands, with all the media for propaganda in the same hands and with the forces of democracy divided and scattered and diffused. It's not impossible to imagine a fascist world."[23]

Throughout his career, Douglas followed up individual cases where citizens had run afoul of the state. He objected in 1961 when the Mounties warned Regina parents not to let their children attend ban-the-bomb marches in Regina. He protested when Gertrude Telford, a founding organizer of the CCF and a pacifist, reported in 1962 that the RCMP visited her house every two years to question her. He spoke out in 1963 when the Mounties persuaded the navy to discharge a sailor because an unrelated man with the same name was a Communist.

Douglas had great faith in the Mounties' ability to catch speeding motorists on Saskatchewan roads. As security and intelligence officers, however, he feared the RCMP saw "Reds under every bed. I have often thought that they became particularly conscious of the Red menace whenever there was any threat of their estimates being cut by the Treasury Board."[24] He joined in the call for a parliamentary inquiry into the Mounties' security activities, and the transfer of their security tasks to a "separate, more sophisticated agency."[25] Eventually, the Pearson government named a special commission, which included Coldwell as a member. This commission called for the creation of a new security agency, separate from the RCMP, but the government took no action. In the late 1970s the news surfaced that the Mounties had committed a long string of burglaries and dirty tricks, and had spied on the Waffle and the Parti Québécois. Along with David Lewis, Douglas signed a covering letter for a Civil Liberties Association petition, calling on the government to prosecute and punish any police officer who had committed a crime.[26]

For his efforts in the field of civil rights, the public rewarded Douglas with a stream of critical and sometimes violently reactionary letters. By far the worst barrage came when Douglas and most of his caucus stood alone in opposing the War Measures declaration of 1970.

The fears that Quebec might separate from Canada had taken on some substance in this year. Lévesque's Parti Québécois, running for the first time, had gathered 23 per cent of the vote in a provincial election, and his following was well-organized and vocal. When some Montreal punks kidnapped James Cross, a British trade commissioner, the event made international headlines. The kidnappers claimed membership in the Front de Libération du Québec, a shadowy entity which had conducted a long campaign of bombings against the Montreal establishment. The apprehension that Canada was entering a period of serious political instability grew when another gang kidnapped Pierre Laporte, the Quebec minister of labour.

In the week after Laporte was kidnapped, the prime minister held a rare series of meetings in his office with the opposition leaders, Douglas, Robert Stanfield, and Réal Caouette. At the last meeting, on the night of October 15, 1970, Trudeau revealed that the War Measures Act would go into force early the next morning, by cabinet order. Trudeau would then ask Parliament to ratify the decision. Premier Bourassa and Mayor Drapeau of Montreal had begged him to act, and Trudeau felt that only the War Measures Act could give the police the powers they would need to find the kidnappers.

Lewis and Knowles were still at work on the sixth floor of the House of Commons when Douglas returned to his own office. Jim Hayes, a caucus aide, recalled their meeting. "Tommy laid it out very clearly. He said he did not have any evidence that the Prime Minister had any reason to impose the War Measures Act. His conclusion was that it would be very bad for the country...Trudeau said the police really didn't know what was going on."[27]

Douglas had seen the Liberals impose the War Measures Act once before, in 1939. He was well aware of the arbitrary powers the act conferred on a government—the power to censor, to seize property and divert shipments of goods, to search without warrant, and to detain people without laying charges. It appalled him that Trudeau should declare war against an invisible enemy—an enemy of whom the RCMP or the Quebec Provincial Police had no knowledge. There was no evidence that radical left-wing leaders in Quebec planned an uprising. On that same evening, several of them had warned a student rally against the use of violence.

When his assistant, Hans Brown, rushed in to work the next morning after hearing the news on the radio, Douglas was already drafting his speech to the Commons. Shortly after nine, the two went down to the caucus room in the basement of the Centre Block. "We went into the meeting, and Tommy didn't say much," Brown said. "David was quite interested in having a discussion, as was Andrew Brewin, as were a number of other people. The nature of the discussion was not so much that we shouldn't oppose the War Measures Act, but David just wished things weren't moving so quickly." Finally, Douglas spoke:

> My position is to oppose it. I know that some of you may not support me, and I'll understand that. There's no question about it: if the Prime Minister calls an election over this, it may devastate the party. You have your own political careers to think about. [When the vote came, fifteen members of the caucus stood with Douglas; four joined the other parties in support of the War Measures declaration.]
>
> I'm going back upstairs now. I have to speak at 11 o'clock. I'm against it, period.[28]

Prime Minister Trudeau, in announcing the imposition of the act, read the letters he had received from the premier of Quebec and the mayor of Montreal. Premier Bourassa had written of "a threat to the security of the state." Mayor Drapeau saw the two kidnappings as the first step in an insurrection. Trudeau said that his government had to move decisively, and it had no legislation besides the War Measures Act to work with. His record in government, Trudeau said, had proved that he was as concerned as anyone to protect civil liberties.

Robert Stanfield, the Conservative leader, expressed some doubts about the use of the act. However, he said, his party was in no position to judge the seriousness of the FLQ threat, and would be forced to trust the government's judgement.

The atmosphere in the House during the speeches of the major party leaders had been grave. When Douglas rose and made it clear that he opposed Trudeau's action, the chamber rocked with howls of anger and cries of "Shame!" He made it clear that he was horrified by the kidnappings. He rejected the proposal from René Lévesque and others in Quebec that the government accede to the kidnappers' demands and release a group of "political prisoners." He suggested how the government might deal with the situation at hand—by moving in troops, by using the Criminal Code. The NDP would allow changes to the code, he said, to make it easier for police to search for weapons. However, he said, using the War Measures Act was going too far. "We are not prepared to use the preservation of law and order as a smokescreen to destroy the liberties and the freedom of the people of Canada...The government, I submit, is using a sledgehammer to crack a peanut."

There had been bombings in Quebec for several years, he said. The Liberals had not acted to stop them:

> The government has panicked and is now putting on a dramatic performance to cover up its own ineptitude...
>
> Right now there is no constitution in this country, no Bill of Rights...The government has the power by Order-in-Council to do anything it wants—to intern any citizen, to deport any citizen, to arrest any person or to declare any organization subversive or illegal...
>
> I suggest, Mr. Speaker, that the action of the government constitutes a victory for the FLQ.[29]

When word of Douglas's speech reached the airwaves, telegrams of condemnation began to pour in. Many of these messages, and the letters that followed, expressed the hope that the police would now crack down on troublemakers of all kinds across Canada. A typical entry read, "Much stronger action should be taken against unionists, professors, students, and other organized groups that defy the law." Someone else wrote, "It would be a most opportune time to take identical measures against you and your party."

The majority of the letters came from people of more moderate views who felt that good citizens had nothing to fear. The Canadian Council of Churches, for example, and the Manitoba Indian Brotherhood sent telegrams to all parties supporting Trudeau's action; a United Auto Workers local branded Douglas's stand as "weak-kneed and disloyal." Many citizens complained that the New Democrat leader was trying to score cheap political points, and making the government look bad at a time of national crisis. A Montreal resident wrote, "What about the civil rights of moral citizens who have been afraid to walk into any bank...for fear of being gunned down?"[30]

A form letter Douglas sent out to hundreds of critics read:

> The decision we made was not taken lightly. We have consistently supported the government in all its efforts to stamp out terrorism, to apprehend the kidnappers of Pierre Laporte and James Cross and bring them to justice.
>
> We maintain, however, that in doing so we must be careful not to destroy the fundamental freedoms and basic rights of Canadians by making it possible to arrest and detain people for 90 days without allowing them to prove their innocence.[31]

The New Democrats continued to propose alternatives to the War Measures Act. Douglas and Lewis insisted that the Criminal Code sections on sedition, offensive weapons, and conspiracy provided adequate cover for a special police operation. The NDP was prepared to see pro-FLQ demonstrations banned, even the outlawing of the FLQ. But this act brought back uneasy memories of the Padlock Law of the late 1930s, with its provisions giving the police the right to move against citizens without cause or trial.

The government's attempts to shore up its case confirmed Douglas's fears. Jean Marchand, the minister for regional economic expansion and Trudeau's one-time political godfather, bandied rumours about recklessly. He warned Ottawa reporters of 3000 armed FLQ members, without providing any evidence. The FLQ, he claimed, had "two tons" of dynamite ready to set off. Marchand also labelled members of FRAP, a radical opposition group contesting the Montreal civic elections, an "FLQ front." During the days leading up to the Montreal vote, police arrested several FRAP leaders.[32]

Brown tried to calm Douglas down, to moderate his language—at least to convince him to avoid mentioning Hitler. But when he appeared on a television forum a week after the act had been declared, Douglas called Marchand's statements about FRAP "a Reichstag fire in miniature. This is an attempt to stampede votes by a smear tactic—guilt by association." The parallel was apt. The Nazis had used the fire at the German parliament, set by a Bolshevik half-wit, as the pretext for a wide-ranging campaign of arrests. The Montreal establishment was using the work of a few thugs to confound a peaceful challenge to Mayor Drapeau. Douglas's aphorism got a bilious reception, however, from Charles Lynch, a member of the television panel:

LYNCH: If the government says, "the nation is in peril, we are acting to save the nation," the people have two options. They rally behind the government or they overthrow them...

DOUGLAS: I'm saying to the government, "You have taken sweeping powers which could undermine the democratic institutions of this country, and before taking those sweeping powers you must give us

some reason. And so far you haven't given us any." Now you ask
me to take this on trust. I want to remind you of something. I
want to remind you that in the 1940s the government of Canada
passed regulations under the War Measures Act to intern all
Canadian-born Japanese. I remember being booed off the platform
in Vancouver for opposing that. People said, "The government
tells us there's a yellow peril, that these Japs are going to blow
up railways and everything else." What happened? We locked
them up and confiscated their property. And at the end of the
war Mr. King said, "There is not a single proven case of sabotage
by any Canadian-born Japanese."

LYNCH: You must be the only man that's slept soundly in the past week
because you're more worried about Trudeau's erosion of freedom
than you are about the insurrection, the revolution.[33]

Some NDP riding associations and party regulars sent letters thank-
ing Douglas and telling him to stick to his principles. But there was
dissent from this quarter, too. Frank Scott offered cautious support
to Trudeau; in her maiden speech in the Senate, former Quebec CCF
leader Thérèse Casgrain lambasted the "malicious criticism and insinua-
tions" of those opposed to the War Measures Act.[34] Premier Ed Schreyer
of Manitoba issued a statement backing Trudeau; he recalled Germany's
Weimar Republic of the 1920s, which had allowed itself to be subverted
by extremists. Douglas replied at a Manitoba NDP convention with the
words of Pastor Niemoller: "When the Nazis came to get the Communists,
I remained silent. When they came to get the socialists, I remained
silent...When they came to get the Jews, I remained silent. When they
came to get me, there was no one left to speak."[35]

Despite the extreme public reaction against the NDP, the prime
minister himself appeared to see some merit in what Douglas was saying. In a letter he sent to the New Democrat leader the day after he
imposed the act, Trudeau promised to draft a new law that would focus
more tightly on the problem at hand. "Our legal fabric is defective in
not enabling the government to deal with [the crisis] speedily and effectively without invoking powers that may be too broad."[36] The NDP caucus
replied that it would support a temporary emergency act—but only if
the government supplied an honest status report on the "insurrection."
The bill should also set up a commission to monitor the treatment of the
accused. When the Temporary Measures Public Order Act came before
the Commons on November 4, the NDP saw serious flaws, but the caucus
voted to send it to committee. The committee rejected all NDP amendments and, three weeks later, the caucus voted against the bill on final
reading, along with two Tories and the Créditistes.

The government never offered any evidence of an insurrection. Of
the 450 Québécois arrested in the police roundup, one was convicted
of a criminal offense.

A public opinion poll, published in December by the Canadian
Institute of Public Opinion, asked: "Did your opinion of these men go
up or down as a result of what they did or said?" Trudeau fared best

among the half a dozen politicians listed: 60 per cent of those responding said their opinion had improved, while 5 per cent said it went down. Douglas finished last in the poll; 8 per cent of those polled had improved their opinion of the NDP leader, while 36 per cent thought less of him.[37] The Gallup Poll also showed support for the NDP bottoming out in December, at 13 per cent, down from 20 per cent in October. After that, support began to revive.

The War Measures Act, in one view, proved the impotence of the NDP in a short-run crisis. Douglas and his caucus did not extract the information they wanted about the alleged uprising; they did not convince the public that it might be dangerous to grant the police unrestricted power; they did not win any concessions when the government drew up a second emergency act.

It might also be argued, however, that the NDP helped to restrain the government in its moment of panic. Beyond its brief period of overreaction in Quebec, the Liberals avoided abusing their powers. The justice minister, John Turner, worked hard to convince the provincial governments not to unleash the kind of anti-radical clean-up campaign that Douglas feared.

The elected representative, Douglas said later, can serve no higher cause than to protect civil rights. His first duty, he told a world parliamentary meeting in 1977, is "to examine every piece of legislation to ensure that the life, liberty, and security of the citizen is safeguarded against the arbitrary power of the state."[38]

In this case, Douglas showed his willingness to endure hatred and abuse in defence of a principle, even if it meant standing alone without the support of his caucus. Donald Brittain, in his documentary film on Douglas's life, concluded that the October Crisis of 1970 was his "finest hour."

27

Who's Next?

ONE MONDAY MORNING in February 1968, Tommy Douglas arrived for work in a foul temper. He stalked into his office, chomped on his pipe through a tense morning briefing from his staff, and then descended to the Commons chamber to deliver a sharp, carping speech. He had met that weekend in Vancouver with Stephen Lewis, a member of the Ontario legislature and the son of David Lewis. Stephen had travelled across Canada to ask the sixty-three-year-old federal leader to resign as soon as possible.

Douglas still believed he could lead the party to new heights. Support among decided voters as measured by the Gallup Poll had reached a new peak in February 1967 at 27 per cent, and he looked forward to fighting a 1968 election. But the Liberal Party was moving to bring in a younger leader, and some felt the New Democrats should also put on a fresh face. "We had moved into a new age, a new era, and Tommy's magnificent appeal from the previous era was just a little out of synch," said Donald MacDonald, who was Ontario NDP leader at the time. "True, as an individual he was not only admired but loved...but it didn't translate into votes."[1]

Douglas, recalled his assistant, Jim Hayes, was "silent and somewhat wounded. He was put in a hell of a dilemma, because if he agreed to step down, how would he pull it off?" Douglas hoped to see the leadership pass to a younger generation. It now seemed more likely that the captain of the Old Guard, a man who outranked even the leader in many ways, would call in the endless debts he was owed and take the job for himself. "There was no natural person to come after Douglas, except one that he could think of," said Hayes, "and he didn't think David Lewis would add anything."[2] Douglas knew, however, that he must put his feelings aside. The federal Conservatives had recently dragged their ageing leader from his job; John Diefenbaker's graceless exit had appalled Douglas, reminding him perhaps of George Williams's departure in Saskatchewan in 1941. He rejected the idea of a snap convention, but he privately informed the party that he was ready to step down at the next regular convention in 1969.

As it turned out, Douglas would stay on for another two-and-a-half years, a time of furious division in the NDP—not over his leadership, but over its identity as a party of social and economic change.

This was the age of the "youth revolution," the time when the mass of North Americans born after the Second World War emerged as a cultural force. Advertisers, journalists, and social philosophers campaigned for the proposition that the values of youth would prevail—that the music, the idealism, the alleged freedom of spirit among young people would overthrow the society of their parents.

For most Canadians, this "revolution" brought only a change in styles; even so, the results were often dramatic. A new informality imposed itself on Christian worship, on higher education, on the workplace. A newborn hope for a Global Village began to dissolve the racism which marked North American life. Aspiring politicians cultivated the qualities of youthfulness, spontaneity, frankness; their political model was John F. Kennedy, martyred by an assassin's bullet, the most popular (as measured by Gallup) American president of the postwar period.

A minority of young people concentrated in the universities took the word "revolution" more literally. One of their models was the Cuban guerilla leader Che Guevara, who waged a dashing struggle far away and died young; Louis Riel also gained status as a Canadian folk hero. In English Canada this subculture of Marxists, anarchists, and romantics adopted a nationalist hostility towards the United States. While they copied the political attitudes and way of life of American youth, they denounced the U.S. establishment for its "militarism abroad and racism at home."[3]

Douglas sympathized with the young radicals; in speeches at colleges across Canada, he linked their pamphleteering and protesting to the struggles of colonized peoples, and to the alienation that accompanied industrial capitalism. "In this contest," he often said, "I am on the side of youth." He wondered, however, whether the university-based radicals wanted only a playtime revolution. "Try escorting the President of General Motors from his office," he told students at McMaster. "You will find yourself in a much tougher league."[4]

The revolution of style in Canada gave us Pierre Elliott Trudeau, who was elected leader of the Liberal Party in April 1968. As in 1919, a year of revolutionary talk and reformist yearnings, the Liberals bypassed their warhorses and chose a relatively young man. Trudeau, like Mackenzie King, combined a progressive appeal with an establishment background. As an intellectual and a former student of Frank Scott in Montreal, Trudeau had agitated against the Duplessis regime during the 1950s. His liberal technocratic ideas now appeared chic, rather than dangerous, and his wealth and polish reassured the country's elite. Above all, he was saleable to an electorate tired of their old politicians, and he embodied the new youthfulness and spontaneity. Ed Broadbent, early in Trudeau's career, called him "a Mackenzie King who likes to dance all night."[5]

The New Democrats also had several youngish leadership prospects who, it was thought, might meet the needs of the times. Laurier Lapierre of Montreal had a national profile as a journalist; Ed Schreyer and Allan Blakeney were gaining reputations in the West, as was provincial secretary John Harney in Ontario. Perhaps the brightest hope was the NDP's own bilingual philosopher, Charles Taylor of McGill University. This list, with some variations, figured often in the speculations of the pundits in 1968 and 1969. None of the names would appear on the final ballot when the NDP held its leadership vote in 1971.

The youth revolution in its more virulent form affected the party in a second way; it gave birth to the Waffle, a radical faction which rocked the NDP boat for a few seasons and then departed.

The first signs of youthful ferment in the NDP came at the federal convention of 1967, when some politically moderate young Ontarians engineered the defeat of John Brockelbank, the party establishment's candidate for president. Stephen Lewis, John Harney, and former assistant federal secretary Terry Grier had spearheaded a modest NDP revival in Ontario, and now they wanted to test their muscles on the federal party. From a room above the meeting hall at the Royal York Hotel they enlisted James Renwick of the Ontario legislature as a candidate, and stormed the convention. Brockelbank had served seventeen years in the Douglas cabinet, but the young men felt his day was past; the federal president's job should not be the NDP equivalent of a Senate appointment. Many prairie New Democrats were furious. They felt that it was their turn to name the president, and saw Brockelbank's defeat as another instance of Ontario and labour domination in the party.

Within weeks, Grier approached others on the federal council to propose an early leadership convention to replace Douglas. Like Douglas Fisher in 1960, Grier argued that an open, contested leadership race would bring new life and momentum to the party. The idea found some favour in Ontario, and in February 1968 some members of the Ontario provincial caucus sent Stephen Lewis to talk with Douglas about stepping down.

The identity of the members of this compact is not clear. Donald MacDonald has suggested the late James Renwick as a key figure. However, after consulting seven former members of his caucus for more names, he reported that "absolutely none of them has any recollection of such a caucus discussion and decision."[6] MacDonald said he personally learned of Stephen's trip through newspaper reports.

Stephen Lewis remembered differently: "I made that trip at the direct request of the caucus," he said. "I remember a very thorough, thoughtful discussion at caucus at which there was an overwhelming consensus, maybe even unanimous, that Tommy should be approached." He denied that his trip was in any way a fronting exercise for his father. He and his Ontario colleagues, he said, wanted a competition among younger men. "David did want the leadership," he said. "It's too innocent by half to pretend otherwise. He felt a tremendous commitment to the party...And given the opportunity, he grabbed it. But he never would have counselled me to talk to Tommy. He would have been horror-struck."[7]

Many in the NDP remained barely aware of the move to unseat Douglas. Clifford Scotton, the federal party secretary, remembered "only mutterings...Anybody who wanted to assail Tommy as leader would have had an immensely difficult job. I mean, he was absolutely worshipped in the party...Because he was at the Last Supper with J. S. Woodsworth, he had all the old CCF, all the trade unions."[8]

If Douglas had accepted the idea of a summer or fall convention for 1968, planning for the meeting would have run into heavy traffic. Within weeks of his talk with Stephen Lewis, the Liberals chose Pierre Trudeau to lead them, and Trudeau called a federal election for June.

Many New Democrats feared that the new prime minister would sweep their party into oblivion. The numbers suggest, though, that Trudeau added mostly first-time voters to the Liberal column in 1968. He also won over some right-wingers in the West who thought he might put French Canada in its place. Altogether, he took about twenty seats from the Tories and Social Credit. The New Democrats chalked up some wins and some losses, and came out with twenty-two seats—one more than in 1965. Trudeaumania, however, cost Tommy Douglas his Burnaby riding.

Douglas entered this campaign, his sixth in nine years, on a low note. His knee had flared up again, party morale was uncertain, and he wondered sometimes whether the NDP was behind him. The turnaround came on June 9, two weeks before election day, with a nationally televised leaders' debate. In ninety minutes before the black-and-white cameras, perched at a little pulpit, Douglas re-established the differences between the NDP and the Liberals. The man who had refused to be coached on his television performances turned in an excellent showing. (It was a mark of the NDP's second-class status that the CBC and CTV wanted to keep Douglas out of the debate; after James Renwick's public protest, they reversed their decision.)

Trudeau and Stanfield set out at the start for the high ground of compassion: Trudeau pledged to work for the poor, the old, housing, and jobs, and Stanfield did the same, with a nod in the direction of "business confidence." Douglas outlined his reasons for wanting a more activist government in Canada. The country, he said, ran the risk of national breakup, with regional squabbling on one hand and the threat of absorption into the United States on the other. "Co-operation must take precedence over competition," he said; "people before profit, planning before drifting."

On the question of rising taxes, Trudeau suggested that, if there was a problem, the provinces and municipalities were to blame. Douglas pointed to the findings of the Carter Commission, that there were too many loopholes for business and the rich, so that the average taxpayer bore the burden. Most specifically, he proposed a tax on oil, insurance, and stock speculators. "I can say to Mr. Trudeau," he said, " that he cannot talk about the just society until he first commits himself to a just tax structure." Trudeau replied, "There is nothing moral or immoral about the absence or presence of a capital gains tax; it is a matter of knowing whether you will raise enough money to make it worthwhile."

Douglas also made use of the Watkins Report, commissioned by the Liberals, which called on Canada to buy back foreign-owned industries, and he proposed a Capital Investment Board to channel investment into priority areas. Trudeau promised in turn to set up a Canada Development Corporation, as Pearson had since 1963. Douglas quoted a Chinese proverb to sum up his attitude to Liberal promises past, present, and future: "A loud noise on the stairs, but no one comes into the room."[9]

"That debate was key in our timing," recalled Douglas aide Jim Hayes. "It did one thing which we weren't able to do up to that point in the election campaign, and that was excite our own workers...Trudeau was working wonders with the psyche of people across the country, even with New Democrats. A lot of them were holding back, and were ready to throw in the towel."[10]

At the David Lewis campaign in York South, they cheered the television set when the debate ended. The federal office staff in Ottawa partied till dawn. The next day a new enthusiasm showed in Douglas's voice as he told a crowd of factory workers from a perch on the bumper of a car: "You've got to hang together or you'll hang separately!"[11]

In Saskatchewan, a desert for the federal NDP since its formation, Diefenbaker's fall had opened up new opportunities. Douglas attracted large and noisy crowds, and the Regina Armouries hosted one of the most enthusiastic rallies of the campaign. In Yorkton-Melville, a twenty-two-year-old candidate named Lorne Nystrom asked for advice on how to clinch what looked like a victory. Douglas told him to hammer away single-mindedly at the most important issue. As it happened, Toronto Tory Dalton Camp had predicted that the proposed national medicare program would fail. Camp "was hated in the West," said Nystrom. "We went back that night and made up a one-page handbill, headlined 'Medicare Dead Duck: Dalton Camp.' " The leaflet highlighted Douglas's role as the father of public health insurance. Nystrom took the seat.[12]

The NDP's success in Saskatchewan was offset by setbacks in Ontario and British Columbia. In central Canada, David Lewis won his seat, but the most prominent of the young prospects—Taylor, Lapierre, Harney— all failed. On the west coast, the New Democrats lost two seats and finished with seven. The Liberals picked up the other sixteen in British Columbia, partly because of a swing away from Social Credit. The Socreds' share of the vote in Burnaby-Seymour, for example, fell from 15 per cent to 2 per cent, allowing Liberal Ray Perrault to squeeze past Douglas.

Douglas had taken Burnaby-Coquitlam with a 10,000 vote margin in 1965. Even with the addition of some affluent neighbourhoods in an electoral redistribution, a poll-by-poll analysis favoured a repeat win for the NDP. As it turned out, he took fully 45 per cent of the vote, more than most of the NDP's winners across the country, but he still lost. Perrault beat him by 138 votes, or about one vote per poll. In retrospect, the small hitches in the Burnaby campaign showed up as fatal flaws. Internal dissension in the riding toppled the first campaign manager and the publicity manager. Many riding workers were suspicious of the organizers sent in from area trade unions. There was also the old problem that had finished Douglas in Regina in 1962: the candidate, said his workers, should have spent more time in his riding. While Douglas rode buses through northern Ontario, the Vancouver-area media questioned his absence from Burnaby election forums.

On election night, the Burnaby NDP wallowed in bitterness and recriminations. Douglas watched the results on television, and then his friend Bert Hill drove him to the local headquarters, where despondent young workers told him they would quit politics. He lectured them hotly on the need to continue the fight. After a few minutes of shaking hands, he left for the last time, and Hill drove him home to Irma. Within two weeks they were packed up and ready to move permanently to their Ottawa apartment.

The headline in the *Globe* read, "Douglas Likely to Quit as NDP Leader." Over the next week the nation's leading columnists and the editorial writers wrote his political obituary. The Edmonton *Journal* proposed Douglas for the Senate; the Toronto *Star* wrote, "Now defeated at 63, he is out of a job, where a man's years of dedication and reputation are so quickly forgotten."[13] Three days after the election, Douglas flew to Ottawa to meet with the national executive. As he passed through Toronto's airport a woman called out to him: "Don't be depressed." "Don't forget," he replied, "I was raised on the story of Bruce and the Spider."[14] The next day he told a news conference in Ottawa of his decision made weeks before: he would retire as leader at the next federal convention. He might, if things worked out, return to Parliament.

Another executive meeting in Winnipeg in mid-July confirmed David Lewis as parliamentary leader. Someone suggested that a sitting member could step aside to let Douglas run in a by-election; he responded with conviction: "I insist I will not take someone else's seat. For somebody to resign with the possibility of us losing the seat would be absolute foolishness."[15] He agreed to consider heading a task force on party reorganization.

Late in the summer, Lewis and party president Renwick announced an October 1969 leadership convention. Lewis added, "My present intention is not to be a candidate as successor to Mr. Douglas. I hope that the leader will come from a younger generation." On this point Allan Blakeney later recalled: "There was a fair amount of speculation at that time as to whether anyone believed that. I said, oh, come on, David wants to be leader of the party, if even for a brief time."[16]

Fate intervened to send Douglas back to Parliament within a few months. In late July 1968, a month after the election, Colin Cameron, the MP for Nanaimo, died at the age of seventy-one. Cameron's New Democrat riding executive decided immediately that Douglas should step in. In early September, he agreed.

Nanaimo-Cowichan-The Islands would be Douglas's political home for the rest of his career. Most of the riding's residents lived along the east coast of Vancouver Island, with the rest scattered on the smaller islands in the Gulf of Georgia. Nanaimo was as safe an NDP seat as any in Canada; its miners and loggers had formed a strong socialist movement before 1900, and the riding had gone CCF in 1935, soon after the party was formed. Cameron had taken every election but one since 1953.

Douglas stepped in cautiously, all the same. Cameron had occupied a leading position on the CCF's left wing, and had jousted openly with the party's leadership on foreign and domestic policy. Mrs. Cameron, still a local power, might resist the coming of the NDP's leader to Nanaimo. He told riding officials he would attend a September nominating meeting; however, "If in the meantime some local candidate emerges who might have a better chance to win the seat for the New Democratic Party, then I would gladly withdraw my name at the convention."[17]

Douglas walked into the candidate's job unchallenged. He spoke at his nominating meeting, among other things, of how an island shipbuilding industry might be revived, and how a tunnel or causeway might link the island to the mainland. An anonymous editor of the Vancouver *Sun* wrote, "No scheme is apparently too outrageous for New Democratic Party leader T. C. Douglas in his carpetbagging attempt to claw and squirm his way back into the House of Commons." The Winnipeg *Free Press* boiled the Douglas doctrine down to one word: "spend."[18]

The Douglases rented an apartment in a tower on the Nanaimo waterfront and waited for Trudeau to call a by-election. The prime minister delayed while the local Liberals got organized; they nominated Eric Winch, whose father and brother had both led the CCF in British Columbia. Finally, Trudeau called a vote for February 1969.

The New Democrats waged the most intense campaign they had ever fought in any constituency. National Secretary Cliff Scotton set up shop on the island and sent out fund-raising letters headlined "Canada Needs Tommy Douglas." Full-time organizers arrived from the Union of Public Employees, the Auto Workers, and the Ontario NDP. Ed Whelan, Lorne Nystrom, Frank Howard, and other experienced campaigners showed up to work, and ferryloads of volunteer canvassers arrived each weekend from Vancouver. The excitement overwhelmed and even angered local party workers. "Bloody zoot-suiters," said one, "they'd sit in the restaurants all day and drink coffee and then charge it to the campaign."[19]

But the NDP refused, this time, to defer to local pride, and the big campaign paid off. Winch increased the Liberals' vote share from 31 to 37 per cent, but Douglas pushed the NDP from 42 to 57 per cent. Already, Trudeaumania was sagging in the West. The Vancouver *Sun* backflipped at the victory, lauding Douglas as "the leading debater of the Commons...his great experience in politics, to say nothing of his practical outlook, is too valuable to be lost."[20] The *Globe and Mail* also praised Douglas, but under the heading "Make Room at the Top," it urged him to "yield the leadership to a new generation without delay."[21]

Douglas returned to the leader's seat in the Commons, and Lewis moved into the deputy's chair. By some accounts, however, Lewis held on to the parliamentary leader's powers in organizing caucus business, and used them to prepare for his leadership campaign. "In the minds of some," a reporter wrote soon after Douglas returned, "[Lewis] runs the show and is preaching for a call even now."[22]

Douglas now encountered Pierre Trudeau for the first time since the television debate. It was said that his sharp jabs had irritated the prime minister on that occasion. In any case, the two regarded each other coldly from here on.

Douglas and Trudeau differed fundamentally on Canada's priorities. Trudeau set out from the first to secure an equal place in the federal system for French-speaking Canadians; Douglas advised him to concentrate on taxes, unemployment, and other bread-and-butter issues. He also felt that Trudeau neglected the West, although perhaps he should have been grateful for that; the Liberals' failure in the West helped keep the NDP alive. Trudeau, said Douglas, was "completely bereft of compassion in personal terms." He viewed members of Parliament as nobodies, and unlike his predecessors, he rarely consulted, at least in Douglas's experience, with opposition leaders, keeping them "at arms' length."[23] Trudeau was also, in Douglas's view, an ex-CCF turncoat, and he held a low opinion of that species of Liberal.

In a speech to the 1977 Liberal convention, Trudeau mocked the New Democrats as a collection of old-timers; the party's leading figures, he said, were only the leftovers of the 1930s. When asked to comment, Douglas said, "Well, I'd sooner be a leftover from the last Depression than be the guy who's going to start the next one."[24]

28

The Waffle

SOON AFTER HIS ELECTION LOSS in Burnaby-Seymour in 1968, Tommy Douglas announced he was stepping down as NDP leader. However, it soon became apparent that an early leadership convention would do the party more harm than good. The next general election was not expected until 1972, and any new leader might have to hang in limbo for up to four years outside the Commons before a winnable seat opened up. With his nomination in Nanaimo, Douglas faced increasing pressure to hold on to the leadership, from trade union groups, the Alberta executive, the Saskatchewan council, and various riding associations. In early 1969 the Ontario Provincial Council, the centre of the earlier unrest over party leadership, sent a letter to Douglas asking him not to retire.

On May 5 Douglas told reporters in Ottawa that he would stay on for reasons of "political strategy"—"under no circumstances" would he remain after 1971.[1] The NDP would wait for Trudeau's popularity to fade before introducing a new leader. That leader, columnists predicted, would be Charles Taylor. One reporter wrote, "Taylor has the fewest enemies within the party, has the brains, the looks and is even well-to-do."[2] The columnists were wrong. The NDP had never taken a seat in Quebec, and Taylor had already suffered three personal defeats in Montreal. He would not contest the leadership.

The party redrafted its plans for its October 1969 convention to emphasize policy. With four elections in eight years, the New Democrats had never had time for a full review of their philosophy and programs. Almost fifty groups and individuals put together briefs for the meeting. But above all, the convention would be remembered for the appearance of a caucus of radical young people, the Waffle.

The Waffle grew out of the "youth revolution." At the same time, it followed in a tradition of noisy dissent on the party's left going back to the Regina Convention of 1933. Sometimes this dissent was the product of Communist provocateurs; more often, it issued from activists working in good faith, people who wanted the party to state the socialist case clearly without regard to short-term electoral popularity.

In 1950, for example, some British Columbia leftists formed a "Socialist Fellowship." The flavour of their rhetoric comes through in a 1947 statement from Colin Cameron, the figurehead of the radical cause in British Columbia. "The revolutionary nature of the CCF program must be clearly understood," he wrote when he was provincial CCF president. "The first task of a CCF administration will be the swift and ruthless removal of the major sources of wealth production from private hands to those of the community."[3] The national party leader, M. J. Coldwell, labelled the fellowship "a threat to liberty and freedom in Canada," and in March 1951 the national executive agreed to ban it from the party.[4]

Through the early 1960s Canada's Trotskyists, especially the League for Socialist Action, fastened on to the NDP as a vehicle for spreading their ideas. In 1965 they formed a "Socialist Caucus" which claimed forty adherents at the federal convention of that year. Their agenda foreshadowed that of the Waffle. It emphasized public ownership of industry, support for the "struggles of colonial peoples," including the Viet Cong, and the liberation of women. Like the Waffle, the Socialist Caucus wanted the NDP to engage in extra-parliamentary politics through tenant groups and street protest. And like the Waffle, the caucus angered the party brass. The caucus complained after the convention that the NDP establishment had blocked its efforts to speak and hand out leaflets. Douglas dismissed the group as a "bunch of screwballs" whose complaints were not worth answering. Several of them, he said, had been expelled from the party in previous years for "deliberate sabotage."[5]

The Waffle, born in 1969, mounted a more credible front. Its theoretical push came from Mel Watkins, political economist at the University of Toronto. Watkins had gained a reputation as a liberal continentalist, but in the late 1960s he shifted rapidly to a radical nationalist position. His highly publicized 1968 report to the federal government on foreign ownership had helped to popularize the term "branch-plant economy." In April 1969 Watkins began to organize informal talk sessions with Ed Broadbent, the MP for Oshawa, and James Laxer, who was then a graduate student at Queen's University. Laxer's network of allies in the universities of Ontario and the West would form the core of the Waffle—a name allegedly coined by Broadbent when he insisted, "If we're going to waffle, let's waffle to the left."

The Waffle sought to move Canada beyond the capitalist welfare state, to create a society where the public, as workers and consumers, would control the major corporations. Douglas sympathized, as he showed when he appeared on a television forum with Cy Gonick, a Winnipeg academic, in May 1969. Gonick, soon to be a prominent Waffler, observed that the old parties had adopted most of the New Democrat platform of the early 1960s, and this left the NDP "sounding more and more like an old line party." Douglas responded, "I would agree with you in part, or almost wholly." With a guaranteed annual income for Canadians, already proposed by Stanfield, "we'll probably hit the peak of welfare democracy. I think we now have to deal with economic control to see who will control the power structure of our society."[6]

The more mainstream members of Watkins's group—Broadbent, Charles Taylor, Gerald Caplan—gradually drifted away as it became clear that Laxer planned to set up an ongoing dissident caucus. In September, Watkins and Laxer issued their manifesto, "Towards an Independent Socialist Canada." It set out the "development of socialist consciousness" as the first priority of the NDP. This must have reminded Douglas of the armchair politics of Carlyle King in the Saskatchewan of the early 1940s, and King's belief that "the main business of socialist parties is not to form governments but to change minds."

The manifesto proposed that the NDP bring about socialism through public ownership combined with worker control of industry, and not through regulation. The party should pursue its strategies not only through Parliament but through a broad range of popular organizations. The manifesto insisted at the same time that Canada should break from the American empire and the NATO alliance, and align itself with the Third World.

Within a month, the 125-member NDP National Council issued a counter document, "For a United and Independent Canada." It offered many of the short-term proposals put forward in the Waffle statement, such as stricter controls on foreign investment in Canada and public ownership of resource industries. Broadbent observed a "curious overlapping" of the two papers; he and Charles Taylor had taken a hand in drafting both.[7]

Douglas expressed reluctance to pass judgement on the Waffle manifesto before a convention debate could take place. "If this document has done nothing else," he wrote, "it has stirred up a great deal of interest, and I think we can anticipate a spirited convention."[8] David Lewis, the party's deputy leader, took a more hostile approach, attacking the manifesto in speeches and articles. It was "short-sighted," he said, in its faith in state ownership, and its description of Canada as a pawn in the American empire was "historically inaccurate and logically invalid."[9]

The differences between the Waffle manifesto and the official party statement now appear largely rhetorical. Both sides favoured federalism, while respecting Quebec's right to self-determination; the question of which should be emphasized was a political judgement call. They were close enough on foreign ownership for Watkins and Gonick to support Broadbent's compromise at the convention. However, the Waffle paper indulged at times in Marxist jargon, which is identified in Canadian English with Stalinism. Douglas openly questioned one catchphrase, "public ownership of the means of production." "I think while there is a place for public ownership," he told a panel of journalists, "that widespread public ownership can be a very blunt instrument that can lead to greater bureaucracy without necessarily solving the economic problem that you're trying to solve."[10]

October 1969 in Winnipeg marked Douglas's last full convention as leader, and on opening night, leader's night, he tried to pull his troops together. He urged all party members to look to a new phase, the struggle to make economic institutions democratic. "We have become mere puppets," he said, "dancing at the end of strings manipulated by invisible hands." At the same time, he warned the ideologues from all factions, "We are not a philosophical society but a political party...I don't think the public are concerned with involved arguments about the various economic tools that are appropriate for social change...We must concern ourselves more with ends than with means, more with goals than with techniques." He encouraged his listeners to take part in "the daily struggle of those who fight against social injustice." He reminded them, though, that Canada was not the United States, and that the political currents which were sometimes stifled in the United States could find a parliamentary voice through the NDP.[11]

The convention acclaimed Douglas as leader. The list of sponsors atop his nominating papers begins with the names Laurier Lapierre, Ed Schreyer, David Lewis; Charles Taylor, Watkins, and Broadbent also signed. But the facade of unity broke down at the resolutions committees into a "silly exercise in superlatives."[12] Waffle and anti-Waffle delegates haggled over such terms as "imperialism," "exploitation," and "socialism." Douglas remained the symbol of the party and his photographs graced the dailies, but his words in debate were quoted less than those of other notables. "Tommy Douglas," said the Montreal *Gazette*, "was no longer a force in the minds of delegates."[13] The Wafflers, with their long hair and their irreverence, got more than their share of attention. When 200 radicals met in a corner of the convention centre, a bystander shouted, "Who's your leader, Mel or Tommy?" Someone shouted back, "Karl Marx!"[14]

The set-piece of the convention was a plenary debate on the Waffle manifesto submitted as a single resolution, carrying the endorsement of twenty-six riding associations, the Saskatchewan Provincial Council, and ninety-four delegates including Laurier Lapierre and Dave Barrett. David Lewis opened for the official side, but Douglas also spoke against the manifesto, for what he labelled its "ambiguous and ambivalent" call for both public ownership and sweeping restrictions on foreign investment. "It's like a man who wants to burn down his house," he said, "because he's got rats in the basement."[15]

Douglas explained after the convention. "I asked what was meant by 'means of production.' Does this mean a farmer's land, his tractor, does it mean a small factory for retreading tires?...I for one am not prepared to stand for something which is so vague and sweeping in its terminology that it's either meaningless or dangerous."[16] He insisted, though, that the debate was a healthy sign of life within the NDP. "A party must never degenerate into a mutual admiration society," he told reporters. "If we get to the place where there is complete agreement, then no social action is possible."[17]

The Waffle lost the vote on its resolution 499 to 286. However, the radicals took seven of the twenty vacant National Council seats, with Watkins elected vice-president.

The rancour between the Waffle and the party's mainstream increased as the months went by. Some in the NDP give the Waffle credit for bringing fresh insight to party debates; others saw mainly a haughty disregard for party solidarity. Soon after the convention, Watkins agreed to serve on an eleven-member policy review committee. At the same time, he wrote a letter to the *Globe* apologizing to his friends for accepting the position.[18]

Scotton, the party secretary, remembers both Laxer and Watkins rejecting the idea of consensus. The Waffle had picked up the American tactic of using the non-negotiable demand; if caucus members failed to persuade a party committee to their point of view, they might issue a minority statement.[19] The Waffle's leaders developed links with the Toronto-based national media and offered their comments freely. It appeared to some that the NDP was offering two positions on every issue.

Tommy Douglas, despite the controversy, retained a sympathy for the Waffle, especially Laxer. His young assistant, Hans Brown, volunteered advice and information to the Waffle from inside Douglas's Parliament Hill suite. Brown recalled, "This perturbed David no end." Lewis felt it was inappropriate for anyone to use the free parliamentary phones on behalf of the Waffle, and he asked Douglas to fire Brown. Douglas—who had never fired anyone—overlooked Lewis's request. "[Tommy] was supportive in the sense that he was glad that I was concerned about political issues," said Brown. "He saw the appeal of the Waffle to the 1960's university crowd, and saw that it was important that these people come into the party."

When Laxer's book *The Energy Poker Game* appeared, Douglas locked himself in his office and read it cover to cover, filling the margins with crabbed notes. A few days later, in a speech to an Ontario NDP convention, Douglas endorsed the book as required reading for party members. "There were all these little old ladies in the audience," said Brown, "whipping out their convention kits and writing, 'Energy Poker Game—James Laxer.' Tommy's speech ends, and up comes the ballot for federal council, and there's James Laxer's name on the ballot. He just went sweeping in!"[20]

However, Douglas also satisfied most anti-Wafflers that he was on their side. Bill Knight, a young Saskatchewan MP, viewed the Waffle as a haven for Trotskyites and "goofballs." In his opinion, "Douglas was every bit as tenacious in his opposition to the Waffle as Lewis. If he'd stayed on, he would have put the sword to them just as Lewis did."[21]

If Douglas navigated the shoals, his good friend Woodrow Lloyd, head of the Saskatchewan NDP, did not. Lloyd had tried to pull his party to the left after two election defeats. Along with several other prominent Saskatchewan New Democrats, he had stood up for the Waffle manifesto in the 1969 vote at Winnipeg. The issue simmered over the winter; Lloyd opposed the formation of an ongoing Saskatchewan Waffle caucus, but he defended the principle of broad debate. In March 1970 most of Lloyd's fellow New Democrat MLAS condemned his actions at a caucus meeting and forced his resignation. The hero of the medicare dispute, the man who had borne the brunt of the doctors' bitterness in 1962, fell in the end to his own colleagues. "I am tired and drained out," Lloyd wrote to Douglas soon after he resigned. "I'm weary of petty bickering and backbiting and backscratching and backstabbing. (Anyone who thinks the so-called 'left' can be tough should go a round with the so-called 'right'.)"[22]

After a period of reflection, Lloyd found a job with the United Nations. On March 30, 1972, he sent a cheerful letter to Douglas on the start of his work in Korea. He died a few days later at the age of fifty-eight. Douglas said at Lloyd's memorial service in Regina, "The older I get, the more I am convinced that one of the rare human virtues is moral courage. It's easy to express kindly sentiments and to profess sympathetic concerns for others if one doesn't endeavor to do anything about it. But to stand almost alone in the face of frenzied hate and hysterical opposition—that takes moral courage."[23]

Douglas continued as party leader for eighteen months after the 1969 convention. Some observers felt he had already relinquished the real power to David Lewis. Allan Blakeney, who was federal president in 1969-70 and knew Douglas's style from Saskatchewan days, saw nothing unusual. Douglas, he said, had always been the public voice of the party. In the backrooms, he often let other people make the decisions on party organization or strategy. "That's how the Douglas-Fines government worked, or on party issues with Carlyle King. Douglas was never the heavy; Douglas said yes, and other people said no."[24]

Douglas shared interim power with Lewis, but he continued to beat the bushes for a younger leader. Lewis went through a period of soul-searching, dropping in on young MPs to seek reassurance and writing to friends about his "deep anxiety to do what is right in the objective and impersonal sense."[25] There was no chance, of course, that Lewis could remain "impersonal" about a party which was virtually his own offspring. In December 1970 he announced he would run for the leadership and that Charles Taylor would manage his campaign. Lewis had held every other important position within the movement; now he would guide it and shape it as leader. Fortunately for the party, he remained a dynamic, eloquent, and astute politician at the age of sixty-one.

Broadbent and Harney also entered the race, as did maverick MP Frank Howard. But the leadership campaign turned largely on the sniping match between Lewis, the embodiment of the old guard, and James Laxer, the youngest and most radical candidate. Lewis charged the Waffle with making "statements and programmes as if it were a separate political party." Laxer replied, "The implication that his proposals represent positive suggestions while ours represent factionalism shows a disrespect for fundamental debate within the party."[26]

Douglas continued, privately, to support the radical wing's right to speak out. "The Waffle group," he wrote, "is making a useful contribution...provided they do not try to form a party within a party." The Waffle oversimplified the issues, said Douglas, owing to lack of experience, but it made more sense to challenge their proposals than to attack their leaders. "I doubt very much that David Lewis, if he is successful, will seek to initiate a 'purge' of the Waffle group."[27]

Tommy Douglas gave his last speech as NDP leader on the opening day of the 1971 federal convention. Ten years before in Ottawa, David Lewis and Claude Jodoin had hoisted him on their shoulders in victory and he had promised to fight his first election on the issue of socialism versus free enterprise. Now he looked back on his achievements. The NDP, he said, had tripled its membership in the House of Commons and doubled its level of popular support. The party had fought for a Canada Pension Plan, national medicare, regional expansion incentives, a Department of the Environment, federal housing programs, and a higher level of Canadian ownership in industry. In the debate over the War Measures Act, the NDP had spoken out unconditionally for civil rights.

In looking to the future, Douglas once again called for a push towards economic democracy—of the kind envisioned by J. S. Woodsworth and William Irvine. "State ownership of monopolies and of the key sectors of the economy is one form of social ownership... But it is not the only form...I look forward to the day when farmers and fishermen will own and control the processing plants that handle their commodities. I see producers and consumers' co-operatives as playing a vital role in a socialist society...Someday we may see industries owned and operated jointly by workers and consumers."

Douglas cautioned the left wing against moving too fast: "There is little value in making programs that appeal only to ourselves. There is nothing to be gained unless we take a large segment of the population with us." Like Lewis, he rejected the view of Canada as a victim. "Our quarrel is not with Americans and we must never descend to racist intolerance or phoney patriotism...Our quarrel is with successive Canadian governments which have supinely acquiesced in the steady erosion of our economic independence."

Douglas ended his speech with a throwback to the social gospel of his boyhood, a prayer from Woodsworth: "May we be the children of the brighter and better day which even now is beginning to dawn. May we not impede, but rather co-operate with the great spiritual forces which we believe are impelling the world onward and upward. For our supreme task is to make our dreams come true and to transform our city into the Holy City—to make this land in reality 'God's own country.' "[28]

The 1971 convention, like the 1969 convention, became a tussle between the Waffle and its opponents. This time, however, the mainstream was organized to impose its will. The Waffle had allied itself with the near-separatist faction that now controlled the NDP's Quebec wing; their joint resolution on Quebec lost by a 2-1 margin. A radical proposal to nationalize all resource industries lost by a 3-1 count. On the final ballot of the leadership contest, David Lewis defeated James Laxer. The strength of the Waffle leader's showing—39.6 per cent of the vote—surprised many observers; however, the lines were drawn so sharply that Laxer could not even get a seat on the federal council.

Douglas expressed his disappointment, in private once again, that the Lewis forces had kept Laxer off the council and Watkins out of the executive. "It seems to me that a party has to represent all points of view within its membership and that these two men represent a considerable portion of our members."[29] Publicly, Douglas fell in behind the new leader. One woman wrote to him to say she cried as she watched "T. C. Douglas Night" televised from the convention. He wrote back, "You need have no fear that Mr. Lewis will be less humane. He was brought up in poverty and knows only too well what deprivation and hardship mean."[30]

The elder Lewis kept a close eye on Waffle activities, but he never moved to outlaw them. The death of the Waffle came at the provincial level, when the Ontario party expelled the radical caucus in 1972. The Waffle's public statements to the media and its autonomous campaign for the half-dozen NDP-Waffle candidates in the 1971 provincial election had worn out the patience of Stephen Lewis, the young Ontario leader. More important, the Waffle made the fatal mistake of poaching on the territory of the big labour leaders.

In late 1971 the Waffle organized a caucus within the Ontario Federation of Labour and attacked the OFL's established leaders as "rightists" propping up the capitalist system. A Waffle-sponsored conference in Windsor in January 1972 attacked the United Auto Workers' leadership. Dennis McDermott, the UAW leader, called publicly for the NDP to repudiate the Waffle; James Laxer, in his reply, suggested that McDermott was a tool of American UAW bosses.

Stephen Lewis has said that the big unions delivered an "unstated ultimatum."[31] In fact, organized labour spoke out openly, at party meetings, in pamphlets, and in press statements—either the Waffle must go or the unions would cancel the mutual support pact that had given birth to the NDP. Some labour leaders used the affair to complain that the whole New Party idea had been a mistake, a deal gone sour. "The simple fact is that the unions have kept their side of the bargain," wrote Murray Cotterill, a long-time Steelworkers' spokesman, "but the super socialists of the CCF and the ultra nationalists of the New Left have not."[32]

In June 1972 the Ontario Provincial Council voted 217 to 88 to order the Waffle to change its name. It also declared that the work of party factions must henceforth remain "non-public and consistent with the principles of the New Democratic Party."[33] In other words, the radicals were welcome to stay—if they quieted down. Some activists immediately severed ties with the Waffle. Those who refused to accept the ruling withdrew to struggle on alone for a few more months. The Saskatchewan Waffle, the second most powerful section, also left the NDP.

A few weeks before the schism, Douglas wrote, "I am greatly disturbed that our party should be engaging in fratricidal strife at a time when we should be concentrating all our efforts on the common enemy."[34] He wanted, he said, to bring opposing sides together. However, there is no evidence that he tried either to mediate or to calm down the union leaders.

Douglas might have chosen to defend the Waffle in the interests of open debate, but this would have affronted Lewis, now the party leader, as well other senior figures in the NDP. Besides, Douglas's ties in Ontario were not especially strong. He had always let David Lewis handle Ontario. Even if Douglas had tried to intervene, he could not have ended the factionalism that worried him so much. "I think he may not always have supported David's organization or tactics," said Allan Blakeney later. "But basically, Tommy was an organization man who felt you couldn't have a party within a party."[35]

Douglas later used this phrase "party within a party" whenever he defended the expulsion of the Ontario Waffle.[36] One local riding executive in Ontario defined such an entity as "a clearly identifiable group who organize, solicit funds, employ staff, hold press conferences to expound their own point of view."[37] Of course, all of these points applied equally to the trade union movement and, unlike other factions, the unions sent delegates directly to party conventions without working through local ridings. Many union delegates to conventions were not even NDP members. Further, union leaders were privileged to hold ongoing secret talks with Liberal and Tory leaders.

The question of labour's special status surfaced only briefly during the Waffle controversy. At the 1969 convention, Dave Barrett of British Columbia proposed that affiliate memberships for members of unions supporting the NDP be cancelled and that the NDP's entire relationship with organized labour be reassessed. John Brockelbank of Saskatchewan called Barrett's suggestions "suicide," and David Lewis also spoke strongly against them.[38]

Labour remained a party within a party, free to cut its own deals with governments and to endorse the corporatist views of industry-labour committees. Such activities, apparently, did not hurt the image of the NDP in the media. Besides, the unions were an important source of funding and election workers. The Waffle, however, was feared as a serious electoral liability, and its lack of respect for party discipline irritated many long-time New Democrats. While Douglas did not make the decision to eject the Waffle, he did not mourn its departure.

Douglas's years as federal leader were in some ways a continuation of his career as a provincial premier. He took a pragmatic approach to public affairs, working for gradual progress in areas such as pensions, regional development, and consumer protection. But he was open to ideas from the left, and members of the Waffle respected him for it.

John Richards, the only Canadian to sit as a Waffle MLA, has written that the Waffle was an attempt to revive the populism and ideological diversity of the early Douglas period in Saskatchewan. It could have restored to the NDP the creative tension that once existed in Saskatchewan—for example, between Joe Phelps, the impulsive radical in cabinet, and George Cadbury, the super-bureaucrat. "Douglas's rhetorical, moralistic, Christian sense of the left sat well with us," Richards said in an interview. "We never thought of him as the enemy."[39]

The critical comments about Douglas's years as leader came from the other side. Desmond Morton, perhaps the leading party intellectual, a man with links to the Ontario moderates and the trade unions, condemned what he called the NDP's pursuit of "fashionable causes" in the 1960s:

> In our search for new slogans and new ideas, we frequently looked foolish, out of breath and irrelevant. We staggered from "Two Nations" to the Bomb to automation. We took up special status, poverty and the housing crisis. When the Hall and Carter Commissions came along, we clung to them because we did not have the time, energy or inclination to do better after our fashionable exertions.
> And who led us on this chase?...It was the radical intellectuals.[40]

For better or worse, it was Tommy Douglas, with his love for new ideas, who led the NDP on "this chase." He was accompanied by an undisciplined federal caucus and a shifting cast of volunteer advisers.

Morton, looking towards 1980, proposed that the NDP change its focus to what he considered the daily concerns of Canadian workers: "low pay, unemployment, bad housing and discrimination." These are almost precisely the problems which Ed Broadbent had characterized as the loose ends left by the welfare state. Broadbent said in a 1969 speech that the old parties could provide decent housing, a guaranteed annual income, regional economic incentives, and fair taxes. The NDP, he said, must move forward to propose economic and industrial democracy, "some form of worker-management partnership in industry."[41]

In the end, Morton's agenda triumphed over those of both Broadbent and the Waffle. Talk of industrial democracy, public ownership, and central planning died within the NDP. The party carried a couple of "fashionable causes," such as world peace, into the 1980s. Otherwise, the NDP under Lewis and Broadbent concerned itself largely with what the young Broadbent saw as Liberal issues.

Did debate within the NDP become flat after the ejection of the Waffle? Some former Wafflers returned to the fold, and party conventions through the 1970s witnessed some lively rows. But a few holdouts, such as Richards, charged that these debates were superficial, and avoided the basic issues of socialism.

Max Saltsman, who worked for fifteen years with Douglas as a member of the NDP caucus, reached the same conclusion. Saltsman was a bitter foe of the Waffle and no great admirer of Douglas as leader. In an interview before his death he suggested that the Waffle was a final, doomed attempt at creative radical politics in Canada. The gifted generalist like Douglas or Broadbent has been eclipsed by the army of professional public servants who can devise government programs to suit every occasion and can analyse them from every angle. The left-wing opposition, said Saltsman, has been reduced to staging political theatre for the television cameras.[42]

Douglas, predictably, remained more optimistic, and continued to believe there was a place for the development of new ideas outside of government. After his retirement from the leadership he accepted the chairmanship of the foundation established in 1971 in his honour and that of his oldest political ally, M. J. Coldwell. The aim of the Douglas-Coldwell Foundation, as he wrote in 1975, was to provide a forum for political discussion removed from the threat of purges, ultimatums, or ad hominem attacks. "The greatest assets to any movement are the gad-flies, who keep reminding us that wisdom is not limited."[43]

29

Energy Critic

DOUGLAS WAS SITTING with a young caucus colleague in the Opposition Lobby—a long corridor of a room, lamp-lit on a winter afternoon, cluttered with easy chairs. Through the open doors, from the Chamber of the House, they heard the voice of the prime minister. "My immediate task, Mr. Speaker," said Pierre Trudeau, "is to place before the House proposals which will set the basis for a new national oil policy. The objective of that policy, to be reached before the end of the decade, is Canadian self-sufficiency in oil and oil products."

The two MPs rose, crossed the lobby, and climbed the steps to peer through the curtains into the parliamentary arena. Trudeau and Douglas had talked on the phone the day before. Douglas, as NDP energy spokesman, had made it clear his party would force an election unless the minority Liberal government agreed to a list of demands.

The government, said Trudeau to the scattering of members in the Commons, would create "a publicly owned Canadian petroleum company principally to expedite exploration and development." This company would lead the way in developing Canada's oil sands, and work with private oil exploration companies on the frontiers. Further, the government was preparing a long-term plan to keep domestic oil prices below the world price, and would reduce eastern Canada's reliance on oil imports with a new Sarnia-Montreal pipeline.[1]

"Well, how do you like that?" Douglas said to his companion when the prime minister finished. "He hardly missed a word."[2]

Perhaps the Liberals would have set up Petro-Canada, the national oil company, without NDP pressure. The near-panic over oil supplies in late 1973 had damaged public confidence in the oil industry, and many Liberals wanted Ottawa to get a view of the business from the inside. But New Democrats, Tories, and editorial writers claimed Trudeau's announcement of December 6, 1973, as a victory for Douglas and his colleagues. Conservative George Hees, replying to Trudeau's speech, mocked the Liberals for embracing ideas that they had rejected for months: "Because the party to the left, the NDP, has put the heat on, the Prime Minister has changed his mind."[3]

The Liberals, with this announcement, avoided a winter election. They also won favour with a growing number of Canadians who supported a nationalist and interventionist approach to energy questions. With the Tories preaching the gospel according to multinational oil, Douglas had been the chief opposition spokesman for the nationalist view. How far the Liberals would have gone if there had been no NDP is a question to which no two observers give the same answer.

Douglas took on the energy critic's job in 1969, while he was still party leader, as a response to the Liberal government's creation of the Department of Energy, Mines and Resources. At this time, nobody had given Canadians any reason to worry about their energy supplies. The price of crude oil had held steady at under $3 a barrel since 1948, with no upward adjustments for inflation. Canada's proven oil reserves had grown sixfold since 1951, and proven reserves of natural gas had grown tenfold. There was a growing belief, however, that while the provinces owned the proven resources, vast new hydrocarbon supplies might be found under federal lands in the Arctic, and that the development of the Alberta oil sands would require a co-ordinated national effort. During his ten years as energy critic, Douglas focused largely on the development of a national oil policy for Canada.

Western Canada had oil pools sitting untapped in the late 1960s and was seeking new markets. In one of his first speeches on energy, delivered in Calgary in June 1969, Douglas called for increased oil exports to the United States. Alberta had to hold oil back, he said, while North American demand was increasing. It was time for the United States to drop its barriers to the export of Canadian oil. This would improve Canada's balance of payments picture and stimulate exploration for new oil on the prairies.[4]

Over the next few years, faced with changing circumstances, Douglas would reverse his position on exports. Even now, when energy appeared limitless, he qualified his pro-export position with some ideas for making better use of Canadian oil within Canada. These concepts—self-sufficiency and Canadian control—would make up the long-term core of New Democrat energy policy.

Douglas regarded oil as a strategic commodity, and he understood that other nations might someday use the threat of an oil embargo as a weapon against Canada. He believed, therefore, that imports should be kept to the minimum. Diefenbaker's government had already moved in the early 1960s to protect Canadian producers against foreign competition. Ontario now depended on crude oil from western Canada rather than on the cheaper supplies available from Venezuela and the Middle East. Douglas, along with the independent oil producers of the West, argued that the federal government had not gone far enough.

As a first step towards increasing self-sufficiency, Douglas demanded an oil pipeline from Ontario into Montreal. This would give western oil producers a new outlet for their product, and increase security of supply in the East. The Liberals replied that such a pipeline would raise energy costs in Montreal, and that private industry would build a pipeline when it made economic sense. Douglas claimed that Venezuela was dumping crude into Canada at unfair prices, and he badgered the government, in vain, to produce an economic study on his pipeline proposal.

In line with the growing nationalism within the NDP, Douglas also called for more Canadian control in the oil and gas industry. Foreign-owned companies produced about 90 per cent of the country's oil and gas; with a few exceptions, they used foreign-designed and foreign-built equipment to funnel raw resources out of Canada. Canadians missed out on management, research, manufacturing, and processing jobs. Even jobs in the oil patch were less secure than they might have been, since the foreign-owned companies often used their Canadian profits to explore elsewhere.

Through 1969 and 1970, with Canadian reserves at their all-time high, Douglas supported the Trudeau government's efforts to increase sales into the restricted American market. However, he feared the Liberals would undervalue Canadian oil and offer concessions to the Americans in return for the privilege of getting rid of Canadian crude.

Trudeau's energy minister, Joe Greene, started talks with Washington in 1969 on "a continental energy policy," a plan to integrate the development and use of Canadian and American energy supplies.* The Liberals acted far more secretively in these free-trade talks than the Mulroney government would in the 1980s; they did not seek public support, and there is no evidence they got it. In the Commons, Douglas could only confront Greene with rumours. Was the minister about to barter away Canada's water, or unchallenged access to the Northwest Passage, in return for the right to export crude to the United States? The Americans, he said, wanted to exchange "a rabbit for a horse. I am afraid that in that kind of trading, the minister will come home pretty badly plucked."[5]

In November 1970 the United States agreed to phase out import restrictions, with no conditions attached. The world's biggest energy consumer was in no position to dicker. As producing states around the world would soon learn, Uncle Sam was running out of oil. Canada, for its part, would act as a willing supplier, but opposition inside and outside the cabinet scuttled the idea that the energy systems of the two countries should be integrated.

Greene labelled Douglas's stand on oil exports "schizophrenic socialism,"[6] and there is some justice to this barb. In the middle of the Canada-U.S. talks the Americans imposed a 30 per cent cutback on oil imports from Canada. Douglas requested an emergency debate in the Commons, warning about the cutback's potentially "serious effect on the

---

* The phrase "continental energy policy" appears to have taken shape in the Nixon administration. It made Canadian officials unhappy, and by early 1970 both governments were denying any knowledge of it.

Canadian economy."[7] A few months later, when Greene announced a long-term natural gas sale to the United States, the New Democrat spokesman opposed it. His reasons were defensible—the amount of gas to be exported amounted to more than twice Canada's annual production, and the government had no estimates on the size of Canadian gas reserves other than those supplied by the exporting companies. All the same, Greene could make the case that Douglas was taking a pro-export stand on oil and an anti-export position on natural gas, which was actually a more abundant resource.

Douglas was caught between two currents of thought. While the energy industry extolled Canada's vast resources, many economists warned that the demand for every commodity was rocketing upwards, and forecast early shortages in food, energy, and minerals.

Like other observers, Douglas was starting to get conflicting signals about the real state of Canada's energy reserves. Greene spoke of "923 years of oil" in the ground. David Cass-Beggs, Douglas's former energy adviser in Saskatchewan, said in 1970 that oil and gas, in combination with hydro and coal supplies, would sustain Canada for 300 years without the development of any new technologies. Douglas later maintained that the industry had "misled and lied" about oil and gas reserves during this period.[8] It is fairer to say that nobody in government, the industry, or in the academic world took an honest look before 1970 at the costs of bringing oil supplies, including those from the oil sands and the frontiers, into production.

When James Laxer published *The Energy Poker Game* in the fall of 1970 he shared the widespread faith in the existence of immense oil and gas reserves. The Waffle leader's work impressed Douglas greatly. As a forecast it turned out to be full of holes, but as a piece of pamphleteering it marked a return to the great old days of William Irvine. Appearing just before the United States opened the gates to imports, it warned that under a continental energy deal the Americans would demand that Canada purchase more U.S. goods, and would prevent Ottawa from nationalizing U.S.-based oil companies. It repeated the conventional predictions that Canada could increase its natural gas exports eightfold by 1980 (they remained constant), and that oil prices would remain constant during the decade (they increased twelve times).

Early in the 1970s independent geologists began to question the oil majors' euphoric predictions of endless energy supplies. At the same time, international forecasting bodies like the Club of Rome warned of a coming acceleration in economic growth and energy consumption, to the point where the world would gobble itself up. The immediate trends seemed to confirm this fear. Canadian natural gas consumption, for example, jumped by almost 10 per cent in 1970. Douglas concluded, "on the basis of a mere 10% increase per annum—I believe the increase will amount to more than that—we shall have reached in 1981 the consumption which the [National Energy Board] estimates for 1990."[9] Douglas and the NDP were now swinging from an attitude of optimism to one of extreme pessimism about the energy outlook.

As it turned out, the growth in Canadian demand for oil and gas would be far less drastic than Douglas feared. Domestic demand for Canadian gas grew by less than 4 per cent per year between 1972 and 1982. Canadian demand for crude oil and oil products, also forecast to mushroom, grew by less than 2 per cent per year after 1972, and fell after 1980.*

Douglas maintained an ambivalent stand on oil exports until 1973, when the OPEC nations began to impose new conditions and higher prices on their customers and American petroleum buyers turned to Canada. By January 1973 the increase in the number of export orders threatened Canadian supplies. Douglas demanded that the government stop the oil hemorrhage. On government instructions, the National Energy Board set a new export limit effective March 1—one and a quarter million barrels a day, two-thirds of Canada's daily crude production. Despite further pressure, the Liberals declined to set the limit any lower. In the year of the global energy scare Canada exported almost 5 per cent of its established oil reserves, and continued to export large amounts of light crude until 1977.

At its 1973 summer convention the NDP adopted a statement based on a Douglas speech condemning "the economic insanity of selling our cheap supplies of oil and gas to the United States."[10] Even this statement was ambivalent. The NDP could pass it off to nationalist voters as a no-export policy. The motion did not, however, oppose the export of energy *at high prices.* Douglas continued to advocate a phase-out, rather than a shutdown, of exports. Nevertheless, from this point on, the New Democrats took the most conservative approach of any party towards oil and gas exports.

In early 1973, with OPEC jacking up the world oil price, the private multinationals operating in Canada served notice that they would do the same. Over a six-month period Imperial Oil raised the price of its Canadian crude by 55 cents a barrel, more than the total of all its price increases during the previous quarter of a century. Douglas was convinced that the industry was gouging consumers. Production costs in Canada were steady, and Imperial Oil had cut staff. The company had simply decided, he said, that Canadians should pay more to consume their own oil.

The NDP, under the leadership of David Lewis, had taken thirty seats in the 1972 federal election and now controlled the balance of power in the Commons. From its position of strength the party began to apply pressure on Trudeau's Liberal minority on the issue of oil prices.

---

* Canada's proven supply of conventional crude oil in 1969, in a reserves/production ratio, amounted to 23.9 years (10.5 billion barrels); by 1974, after a period of high export volumes, this had dropped to fourteen years. By 1981, with demand for petroleum falling, Canada had a thirteen years' proven supply of conventional crude oil on hand.

Canada's proven supply of natural gas rose sharply during the 1970s, despite increased demand, from 57 trillion cubic feet (thirty-seven years' worth) in 1969 to 92 trillion cubic feet (forty-two years' worth) in 1983.

(Canadian Petroleum Association figures supplied by the federal energy department.)

Douglas saw no reason to let the industry collect windfall profits. He proposed to the Commons on May 28 that the Liberals should freeze domestic crude prices. He had first put forward the idea of oil price controls in 1971, and industry department officials had since offered the government the same advice. In addition, Douglas added a twist that would allow Canada to profit from the OPEC offensive. His research assistant, Richard Kerr, had convinced him of the need for an export tax—a device that would allow Ottawa to collect the difference between the Canadian price and the world price as oil crossed the border. The Americans should pay the world price for what they took from Canada, but Ottawa, not the oil companies, would get the gravy.

Trudeau had named Donald S. Macdonald, a lawyer from Toronto, as energy minister in the new government. Macdonald paid close attention to his critics in the opposition and the media. In this case, he cautioned Douglas that domestic oil price controls would encounter strong opposition in the West. Perhaps in response, Douglas proposed to his caucus energy committee two weeks later that the "entire surplus" of the oil export tax should go to the producing provinces.[11] The Liberals would ignore the idea. When they imposed the tax in the fall, they used the proceeds to pay for oil imports into the East.

Douglas pushed for domestic oil price controls all summer, along with his colleagues on the NDP caucus energy committee, Max Saltsman and Cyril Symes. In August 1973 the major oil companies announced their biggest price hike yet. Within a few weeks, Trudeau announced an oil price freeze as part of a package of anti-inflation measures. Soon after, Ottawa imposed an export tax on oil flowing south. Perhaps the NDP had set the course for these changes. Economic conditions, along with public hostility to the oil companies, provided the push.

The made-in-Canada oil price proved unpopular in Alberta and got a lukewarm response in Saskatchewan. For a decade, the low domestic oil price would provide a weapon for western Tories, who accused the NDP of standing with the Liberals in a discriminatory anti-western grab. It also stirred up dissent in some sections of the NDP. The federal government did not control the price of Ontario nickel, or levy an export tax on B.C. power—why should oil from the prairies be singled out for special treatment?

Allan Blakeney, the premier of Saskatchewan, confronted the NDP federal council with these questions at a meeting in Toronto's King Edward Hotel in January 1974. Douglas, as a former premier and a former federal leader, was caught in the middle. He stayed mostly silent, speaking only briefly for the federal caucus. Lorne Nystrom, a Saskatchewan MP, recalled, "I was a bit upset that he didn't really get involved. But it was Blakeney on one side, and Lewis on the other."[12]

David Lewis presented the federal party's case. To let oil prices skyrocket, he said, would be politically and economically indefensible. It would enrich provincial and federal coffers, true enough, but it would also bring fabulous profits to the national villains, the oil majors. At the same time, many central Canadians, including trade union leaders, hoped that lower energy prices would make Canada more competitive and create jobs. Lewis believed that the federal NDP's electoral future lay in Ontario, and he argued forcefully for the Ontario consumer.

Blakeney replied that under the constitution it was the provinces, not Ottawa, that should manage natural resources. If the oil companies applied too high a mark-up on their product, he said, it was up to the provinces to respond with higher royalty rates. As for prices, he said, Canada could afford to pay the going rate. "The argument that Ontario industry would be hurt is surely an unjust reflection on the ability and energy of the people of Ontario. Two years ago they paid the world price...you're suggesting that in the last two years these folk have become indolent and uncompetitive."

Blakeney understood, at the same time, that most Canadians viewed his defence of high oil prices as a defence of the oil majors. Douglas was forced into advocating low oil prices along with Lewis. "The political reality," Blakeney said later, "was that our position was seen to be a simple echo of Peter Lougheed, the Blue-Eyed Sheik, and all the rest, and that couldn't be a very popular position."[13]

Over the next few years federal-provincial agreements led to step-by-step increases in the price of Canadian oil. The NDP's response reflected the pulls of East and West. Lewis and then Broadbent defended the consumer's right to low-cost energy. Douglas said that he would support energy price increases—but only if the new revenues went into research and exploration, to make Canada self-sufficient. The federal NDP never admitted that the campaign for cheap energy clashed with the call for self-sufficiency in a country where future domestic oil supplies will be dug out of the ground or piped in from the frontiers.

Blakeney's advisers came up with the idea of a "Canadian resources security fund," and Douglas put it before the Commons in 1975.[14] Every cent from oil price increases after April 16, 1975, should go into this fund, he said. Ottawa and the producing provinces would then work together to spend the money finding energy reserves. Nothing remotely like this scheme ever came into existence. In practice, Douglas would oppose every oil price hike.

Douglas also argued that if Ottawa was going to control oil prices, it should control prices for other commodities too. He spoke as a western Canadian: "Whenever we have something the rest of the country needs, there is a price control imposed as soon as it crosses provincial boundaries. But whenever we buy farm machinery, trucks, automobiles, cement, and a host of other commodities which enter into our cost of production, we are forced to pay the going price."[15] The Liberals introduced a form of wage and price controls in 1975, but there is no evidence that they took the NDP's complaints into account.

The domestic energy price increases of the 1970s, despite the NDP's resistance, had some positive results. They pushed Canadians into conserving oil and gas—an effect that Douglas doubted would ever take hold.

They also stimulated exploration for new reserves and promoted oil sands development. However, when oil prices fell in the mid-1980s, this exploration and development activity came to a halt. It was questionable whether Canadians had any real commitment to energy self-sufficiency.

Through the early 1970s, the New Democrats supported public owner-ship in general terms, as a tool for providing both secure energy and more research and processing jobs for Canada. The first solid proposal for a national oil company came only in June 1973. This was more than a year after Energy Department officials had reported favourably on the idea, and two months after the Trudeau cabinet first considered it. On June 2 David Lewis told a party banquet in Vancouver that the federal govern-ment should set up an integrated national oil company. It would operate, he said, in every branch of the industry, in exploration, production, pipelines, refining, and marketing.[16]

Douglas favoured a takeover of the largest privately owned oil com-pany, Imperial Oil, the Canadian subsidiary of Exxon. Imperial, of all the multinationals, had done the best job of developing a research and management base in Canada, and was ripest for nationalization. More parasitic outfits like Texaco, which simply pumped out oil and gas and developed few new products or ideas in Canada, were safe, ironically, from NDP designs. The instrument for buying into the energy industry was to be a "National Energy Finance Corporation." Douglas suggested to the caucus that the same corporation would also supervise major energy investment decisions in the private sector. In other words, the new national oil company's parent should have the power to regulate its competitors.[17]

The federal NDP's summer convention approved the creation of "a government-owned Canadian Petroleum Corporation,"[18] and the item ranked high on the caucus agenda when Parliament reconvened. However, some caucus members felt that defeating the government should come above all else. The longer the NDP propped Trudeau up, they complained, the more it would anger the West. (They were probably right. The NDP lost fifteen of its thirty-one seats the next year, thirteen of them in western Canada.) Lewis's advisers were among the militants, and the leader grew restless. He proposed dumping the Liberals in September 1973, but he chose the wrong issue—high food prices—and walked into another East-West disagreement. The Saskatchewan members argued that prairie farmers were enjoying their first real profit increases in a genera-tion, and squelched the idea. Instead, the NDP caucus agreed that it would turn the government out unless Trudeau moved on the energy issue.

On October 25, a few days after Exxon had diverted a Canadian-bound oil tanker to the United States, Douglas moved a resolution in the Commons demanding "a publicly-owned National Petroleum Corpora-tion." The corporation's first task, he said, would be to bypass private companies and arrange secure import contracts with state agencies in producing countries. He also insisted that a joint federal-provincial crown corporation should undertake development of the Canadian oil sands. He would "fight to the death," he said, against any move to turn the oil sands over to private companies.[19]

The NDP caucus gave the cabinet a month to act. In the Middle East, war broke out. The Arab oil states announced a 25 per cent production cut and a boycott against Israel's strongest allies, the United States and Holland. Because there was no eastern pipeline, Canada too was vulnerable, and the government began to draw up rationing and emergency oil-shipping plans. Energy Minister Macdonald spoke of a "breakdown in the private supply system."[20]

When the month passed without government action, Lewis told Cliff Scotton, the NDP federal secretary, to gear up the party election machine. While Douglas tried to get through to Trudeau, Lewis flew to the West with Cyril Symes, an Ontario MP, to make some pre-election speeches on energy. The New Democrats planned to vote with the Tories in an upcoming no-confidence motion on oil supplies.

Lewis and Symes were in Edmonton when Trudeau told the Commons of his intentions for a national oil company. The new corporation, he said, would function both as an oil importer and as a partner in Canadian energy development, especially in the oil sands. When the prime minister had finished speaking, Douglas picked up a phone in the opposition lobby and called Lewis at his Edmonton hotel. "I remember David getting off the phone with Tommy," said Symes, "and saying that the Liberals had capitulated and granted us almost everything we had asked for...We would look like medieval philosophers splitting hairs if we said it wasn't good enough."[21]

Douglas walked out from the lobby to announce to reporters in the corridor that the election threat had lifted. In the House, Nystrom was saying that the NDP wanted more, that the oil industry should be converted wholesale into a public utility. Outside, Douglas committed his party to voting with the government and against the Tories' no-confidence motion.

At a caucus meeting the next week, most MPs expressed relief, although a few grumblers predicted trouble ahead. Caucus member Terry Grier said later, "My recollection is one of absolute elation. It was the cleanest and most complete capitulation by the government to any of our demands."[22]

Some observers have disagreed. Larry Pratt has suggested that the political differences between the Liberals and the NDP on Petro-Canada were unimportant. He notes that the Liberals did not set up the state oil company until 1975, after the NDP had lost the balance of power. The Sarnia-Montreal pipeline, another item on the Douglas shopping list, was also delayed until 1975.[23] Donald Macdonald, the former energy minister, has said the Trudeau cabinet responded to public opinion, rather than the NDP. "The government had hold of a good issue—I don't think the opposition ever really caught up." When the time came to frame the

Petro-Canada legislation in 1975, he said, Douglas missed many of the committee sessions.[24]

Senior officials in the Energy Department have said that Douglas never tried to apply pressure on them, either during the energy crisis of 1973 or at any other time. Tommy Shoyama, the man who supplied chicken soup and research for Douglas on the first NDP leader's tour in 1961, served for a time as deputy minister of energy. But Shoyama said that Douglas always kept his distance from the bureaucrats, never phoning or visiting them, because he did not want to put them in a compromising position.

Trudeau, addressing Parliament a few weeks after his energy statement, compared Douglas and his colleagues to a flock of seagulls. "Because they were squawking and making a lot of noise," he said, "they thought they were actually running the ship." Douglas replied, "I think when the people of Canada review the steps that have been taken with respect to the oil crisis during the past 12 months, they will be inclined to say, 'Thank God for the seagulls.' "[25]

The influence of the NDP, or at least the similarities between Liberal and NDP energy policy, grew less marked after 1973. In a mid-1974 general election the voters turned against the New Democrats and restored the Liberal majority.

In February 1975 the federal government entered into an agreement with the oil multinationals that Douglas viewed as a major setback for Canada. Along with Alberta and Ontario, Ottawa took a minority interest in the Syncrude project, a privately controlled oil sands project. Douglas felt that the prime minister had broken his promises of late 1973.

The oil sands of northern Alberta contain hundreds of billions of barrels of crude oil, a deposit on the scale of the Persian Gulf reserves. For years, Douglas had seen their public development as the key to Canadian energy self-sufficiency. The Syncrude agreement now suggested to him that foreign-based companies should be granted control of this resource. The original Syncrude consortium, a group of private companies, began to fall apart because of cost overruns and delays in late 1974. A $900 million cost estimate had ballooned to $2 billion. Douglas saw a chance for Ottawa to take over the project—preferably in concert with the provinces. The Liberals, though, had no intention of taking a lead role. Who in Ottawa knew anything about oil sands? Who had ever heard of a joint federal-provincial crown corporation? The CCF premier of Saskatchewan had suggested one back in the 1950s, at the time of the Trans-Canada pipeline debate, but the idea had gone nowhere.

Trudeau had promised that his government's new oil revenues would go to make the country self-sufficient. But money from Ottawa's export tax was committed to keeping oil prices down in the East, through a refinery subsidy which Douglas viewed as a rip-off. The prime minister had also promised that the national petroleum corporation would go to work in the oil sands; however, the Petro-Canada bill was still on the drawing board. Energy Minister Macdonald confessed, "We have no policy specifically directed at federal investment in the oil sands."[26] A few weeks after this statement, in January 1975, Macdonald and Treasury Board president Jean Chrétien went into emergency negotiations with the Syncrude group. By the time they finished, they had promised to assist the oil sands project with a $300 million investment, in addition to several important tax concessions.

The agreement allowed the surviving private sector partners in Syncrude—Imperial, Shell, and Canada Cities-Service—to write off all their Syncrude expenses against income from any source. They could also deduct provincial royalty payments from their federal taxes, a privilege which Ottawa had just stripped from oil companies working in conventional areas. Most important, Syncrude oil was to fetch the world price. Douglas feared that future oil sands projects would win the same terms and erode the principle of a special domestic price. Moments after Macdonald announced the deal in the Commons, Douglas labelled it "the greatest sell-out of our natural resources in the history of Canada...The people of Canada will pay the world price set by the OPEC countries for the privilege of using their own oil."[27]

"The concessions that were wrung out of the government," said Cyril Symes, "went far beyond what anyone, including the cabinet, expected...I remember how angry we were, especially Tommy, about the deal, and how important it was for Canada's future to try to raise public consciousness about this...I remember Tommy rallying the caucus around it. During those years there were few causes that got the caucus together."[28] The episode strained relations between Douglas and Macdonald, who denounced the NDP spokesman's "contemptible falsehoods."[29] Douglas insisted, however, that the taxpayer, one way or another, would pick up 80 per cent of the cost of the Syncrude plant.

In the Liberals' defence, the final agreement looked better than the bizarre schemes that some in the cabinet had played with. These would have seen migrant Korean labourers working round the clock to build an oil export plant for the Americans. As it was, Ottawa, Alberta, and Ontario took 30 per cent of the shares in the project, so at least they could look over the private companies' shoulders. When Petro-Canada finally came into being, in 1976, its share in Syncrude was its plum asset. As for the long-term effect on Canadian oil prices, Syncrude did not set a precedent—it was the last of the oil sands megaprojects until at least the late 1980s.

The deal showed Douglas, however, that the Liberals had not changed their ways. The government was committed to subsidized private activity rather than public resource development. His attacks on big oil became even sharper. The title of one speech, "The Mask is Off," suggested demons or robbers.[30] "The country is getting a little fed up," he told the Commons a few weeks after the Syncrude announcement, "with these entrepreneurs who read us lectures about 'standing on your own feet,' 'no government intervention,' 'no government subsidies,' 'welfare bums'...but the moment there is an election in the offing they are the first people to the trough wanting subsidies, tax concessions, protective tariffs, quotas."[31] After finishing this speech, Douglas collapsed with a bleeding ulcer, and was carried from the House on a stretcher.

After its establishment in 1976, Petro-Canada grew helter-skelter to become one of the largest energy companies in the country. It became a leader in Canadian-based petroleum research and helped to nurture the Canadian oilfield equipment and servicing industries. It took a central part in the largely government-financed effort to find oil on the frontiers.

As it matured, Petro-Canada came more and more to resemble its private competitors, and to move away from the goals that Trudeau had originally set out. It followed passively behind Esso and Texaco in setting its retail prices and copied their marketing gimmicks. It shipped large volumes of sulphur to South Africa, despite Ottawa's alleged opposition to apartheid. It joined in pillaging the lands of Alberta's Lubicon Cree, an exercise the World Council of Churches condemned as "cultural genocide."

Douglas defended Petro-Canada to the end of his life. He drew a distinction between its origins, as a Liberal "charade to soothe public indignation" against the majors, and what it might someday achieve as a national symbol and as a public enterprise.[32] Perhaps his last passionate cause in Parliament was to warn Canadians about Joe Clark's plans to dismantle the corporation: "On the eve of an election, the Tory party is psychopathic on the subject of Petro-Canada. They are psychotic about the whole idea of public ownership. They have spent most of the time in the last few days pimping for the oil companies."[33]

He continued to hope that Petro-Canada might absorb some of the largest oil companies and curb the multinationals' influence. He hoped that the corporation might become the sole distributor of imported oil in Canada, and thus gain some control over consumer prices. All this, however, remained in the realm of potential.

While most Canadians were becoming aware during the 1970s of the fragile state of their oil and gas reserves, they also developed grave concerns about nuclear power. Douglas, unlike many New Democrats, never took a hard line against nuclear development. However, he fought against efforts to export CANDU reactors, and in this he played a part in generating the anti-nuclear mood of the 1980s.

Along with other leftists, Douglas and the CCF had high hopes for "the peaceful atom" after the Second World War. Nuclear power was to provide a cheap, decentralized energy technology. It would bring developing countries and remote areas of Canada into the twentieth century. "The development of atomic energy," said Coldwell in 1950, "brings nearer the human ability to completely eliminate poverty, misery and want, more than any other discovery in the long history of scientific research."[34]

When he came to Ottawa, Douglas's main concern was to see that Uranium City, Saskatchewan, got the same share of federal development money as rival towns in northern Ontario. However, some activists within the NDP began to question the safety and long-term health effects of nuclear reactors, and in 1967 the party called for a full-scale federal inquiry. Douglas pressed the government unsuccessfully for such an inquiry during his entire career as energy critic.

During the 1970s he never clearly expressed his personal views on the subject. He could write to one citizen, "Nuclear power may very well be the answer to our needs," but it appears from other letters that he viewed atomic power as an energy technology of last resort. He once told the Commons, "I agree with Mr. Maurice Strong, who said that we are in danger of becoming a prisoner to reliance on nuclear energy before we understand the risks."[35] One of the risks became obvious on May 18, 1974, when India exploded an atomic bomb using reprocessed fuels taken from a CANDU research reactor. Would every country with a nuclear plant take the same route?

Ottawa and the nuclear industry wanted exports. Atomic Energy of Canada officials spoke for propaganda purposes of selling 115 reactors in Canada by the year 2000, but they knew that they must find offshore buyers if they were to profit from the money invested in Canadian research. During the years of cheap oil the crown corporation's sales efforts flopped, but, eventually, Canadian officials entered serious negotiations with South Korea and Argentina—both countries which Douglas regarded as fascist states.*

As news of the talks surfaced, Douglas warned that both prospective customer nations were developing the ability to turn nuclear fuel into atomic weapons. He raised the question of safeguards with the government many times during 1974 and 1975. All countries buying a CANDU, he said, should be required to sign the international nuclear weapons nonproliferation treaty, and should agree to return all spent fuel rods to Canada. The Liberals avoided imposing either condition. When Douglas asked Allan MacEachen if the government wanted peace or increased reactor sales, the minister of external affairs replied, "We are primarily interested in both."[36]

The final agreements with Argentina and South Korea set out some safeguards on the use of spent fuel, but it made no provision for what Canada would do if either country broke the rules. "The fact is that the world is living on the edge of Armageddon," said Douglas when the government announced the two treaties. "It may be that the contributions we have made to that situation up until now has been made unknowingly, but the step now being taken by the government is being taken deliberately and the government has a very heavy burden on its conscience."[37]

---

* In 1987 there were seventeen commercial-scale CANDU reactors operating at four sites in Canada. One projection put the cost of a fifth complex then under construction near Oshawa at $11 billion. There were six commercial-scale CANDU reactors at work abroad, in Pakistan, South Korea, and Argentina.

When the sordid details behind the two contracts emerged in the media, the Liberals appeared as surprised as anyone. Parliament never learned what happened to the $20 million AECL spent on "agents' fees" in the Korean sale. In the Argentine sale, it appears at least $2.5 million went to pay off Argentine ex-cabinet ministers.

AECL's annual report for 1977 showed that, after bribing the Argentines to choose the CANDU, Canada lost $130 million on the sale. Once again, the Liberal front bench expressed surprise. Once again, the question is raised as to whether Atomic Energy's identity as a state corporation went any distance in protecting the public interest. Douglas was intensely irritated with AECL's management. "They go on spending public funds, carrying out policies and introducing programs not only with no reference to Parliament but in many cases with no reference to the minister to whom they are supposed to report."[38]

As a leading nationalist and a popular public figure, Douglas raised the profile of the energy issue during the 1970s. He helped to bring about a shift in public attitudes, as more people adopted the idea that the consumer and the taxpayer, and not oil companies, should control the key decisions on energy policy. As an example, the multinationals' plan to ship Alaska natural gas by pipeline through the Mackenzie Valley generated enormous public opposition. Douglas's statements in the Commons were overshadowed by the protests from church and labour groups, and by the news coverage of the commission of inquiry set up by Trudeau and chaired by Thomas Berger, a former New Democrat MP.

The Trudeau Liberals, nudged along by public opinion and by the NDP and their own left wing, put together some of the components of a social democratic energy system. Ottawa imposed controls on oil and gas prices. Petro-Canada became a giant enterprise. The government set up a monitoring agency to keep track of profits and investment levels among private energy companies, and made the National Energy Board into an effective regulator.

Unfortunately, the public's desire to assert control over the energy sector began to wane soon after Douglas left Parliament. The National Energy Program of 1980 highlighted the principles of self-sufficiency and Canadian ownership, ideas that Douglas had talked about for a decade. The program imposed new taxes on oil and gas production that were intended to pay for frontier drilling grants and energy conservation schemes. The oil companies hated the NEP, and launched a long-term public relations program to discredit the Liberals and improve their own image. The nationalist, interventionist forces went into retreat—perhaps because they lacked a consensus on how the public and private sectors should work together for the national good.

It became increasingly clear that the NDP's desire for cheap energy contradicted the Douglas rhetoric of self-sufficiency. Even with OPEC setting a high world price for oil, it remained cheaper to import crude oil than to develop sources on the Canadian frontiers. Ottawa spent several billion dollars helping the private sector explore in the Beaufort, but it made no economic sense to ship the new oil to market. At the same time, Canadians lost sight of the reasons why they had supported domestic ownership of the energy industry. Douglas had railed against the foreign-owned multinationals as organizations that "exploited our people and ravaged our resources without any regard for the well-being of this country."[39] It was hard to see, though, whether the new Canadian-based firms that grew up in Calgary after 1975 behaved any differently.

The growth in the big state energy corporations, Petro-Canada and Atomic Energy, together with their perceived indifference to public concerns, brought widespread disillusionment and cynicism. For the young Douglas of the 1930s, state ownership had symbolized efficiency and democracy, and he remained a strong advocate of public enterprise. Some outside the party wondered, as Petro-Canada enlisted as a model member of the corporate club, why Douglas and his successors continued to treat federal businesses as sacred cows. They appeared to be out of control, and not clearly accountable to anyone. By the late 1980s it appeared very possible that the assets of Petro-Canada—along with those of other leading state businesses like Air Canada and the CBC—would soon be dispersed on the stock exchanges without a public outcry.

30
Life Begins at 75

DOUGLAS LEFT the House of Commons early in 1979, at the age of seventy-four. He could have fought and won another election in Nanaimo, but he had seen too many old men cling to their political careers to the point of decay. He stepped aside for a much younger man, a schoolteacher named Ted Miller. He did not, however, drift into retirement. Instead, he moved about a mile down Metcalfe Street, to an office at Woodsworth House, the national headquarters of the NDP. Here he worked as an independent missionary in the cause of socialism.

The vehicle for his crusade was to be the organization that Laurier Lapierre and some fellow activists had set up in 1971 to honour two leaders of the movement. Douglas assumed the role of chairman of the Douglas-Coldwell Foundation, and soon became its driving force.

Despite his years, Douglas still sought new horizons and the regeneration of the ideals of his movement. In many ways, his mind was that of a young man, and he searched out and encouraged young leaders and thinkers to come forward. He saw in the foundation a base for building in Canada the counterpart of the British Fabian organization. It would stay clear from any party affiliation, and function as a think-tank for the Canadian left. In his words, it would "make it possible for those with radically different ideas about democratic socialism to submit them to consideration without fear of being labelled either heretics, or having any political party accept responsibility for the ideas which they are advancing...it is out of this hurly-burly of controversy that new lines of thought will eventually emerge."[1]

Douglas hoped that the foundation could sponsor a series of exchanges between Canadian socialists and left-wing movements in other countries, including those under Communist rule. Among senior Canadian politicians, Douglas had been the first to call for recognition of Red China and its admission to the United Nations. He spoke to this issue in the 1962 federal election, more than eight years before the Trudeau government concluded their arrangement with mainland China. He continued to press the matter during the Pearson years. His stand won him the lasting friendship of the Chinese. In the fall of 1979, at a time when entry to mainland China was not easy, Douglas led a delegation from the foundation on a visit to the People's Republic.

The nineteen-member group comprised New Democrat MPs, farm and co-operative leaders from the West, and labour leaders from the East. They spent three weeks visiting farms and factories, talking to trade unionists, and meeting with senior government officials. Kalmen Kaplansky, a long-time director of the foundation, recollected that Douglas was still at his spry best—he even walked the Great Wall faster than the younger members of the delegation.[2]

After this visit, Douglas was a frequent guest at the table of the Chinese ambassador to Canada, and the embassy staff expressed great concern in the last weeks of his illness. The ambassador attended the Ottawa memorial service held in Douglas's memory, and Irma received a long message of condolence from the president of the People's Republic of China.

Unfortunately, the China trip was the last of the exchanges. Douglas's ambitions for the foundation, in this and other respects, were frustrated by the decline in his health after 1981. This was one of his great disappointments. He continued, though, to hope for the best. In a last Sunday afternoon chat a few days before his death, he spoke of the membership sweep that we planned to make through western Canada as soon as he recovered.

Douglas remained a popular public figure in his retirement. Every day he went for lunch at the Colonnade Restaurant on Metcalfe Street, where he invariably consumed a fried egg sandwich on brown toast and a pot of tea. Almost every day a well-wisher or two would step up to his table and launch him into an animated conversation with the mention of a cousin or a village in the Maritimes. In 1978 the Saskatchewan NDP took a poll to find out which provincial politicians were known to the voters. Douglas—seventeen years after leaving provincial politics—scored higher than anyone else except for Premier Blakeney.

The party used this popularity to good advantage, and Douglas headlined at rallies, nominating conventions, fundraising dinners, and during election campaigns. He found a soul-mate in Grant Notley, the Alberta party leader, and he travelled often to work in the mission fields of Alberta. Douglas greatly admired Notley, who appeared to carry the cause of socialism in Alberta almost single-handedly. When Notley died in a 1984 airplane crash it was like a death in the family. Douglas was crushed.

In his earlier days in politics he had written many columns and articles for the party press and for special-interest journals. Now he turned his attention again to writing, producing articles for small magazines and a chapter for a collection of essays called *My Canada*. He prepared a slim volume of his favourite political stories, a work that remained unedited and unpublished when he died. In the face of considerable prodding— from Mel Hurtig and Jack McClelland among others—he resisted the idea of writing his memoirs.

The files he left behind also contained, on a foolscap pad, the outline for a book he intended to write under the title *A New Democracy*. He never made a real start on this work, though the outline signals the problems that he wanted to address.

In part, the book would have answered the critics who felt that Douglas's words and thoughts were a hangover from the 1930s. The outline recognizes the drastic effects of new technologies, and the changes in our social and political system over the past few decades. At the same time, it points out that Canadians still suffer unemployment and poverty, and that the gap between rich and poor has increased rather than diminished. Douglas found the fact of poverty in the midst of plenty harder to explain with every passing year, as he watched Canada's resources, its factories, and its young men and women sitting idle.

The Saskatchewan CCF had issued a popular pamphlet called "Who Owns Canada?" in the 1930s, and answered the question with a list of 200 large corporations. Douglas posed the same question, and suggested that a similar list would provide the answer—although some of the company names would be different, reflecting a shift towards American control. The outline for *A New Democracy* suggested familiar points of departure: planning, the rational use of new knowledge and technology, and the commitment to build a moral society. The final chapter was to be entitled "Canada—Good Neighbor in a World Community."

The problems of the world community caused Douglas greater anguish in his last years. He frequently spoke of his concern about the arms race, and about the gap between the developed nations and the Third World. Even so, he held on to his optimistic view of man's possibilities, his belief that humanity could build on the teaching that "I am my brother's keeper." His faith in the idea of collective action and even world government remained unshaken, and he continued to support the work of the United Nations, in spite of its flaws.

Douglas took great satisfaction from the resurgence of social activism in the Christian churches. His roots remained firmly fixed in the social gospel. His conversation returned frequently to earlier days and the activities of the Fellowship for a Christian Social Order—a group that had provided early support in the development of his social philosophy. Talk revolved around the possibilities for calling together such survivors of the old group as King Gordon and Eugene Forsey, together with such representatives of the new social gospelers as Richard Allen and Bill Blaikie. The dream never materialized. Douglas was especially pleased that the Catholic church, which had shown such hostility to the CCF in the 1930s, was now taking a position of leadership in Canadian social thinking. He met with some of the Catholic bishops while they were preparing their paper *Ethical Reflections on the Economic Crisis* and was particularly impressed with Remi De Roo, the bishop of Victoria. He said afterwards, "They have moved well ahead of us."

For Douglas, the role of elder statesman carried more than nominal duties. With Eleanor McKinnon, he churned out letters of congratulation, sympathy, and thanks—covering everything from Bar Mitzvahs through Golden Wedding anniversaries—even though it was no longer a duty of office. He granted countless interviews to journalists, political scientists, archivists, historians, and students of all ages writing class papers. Charitable groups sought to adorn their letterheads with his name. He spoke to Protestant, Catholic, and Jewish groups, to students, teachers, professionals, and interest groups. He remained a Burns' Night favourite, though more and more he delivered his address to the poet's immortal memory on Parliament Hill, before a small group of card-carrying Scots colleagues.

In 1979, soon after his retirement from the Commons, Douglas took a step which surprised many of his supporters, and joined the Board of Directors of Husky Oil, a Calgary-based subsidiary of Alberta Gas Trunk Ltd. Some New Democrats were surprised to see Douglas in bed with the capitalists, on a board that had included such right-wing Albertans as Ernest Manning and Don Getty. The confusion is understandable, and points up the tension between Douglas's role as a populist preacher and his outlook as a social democrat. As a populist, he had denounced large oil companies, and sometimes questioned the motives and the integrity of their executives. As a social democrat, he hoped that leaders from the public and private sectors could plan the economy together, as they had in West Germany and Sweden.

Husky was a Canadian company operating in a field that was dominated by foreign capital. It had also been one of the most important oil producers in Saskatchewan since the early 1950s. In the days when multinationals like Imperial Oil were boycotting Saskatchewan, Husky (then based in Wyoming) maintained its holdings in the province. Of course, Husky had tried to maximize its profits, but the company had taken a negotiating position, rather than a hostile stance, towards the CCF government. Douglas's feeling towards Husky, even thirty years later, could not be wholly unkind. Robert Blair, the chairman of Alberta Gas Trunk—now renamed Nova, an Alberta Corporation—has said that "pure personal respect" moved him to invite Douglas to sit on the Husky board. In addition, the former premier knew every back road and hamlet in Saskatchewan, at a time when Husky was intensifying its work in the heavy oil fields around Lloydminster.

Blair was starting work in the late 1970s on plans for a heavy oil upgrading plant, a capital project worth hundreds of millions of dollars. He hoped to get help with the scheme from the NDP government in Saskatchewan. He denied in 1986 that he ever used Douglas as a go-between, and said that Husky always dealt directly with Premier Allan Blakeney and his cabinet. Blakeney has confirmed this, saying that he never discussed Husky business with Douglas.[3] However, Douglas believed that he could influence Blair and the other directors. The government of Alberta was eager to have the upgrader built on its side of the provincial border, and Douglas was determined to put the case for locating in Saskatchewan.

Douglas and Blair had a similar outlook, as it turned out, on many Canadian energy issues. Douglas had long advocated that Canadians should assert more control over the oil industry. When the Trudeau Liberals moved to promote Canadian ownership, with the National Energy Program of 1980, Blair was one of the few industry leaders who accepted rather than opposed the decision. Douglas was able to back Blair up from within Husky. This partnership grew into a friendship, and Blair took care to see that the ailing Douglas was well looked after on his visits to Calgary.

Although, in retirement, Douglas worked hard—in his own words, "I find it takes longer and longer to do less and less"—he also found time to relax. During the 1970s, he and Irma bought a summer cottage on the shore of the Gatineau River near Wakefield, Quebec. The cottage, which was slightly rickety when they bought it, proved a challenge to Irma's homemaking talents. Moreover, it gave her the opportunity to spend time in the outdoors, watching for birds and wildlife. The cottage also became a favourite retreat for the Douglas grandchildren.

He now had a chance to indulge in the retiree's favourite occupation, "puttering"—repairing the cottage, cleaning out the surrounding woods, tidying up the shore-line. Even his puttering had to have some purpose, although it almost cost him dearly. Soon after they bought the cottage, Douglas was working on the chimney and fell from the roof onto a stump. Fortunately, the fall left him only with sore ribs.

Retirement also gave the Douglases the time to flee from the Canadian winter. After trying both Jamaica and Spain, they settled on Florida as their winter vacation spot, and their annual six-week trek became a ritual.

Sadly, only two years after he left politics, a shadow fell across Douglas's life. In the summer of 1981 a doctor told him that he had an incurable cancer and that it might cut him down at any time. His illness remained a family secret, and Douglas maintained both his arduous schedule and his sense of humour. It was not a matter of putting up a brave front. He simply did not know how to live life any other way. Two years before the end, he revealed his condition to his closest associates, pledging them to secrecy. At almost the same time a new drug therapy arrested the progress of the cancer, and he was able to function with somewhat greater energy.

Honours and awards continued to arrive on Douglas's desk from all points of the political compass. He had already been awarded honorary doctorates from many universities, from Vancouver to Halifax—something that had made him ponder the question of whether he was at last "becoming respectable." Now, in the final days of the Trudeau regime, he was named Companion of the Order of Canada, and early in the life of the Mulroney government he was made a Privy Councillor.

On December 5, 1985, he made his last journey to Regina, accompanied by his granddaughter Rachel, to receive the Saskatchewan Award of Merit. At the evening ceremonies he found the strength to answer the call and responded on behalf of all of the recipients. It was his last public appearance.

Douglas had always kept fit, and had found time for a brisk walk even on his busiest days. In the days of train travel, those who crossed the country with him to Ottawa suffered the indignity of being rooted out at every divisional point, regardless of the weather, for a quick march up and down the station platform. As in everything else, he paced far ahead of his troops. In retirement, he took a walk every day. On a hot afternoon in July 1984 he stepped out to cross the Western Parkway in Ottawa and was knocked flying by a municipal bus.

Weakened by his cancer and his medication, the collision should have been the end, but in the true Douglas tradition he fought back. After several weeks on his back he began to move about and joked, "If you think I'm in bad shape, you should see the bus." His recovery was, in its own way, miraculous, but the dread enemy set to work again. In the latter part of 1985 the doctors found that his cancer was spreading. The flame that had shone for a nation grew dimmer, flickered for a while, and then on February 24, 1986, was extinguished forever.

Before passing on, Douglas had made one more visit to the Hill. A few weeks before his death he dressed himself and told Shirley that he wanted to go to the parliamentary barber shop to have his hair cut. Shirley said later that he mustered every ounce of strength to take this ride. The barbers and the staff at the House of Commons made a great fuss over him, and he returned home satisfied. It was his last trip into the outside world.

Douglas's last years were marred, to some extent, by his knowledge that the New Democratic Party faced a growing list of internal disagreements. The oil price issue had caused sharp debate within the party in the 1970s. In 1981 Ed Broadbent's decision to support Trudeau's constitutional package—whether or not the provincial governments agreed to it—caused an open split in the parliamentary caucus.

Douglas remained faithful in these disputes to Broadbent and the federal party leadership. In Broadbent's view, Douglas's support helped to keep the party together, and to show that the federal party position had the support of some westerners. Broadbent's critics disagreed, saying that Douglas belonged to everyone and that he should have stayed above the fray. Douglas, in fact, had acted as honorary chairman for Broadbent's leadership campaign in 1975. Lorne Nystrom, who also contested the leadership, said later that he was "grieved" at Douglas's action, and that "a lot of Saskatchewan people were cheesed off he'd take a stand openly against a Saskatchewan member."[4]

At the summer 1981 federal convention, Douglas and Stanley Knowles spoke in favour of Broadbent's position on the constitution. More than a third of the delegates, including most of those from Saskatchewan, voted against it. Once again, complained Bill Knight of Saskatchewan later, Douglas and Knowles "should have been anchors for the whole party," while Nystrom thought it unfair for Broadbent to "drag" the old leaders into the debate.[5]

Perhaps the lowest moment came early in 1981, when Broadbent and Blakeney met at a hotel in Hull to discuss their differences over the constitution. The tone was grim and the discussion went nowhere. Douglas and David Lewis, who was close to death from cancer, sat almost helplessly by. "David Lewis attempted to meet my intellectual argument," Blakeney said tartly, "but Tommy was just saying, well, I'm for the Charter of Rights. To which I would say, we're not talking about the Charter of Rights, we're talking about how we get there."[6] Afterwards, Broadbent came upon David Lewis weeping in the street outside the hotel, with Douglas standing forlornly at his side. Lewis felt that "something he and Tommy had worked for all their lives was coming undone."[7]

The party faced another East-West wrangle at its 1983 convention in Regina, but at a key moment Douglas stepped forward, and this time spoke—unmistakably—for the whole party. It was one of the great speeches of his life, and was remembered after as one of the great moments in the history of the movement. His health was failing, and he knew that he might not have long to live. As soon as he stepped up to the microphones and grasped the lectern, a transformation took place. The Douglas that crowds had cheered hundreds of times stood before the hall. The standing ovation which followed his speech lasted for close to half an hour.

Douglas had been wheeled into the hall on a golf cart which pulled an enormous cake, made up to celebrate the fiftieth anniversary of the Regina Manifesto. As he spoke, he looked back over those fifty years, back to Woodsworth and Coldwell and the days when the young movement had nothing but dreams to keep it alive. But this history, he suggested, was instructive only as a key to the future. The greatest work remained yet to be done, the building of a productive, caring, and peaceful world. The fires of the old social gospel crusader still burned brightly as he admonished the crowd:

> The growth and development of the New Democratic Party must never allow us to forget our roots. Don't sacrifice conviction for success. Don't ever give up quality for quantity.
> In a movement like ours, as socialist movements around the world have demonstrated, we're not just interested in getting votes...We are seeking to get people who are willing to dedicate their lives to building a different kind of society...a society founded on the principles of concern for human well being and human welfare.[8]

Word of Tommy Douglas's death evoked a response which showed clearly that though he may not have been one of Canada's most successful politicians, he was beyond all doubt one of its most loved. Tributes poured into his home and office at the foundation from all parts of the country and from Canadians in all walks of life and of all political persuasions. The media—the greater part of which had never supported his political causes—found much in his passing from the Canadian scene to be mourned. In churches and assembly halls across the country, people gathered in large numbers to bid him a last farewell.

Typical was the scene in the city where he had spent more than half of his political career. On an afternoon in late February 1986 more than 800 people joined together in Dominion-Chalmers United Church in Ottawa to honour the memory of Tommy Douglas. The eulogist was that veteran of the battles of the Canadian left, a member of both the League for Social Reconstruction and the Fellowship for a Christian Social Order and also one of the small group that drafted the Regina Manifesto, J. King Gordon. The service was conducted and the lament played on the pipes by Bill Blaikie, MP, who Douglas hoped would carry on the mission of the social gospel in Canadian left-wing politics. The soloist, Bill Haney, had been a member of Douglas's own "Saskatchewan Mafia," and the organist, Dan Crone, had been a friend in Weyburn days. As the family and immediate friends were withdrawing at the end of the service, Crone began to play "The Battle Hymn of the Republic." Of its own accord, the gathering, at first tentatively but soon in full voice, sang out, "Mine eyes have seen the glory of the coming of the Lord." On the steps outside the church a small elderly lady took Irma's hand and said, "He was one of us."

Postscript

This has been an attempt to follow the footsteps of a great Canadian. It has been necessary to be selective, to set aside incidents, episodes, and individuals that others might have given a place to in this narrative. We can only say that, in making our selections, we have tried to choose the events that most clearly reflect the real Tommy Douglas, that illuminate his development as a politician, and give some measure of his impact on the province and the nation that he loved.

In a real sense it has been a personal journey. Over a period of more than a half a century it was my privilege to walk some part of the course with him. As a high school student in Weyburn I was a member of that boy's club of which mention is made later. I was active in his first election in 1934—as active as any near-sixteen-year-old can be who goes out after dark with his father to tack up posters announcing public meetings. Diligence in this task brought promotion, and in the 1935 election I was allowed to carry the message to hamlets and schoolhouses in the constituency where it seemed unlikely that the candidate could do much good or I could do much harm.

From that time on, our paths crossed and re-crossed. I like to entertain the idea that I helped him win his first majority in the city of Weyburn when he and his party won the astounding 1944 victory. From 1944 to 1952 I joined him at the centre of the action during what were for me, and I believe for the CCF, our most exciting years.

Later, as the journey moved towards its end, I was closely associated with him in the work of the Douglas-Coldwell Foundation. A loop seemed to close. I commented to my wife Beryl that I had begun my adult life as Tommy Douglas's spear-carrier, and it was beginning to look as though I would finish it the same way. I hasten to add that this was regarded as a matter of privilege, not of duty.

In writing the Tommy Douglas story, the friendship of more than half a century cannot be set aside. Neither is there need for sycophancy. We have been conscious of the fact that nothing we might say could in any way add to or detract from the greatness of the man himself. We have attempted to "tell it as it was." Evaluation of the contributions he made to public life and selection of the niche he will occupy in Canadian history are tasks we have eschewed—both because we have stood too close to our subject and because we lack the courage or the arrogance to presume on the future. As my Scottish grandmother used to say, "Time will tell and frost will try the 'taties."

He was a simple and humble person, with a great sensitivity to those around him. He brought to the political life of the country a civility that enriched the Canadian scene. He carried a remarkably light load of ideological dogma. His basic principles were as uncomplicated as he was, stemming from the social gospeller's dedication to the ideas of the fatherhood of God and the brotherhood of man—ideas that provided both the goal of his political endeavours and the measure of his success. The ideals of his youth guided him consistently throughout his political career, being truly reflected in the last speech he made. For his principles he was prepared to stand alone, saying, like Martin Luther, "Here I stand, I cannot do otherwise."

Being human, he made what some would regard as errors in judgement. Critics outside the party, denied the juice of scandal that is too often associated with high political office, and critics within the party whose professions of ideological purity usually reflect the fact that they have never had to make a major decision, have seized on them from time to time, as though relieved that the god, indeed, had at least one clay foot. Without disputing the claims made, the record shows that the errors, such as they were, stemmed usually from Douglas characteristics that were more often the source of much of his political strength—a desire to follow the best advice available and his desire to keep his party free from internal strife and factionalism.

The Douglas sense of humour—the mastery of what King Gordon in his eulogy described as the balance between reality and the absurd—was legend. It was not merely a tool to be used in speech-making, or a weapon in debate. As anyone who worked with him could testify, humour was part of his very being. Its foundation was in his simplicity and in his lack of preoccupation with self-regard. He was able to laugh at himself, and this made him sensitive in laughing at others.

Despite the differences of opinion which may have existed between Tommy Douglas and his opponents—usually outside, but at times within, his party—few would contend that he did not establish for himself a unique place in the political history of his beloved Canada.

T. H. McLeod
October, 1987

NOTES

All interviews were conducted by Ian McLeod unless otherwise noted.

CHAPTER 1: NOTHING OF EVERYTHING

1 *Weyburn Review*, April 30, 1930
2 Ibid., Oct. 23, 1930
3 Saskatoon *Star-Phoenix*, Regina *Leader-Post*, Winnipeg *Free Press*, Sept. 1937
4 T. C. Douglas (TCD) interview, Jan. 29, 1985

CHAPTER 2: SOCIALIST BEGINNINGS

1 Kate Waterhouse interview, Sept. 18, 1984
2 TCD interview, April 26, 1985
3 Ibid.
4 David Daiches, ed., *Robert Burns* (London, 1957), 142
5 Psalm 24:3-4
6 Daiches, *Robert Burns*, 22
7 Public Archives of Canada, TCD Papers, MG 32, C 28, vol. 152, TCD to L. Lebam, March 16, 1967
8 Grace MacInnis interview, April 18, 1985
9 Daiches, *Robert Burns*, 16
10 TCD interview, April 26, 1985
11 Arthur Conner, "James Keir Hardie's Life Story" (pamphlet), 1917, Woodsworth Collection, Thomas Fisher Library, University of Toronto
12 TCD interview, April 26, 1985
13 Ibid.
14 TCD Papers, Ottawa, vol. 148, TCD's review of Richard Allen's *The Social Passion*, manuscript
15 TCD Papers, Ottawa, vol. 148, TCD address, March 24, 1976
16 John S. Moir, "The Canadian Baptist and the Social Gospel," in Harold Zeman, ed., *The Baptists in Canada* (Burlington, 1980), 149-57
17 TCD Papers, Ottawa, vol. 146, TCD address, Nov. 8, 1964
18 Walter Rauschenbusch, quoted in Ronald White and Edward Hopkins, *The Social Gospel* (Philadelphia, 1976), 41
19 United Church Archives, Toronto, Salem Bland Papers, "The New Deal and The New Party," address, 1913, reconstructed from notes
20 Glenbow Library, Calgary, J. S. Woodsworth, "The Holy City," 1916, in "Towards Socialism" (pamphlet), Ontario Woodsworth Memorial Foundation, 1958
21 Isobel Bergstrom interview, Feb. 8, 1987
22 TCD interview, April 26, 1985

23 United Church Archives, *Methodist Acts and Proceedings*, 1919
24 J. S. Woodsworth, quoted in Anthony Mardiros, *William Irvine* (Toronto, 1979), 65
25 Lewis Thomas, ed., *The Making of a Socialist* (Edmonton, 1982), 32
26 William Irvine, *The Farmers in Politics* (Toronto, 1976), 147-48
27 Ibid., 52-53
28 *Weekend Magazine*, Sept. 9, 1961
29 TCD interview, April 26, 1985
30 Mark Talney, taped memoir, May 1986
31 Saskatchewan Archives, Saskatoon, taped recordings, TCD radio address, "Christianity and the CCF," Nov. 2, 1943
32 University of British Columbia Special Collections, British Columbia NDP Papers, vol. 22-4, TCD address, July 3, 1967
33 TCD interview, Jan. 29, 1985

CHAPTER 3: COLLEGE YEARS

1 Baptist Archives, McMaster University, Hamilton, Brandon College Commission files, J. R. C. Evans to Horace Whidden, Dec. 21, 1936
2 Edgar Bailey interview, July 24, 1985
3 Baptist Archives, Brandon College Commission files, "Some Facts Concerning Brandon College," and "Jesuit Methods," pamphlets, 1922
4 Baptist Archives, Baptist Union of Western Canada, *Year Book*, 1922
5 TCD conversation with T. H. McLeod, 1985
6 TCD interview, April 24, 1985
7 Ibid.
8 Edgar Bailey interview, July 24, 1985
9 Brandon University Archives, *The Quill*, Dec. 1925
10 Ibid.
11 Mac Rogers interview with T. H. McLeod, June 1985
12 Carberry *News-Express*, various dates, 1928
13 Ibid., Sept. 19, 1927
14 Mac Rogers interview, June 1985
15 TCD conversation with T. H. McLeod, 1985
16 Brandon University Archives, TCD address to Brandon University Convocation, May 15, 1970

CHAPTER 4: DUSTBOWL PREACHER

1 T. C. Douglas Calvary Centre, Weyburn, *Minute Book*, 1928-33
2 Ibid., Board of Deacons, *Annual Report*, 1932
3 Jun Staveley interview, June 14, 1985
4 Based on TCD interview, April 24, 1985; also Jun Staveley interview, June 14, 1985
5 United Church Archives, Toronto, Charles Gordon, ed., *Proceedings of the Social Service Congress* (Ottawa, 1914), vi
6 TCD interview, April 24, 1985
7 Ibid.
8 TCD in Thomas, ed., *The Making of a Socialist*, 65
9 TCD in Kenneth Falconer, "Tommy Douglas, 1930-1944," MA thesis, University of Regina, 1979, 124-25
10 Fred Steininger, "George H. Williams," MA thesis, University of Regina, 1976, 47.
11 Regina *Leader-Post*, Sept. 24, 1931
12 *Weyburn Review*, Sept. 24, 1931; also T. C. Douglas letter to George Williams, Jan. 9, 1935, quoted in Falconer, "Tommy Douglas," 140-43
13 *Weyburn Review*, Sept. 24, 1931
14 TCD interview, April 24, 1985
15 Ibid.
16 TCD interview, May 14, 1985
17 *Weyburn Review*, March 30 and April 13, 1933
18 TCD interview, April 24, 1985
19 Harry Laughlin, "A Model Eugenical Sterilization Law," in Carl Bajema, ed., *Eugenics Then and Now* (Philadelphia, 1976), 138-52
20 Saskatchewan Archives, Regina, T. C. Douglas, "The Mentally and Morally Subnormal Family," MA thesis, microfilm

21 *CCF Research Review*, Regina, June 1934
22 TCD with Jack Scott in *The Courier* (Vancouver), Dec. 16, 1969
23 *Weyburn Review*, April 28, 1932
24 Ibid., May 5, 1932
25 T. C. Douglas private files, Karen Shelton Southern to TCD, nd
26 Joan Tulchinsky to T. H. McLeod, Feb. 1987
27 Shirley Douglas interview, May 14, 1985
28 T. C. Douglas private files, TCD interview with Grant Maxwell, transcript, Nov. 1980
29 Edgar Bailey interview, July 24, 1985
30 *Weyburn Review*, Feb. 11, 1932
31 Helen Davidson interview, May 16, 1984
32 TCD interview, Jan. 29, 1985
33 Grace MacInnis interview, April 18, 1985

CHAPTER 5: THE 1934 ELECTION

1 Public Archives of Canada, sound recordings, TCD interview with Peter Stursberg, Dec. 4, 1972
2 The Regina Manifesto has been widely reprinted, for example in Kenneth McNaught, *A Prophet in Politics* (Toronto, 1959), Appendix
3 United Church Archives, Toronto, Salem Bland Papers, address to the CCF meeting at Alhambra Hall, Oct. 3, 1933, reconstructed from notes
4 TCD interview, Jan. 29, 1985
5 *Weyburn Review*, July 27, 1933
6 Saskatchewan Archives, Saskatoon, Saskatchewan CCF Papers, vol. II-142, Frank Eliason to Clarence Fines, May 8, 1934
7 Public Archives of Canada, Coldwell Papers, vol. 58, unpublished memoir by M. J. Coldwell, c. 1964, copy in University of British Columbia Special Collections, Walter Young Papers, vol. 5-14; see also Saskatchewan Archives, Regina, Clarence Fines, "The Impossible Dream," unpublished memoir, 1981
8 CCF Papers, Saskatoon, 3146; also vol. II-142
9 *Weyburn Review*, Nov. 9, 1933
10 Ibid., May 24, 1934
11 Hugh Alexander interview, Sept. 17, 1985
12 CCF Papers, Saskatoon, vol. II-142, Clarence Fines to Frank Eliason, Nov. 12, 1933
13 Evelyn Eager, "The Conservatism of the Saskatchewan Electorate," in Norman Ward and Duff Spafford, eds., *Politics in Saskatchewan* (Toronto, 1968), 12
14 Unpublished memoir by M. J. Coldwell. Douglas encountered the Klan in 1929 when he was the head of the student body at Brandon. "I incurred the wrath of the Klan by denouncing them and forestalling their attempt to organize on campus," he wrote later. By the time he arrived in Weyburn in 1930 the Klan's membership had shrunk to half a dozen, all of them Tory Orangemen. Public Archives of Canada, T. C. Douglas Papers, vol. 88, TCD to Norman Ward, Sept. 29, 1973
15 *Weyburn Review*, May 31, 1934
16 William Irvine, "The Forces of Reconstruction," Ottawa, 1934
17 TCD interview, May 9, 1985
18 *Weyburn Review*, June 7, 1934
19 Regina *Leader-Post*, June 11, 1934
20 Archbishop Gauthier, pastoral letter, in *Prairie Messenger*, five issues, Feb. 21 to April 11, 1934
21 Frank Eliason to George Williams, March 31, 1932, quoted in George Hoffman, "The Saskatchewan Provincial Election of 1934," MA thesis, University of Regina, 1934, 172
22 TCD interview, May 14, 1985
23 *Weyburn Review*, June 14, 1934
24 TCD quoted in Falconer, "Tommy Douglas," 160
25 Unpublished memoir by M. J. Coldwell; also Saskatchewan Archives, Saskatoon, George Williams Papers, Williams memo to provincial executive, Dec. 12, 1936

CHAPTER 6: THE 1935 ELECTION

1 Saskatchewan Archives, Saskatoon, Saskatchewan CCF Papers, vol. II-35, transcript of special CCF executive meeting, Oct. 9, 1935

2 Frank Underhill to J. S. Woodsworth, quoted in Michiel Horn, *The League for Social Reconstruction* (Toronto, 1980), 60
3 Public Archives of Canada, Louise Lucas Papers, Minutes of CCYM Convention, 1934
4 TCD interview, May 9, 1985
5 Ernest Watkins, *R. B. Bennett* (London, 1963), 134
6 Glenbow Archives, Calgary, George Coote Papers, vol. 4, G. G. Coote radio broadcast, transcript, Oct. 1935
7 *Weyburn Review*, Aug. 22, 1935
8 CCF Papers, Saskatoon, vol. II-28, M. J. Coldwell to George Williams, June 16, 1935
9 *Weyburn Review*, Aug. 22, 1935
10 T. C. Douglas Calvary Centre, Weyburn, 1935 campaign blotting paper
11 CCF Papers, Saskatoon, vol. II-23, joint statement from M. J. Coldwell and George Williams, Sept 3, 1935
12 *Weyburn Review*, Sept. 3, 1935
13 Regina *Leader-Post* Sept. 26, 1935
14 Ibid., Sept. 30, 1935
15 TCD interview, May 14, 1985; Wally Stinson interview, June 25, 1985
16 CCF Papers, Saskatoon, vol. II-23, George Williams to TCD, Sept. 19, 1935
17 Ibid., TCD to George Williams, Oct. 1, 1935
18 Weekly columns by TCD, *Weyburn Review*, Aug. 22 to Oct. 10, 1935
19 *Weyburn Review*, Oct. 3, 1935
20 Saskatchewan Archives, Saskatoon, TCD interview with A. M. Nicholson, transcript, Feb. 11, 1975
21 CCF Papers, Saskatoon, vol. II-23, Andy Macauley memo to CCF executive, nd
22 *Leader-Post*, Oct. 1, 1935
23 Ibid., Oct. 5, 1935
24 CCF Papers, Saskatoon, vol. II-23, transcript of special CCF executive meeting, Oct. 9, 1935
25 Ibid., M. J. Coldwell telegram to George Williams, Oct. 10, 1935; also M. J. Coldwell form letter to members of CCF executive, Oct. 11, 1935
26 *Leader-Post*, Oct. 10, 1935
27 *Weyburn Review*, Oct. 17, 1935
28 CCF Papers, Saskatoon, vol. II-23, minutes of executive meeting, Oct. 21, 1935
29 *Social Credit Chronicle*, Edmonton, Sept. 18, 1935
30 CCF Papers, Saskatoon, vol. II-23, minutes of Political Directive Board meeting, Dec. 21, 1935
31 George Williams to Mrs. V. Kavaner, quoted in Steininger, "George H. Williams"
32 TCD interview, May 14, 1985
33 Baptist Archives, McMaster University, Hamilton, T. C. Douglas file, James E. Smith to H. R. Hobbs, April 21, 1983

CHAPTER 7: A WESTERN MP

1 T. C. Douglas, "Ottawa in Retrospect," Ottawa *Journal*, Nov. 26, 1973
2 Ottawa letter, *Canadian Forum*, April 1923
3 Saskatchewan Archives, Saskatoon, Saskatchewan CCF Papers, vol. II-235, M. J. Coldwell and TCD to Saskatchewan CCF executive, nd [1936]
4 Grace MacInnis interview, April 18, 1985
5 Canada, House of Commons, *Debates*, Jan. 24, 1939, 271
6 Ibid., March 8, 1937, 1564
7 *Maclean's*, Aug. 1, 1944
8 House of Commons, *Debates*, Feb. 24, 1936, 453
9 University of British Columbia Special Collections, Walter Young Papers, box 3, John Saywell, unpublished essay on the CCF and the Communists
10 TCD interview, Nov. 19, 1984
11 TCD interview, May 9, 1985
12 TCD in Thomas, ed., *The Making of a Socialist*, 104
13 Saskatchewan *Commonwealth*, Jan. 3, 1940
14 House of Commons, *Debates*, Feb. 24, 1936, 475; also Jan. 24, 1939, 277
15 TCD interview, Nov. 19, 1984
16 CCF Papers, Saskatoon, vol. VI-5, TCD radio address, "Liberalism Unmasked," transcript, April 15, 1938
17 TCD interview, Nov. 19, 1984

18 CCF Papers, Saskatoon, vol. VI-5, TCD radio address, transcript, April 15, 1938
19 House of Commons, *Debates*, April 28, 1938, 2353-57
20 Ibid., Feb. 7, 1938, 229
21 Ibid., May 11, 1939, 3885
22 Ibid., Jan. 31, 1939, 516
23 Ibid., Feb. 11, 1937, 202-08
24 Ibid., June 16, 1936, 3791
25 Ibid., May 1, 1939, 3389-96; in article form, CCF Papers, Saskatoon, vol. VII-c-17-d (T. C. Douglas clippings)
26 House of Commons, *Debates*, March 30, 1937, 3219
27 Ibid., Nov. 14, 1941, 4434
28 Ibid., May 11, 1939, 3905
29 Ibid., July 25, 1940, 1947

CHAPTER 8: NOT PEACE...BUT A SWORD

1 Public Archives of Canada, CCF Papers, MG 28 IV-1, vol. 1, National Council minutes
2 *CCF Research Review*, Regina, June 1934
3 Canada, House of Commons, *Debates*, June 18, 1936, 2862
4 CCF Papers, Ottawa, vol. 1, 1934 convention minutes
5 House of Commons, *Debates*, June 18, 1936, 3873ff
6 Ibid., Jan. 25, 1937, 257ff
7 CCF Papers, Ottawa, vol. 1, 1936 convention minutes
8 House of Commons, *Debates*, Feb. 19, 1937, 1059ff
9 CCF Papers, Ottawa, vol. 3, National Council minutes, Feb. 26-27, 1938
10 H. Blair Neatby, *William Lyon Mackenzie King*, vol. III (Toronto, 1976), 292
11 House of Commons, *Debates*, Jan. 24, 1939, 270
12 Ibid., April 3, 1939, 2517. (Our emphasis)
13 CCF Papers, Ottawa, vol. 3, National Council minutes, Sept. 6-7, 1939
14 TCD with Ralph Allen, *Maclean's*, April 8, 1961
15 TCD interview, April 26, 1985
16 Saskatchewan *Commonwealth*, Oct. 14, 1939, and Dec. 6, 1939

CHAPTER 9: "THE CANADIAN PEOPLE ARE PREPARED TO FIGHT"

1 J. L. Granatstein, *Canada's War* (Toronto, 1975), 84
2 Canada, House of Commons, *Debates*, May 30, 1940, 1550ff
3 Roy Borrowman interview, Sept. 18, 1985
4 House of Commons, *Debates*, May 30, 1940, 1550ff
5 Ibid., April 29, 1942, 1992ff
6 Ibid.
7 Ibid., June 18, 1940, 898ff
8 Ibid., Jan. 26, 1942, 51
9 Ibid., Feb. 12, 1942, 523
10 Ibid., Jan. 26, 1942, 56
11 Saskatchewan Archives, Saskatoon, Saskatchewan CCF Papers, vol. II-98, TCD to Clarence Fines, March 11, 1942
12 T. C. Douglas with Ralph Allen, *Maclean's*, April 8, 1961
13 House of Commons, *Debates*, June 11, 1940, 673
14 Ivan Avakumovic, *Socialism in Canada* (Toronto, 1978), 74
15 House of Commons, *Debates*, June 13, 1940, 751ff
16 Ibid., Nov. 28, 1940, 4970ff
17 Ibid., May 2, 1942, 2091-92
18 Ibid., June 5, 1940, 533
19 Ken Adachi, *The Enemy That Never Was* (Toronto, 1976), 228
20 House of Commons, *Debates*, Feb. 17, 1941, 788-89
21 Maurice A. Pope, *Soldiers and Politicians*, (Toronto, 1962), 176ff
22 House of Commons, *Debates*, July 29, 1942, 1018
23 *The Federationist*, March 5 and 19, 1942
24 Saskatchewan Archives, Regina, TCD Premier's Papers, vol. 860, TCD to Rev. Scott Leith, Dec. 5, 1945
25 Winnipeg *Free Press*, March 28, 1946
26 TCD Premier's Papers, Regina, vol. 137, Tamaki file

CHAPTER 10: RETURN TO THE PRAIRIES

1 Saskatchewan Archives, Saskatoon, Saskatchewan CCF Papers, vol. II-97, George Williams to TCD, June 24, 1936
2 Ibid., CCF Convention minutes, 1936, 1937
3 Ibid., vol. II-97, TCD to George Williams, Jan. 25, 1938
4 Ibid., March 26, 1938
5 Ibid., May 16, 1938
6 Ibid., vol. II-300, George Williams to J. S. Woodsworth, June 23, 1938
7 TCD interview, May 23, 1985
8 CCF Papers, Saskatoon, vol. II-97, March 26, 1938
9 Clarence Fines interview, Feb. 10, 1986; Saskatchewan Archives, Regina, Clarence Fines interview with Jean Larmour, transcript, Oct. 22, 1981; *Weyburn Review*, April 28, 1938
10 Clarence Fines interview, Feb. 10, 1986
11 CCF Papers, Saskatoon, vol. II-300, J. S. Woodsworth to George Williams, June 10, 1938
12 Ibid., vol. II-97, TCD to George Williams, Aug. 19, 1938
13 Ibid., George Williams to TCD, March 30, 1939
14 Ibid., convention minutes, 1939
15 Regina *Leader-Post*, Sept. 20, 1939
16 Saskatchewan Archives, Saskatoon, Carlyle King Papers, vol. 20, Carlyle King to Gladys Strum, March 29, 1940
17 Saskatchewan Archives, Regina, Clarence Fines, "The Impossible Dream," unpublished memoir, 1981
18 T. C. Douglas private files, A. M. Nicholson interview with TCD, tape recording, June 15, 1980
19 Falconer, "Tommy Douglas," 302
20 Saskatchewan Archives, Saskatoon, George Williams Papers, vol. 7, text of undelivered speech by George Williams, Dec. 26, 1940
21 CCF Papers, Saskatoon, vol. II-49, MPS' brief on party structure, nd [1940]
22 *Leader-Post*, July 20, 1940
23 Carlyle King Papers, vol. 20, Carlyle King to "E. B.," Dec. 2, 1939
24 Steininger, "George H. Williams," 421
25 CCF Papers, Saskatoon, vol. II-131, Oak Valleau to Provincial Council, Jan. 9, 1942
26 Saskatchewan Archives, Regina, Carlyle King interview with Jean Larmour, transcript, 1981
27 Robert Walker interview, Jan. 16, 1986
28 CCF Papers, Saskatoon, CCF Convention minutes, 1942
29 Ibid.

CHAPTER 11: VICTORY

1 Saskatchewan Archives, Saskatoon, Saskatchewan CCF Papers, vol. VI-5, TCD radio broadcast, transcript, June 12, 1944
2 Saskatchewan *Commonwealth*, Feb. 9, 1944
3 Ibid., Sept. 9, 1942
4 TCD interview, Oct. 30, 1985
5 Public Archives of Canada, F. R. Scott Papers, vol. 12, F. R. Scott to TCD, Jan. 6, 1943
6 CCF Papers, Saskatoon, vol. VI-5, TCD radio broadcast, transcript, May 4, 1943
7 Carlyle King article in *Canadian Forum*, quoted in Walter Young, *The CCF: Anatomy of a Party* (Toronto, 1969), 127
8 Saskatchewan Archives, Saskatoon, Carlyle King Papers, vol. 5, M. J. Coldwell to Carlyle King, Oct. 30, 1943
9 Carlyle King, in Donald Kerr, ed., *Western Canadian Politics* (Edmonton, 1981), 40
10 CCF Papers, Saskatoon, vol. VI-5, TCD radio broadcast, transcript, Dec. 14, 1943
11 Ibid., TCD radio broadcast, transcript, "Socialized Health Services," 1943
12 Ibid., TCD radio broadcast, transcript, May 9, 1944
13 Regina *Leader-Post*, June 12, 1944

CHAPTER 12: THE FIRST CABINET

1 Saskatchewan Archives, Saskatoon, Saskatchewan CCF Papers, vol. VI-5, TCD radio broadcast, transcript, July 12, 1944
2 Saskatchewan Archives, Regina, TCD Premier's Papers, R 33.1, file 938 ("Crackpots")

3 Ibid., file 815, TCD to William Patterson, Sept. 18, 1944, and reply from Patterson, Oct. 3, 1944
4 Saskatchewan Archives, Saskatoon, tape recording VI-171a, TCD at Woodrow Lloyd dinner
5 Carlyle King conversation with T. H. McLeod, 1985
6 TCD interview, Oct. 24, 1985
7 TCD private files, Jack Corman to TCD, Dec. 1963
8 TCD interview, Oct. 24, 1984
9 Stephen Lewis interview, Sept. 9, 1985

CHAPTER 13: WHO'S IN CHARGE?

1 Al Johnson, "Biography of a Government," PhD thesis, Harvard University, 1963, 120
2 Clarence Fines interview, Feb. 12, 1986
3 Saskatchewan *Commonwealth*, July 7, 1943
4 Saskatchewan Archives, Saskatoon, CCF Papers, CCF Convention minutes, 1946
5 Regina *Leader-Post*, June 17, 1944
6 Saskatchewan Archives, Regina, TCD Premier's Papers, R 33.1, file 395, T. H. McLeod memo to cabinet, nd [1944]
7 CCF Papers, Saskatoon, vol. VI-5, TCD radio broadcast, transcript, July 12, 1944
8 TCD Premier's Papers, Regina, file 400, unsigned memo, nd [1945?]
9 Ibid., TCD letter to Lambert Wiggins, Jan. 22, 1946
10 TCD interview, Oct. 24, 1984
11 *Journals of the Saskatchewan Legislature*, 1944, Speech from the Throne
12 TCD interview, Oct. 24, 1984
13 Ottawa *Journal*, April 12, 1952

CHAPTER 14: THE POLITICS OF FEDERALISM

1 Public Archives of Canada, sound recordings, TCD interview with Peter Stursberg, Dec. 4, 1972
2 Saskatchewan Archives, Saskatoon, CCF Papers, II-247, TCD to David Lewis, Dec. 27, 1937
3 CCF Papers, Saskatoon, II-247, George Williams to David Lewis, Oct. 21, 1937
4 Public Archives of Canada, sound recordings, TCD interview with Richard Alway, c1976
5 University of British Columbia Special Collections, Walter Young Papers, vol. 5-1, TCD radio broadcast, Feb. 11, 1944
6 Saskatchewan Archives, Regina, TCD Premier's Papers, file 671, TCD to Harold Thayer, June 20, 1955
7 TCD conversation with T. H. McLeod, 1985
8 Public Archives of Canada, F. R. Scott Papers, vol. 28, public statement from M. J. Coldwell, Feb. 7, 1945
9 CCF Papers, Saskatoon, vol. VI-5, TCD radio address, transcript, Sept. 13, 1944
10 Sources on the seed-grain dispute include Clarence Fines, "The Impossible Dream," unpublished manuscript, at the Saskatchewan Archives, Regina, and "The Seed Grain Dispute," in TCD Premier's Papers, file 327.
11 TCD in Thomas, ed., *The Making of a Socialist*, 216
12 Saskatchewan Archives, Regina, 33.1 XXVII 866, memo, TCD to all CCF MLAS
13 Ibid., M. J. Coldwell to TCD, Oct. 4, 1945
14 F. R. Scott Papers, vol. 11, F. R. Scott to TCD, Feb. 20, 1950
15 Saskatchewan Archives, "The Record of the Establishment of Indian Unity in Saskatchewan," booklet
16 Saskatchewan Archives, Regina, TCD Executive Assistant Papers, R 33.3, file 409, James McKinnon to TCD, July 19, 1949. File 404 contains a record of individual cases
17 TCD Premier's Papers, Regina, file 864, Jack Sturdy speech to the legislature, March 27, 1957
18 *The Westerner*, Oct. 9, 1958
19 Canada, House of Commons, *Debates*, Feb. 21, 1938, 636
20 House of Commons, *Debates*, Dec. 8, 1945, 3191
21 P. C. 2298, June 19, 1947
22 Paul Martin, *A Very Political Life* (Toronto, 1985), 19-20

23 Saskatchewan Archives, Regina, South Saskatchewan River Project file, internal government memo reviewing discussions concerning the project, May 1953
24 Saskatchewan Archives, Regina, 33.1 file 19, June 1950
25 TCD Premier's Papers, Regina, file 19, TCD to James Gardiner, July 26, 1951
26 "Report of the Royal Commission on the South Saskatchewan River Dam Project," Jan. 19, 1953
27 TCD Premier's Papers, Regina, file 19, TCD press release, Jan. 19, 1953
28 Ibid., M. J. Coldwell to TCD, 1951
29 Saskatchewan Archives, Regina, South Saskatchewan River Project file, J. T. Douglas memo, acting premier reporting to TCD on discussions with J. G. Gardiner, June 22, 1954
30 TCD Premier's Papers, Regina, file 19, TCD to Louis St. Laurent, Jan. 23, 1953
31 Ibid., TCD press release, April 28, 1953
32 Ibid., July 7, 1954
33 Martin, *A Very Political Life*, vol. II (Toronto, 1985), 20
34 TCD Premier's Papers, Regina, file 19, TCD press release, April 29, 1955
35 Ibid., TCD to Alvin Hamilton, July 6, 1950
36 Public Archives of Canada, TCD Papers, vol. 147, TCD speech at Gardiner Dam opening, July 24, 1967

CHAPTER 15: MINISTER OF PUBLIC HEALTH

1 TCD private papers, Ottawa, TCD speech to 1983 NDP Convention, tape recording, July 2, 1983
2 Saskatchewan Legislature, *Debates and Proceedings*, 1961 Special Session, vol. 11, 96
3 Saskatchewan Archives, Saskatoon, Hugh MacLean Papers, vol. 12, correspondence between TCD and Hugh MacLean
4 TCD private papers, TCD interview with A. M. Nicholson, tape recording, June 15, 1980
5 Hugh MacLean Papers, vol. 12, TCD to Hugh MacLean, Nov. 6, 1952
6 *Report of Saskatchewan Health Services Survey Commission* (Sigerist Report), 1944. (Our emphasis)
7 Malcolm Taylor, *Health Insurance and Canadian Public Policy* (Montreal, 1978), 83
8 Saskatchewan Archives, Saskatoon, Carlyle King Papers, vol. 1, CCF executive resolution, nd
9 Taylor, *Health Insurance*, 77
10 Ibid., 319
11 *Journal of the Canadian Medical Association*, May 1971
12 Sigerist Report
13 Taylor, *Health Insurance*, 103
14 TCD interview, Oct. 19, 1985
15 *American Journal of Public Health*, Dec. 1947
16 Saskatchewan Archives, Saskatoon, CCF Papers, VII-1, Fred Mott to F. G. Hanson, Feb. 22, 1949
17 University of Saskatchewan library, government documents, C. M. Hincks, "A Mental Hygiene Program for Saskatchewan," 1945
18 Saskatchewan Archives, Regina, TCD Premier's Papers, file 105, "Report on the North Battleford Hospital"
19 Harley Dickinson, "Community Psychiatry: The Transformation of Psychiatric Work," PhD thesis, University of Lancaster, 1984, 183
20 TCD Premier's Papers, Regina, file 554, Eiling Kramer to TCD, Dec. 22, 1960
21 Dickinson, "Community Psychiatry," 228

CHAPTER 16: LABOUR REFORM

1 "When we make one of these moves forward, there's a great tendency to sit down and catch our breath and say, 'oh boy, that was tough, but we won.' We didn't win. All we did was get back a little of the fruit of people's labour and give them a chance to enjoy it." TCD interview, Jan. 29, 1985
2 CCF Papers, Ottawa, vol. 3, National Council minutes, 1940
3 Saskatchewan Archives, Regina, TCD Premier's Papers, file 307, memo from Morris Shumiatcher to TCD, nd [1946]
4 Ibid., file 295, David Lewis to TCD, July 19, 1944
5 Ibid., file 672, David Lewis to TCD, Aug. 23, 1944

6 Ed Whelan interview, Nov. 28, 1985
7 TCD Premier's Papers, Regina, file 672, TCD to David Lewis, Aug. 18, 1944
8 William Davies interview, Nov. 4, 1986
9 TCD Premier's Papers, file 307, memo from George Cadbury to TCD, June 9, 1950
10 Ibid., file 318, TCD to J. K. McGregor, Dec. 3, 1948
11 Ibid., file 318, TCD to Aaron Mosher, Dec. 21, 1948
12 Ibid.
13 Regina *Leader-Post*, April 28 and 29, 1950
14 TCD Premier's Papers, file 307, TCD public statement, Nov. 30, 1954
15 Walter Smishek interview, Nov. 29, 1985
16 Saskatchewan Archives, Regina, Clarence Fines interview with Jean Larmour, transcript, Sept. 10, 1982
17 William Davies interview, Nov. 4, 1986
18 TCD interview, Sept. 12, 1985

CHAPTER 17: PLANNING FOR DEVELOPMENT

1 Regina Manifesto
2 Meyer Brownstone, "The Douglas-Lloyd Governments: Innovation and Bureaucratic Adaptation," in L. Lapierre et al., eds., *Essays on the Left* (Toronto, 1971), 66
3 Al Johnson interview with T. H. McLeod, Feb. 6, 1987
4 Ibid.
5 Saskatchewan Archives, Saskatoon, Saskatchewan CCF Papers, vol. VI-5, TCD radio address, Sept. 13, 1944
6 Saskatchewan *Commonwealth*, April 5, 1944
7 CCF Papers, Saskatoon, vol. VI-5, TCD radio address, Sept. 13, 1944
8 Johnson, "Biography of a Government," 135
9 Saskatchewan Archives, T. C. Douglas Economic Advisory and Planning Board Papers, R 33.4, part III, minutes of joint cabinet-planning board meeting, Sept. 9, 1946
10 Johnson, "Biography of a Government," 112
11 Ibid., 357
12 *Globe and Mail*, Jan. 26, 1957
13 Saskatchewan Archives, Regina, *Report of the Royal Commission on Certain Mineral Transactions*, 1957, with background papers; also Ray Cugnat interview, Nov. 26, 1986
14 Ibid.
15 Public Archives of Canada, TCD Papers, vol. 43, exchange of letters between TCD and Clinton White, 1975
16 TCD Papers, Ottawa, vol. 142, TCD speech, Saskatchewan Throne Speech debate, 1952
17 Al Johnson, in *A Nosegay of Memories*, a booklet prepared for the retirement of TCD from Parliament, 1979

CHAPTER 18: MINISTER OF CO-OPERATIVE DEVELOPMENT

1 T. K. Shoyama, in *A Nosegay of Memories*
2 Canada, House of Commons, *Debates*, March 22, 1943, 1441
3 Public Archives of Canada, TCD Papers, vol. 142, speech by TCD, Sept. 10, 1958
4 Saskatchewan Archives, Regina, TCD Ministerial Papers, file 10, TCD to Marjorie Barmby, May 30, 1951
5 Saskatchewan Archives, Regina, Clarence Fines papers, TCD clippings file, press clipping, April 27, 1951
6 Barney Arnason to T. H. McLeod, Feb. 1987
7 Ibid.
8 Saskatchewan Archives, Regina, TCD Premier's Papers, file 413, Economic Advisory and Planning Board Four-Year Plan, Nov. 1947
9 Saskatchewan Archives, Regina, TCD Executive Assistant files, file 72, J. Graham report to the Planning Board, Nov. 22, 1949
10 TCD Ministerial Papers, Regina, file 30, TCD to Bob von Pilis, April 23, 1958

CHAPTER 19: THE PERILS OF POWER

1 Saskatchewan Archives, Regina, TCD Premier's Papers, file 130, Lewie Lloyd to TCD, Sept. 23, 1956
2 Saskatchewan Archives, Saskatoon, CCF Papers, vol. VI-5, TCD radio address, transcript, June 12, 1944

3 Regina *Leader-Post*, April 10, 1947
4 *Sunday News* (U.S.A.), April 9, 1950
5 Vancouver *Sun*, series of articles on Saskatchewan, May 1960
6 Joan Tulchinsky to T.H. McLeod, Feb. 1987
7 Shirley Douglas interview, May 14, 1985
8 Ibid.
9 Public Archives of Canada, TCD Papers, vol. 142, "Fireside Chats"
10 Saskatchewan Archives, Regina, TCD Ministerial Papers, file 150, TCD to M. J. Coldwell, June 28, 1948
11 Saskatchewan Archives, Saskatoon, Hugh MacLean Papers, vol. 12, TCD to Hugh MacLean, Dec. 12, 1950
12 TCD Premier's Papers, Regina, file 115, report from Graham Spry, 1952
13 *Leader-Post*, April 8, 1957
14 TCD private papers, Ottawa, correspondence between TCD and Mackenzie King, 1944-48
15 *Leader-Post*, Saskatoon *Star-Phoenix*, July 14, 1947
16 *Leader-Post*, April 3, 1948
17 *Star-Phoenix*, Oct. 28, 1948
18 TCD interview, May 23, 1985
19 Clarence Fines interview, Feb. 12, 1986
20 *Star-Phoenix*, Feb. 29, 1952; also Saskatchewan Archives, Regina, Clarence Fines Papers, "Theatre Under the Stars" file
21 Saskatchewan Archives, Regina, Rawluk inquiry records, March 12, 1953
22 TCD Premier's Papers, file 848, report of the Standing Committee on Crown Corporations, April 1953
23 Saskatchewan Legislature, *Debates and Proceedings*, April 13, 1953
24 TCD private papers, Jack Corman radio address, transcript, May 12, 1953
25 Saskatchewan Legislature, *Debates and Proceedings*, April 14, 1953
26 Hugh MacLean Papers, vol. 12, TCD to Hugh MacLean, May 15, 1953
27 Saskatchewan Archives, Saskatoon, Saskatchewan NDP Papers, vol. II-21, TCD to Mrs. E. W. Turner, March 18, 1958
28 Clarence Fines Papers, Liquor Board, Brewers, and Distillers file, Clarence Fines to C. M. Suggitt, Nov. 29, 1958
29 Walter Smishek interview, Nov. 29, 1985
30 TCD Premier's Papers, Regina, file 960, *Leader-Post* clipping c Aug. 1958
31 *Leader-Post*, May 21, 1957; Robert Tyre, *Douglas in Saskatchewan* (Vancouver, 1962), 123
32 Vancouver *Sun* series on Saskatchewan, May 1960
33 *Union Farmer*, June 1960
34 Saskatchewan NDP Papers, Saskatoon, vol. II-22, TCD speech to the CCF annual convention, 1959
35 TCD Premier's Papers, Regina, file 675, report from Graham Spry, April 9, 1960
36 Saskatchewan Archives, Regina, Homer Lane Papers, TCD to Homer Lane, June 14, 1960

CHAPTER 20: MEDICARE

1 Saskatchewan Archives, Regina, TCD Ministerial Papers, file 154, TCD radio broadcast, transcript, April 29, 1952
2 Allan Blakeney interview, Sept. 18, 1985
3 Saskatchewan *Commonwealth*, Dec. 23, 1959
4 Ken MacTaggart, *The First Decade* (Ottawa, 1973), 32
5 Saskatchewan Archives, Regina, TCD Premier's Papers, file 574, correspondence between TCD and Dr. G. W. Peacock, March 1960
6 TCD Premier's Papers, Regina, file 574, TCD television debate with Dr. E. W. Barootes, transcript, March 1960
7 Robin Badgeley and Samuel Wolfe, *Doctors' Strike* (Toronto, 1967), 31-33
8 TCD Premier's Papers, file 573, TCD to Dr. Humphrey Osmond, July 13, 1960
9 MacTaggart, *The First Decade*, 83
10 TCD Premier's Papers, file 576, correspondence between TCD and W. P. Thompson, Nov. 1960
11 Robert Walker interview, Jan. 16, 1985
12 W. P. Thompson, *Medical Care: Programs and Issues* (Toronto, 1964), 65
13 Saskatchewan Legislature, *Debates and Proceedings*, Oct. 13, 1961, 19
14 William Davies interview, Nov. 3, 1986

15 E. A. Tollefson, *Bitter Medicine* (Saskatoon, nd), 63
16 Johnson, "Biography of a Government," 636
17 Saskatchewan Archives, Saskatoon, TCD interview with E. A. Tollefson, transcript
18 William Davies interview, Nov. 3, 1986
19 Toronto *Star*, July 14, 1962
20 Ibid., July 9, 1962
21 Regina *Leader-Post*, June 15, 1962
22 Douglas private papers, TCD interview with Sandy Nicholson, tape recording, June 15, 1980
23 Saskatchewan Archives, Saskatoon, NDP Papers, vol. II-356, TCD speech to 1964 provincial convention, July 15, 1964

CHAPTER 21: NEW START, FALSE START?

1 Walter Young, *The Anatomy of a Party: The National CCF* (Toronto), 137
2 *Maclean's*, Sept. 15, 1956
3 University of British Columbia Special Collections, Walter Young Papers, vol. 6-32, TCD radio addresses, transcripts, Oct., Nov. 1956
4 Saskatchewan Archives, Regina, TCD Premier's Papers, file 949, George Cadbury to TCD, Oct. 25, 1956
5 Public Archives of Canada, M. J. Coldwell Papers, vol. 59, David Lewis to M. J. Coldwell, May 19, 1958
6 Public Archives of Canada, TCD Papers, vol. 1, CLC news release, April 1958
7 Public Archives of Canada, CCF-NDP Papers, vol. 373, New Party Committee minutes
8 Glenbow Archives, Alberta CCF Papers, file 226, TCD to William Irvine, Oct. 21, 1959
9 Queen's University Archives, Donald MacDonald Papers, II-54-314, Donald MacDonald to Stanley Knowles, Oct. 14, 1958
10 Douglas Fisher interview, Feb. 26, 1985
11 *Financial Post*, Dec. 6, 1958
12 Walter Young Papers, vol. 8-9A, Howard Pawley and Al Mackling to CCF national executive, Feb. 17, 1959
13 M. J. Coldwell Papers, vol. 58, Clarence Fines to M. J. Coldwell, June 16, 1959
14 Ibid., Coldwell to Fines, June 13, 1959
15 TCD Papers, Ottawa, vol. 1, Woodrow Lloyd to M. J. Coldwell, Nov. 19, 1959
16 Saskatchewan *Commonwealth*, Sept. 14, 1960
17 TCD interview, May 23, 1985
18 TCD Papers, Ottawa, vol. 1, TCD to N. P. Finnemore, Sept. 18, 1959
19 Ibid., TCD to S. E. Ellwood, Aug. 25, 1959
20 Ibid., TCD to Carl Hamilton, Aug. 26, 1959
21 Ibid., TCD to Stanley Knowles, April 3, 1961
22 Ibid., TCD to Bert Herridge, Feb. 10, 1959
23 Ibid., TCD to David Lewis, Oct. 7, 1959
24 Alberta CCF Papers, vol. 228, William Irvine to Hazen Argue, March 11, 1960
25 Manitoba Archives, Magnus Eliason Papers, MG 14, B 64, file 39
26 TCD Papers, Ottawa, vol. 1, TCD to Stanley Knowles, May 4, 1959
27 Donald MacDonald interview, July 25, 1985
28 TCD Papers, Ottawa, vol. 1, TCD to Stanley Knowles, May 4, 1959 (same letter as note 26)
29 Queen's University Archives, Ontario CCF Papers, box 4, Sask. NDP file, Peg Stewart and Ken Bryden to Woodrow Lloyd, June 24, 1960
30 TCD Papers, Ottawa, vol. 1, TCD to Hazen Argue, Feb. 24, 1960
31 Saskatchewan Legislature, *Debates and Proceedings*, March 9, 1960
32 *Financial Post*, Aug. 13, 1960

CHAPTER 22: HIGH NOON

1 Toronto *Star*, series on the CCF, Aug. 1956
2 Public Archives of Canada, M. J. Coldwell Papers, vol. 59, David Lewis to M. J. Coldwell, Jan. 30, 1958
3 Thomas, ed., *The Making of a Socialist*, 256
4 Carl Hamilton interview, July 22, 1985
5 Douglas Fisher interview, Feb. 26 1985
6 Toronto *Telegram*, letter from Andrew Brewin, Feb. 28, 1966

7 Queen's University Archives, Donald MacDonald Papers, 47-249, circular from Fisher, Peters, Howard, and Herridge, Aug. 1, 1960
8 Arnold Peters interview, May 29, 1985
9 Saskatchewan *Commonwealth*, Aug. 17, 1960
10 Toronto *Telegram*, letter from Andrew Brewin, Feb. 28, 1966
11 Terry Grier interview, July 25, 1985
12 Douglas Fisher interview, Feb. 26, 1985
13 Stephen Lewis interview, Sept. 9, 1985
14 Public Archives of Canada, TCD Papers, vol. 1, Stanley Knowles to TCD, July 13, 1959
15 Ibid., TCD to Sam Laycock, Oct. 12, 1960
16 Ibid., TCD to Andrew Brewin, Nov. 9, 1960
17 TCD Papers, Ottawa, vol. 2, TCD to David Lewis, April 10, 1961
18 TCD Papers, Ottawa, vol. 1, TCD to Andrew Brewin, Nov. 9, 1960
19 Public Archives of Canada, sound recordings, TCD interview with Peter Stursberg, Sept. 3, 1976
20 Glenbow Archives, Alberta CCF Papers, file 228, David Lewis to Nellie Peterson, Feb. 3, 1960
21 TCD Papers, Ottawa, vol. 2, letters on New Party leadership
22 Public Archives of Canada, sound recordings, TCD interview with Peter Stursberg, Sept. 3, 1976
23 Terry Grier interview, July 25, 1985
24 Hazen Argue interview, Aug. 27, 1985
25 Queen's University Archives, Ontario CCF-NDP Papers, vol. 2, Murdo Martin to Leo Behie, July 4, 1961
26 TCD Papers, Ottawa, vol. 2, Allan Blakeney to TCD, March 31, 1961
27 Saskatchewan Archives, Regina, John Brockelbank Papers, vol. IX 21, TCD to John Brockelbank, April 2, 1961
28 TCD Papers, Ottawa, vol. 2, correspondence between TCD and David Lewis, April 1961
29 Ibid., TCD news release, June 28, 1961
30 Ibid., TCD to Elmer Roper, April 11, 1961
31 *Globe and Mail*, June 30, 1961
32 TCD Papers, Ottawa, vol. 1, TCD to R. E. Spencer, April 14, 1961
33 TCD Papers, Ottawa, vol. 91, TCD to Emlyn Davies, Aug. 17, 1961
34 Arnold Peters interview, May 29, 1985
35 CBC radio archives, Toronto, TCD acceptance speech, NDP founding convention, 1961
36 Hazen Argue interview, Aug. 27, 1985
37 Regina *Leader-Post*, Nov. 7, 1961
38 T. K. Shoyama interview, Jan. 16, 1986
39 TCD interview, May 23, 1985
40 Ontario CCF-NDP Papers, vol. 2, Terry Grier to Peg Stewart, Jan. 11, 1962
41 TCD Papers, Ottawa, vol. 145, TCD television address, transcript, Oct. 11, 1961
42 Niagara Falls *Review*, April 2, 1962
43 *Leader-Post*, Dec. 10, 1961
44 *Globe and Mail*, Feb. 19, 1962
45 TCD interview, May 14, 1985

CHAPTER 23: THE BITTER TASTE

1 Pemrose Whelan interview, Nov. 28, 1985
2 TCD interview, May 23, 1985
3 Public Archives of Canada, sound recordings, TCD interview with Peter Stursberg, Sept. 3, 1976
4 Terry Grier interview, July 25, 1985
5 Queen's University Archives, Donald MacDonald Papers, 60-423, TCD speech, Jan. 15, 1962
6 Regina *Leader-Post*, June 2, 6, 1962
7
8 Public Archives of Canada, TCD Papers, vol. 94, letters on the 1962 defeat
9 TCD interview, May 23, 1985
10 TCD private papers, TCD letter to Morinne More, Feb. 1982
11 Ed Whelan interview, Nov. 28, 1985

CHAPTER 24: A MINOR PARTY

1 Clifford Scotton interview, Sept. 12, 1985
2 Bert Hill interview, Jan. 21, 1986
3 University of British Columbia Special Collections, B.C. NDP Papers, vol. 33-3, Vancouver Burrard CCF newsletter, Sept. 1963
4 Max Saltsman interview, July 17, 1985
5 Clifford Scotton interview, Sept. 12, 1985
6 Arnold Peters interview, May 29, 1985
7 Clifford Scotton interview, Sept. 12, 1985
8 Douglas Fisher interview, Feb. 26, 1985
9 Stephen Lewis interview, Sept. 9, 1985
10 Grace MacInnis interview, April 21, 1985
11 *Globe and Mail*, June 18, 1962
12 *Canadian Annual Review*, 1965, 72
13 Ottawa *Citizen*, Feb. 25, 1986
14 Public Archives of Canada, sound recordings, TCD interview with Peter Stursberg, Dec. 4, 1972
15 Ibid.
16 University of British Columbia Special Collections, Walter Young Papers, vol. 8-5, TCD election telecast, transcript, March 13, 1963
17 Vancouver *Sun*, April 4, 1963
18 Public Archives of Canada, sound recordings, TCD interview with Richard Alway, nd [1966?]
19 Public Archives of Canada, TCD Papers, vol. 130, TCD to Woodrow Lloyd, April 12, 1963
20 Canada, House of Commons, *Debates*, Nov. 12, 1963, 4631
21 TCD Papers, Ottawa, vol. 145, report to the 1963 federal convention, Aug. 8, 1963
22 Public Archives of Canada, sound recordings, TCD interview with Peter Stursberg, Sept. 3, 1976
23 House of Commons, *Debates*, June 12, 1966, 7556
24 Ibid., March 8, 1966, 2370, 2375
25 TCD Papers, Ottawa, TCD, "Labour in a Free Society," unpublished article, Jan. 6, 1970
26 *The Barker*, Industrial Woodworkers of America, July 24, 1968
27 Clifford Scotton interview, Oct. 24, 1986
28 TCD speech, *CUPE Journal*, Sept. 1968
29 TCD, "Labour in a Free Society," unpublished article
30 Ed Broadbent interview, Oct. 25, 1986
31 *Weyburn Review*, Sept. 12, 1935
32 Public Archives of Canada, NDP Papers, vol. 4, approved resolutions, 1971

CHAPTER 25: IN THE EAGLE'S CLAWS

1 Saskatchewan Archives, Regina, Woodrow Lloyd Papers, vol. XIX.94, TCD's "Canadian Credo," Feb. 1, 1965
2 Vancouver *Sun*, April 10, 1965
3 Ibid., April 4, 1963
4 Saskatoon *Star-Phoenix*, Nov. 29, 1962
5 *Globe and Mail*, Jan. 14, 1963
6 Public Archives of Canada, TCD Papers, vol. 125, State Department memo, Jan. 30, 1963
7 *Globe and Mail*, Feb. 1, 1963
8
9 TCD Papers, Ottawa, vol. 125, Harry Pope memo to TCD, Nov.-Dec. [?] 1962
10 Queen's University Archives, Ontario CCF/NDP Papers, vol. 5, TCD to Stan Hall, July 2, 1963
11 A.E. Safarian, *Foreign Ownership of Canadian Industry* (Toronto, 1966)
12 Canada, House of Commons, *Debates*, June 16, 1964, 4347-52
13 Regina *Leader-Post*, July 21, 1933
14 Frank Scott et. al., *Social Planning for Canada*, 56
15 Queen's University Archives, Donald MacDonald Papers, 48-260, TCD to Louis St. Laurent, Nov. 29, 1955
16 Public Archives of Canada, sound recordings, TCD interview with Richard Alway, 1966 [?]

17 TCD Papers, Ottawa, vol. 145, speech at Laval University, Nov. 21, 1962; also vol. 152, article by TCD, *Bay Street Journal*, March 1962
18 TCD Papers, Ottawa, vol. 146, speech by TCD, May 4, 1964
19 House of Commons, *Debates*, Nov. 28, 1962, 2113; Nov. 12, 1963, 4630; April 6, 1965, 48; Jan. 20, 1966, 80
20 Public Archives of Canada, sound recordings, TCD interview with Peter Stursberg, Sept. 3, 1976
21 *Globe and Mail*, May 29, 1969
22 House of Commons, *Debates*, April 28, 1964, 2685
23 TCD Papers, Ottawa, vol. 146, TCD speech to Saskatchewan NDP, Nov. 19, 1965
24 *Globe and Mail*, Feb. 2, 1965
25 House of Commons, *Debates*, March 2, 1971, 3878ff
26 Toronto *Telegram*, July 6, 1967
27 Max Saltsman interview, July 17, 1985
28 University of British Columbia Special Collections, B.C. NDP papers, vol. 22-4, TCD news release, Feb. 19, 1968
29 House of Commons, *Debates*, March 2, 1971, 3878ff
30 Allan Blakeney interview, Sept. 18, 1985
31 Clifford Scotton interview, Sept. 12, 1985
32 TCD Papers, Ottawa, vol. 148, TCD radio address, May 10, 1972
33 B.C. NDP Papers, vol. 22-4, TCD speech to B.C. NDP, July 3, 1967
34 Victoria *Daily Times*, July 10, 1967
35 Public Archives of Canada, M. J. Coldwell Papers, vol. 58, TCD to M. J. Coldwell, Jan. 31, 1955
36 TCD Papers, Ottawa, vol. 3, Edmonton *Journal* clipping, nd
37 House of Commons, *Debates*, May 28, 1965, 1790-96
38 Ibid., Eldon Woolliams, Feb. 8, 1966, 886
39 Ibid., Feb. 13, 1967, 12998-99
40 TCD Papers, Ottawa, vol. 3, Vietnam files
41 House of Commons, *Debates*, Feb. 13, 1967, 12993; also St. John's *Telegraph-Journal*, Nov. 14, 1967
42 Jim Hayes interview, Sept. 5, 1985
43 TCD Papers, Ottawa, vol. 88, TCD form letter
44 Lorne Nystrom interview, Sept. 10, 1985; also Jim Hayes interview, Sept. 5, 1985
45 TCD Papers, Ottawa, vol. 112, TCD statement, Oct. 5, 1969
46 TCD private papers, TCD to Woodrow Lloyd, Oct. 14, 1969

CHAPTER 26: RIGHTS AND POWERS

1 Public Archives of Canada, F. R. Scott Papers, vol. 11, minutes of first ministers' conference, Sept. 27, 1950
2 F. R. Scott, "Centralization and Decentralization in Canadian Federalism," *Canadian Bar Review*, 1951, 1123
3 Public Archives of Canada, TCD Papers, vol. 147, TCD report to NDP federal council, May 30, 1969
4 *Globe and Mail*, Jan. 5, 1955
5 University of British Columbia Special Collections, Walter Young Papers, vol. 5-14, M. J. Coldwell to D. H. Black, Feb. 10, 1955
6 TCD Papers, Ottawa, vol. 152, "Question Period," CTV, transcript, Oct. 17, 1969
7 TCD interview, Oct. 19, 1984
8 Saskatchewan Archives, Saskatoon, Saskatchewan NDP Papers, vol. II-132, NDP founding program, 1961
9 John Harney interview, Oct. 26, 1986
10 Saskatchewan NDP Papers, vol. II-673, TCD news release, Feb. 20, 1962
11 *Globe and Mail*, Feb. 11, 1967
12 Public Archives of Canada, sound recordings, TCD interview with Peter Stursberg, Sept. 3, 1976
13 Ibid.
14 Canada, House of Commons, *Debates*, June 16, 1964, 4349
15 Ibid., Sept. 8, 1964, 7738
16 Ibid., Dec. 14, 1964, 11109
17 Walter Young Papers, vol. 7-24, NDP federal council statement on Confederation, Nov. 22, 1964

18 TCD Papers, Ottawa, vol. 146, TCD nominating speech, Sept. 24, 1965
19 Jim Hayes interview, Sept. 5, 1985
20 University of British Columbia Special Collections, B.C. NDP Papers, vol. 22-4, TCD speech to B.C. NDP, July 3, 1967
21 Ibid., TCD article, "On Parliament Hill," Feb. 12, 1968
22 TCD Papers, Ottawa, vol. 151, TCD speech, Nov. 21, 1978
23 TCD interview, Jan. 29, 1985
24 TCD Papers, Ottawa, vol. 69, TCD to A. R. M. Lower, April 22, 1959
25 *Globe and Mail*, June 6, 1963
26 TCD Papers, Ottawa, vol. 69, TCD letter co-signed with David Lewis, 1977 [?]
27 Jim Hayes interview, Sept. 5, 1985
28 Hans Brown interview, Jan. 20, 1986; also Jim Hayes interview, Sept. 5, 1985
29 House of Commons, *Debates*, Oct. 16, 1970, 193-99
30 TCD Papers, Ottawa, vol. 31, letters to TCD on the War Measures Act, 1970
31 Ibid., TCD form letter
32 *Canadian Annual Review*, 1970, 111
33 TCD Papers, Ottawa, vol. 120, "Encounter," CBC television, transcript, Oct. 1970
34 Montreal *Gazette*, Nov. 7, 1970
35 Calgary *Herald*, Nov. 2, 1970
36 TCD Papers, Ottawa, vol. 133, Pierre Trudeau to TCD, Oct. 17, 1970
37 *Canadian Annual Review*, 1970, 118
38 TCD Papers, Ottawa, vol. 150, TCD speech to world parliamentarians, Sept. 21, 1977

CHAPTER 27: WHO'S NEXT?

1 Donald MacDonald interview, July 25, 1985
2 Jim Hayes interview, Sept. 5, 1985
3 "Towards an Independent Socialist Canada," manifesto of the NDP Waffle caucus, Sept. 1969
4 Public Archives of Canada, TCD Papers, vol. 147, TCD speech, "The Triple Revolution," May 30, 1969
5 TCD Papers, Ottawa, vol. 152, Ed Broadbent speech to the United Auto Workers, Feb. 9, 1969
6 Donald MacDonald to Ian McLeod, May 14, 1986
7 Stephen Lewis interview, Sept. 9, 1985
8 Clifford Scotton interview, Sept. 12, 1985
9 TCD Papers, Ottawa, vol. 147, leaders' television debate, transcript, June 9, 1968
10 Jim Hayes interview, Sept. 5, 1985
11 *Globe and Mail*, June 11, 1968
12 Lorne Nystrom interview, Sept. 10, 1985
13 *Globe and Mail*, June 28, 1968; Toronto *Star*, June 28, 1968; TCD Papers, Ottawa, vol. 122, Edmonton *Journal* clipping, nd
14 *Globe and Mail*, June 29, 1968
15 Clifford Scotton interview, Sept. 12, 1985
16 *Globe and Mail*, Sept. 9, 1968; Allan Blakeney interview, Sept. 18, 1985
17 TCD Papers, Ottawa, vol. 70, TCD to Joyce Nash, Aug. 1, 1968
18 University of British Columbia Special Collections, B.C. NDP Papers, vol. 20-9, Vancouver *Sun* clipping, nd; Winnipeg *Free Press*, Sept. 11, 1968
19 Peter McCusker interview, Jan. 17, 1986
20 Vancouver *Sun*, Feb. 11, 1969
21 *Globe and Mail*, Feb. 12, 1969
22 Ibid., March 20, 1969
23 Ottawa *Citizen*, March 27, 1971; Barrie *Examiner*, Aug. 7, 1970
24 Peter McCusker interview, Jan. 17, 1986

CHAPTER 28: THE WAFFLE

1 Public Archives of Canada, TCD Papers, vol. 12, TCD news release, May 5, 1969
2 Toronto *Telegram*, March 26, 1969
3 University of British Columbia, Colin Cameron Papers, vol. 1, Colin Cameron statement, April 11, 1947
4 University of British Columbia Special Collections, Walter Young Papers, vol. 5, M. J. Coldwell to Grant MacNeil, March 8, 1951

5 McMaster University Archives, CCF Papers, vol. 1, Socialist Caucus Bulletins, news clippings
6 TCD Papers, Ottawa, vol. 109, "Twenty Million Questions," CBC television, transcript, May 6, 1969
7 Winnipeg *Tribune*, Oct. 29, 1969
8 TCD Papers, Ottawa, vol. 110, TCD to Lorne Ingle, Oct. 15, 1969
9 Toronto *Star*, Oct. 17, 1969
10 TCD Papers, Ottawa, vol. 152, "Question Period," CTV, transcript, Oct. 17, 1969
11 Walter Young Papers, vol. 8-3B, TCD convention speech, Oct. 28, 1969
12 Winnipeg *Free Press*, Oct. 30, 1969
13 Montreal *Gazette*, Oct. 30, 1969
14 Winnipeg *Tribune*, Oct. 29, 1969
15 Ottawa *Journal*, Toronto *Star*, Oct. 31, 1969
16 TCD Papers, Ottawa, vol. 110, TCD to Carol Gudmundson, Nov. 16, 1969
17 *Globe and Mail*, Oct. 29, 1969
18 Ibid., Feb. 6, 1970
19 Clifford Scotton interview, Sept. 12, 1985
20 Hans Brown interview, Jan. 20, 1986
21 Bill Knight interview, June 2, 1985
22 TCD Papers, Ottawa, vol. 130, Woodrow Lloyd to TCD, March 29, 1970
23 Ibid., TCD memorial address for Woodrow Lloyd, April 16, 1972
24 Allan Blakeney interview, Sept. 18, 1985
25 Saskatchewan Archives, Regina, John Brockelbank Papers, vol. IX-53, David Lewis to John Brockelbank, Aug. 6, 1970
26 TCD Papers, Ottawa, vol. 110, Jim Laxer news release, nd
27 Ibid., TCD to Paul MacEwen, April 6, 1971
28 TCD Papers, Ottawa, vol. 148, TCD convention speech, April 21, 1971
29 TCD Papers, Ottawa, vol. 92, TCD to Gordon Schurman, May 6, 1971
30 TCD Papers, Ottawa, vol. 101, TCD to Elva Hennessey, May 7, 1971
31 Robert Hackett, "Pie in the Sky: A History of the Ontario Waffle," *Canadian Dimension*, Oct.-Nov. 1980, 55
32 Toronto *Star*, June 22, 1972
33 TCD Papers, Ottawa, vol. 110, Ontario NDP council resolution, June 24, 1972
34 Ibid., TCD to Robert Dumont, May 12, 1973
35 Allan Blakeney interview, Sept. 18, 1985
36 For example, TCD Papers, Ottawa, vol. 110, TCD to B. G. Swentz, Jan. 30, 1973
37 Ibid., CLC document on the Waffle, 1972
38 *Globe and Mail*, Oct. 29, 1969
39 Donald Kerr, ed., *Western Canadian Politics* (Edmonton, 1981), 69-75; John Richards interview, Aug. 15, 1986
40 TCD Papers, Ottawa, vol. 113, Desmond Morton, "Socialism/Canada/'70's: A Critique," nd
41 TCD Papers, Ottawa, vol. 152, Ed Broadbent speech, Feb. 9, 1969
42 Max Saltsman interview, July 17, 1985
43 Shortt Library, University of Saskatchewan, "Instrument for Change," pamphlet

CHAPTER 29: ENERGY CRITIC

1 Canada, House of Commons, *Debates*, Dec. 6, 1973, 8479-82
2 Bill Knight interview, June 2, 1985
3 House of Commons, *Debates*, Dec. 6, 1973, 8484
4 Calgary *Herald*, June 7, 1969
5 House of Commons, *Debates*, Jan. 13, 1970, 2334
6 Ibid., March 10, 1970, 4580
7 Ibid., March 10, 1970, 4578
8 Bruce Doern and Glen Toner, *The Politics of Energy* (Agincourt, 1975), 85; Public Archives of Canada, TCD Papers, vol. 124, speech by David Cass-Beggs, May 26, 1970; ibid., vol. 149, TCD speech, Nov. 28, 1975
9 House of Commons, *Debates*, Oct. 9, 1970, 39
10 Public Archives of Canada, NDP Papers, vol. 4, approved resolutions, 1973 federal convention
11 TCD Papers, Ottawa, vol. 124, caucus discussion paper, June 12, 1973
12 Lorne Nystrom interview, Sept. 10, 1985

13 Allan Blakeney interview, Sept. 18, 1985

14 House of Commons, *Debates*, April 24, 1975, 5192

15 Ibid., Nov. 13, 1974, 1296

16 Vancouver *Sun*, June 3, 1973

17 TCD Papers, Ottawa, vol. 124, caucus discussion paper, June 12, 1973

18 TCD Papers, Ottawa, vol. 4, approved resolutions, 1973 federal convention

19 House of Commons, *Debates*, Oct. 25, 1973, 7215-17

20 Ibid., Nov. 5, 1973, 7545

21 Cyril Symes interview, Sept. 16, 1985

22 Terry Grier interview, July 25, 1985

23 Larry Pratt, "Petro-Canada," in Alan Tupper and Bruce Doern, eds., *Public Corporations and Public Policy in Canada* (Montreal, 1981)

24 Donald S. Macdonald interview, Feb. 24, 1987

25 House of Commons, *Debates*, Feb. 24, 1974, 28; ibid., March 5, 1974, 185

26 Ibid., Dec. 2, 1974, 1835

27 Ibid., Feb. 4, 1975, 2898

28 Symes interview, Sept. 16, 1985

29 House of Commons, *Debates*, Feb. 25, 1975, 3568

30 TCD Papers, Ottawa, vol. 151, TCD radio address, Dec. 1, 1978

31 House of Commons, *Debates*, March 12, 1975, 4044

32 Ibid., 4043

33 Ibid., Feb. 16, 1979, 3437

34 Montreal *Gazette*, March 11, 1950

35 TCD Papers, Ottawa, vol. 43, TCD to R. K. Brown, March 6, 1978; House of Commons, *Debates*, June 17, 1975, 6847

36 House of Commons, *Debates*, June 10, 1975, 6600

37 Ibid., Jan. 30, 1976, 10491

38 Ibid., July 7, 1977, 7421

39 TCD Papers, Ottawa, vol. 123, "The Great Debate," Global Television, transcript, Dec. 12, 1974

CHAPTER 30: LIFE BEGINS AT 75

1 University of Saskatchewan, Shortt Library, "Instrument for Change," (pamphlet), Douglas-Coldwell Foundation, 1975

2 Kalmen Kaplansky conversation with T. H. McLeod, Feb. 27, 1987

3 Robert Blair interview, May 5, 1986; Allan Blakeney conversation with T. H. McLeod, Feb. 27, 1987

4 Lorne Nystrom interview, Sept. 10, 1985

5 Bill Knight interview, June 2, 1985; Lorne Nystrom interview, Sept. 10, 1985

6 Allan Blakeney interview, Sept. 18, 1985

7 Ed Broadbent interview, Oct. 25, 1986

8 TCD private papers, speech to federal NDP convention, tape recording, July 2, 1983

INDEX

Printed in Canada